Cultural Theory and Popular Culture: An Introduction, Eighth Edition

The companion website for this new edition features:

- Extension activities for each chapter
- Additional questions for discussion
- Interactive quizzes covering the topics discussed within each chapter
- Annotated links to relevant websites and further reading
- A complete glossary of key terms.

Please visit the website at www.routledge.com/cw/storey to access these additional resources.

Cultural Theory and Popular Culture

In this eighth edition of his award-winning *Cultural Theory and Popular Culture: An Introduction*, John Storey presents a clear and critical survey of competing theories of, and various approaches to, popular culture. Its breadth and theoretical unity, exemplified through popular culture, means that it can be flexibly and relevantly applied across a number of disciplines.

Retaining the accessible approach of previous editions, and using appropriate examples from the texts and practices of popular culture, this new edition remains a key introduction to the area.

New to this edition:

- revised, rewritten and updated throughout
- brand-new chapter on class and popular culture
- updated student resources at www.routledge.com/cw/storey.

The new edition remains essential reading for undergraduate and postgraduate students of cultural studies, media studies, communication studies, the sociology of culture, popular culture and other related subjects.

John Storey is Emeritus Professor of Cultural Studies at the Centre for Research in Media and Cultural Studies at the University of Sunderland, UK. He has published widely in cultural studies, including twelve books. The most recent is *Theories of Consumption* (2017).

Cultural Theory and Popular Culture
An Introduction

Eighth Edition

John Storey

Routledge
Taylor & Francis Group

LONDON AND NEW YORK

Eighth edition published 2018
by Routledge
2 Park Square, Milton Park, Abingdon, Oxon, OX14 4RN

and by Routledge
711 Third Avenue, New York, NY 10017

Routledge is an imprint of the Taylor & Francis Group, an informa business

First edition published by Pearson Education Limited 1997
Seventh edition published by Routledge 2015

British Library Cataloguing-in-Publication Data
A catalogue record for this book is available from the British Library

Library of Congress Cataloging-in-Publication Data
Names: Storey, John, author.
Title: Cultural theory and popular culture : an introduction / John Storey.
Description: Eighth edition. | London ; New York : Routledge, [2018] | Includes
    bibliographical references and index.
Identifiers: LCCN 2017034776 | ISBN 9780415786621 (hardback : alk. paper) |
    ISBN 9780415786638 (pbk. : alk. paper) | ISBN 9781315226866 (ebook : alk. paper)
Subjects: LCSH: Popular culture—Philosophy. | Culture—Philosophy. | Culture—History.
Classification: LCC CB19 .S743 2018 | DDC 306.01—dc23
LC record available at https://lccn.loc.gov/2017034776

ISBN: 978-0-415-78662-1 (hbk)
ISBN: 978-0-415-78663-8 (pbk)
ISBN: 978-1-315-22686-6 (ebk)

Typeset in Giovanni Std
by Apex CoVantage, LLC

Visit the companion website: www.routledge.com/cw/storey

For Charlie

Contents

Preface/Acknowledgements   xiii
Publisher's acknowledgements   xvii

1 What is popular culture?   1
Culture   1
Ideology   2
Popular culture   5
Popular culture as *other*   13
The contextuality of meaning   14
Notes   16
Further reading   16

2 The 'culture and civilization' tradition   18
Matthew Arnold   19
Leavisism   23
Mass culture in America: the post-war debate   29
The culture of other people   34
Notes   36
Further reading   36

3 Culturalism   38
Richard Hoggart: *The Uses of Literacy*   39
Raymond Williams: 'The analysis of culture'   45
E.P. Thompson: *The Making of the English Working Class*   50
Stuart Hall and Paddy Whannel: *The Popular Arts*   52
The Centre for Contemporary Cultural Studies   58
Notes   59
Further reading   59

4 Marxisms   61
Classical Marxism   61
The English Marxism of William Morris   64
The Frankfurt School   66
Althusserianism   74

Hegemony   83
Post-Marxism and cultural studies   86
Notes   93
Further reading   93

5   Psychoanalysis   95
Freudian psychoanalysis   95
Lacanian psychoanalysis   105
Cine-psychoanalysis   109
Slavoj Žižek and Lacanian fantasy   111
Notes   113
Further reading   114

6   Structuralism and post-structuralism   116
Ferdinand de Saussure   116
Claude Lévi-Strauss, Will Wright and the American Western   119
Roland Barthes: *Mythologies*   123
Post-structuralism   131
Jacques Derrida   131
Discourse and power: Michel Foucault   133
The panoptic machine   135
Notes   138
Further reading   138

7   Class and class struggle   140
Class and popular culture   140
Class in cultural studies   140
Class struggle   141
Consumption as class distinction   144
Class and popular culture   146
The ideological work of meritocracy   149
Notes   151
Further reading   151

8   Gender and sexuality   152
Feminisms   152
Women at the cinema   153
Reading romance   157
Watching Dallas   164
Reading women's magazines   170
Post-feminism   175
Men's studies and masculinities   178
Queer theory   179
Notes   184
Further reading   185

9 'Race', racism and representation 187
    'Race' and racism 187
    The ideology of racism: its historical emergence 189
    Orientalism 192
    Whiteness 199
    Anti-racism and cultural studies 200
    Notes 201
    Further reading 202

10 Postmodernism 204
    The postmodern condition 204
    Postmodernism in the 1960s 205
    Jean-François Lyotard 207
    Jean Baudrillard 209
    Fredric Jameson 214
    Postmodern pop music 220
    Postmodern television 221
    Postmodernism and the pluralism of value 224
    The global postmodern 227
    Convergence culture 233
    Afterword 234
    Notes 234
    Further reading 235

11 The materiality of popular culture 237
    Materiality 237
    Materiality as actor 238
    Meaning and materiality 240
    Materiality without meaning 244
    Material objects in a global world 247
    Notes 249
    Further reading 249

12 The politics of the popular 251
    The cultural field 253
    The economic field 264
    Post-Marxist cultural studies: hegemony revisited 270
    The ideology of mass culture 271
    Notes 273
    Further reading 274

    Bibliography 276
    Index 289

Preface/Acknowledgements

Preface to eighth edition

In writing the eighth edition I have revised, rewritten, edited and added throughout. The most obvious addition is a new chapter called 'Class and class struggle'. Altogether, the size of the book has increased by more than 6,500 words.

The eighth edition is best read in conjunction with its companion volume, *Cultural Theory and Popular Culture: A Reader*, fifth edition (Routledge, forthcoming).

Preface to seventh edition

In writing the seventh edition I have revised, rewritten and edited throughout. I have also added new material to most of the chapters. The most obvious additions are a new section on the contextuality of meaning at the end of Chapter 1 and a new chapter called 'The materiality of popular culture'. Altogether I have added more than 8,500 words.

The seventh edition is best read in conjunction with its companion volume, *Cultural Theory and Popular Culture. A Reader*, fourth edition (Routledge, 2009).

Preface to sixth edition

In writing the sixth edition I have revised, rewritten and edited throughout. I have also added new material to most of the chapters (the book has grown from a first edition of around 65,000 words to a sixth edition that is in excess of 120,000 words). The most obvious additions are the new sections on the English Marxism of William Morris (Chapter 4), Post-feminism (Chapter 7) and Whiteness (Chapter 8).

The sixth edition is best read in conjunction with its companion volume, *Cultural Theory and Popular Culture: A Reader*, fourth edition (Pearson, 2009).

Preface to fifth edition

In writing the fifth edition I have revised, rewritten and edited throughout. I have also added new material to most of the chapters (the book has grown from a first edition of around 65,000 words to a fifth edition that is in excess of 114,000 words). The most obvious additions are the new chapter '"Race", racism and representation' and the new sections on the panoptic machine (Chapter 6) and convergence culture (Chapter 9). I have also added more diagrams and illustrations.

The fifth edition is best read in conjunction with its companion volume, *Cultural Theory and Popular Culture: A Reader*, fourth edition (Pearson, 2009).

Preface to fourth edition

In writing the fourth edition I have revised, rewritten and edited throughout. I have also added new material to most of the chapters (the book has grown from a first edition of around 65,000 words to a fourth edition that is well in excess of 100,000 words). The most obvious additions are the new chapter on psychoanalysis and the sections on post-Marxism (Chapter 4) and the global postmodern (Chapter 8). I have also added more diagrams and illustrations. Finally, I have changed the running order of the chapters. The chapters are now chronological in terms of where each begins. However, where each chapter ends may sometimes disrupt chronology. For example, Marxism begins before post-structuralism, but where the discussion of Marxism ends is more contemporary than where the discussion of post-structuralism ends. There seems to be no obvious solution to this problem.

Preface to third edition

In writing the third edition I have sought to improve and to expand the material in the first two editions of this book. To achieve this I have revised and I have rewritten much more extensively than in the second edition. I have also added new material to most of the chapters. This is most evident in the renamed, and reorganized, Chapter 6, where I have added a new section on queer theory, and where I have extended the section on reading women's magazines. Perhaps the most visible change is the addition of illustrations, and the inclusion of a list of websites useful to the student of cultural theory and popular culture.

Preface to second edition

In writing the second edition I have sought to improve and to expand the material in the first book. To achieve this I have revised and I have rewritten. More specifically, I have added new sections on popular culture and the carnivalesque, postmodernism and the pluralism of value. I have also extended five sections, neo-Gramscian cultural studies, popular film, cine-psychoanalysis and cultural studies, feminism as reading, postmodernism in the 1960s, the cultural field.

Preface to first edition

As the title of this book indicates, my subject is the relationship between cultural theory and popular culture. But as the title also indicates, my study is intended as an *introduction* to the subject. This has entailed the adoption of a particular approach. I have not tried to write a history of the encounter between cultural theory and popular culture. Instead, I have chosen to focus on the theoretical and methodological implications and ramifications of specific moments in the history of the study of popular culture. In short, I have tended to treat cultural theory/popular culture as a discursive formation, and to focus less on historical provenance and more on how it functions ideologically in the present. To avoid misunderstanding and misrepresentation, I have allowed critics and theorists, when and where appropriate, to speak in their own words. In doing this, I am in agreement with the view expressed by the American literary historian Walter E. Houghton: 'Attitudes are elusive. Try to define them and you lose their essence, their special colour and tone. They have to be apprehended in their concrete and living formulation.' Moreover, rather than simply surveying the field, I have tried through quotation and detailed commentary to give the student of popular culture a 'taste' of the material. However, this book is not intended as a substitute for reading first-hand the theorists and critics discussed here. And, although each chapter ends with suggestions for further reading, these are intended to supplement the reading of the primary texts discussed in the individual chapters (details of which are located in the Notes at the end of the book).

Above all, the intention of this book is to provide an introduction to the academic study of popular culture. As I have already indicated, I am under no illusion that this is a *fully* adequate account, or the only possible way to map the conceptual landscape that is the subject of this study. My hope is that this version of the relationship between popular culture and cultural theory will encourage other students of popular culture to begin their own mapping of the field.

Finally, I hope I have written a book that can offer something to both those familiar with the subject and those to whom – as an academic subject at least – it is all very new.

Acknowledgements

I would like to thank students on the 'Cultural Theory and Popular Culture' modules at the University of Sunderland, Wuhan University, the University of Vienna, and Dresden University with whom I have rehearsed many of the ideas contained in this book. I would also like to thank colleagues in the (University of Sunderland) Centre for Research in Media and Cultural Studies, and friends at other institutions, for ideas and encouragement. I would also like to thank Natalie Foster of Routledge for giving me the opportunity to write an eighth edition.

Publisher's acknowledgements

The publisher would like to thank the following for their kind permission to reproduce their photographs:

Photo 2.1 A day trip to Blackpool in the early 1950s. Author's own.

Photo 4.1 Advertising as an example of the 'problematic'. Courtesy of The Advertising Archives.

Photo 4.2 Two figures on a beach. Author's own.

Photo 5.1 The Mirror Stage. Author's own.

Photo 6.1 Black soldier saluting the flag. Courtesy of IZIS/Paris Match Archive/Getty Images.

Photo 6.2 Rock-a-day Johnny 'My baby done me wrong' from the album *Dogbucket Days*. Author's own.

Photo 6.3 Rock-a-day Johnny 'Drugs killed my best friend'. Author's own.

Photo 6.4 Advertising for teachers. Courtesy of Department of Education. Crown copyright material is reproduced with the permission of the Controller, Office of Public Sector Information (OPSI).

Photo 6.5 The panoptic machine.

Photo 8.1 Post-feminism and the Wonderbra. Courtesy of The Advertising Archives.

Photo 10.1 An example of hyperrealism. Courtesy of Daily Express/N&S Syndication and Licensing.

Photo 10.2 The Coca-Colonization of China. Author's own.

Photo 10.3 'Imagine there's no countries'. Author's own.

Photo 11.1 Begin the revolution. Author's own.

Photo 11.2 Christmas in China. Author's own.

Photo 12.1 For the benefit of striking bookbinders. Courtesy of Arts Library Manchester.

Every effort has been made to trace the copyright holders and we apologize in advance for any unintentional omissions. We would be pleased to insert the appropriate acknowledgement in any subsequent edition of this publication.

1 What is popular culture?

Before we consider in detail the different ways in which popular culture has been defined and analysed, I want to outline some of the general features of the debate that the study of popular culture has generated. It is not my intention to pre-empt the specific findings and arguments that will be presented in the following chapters. Here I simply wish to map out the general conceptual landscape of popular culture. This is, in many ways, a daunting task. Part of the difficulty stems from the implied *otherness* that is always absent/present when we use the term 'popular culture'. As we shall see in the chapters that follow, popular culture is always defined, implicitly or explicitly, in contrast to other conceptual categories: folk culture, mass culture, high culture, dominant culture, working-class culture. A full definition must always take this into account. Moreover, as we shall also see, whichever conceptual category is deployed as popular culture's *absent other*, it will always powerfully affect the connotations brought into play when we use the term 'popular culture'.

Therefore, to study popular culture we must first confront the difficulty posed by the term itself. For it will almost certainly be the case that the kind of analysis we do and the theoretical frame we employ to do this analysis will be largely shaped by the definition of popular culture we use. The main argument that I suspect readers will take from this book is that popular culture is in effect an *empty conceptual category*, one that can be filled in a wide variety of often conflicting ways, depending on the context of use.

Culture

In order to define popular culture we first need to define the term 'culture'. Raymond Williams (1983) calls culture 'one of the two or three most complicated words in the English language' (87). Williams suggests three broad definitions. First, culture can be used to refer to 'a general process of intellectual, spiritual and aesthetic development' (90). We could, for example, speak about the cultural development of Western Europe and be referring only to intellectual, spiritual and aesthetic factors – great philosophers, great artists and great poets. This would be a perfectly understandable formulation. A second use of the word 'culture' might be to suggest 'a particular way of life, whether of a people, a period or a group' (ibid.). Using this definition, if we speak of the cultural development of Western Europe, we would have in mind not just intellectual and aesthetic factors, but the development of, for example, literacy, holidays, sport, religious festivals. Finally, Williams suggests that culture can be used to refer to 'the works and practices of intellectual and especially artistic activity' (ibid.). In other words, culture here means the texts and practices whose principal function is to signify, to produce or to be the occasion for the production of meaning. Culture in this third definition is synonymous with what structuralists and post-structuralists call 'signifying practices' (see Chapter 6). Using this definition, we would probably think of examples such as poetry, the novel, ballet, opera and fine art. To speak of popular culture usually means to mobilize the second and third meanings of the word 'culture'. The second meaning – culture as a particular way of life – would allow us to speak of such practices as the seaside holiday, the celebration of Christmas, and youth subcultures, as examples of culture. These are usually referred to as *lived* cultures or practices. The third meaning – culture as signifying practices – would allow us to speak of soap opera, pop music, and comics as examples of culture. These are usually referred to as texts. Few people would imagine Williams's first definition when thinking about popular culture.

Ideology

Before we turn to the different definitions of popular culture, there is another term we have to think about: ideology. Ideology is a crucial concept in the study of popular culture. Graeme Turner (2003) calls it 'the most important conceptual category in cultural studies' (182). James Carey (1996) has even suggested that 'British cultural studies could be described just as easily and perhaps more accurately as ideological studies' (65). Like culture, ideology has many competing meanings. An understanding of this concept is often complicated by the fact that in much cultural analysis the concept is used interchangeably with culture itself, and especially popular culture. The fact that ideology has been used to refer to the same conceptual terrain as culture and popular culture makes it an important term in any understanding of the nature of popular culture. What follows is a brief discussion of just five of the many ways of understanding ideology. We will consider only those meanings that have a bearing on the study of popular culture.

First, ideology can refer to a systematic body of ideas articulated by a particular group of people. For example, we could speak of 'professional ideology' to refer to the ideas that inform the practices of particular professional groups. We could also speak of the 'ideology of the Labour Party'. Here we would be referring to the collection of political, economic and social ideas that inform the aspirations and activities of the party.

A second definition suggests a certain masking, distortion or concealment. Ideology is used here to indicate how some texts and practices present distorted images of reality.

They produce what is sometimes called 'false consciousness'. Such distortions, it is argued, work in the interests of the powerful against the interests of the powerless. Using this definition, we might speak of capitalist ideology. What would be intimated by this usage would be the way in which ideology conceals the reality of domination from those in power: the dominant class do not see themselves as exploiters or oppressors. And, perhaps more importantly, the way in which ideology conceals the reality of subordination from those who are powerless: the subordinate classes do not see themselves as oppressed or exploited. This definition derives from certain assumptions about the circumstances of the production of texts and practices. It is argued that they are the superstructural 'reflections' or 'expressions' of the power relations of 'the economic structure of society'. This is one of the fundamental assumptions of classical Marxism. Here is Karl Marx's (1976a) famous formulation:

> In the social production of their existence men enter into definite, necessary relations, which are independent of their will, namely, relations of production corresponding to a determinate stage of development of their material forces of production. The totality of these relations of production constitutes the economic structure of society, the real foundation on which there arises a legal and political superstructure and to which there correspond definite forms of social consciousness. The mode of production of material life conditions the social, political and intellectual life process in general (3).

What Marx is suggesting is that the way a society organizes the means of its material production will have a determining effect on the type of culture that society produces or makes possible. The cultural products of this so-called base/superstructure relationship are deemed ideological to the extent that, as a result of this relationship, they implicitly or explicitly support the interests of dominant groups who, socially, politically, economically and culturally, benefit from this particular economic organization of society. In Chapter 4, we shall consider this formulation in more detail.

We can also use ideology in this general sense to refer to power relations outside those of class. For instance, feminists speak of the power of patriarchal ideology, and how it operates to conceal, mask and distort gender relations in our society (see Chapter 8). In Chapter 9 we shall examine the ideology of racism.

A third definition of ideology (closely related to, and in some ways dependent on, the second definition) uses the term to refer to 'ideological forms' (Marx, 1976a: 5). This usage is intended to draw attention to the way in which texts (television fiction, pop songs, novels, feature films, etc.) always present a particular image of the world. This definition depends on a notion of society as conflictual rather than consensual, structured around inequality, exploitation and oppression. Texts are said to take sides, consciously or unconsciously, in this conflict. The German playwright Bertolt Brecht (1978) summarizes the point: 'Good or bad, a play always includes an image of the world. . . . There is no play and no theatrical performance which does not in some way affect the dispositions and conceptions of the audience. Art is never without consequences' (150–1). Brecht's point can be generalized to apply to all texts. Another way of saying this would be simply to argue that all texts are ultimately political. That is, they offer competing ideological significations of the way the world is or should be. Popular culture is thus, as Hall (2009a) claims, a site where 'collective social understandings are created': a terrain on which 'the politics of signification' are played out in attempts to win people to particular ways of seeing the world (122–3).

A fourth definition of ideology is one associated with the early work of the French cultural theorist Roland Barthes (discussed in more detail in Chapter 6). Barthes argues that ideology (or 'myth' as Barthes himself calls it) operates mainly at the level of connotations, the secondary, often unconscious, meanings that texts and practices carry, or can be made to carry. For example, a Conservative Party political broadcast transmitted in 1990 ended with the word 'socialism' being transposed into red prison bars. What was being suggested is that the socialism of the Labour Party is synonymous with social, economic and political imprisonment. The broadcast was attempting to fix the connotations of the word 'socialism'. Moreover, it hoped to locate socialism in a binary relationship in which it connoted unfreedom, whilst conservatism connoted freedom. For Barthes, this would be a classic example of the operations of ideology, the attempt to make universal and legitimate what is in fact partial and particular; an attempt to pass off that which is cultural (i.e. humanly made) as something which is natural (i.e. just existing). Similarly, it could be argued that in British society white, masculine, heterosexual, middle class, are unmarked in the sense that they are the 'normal', the 'natural', the 'universal', from which other ways of being are an inferior variation on an original. This is made clear in such formulations as a female pop singer, a black journalist, a working-class writer, a gay comedian. In each instance the first term is used to qualify the second as a deviation from the 'universal' categories of pop singer, journalist, writer and comedian.

A fifth definition is one that was very influential in the 1970s and early 1980s. It is the definition of ideology developed by the French Marxist philosopher Louis Althusser. We shall discuss Althusser in more detail in Chapter 4. Here I will simply outline some key points about one of his definitions of ideology. Althusser's main contention is to see ideology not simply as a body of ideas, but as a material practice. What he means by this is that ideology is encountered in the practices of everyday life and not simply in certain ideas about everyday life. Principally, what Althusser has in mind is the way in which certain rituals and customs have the effect of binding us to the social order: a social order that is marked by enormous inequalities of wealth, status and power. Using this definition, we could describe the seaside holiday or the celebration of Christmas as examples of ideological practices. This would point to the way in which they offer pleasure and release from the usual demands of the social order, but, ultimately, return us to our places in the social order, refreshed and ready to tolerate our exploitation and oppression until the next official break comes along. In this sense, ideology works to reproduce the social conditions and social relations necessary for the economic conditions and economic relations of capitalism to continue.

So far we have briefly examined different ways of defining culture and ideology. What should be clear by now is that culture and ideology do cover much the same conceptual landscape. The main difference between them is that ideology brings a political dimension to the shared terrain. In addition, the introduction of the concept of ideology suggests that relations of power and politics inescapably mark the culture/ ideology landscape; it suggests that the study of popular culture amounts to something more than a simple discussion of entertainment and leisure.

Popular culture

There are various ways to define popular culture. This book is of course in part about that very process, about the different ways in which various critical approaches have attempted to fix the meaning of popular culture. Therefore, all I intend to do for the remainder of this chapter is to sketch out six definitions of popular culture that, in their different, general ways, inform the study of popular culture. But first a few words about the term 'popular'. Williams (1983) suggests four current meanings: 'well liked by many people'; 'inferior kinds of work'; 'work deliberately setting out to win favour with the people'; 'culture actually made by the people for themselves' (237). Clearly, then, any definition of popular culture will bring into play a complex combination of the different meanings of the term 'culture' with the different meanings of the term 'popular'. The history of cultural theory's engagement with popular culture is, therefore, a history of the different ways in which the two terms have been connected by theoretical labour within particular historical and social contexts.

An obvious starting point in any attempt to define popular culture is to say that popular culture is simply culture that is widely favoured or well liked by many people. And, undoubtedly, such a quantitative index would meet the approval of many people. We could examine sales of books, sales of CDs and DVDs. We could also examine attendance records at concerts, sporting events and festivals. We could also scrutinize market research figures on audience preferences for different television programmes. Such counting would undoubtedly tell us a great deal. The difficulty might prove to be that, paradoxically, it tells us too much. Unless we can agree on a figure over which something becomes popular culture, and below which it is just culture, we might find that widely favoured or well liked by many people included so much as to be virtually useless as a conceptual definition of popular culture.

Despite this problem, what is clear is that any definition of popular culture must include a quantitative dimension. The *popular* of popular culture would seem to demand it. What is also clear, however, is that on its own, a quantitative index is not enough to provide an adequate definition of popular culture. Such counting would almost certainly include 'the officially sanctioned "high culture" which in terms of book and record sales and audience ratings for television dramatisations of the classics, can justifiably claim to be "popular" in this sense' (Bennett, 1980: 20–1).

A second way of defining popular culture is to suggest that it is the culture that is left over after we have decided what is high culture. Popular culture, in this definition, is a residual category, there to accommodate texts and practices that fail to meet the required standards to qualify as high culture. In other words, it is a definition of popular culture as inferior culture. What the culture/popular culture test might include is a range of value judgements on a particular text or practice. For example, we might want to insist on formal complexity. In other words, to be real culture, it has to be difficult. Being difficult thus ensures its exclusive status as high culture. Its very difficulty literally excludes, an exclusion that guarantees the exclusivity of its audience. The French sociologist Pierre Bourdieu argues that cultural distinctions of this kind are often used to support class distinctions. Taste is a deeply ideological category: it functions as a marker of 'class' (using the term in a double sense to mean both a social economic category and the suggestion of a particular level of quality). For Bourdieu (1984), the consumption of culture is 'predisposed, consciously and deliberately or not, to fulfil a social function of legitimating social differences' (5). This will be discussed in more detail in Chapters 7, 10, and 12.

This definition of popular culture is often supported by claims that popular culture is mass-produced commercial culture, whereas high culture is the result of an individual act of creation. The latter, therefore, deserves a moral and aesthetic response; the former requires only a fleeting sociological inspection to unlock what little it has to offer. Whatever the method deployed, those who wish to make the case for the division between high and popular culture generally insist that the division between the two is absolutely clear. Moreover, not only is this division clear, it is trans-historical – fixed for all time. This latter point is usually insisted on, especially if the division is dependent on supposed essential textual qualities.

There are many problems with this certainty. For example, William Shakespeare is now seen as the epitome of high culture, yet as late as the nineteenth century his work was very much a part of popular theatre.[1] The same point can also be made about Charles Dickens's work. Similarly, film noir can be seen to have crossed the border supposedly separating popular and high culture: in other words, what started as popular cinema is now the preserve of academics and film clubs.[2] One recent example of cultural traffic moving in the other direction is Luciano Pavarotti's recording of Puccini's 'Nessun Dorma'. Even the most rigorous defenders of high culture would not want to exclude Pavarotti or Puccini from its select enclave. But in 1990, Pavarotti managed to take 'Nessun Dorma' to number one in the British charts. Such commercial success on any quantitative analysis would make the composer, the performer and the aria popular culture.[3] In fact, one student I know actually complained about the way in which the aria had been supposedly devalued by its commercial success. He claimed that he now found it embarrassing to play the aria for fear that someone should think his musical taste was simply the result of the aria being 'The Official BBC Grandstand World Cup Theme'. Other students laughed and mocked. But his complaint highlights something very significant about the high/popular divide: the elitist investment that some put in its continuation.

On 30 July 1991, Pavarotti gave a free concert in London's Hyde Park. About 250,000 people were expected, but because of heavy rain, the number of those who actually attended was around 100,000. Two things about the event are of interest to a student of popular culture. The first is the enormous popularity of the event. We could connect this with the fact that Pavarotti's previous two albums (*Essential Pavarotti 1* and *Essential Pavarotti 2*) had both topped the British album charts. His obvious popularity would appear to call into question any clear division between high and popular culture. Second, the extent of his popularity would appear to threaten the class exclusivity of a high/popular divide. It is therefore interesting to note the way in which the event was reported in the media. All the British tabloids carried news of the event on their front pages. The *Daily Mirror*, for instance, had five pages devoted to the concert. What the tabloid coverage reveals is a clear attempt to define the event for popular culture. The *Sun* quoted a woman who said, 'I can't afford to go to posh opera houses with toffs and fork out £100 a seat.' The *Daily Mirror* ran an editorial in which it claimed that Pavarotti's performance 'wasn't for the rich' but 'for the thousands . . . who could never normally afford a night with an operatic star'. When the event was reported on television news programmes the following lunchtime, the tabloid coverage was included as part of the general meaning of the event. Both the BBC's *One O'clock News* and ITV's *12.30 News* referred to the way in which the tabloids had covered the concert, and, moreover, the *extent* to which they had covered the concert. The old certainties of the cultural landscape suddenly seemed in doubt. However, there was some attempt made to reintroduce the old certainties: 'some critics said that a park is no place for opera' (*One O'clock News*); 'some opera enthusiasts might think it all a bit vulgar' (*12.30 News*). Although such comments invoked the spectre of high-culture exclusivity, they seemed strangely at a loss to offer any purchase on the event. The apparently obvious cultural division between high and popular culture no longer seemed so obvious. It suddenly seemed that the cultural had been replaced by the economic, revealing a division between 'the rich' and 'the thousands'. It was the event's very popularity that forced the television news to confront, and ultimately to find wanting, old cultural certainties. This can be partly illustrated by returning to the contradictory meaning of the term 'popular'.[4] On the one hand, something is said to be good because it is popular. An example of this usage would be: it was a popular performance. Yet, on the other hand, something is said to be bad for the very same reason. Consider the binary oppositions in Table 1.1. This demonstrates quite clearly the way in which popular and popular culture carries within its definitional field connotations of inferiority; a second-best culture for those unable to understand, let alone appreciate, real culture – what Matthew Arnold refers to as 'the best that has been thought and said in the world' (see Chapter 2). Hall (2009b) argues that what is important here is not the fact that popular forms move up and down the 'cultural escalator'; more significant are 'the forces and relations which sustain the distinction, the difference . . . [the] institutions and institutional processes . . . required to sustain each and to continually mark the difference

Table 1.1 Popular culture as 'inferior' culture.

Popular press	Quality press
Popular cinema	Art cinema
Popular entertainment	Art

between them' (514). This is principally the work of the education system and its promotion of a selective tradition (see Chapter 3).

A third way of defining popular culture is as 'mass culture'. This draws heavily on the previous definition. The mass culture perspective will be discussed in some detail in Chapter 2; therefore all I want to do here is to suggest the basic terms of this definition. The first point that those who refer to popular culture as mass culture want to establish is that popular culture is a hopelessly commercial culture. It is mass-produced for mass consumption. Its audience is a mass of non-discriminating consumers. The culture itself is formulaic, manipulative (to the political right or left, depending on who is doing the analysis). It is a culture that is consumed with brain-numbed and brain-numbing passivity. But as John Fiske (1989a) points out, 'between 80 and 90 per cent of new products fail despite extensive advertising . . . many films fail to recover even their promotional costs at the box office' (31). Simon Frith (1983: 147) also points out that about 80 per cent of singles and albums lose money. Such statistics should clearly call into question the notion of consumption as an automatic and passive activity (see Chapters 8 and 12).

Those working within the mass culture perspective usually have in mind a previous 'golden age' when cultural matters were very different. This usually takes one of two forms: a lost organic community or a lost folk culture. But as Fiske (1989a) points out, 'In capitalist societies there is no so-called authentic folk culture against which to measure the "inauthenticity" of mass culture, so bemoaning the loss of the authentic is a fruitless exercise in romantic nostalgia' (27). This also holds true for the 'lost' organic community. The Frankfurt School, as we shall see in Chapter 4, locate the lost golden age not in the past, but in the future.

For some cultural critics working within the mass culture paradigm, mass culture is not just an imposed and impoverished culture – it is, in a clear identifiable sense, an imported American culture: 'If popular culture in its modern form was *invented* in any one place, it was . . . in the great cities of the United States, and above all in New York' (Maltby, 1989: 11; my italics). The claim that popular culture is American culture has a long history within the theoretical mapping of popular culture. It operates under the term 'Americanization'. Its central theme is that British culture has declined under the homogenizing influence of American culture. There are two things we can say with some confidence about the United States and popular culture. First, as Andrew Ross (1989) has pointed out, 'popular culture has been socially and institutionally central in America for longer and in a more significant way than in Europe' (7). Second, although the availability of American culture worldwide is undoubted, how what is available is consumed is at the very least contradictory (see Chapter 10). What is true is that in the 1950s (one of the key periods of Americanization), for many young people in Britain, American culture represented a force of liberation against the grey certainties of British everyday life. What is also clear is that the fear of Americanization is closely related to a distrust (regardless of national origin) of emerging forms of popular culture. As with the mass culture perspective generally, there are political left and political right versions of the argument. What are under threat are either the traditional values of high culture, or the traditional way of life of a 'tempted' working class.

There is what we might call a benign version of the mass culture perspective. The texts and practices of popular culture are seen as forms of public fantasy. Popular culture is understood as a collective dream world. As Richard Maltby (1989) claims, popular culture provides 'escapism that is not an escape from or to anywhere, but an escape of our utopian selves' (14). In this sense, cultural practices such as Christmas and the seaside holiday, it could be argued, function in much the same way as dreams: they articulate, in a disguised form, collective (but repressed) wishes and desires. This is a benign version of the mass culture critique because, as Maltby points out, 'If it is the crime of popular culture that it has taken our dreams and packaged them and sold them back to us, it is also the achievement of popular culture that it has brought us more and more varied dreams than we could otherwise ever have known' (ibid.).

Structuralism, although not usually placed within the mass culture perspective, and certainly not sharing its moralistic approach, nevertheless sees popular culture as a sort of ideological machine that more or less effortlessly reproduces the prevailing structures of power. Readers are seen as locked into specific 'reading positions'. There is little space for reader activity or textual contradiction. Part of post-structuralism's critique of structuralism is the opening up of a critical space in which such questions can be addressed. Chapter 6 will consider these issues in some detail.

A fourth definition contends that popular culture is the culture that originates from 'the people'. It takes issue with any approach that suggests that it is something imposed on 'the people' from above. According to this definition, the term should be used only to indicate an 'authentic' culture of 'the people'. This is popular culture as folk culture: a culture of the people for the people. As a definition of popular culture, it is 'often equated with a highly romanticised concept of working-class culture construed as the major source of symbolic protest within contemporary capitalism' (Bennett, 1980: 27). One problem with this approach is the question of who qualifies for inclusion in the category 'the people'. Another problem with it is that it evades the 'commercial' nature of much of the resources from which popular culture is made. No matter how much we might insist on this definition, the fact remains that people do not spontaneously produce culture from raw materials of their own making. Whatever popular culture is, what is certain is that its raw materials are those that are commercially provided. This approach tends to avoid the full implications of this fact. Critical analysis of pop and rock music is particularly replete with this kind of analysis of popular culture. At a conference I once attended, a contribution from the floor suggested that Levi's jeans would never be able to use a song from the Jam to sell its products. The fact that they had already used a song by the Clash would not shake this conviction. What underpinned this claim was a clear sense of cultural difference – television commercials for Levi's jeans are mass culture; the music of the Jam is popular culture defined as an oppositional culture of 'the people'. The only way the two could meet would be through the Jam 'selling out'. As this was not going to happen, Levi's jeans would never use a song by the Jam to sell its products. But this had already happened to the Clash, a band with equally sound political credentials. This circular exchange came to a stop. The cultural studies use of the concept of hegemony would, at the very least, have fuelled further discussion (see Chapter 4).

A fifth definition of popular culture, then, is one that draws on the political analysis of the Italian Marxist Antonio Gramsci, particularly on his development of the concept of hegemony. Gramsci (2009) uses the term 'hegemony' to refer to the way in which dominant groups in society, through a process of 'intellectual and moral leadership' (75), seek to win the consent of subordinate groups in society. This will be discussed in some detail in Chapter 4. What I want to do here is to offer a general outline of how cultural theorists have taken Gramsci's political concept and used it to explain the nature and politics of popular culture. Those using this approach see popular culture as a site of struggle between the 'resistance' of subordinate groups and the forces of 'incorporation' operating in the interests of dominant groups. Popular culture in this usage is not the imposed culture of the mass culture theorists, nor is it an emerging from below, spontaneously oppositional culture of 'the people' – it is a terrain of exchange and negotiation between the two: a terrain, as already stated, marked by resistance and incorporation. The texts and practices of popular culture move within what Gramsci (1971) calls a 'compromise equilibrium' (161) – a balance that is mostly weighted in the interests of the powerful. The process is historical (labelled popular culture one moment, and another kind of culture the next), but it is also synchronic (moving between resistance and incorporation at any given historical moment). For instance, the seaside holiday began as an aristocratic event and within a hundred years it had become an example of popular culture. Film noir started as despised popular cinema and within thirty years had become art cinema. In general terms, those looking at popular culture from the perspective of hegemony theory tend to see it as a terrain of ideological struggle between dominant and subordinate classes, dominant and subordinate cultures. As Bennett (2009) explains,

> The field of popular culture is structured by the attempt of the ruling class to win hegemony and by forms of opposition to this endeavour. As such, it consists not simply of an imposed mass culture that is coincident with dominant ideology, nor simply of spontaneously oppositional cultures, but is rather an area of negotiation between the two within which – in different particular types of popular culture – dominant, subordinate and oppositional cultural and ideological values and elements are 'mixed' in different permutations (96).

The compromise equilibrium of hegemony can also be employed to analyse different types of conflict within and across popular culture. Bennett highlights class conflict, but hegemony theory can also be used to explore and explain conflicts involving ethnicity, 'race', gender, generation, sexuality, disability, etc. – all are at different moments engaged in forms of cultural struggle against the homogenizing forces of incorporation of the official or dominant culture. The key concept in this use of hegemony theory, especially in post-Marxist cultural studies (see Chapter 4), is the concept of 'articulation' (the word being employed in its double sense to mean both to express and to make a temporary connection). Popular culture is marked by what Chantal Mouffe (1981) calls 'a process of disarticulation–articulation' (231). The Conservative Party political broadcast, discussed earlier, reveals this process in action. What was being attempted was the disarticulation of socialism as a political movement concerned with economic, social and political emancipation, in favour of its articulation as a political movement concerned to impose restraints on individual freedom. Also, as we shall see in Chapter 8, feminism has always recognized the importance of cultural struggle within the contested landscape of popular culture. Feminist presses have published science fiction, detective fiction and romance fiction. Such cultural interventions represent an attempt to articulate popular genres for feminist politics. It is also possible, using hegemony theory, to locate the struggle between resistance and incorporation as taking place within and across individual popular texts and practices. Raymond Williams (1980) suggests that we can identify different moments within a popular text or practice – what he calls 'dominant', 'emergent' and 'residual' – each pulling the text in a different direction. Thus a text is made up of a contradictory mix of different cultural forces. How these elements are articulated will depend in part on the social circumstances and historical conditions of production and consumption. Hall (1980a) uses Williams's insight to construct a theory of reading positions: 'subordinate', 'dominant' and 'negotiated'. David Morley (1980) has modified the model to take into account discourse and subjectivity: seeing reading as always an interaction between the discourses of the text and the discourses of the reader (see Storey, 2010a).

There is another aspect of popular culture that is suggested by hegemony theory. This is the claim that theories of popular culture are really theories about the constitution of 'the people'. Hall (2009b), for instance, argues that popular culture is a contested site for political constructions of 'the people' and their relation to 'the power bloc' (see Chapter 4):

> 'the people' refers neither to everyone nor to a single group within society but to a variety of social groups which, although differing from one another in other respects (their class position or the particular struggles in which they are most immediately engaged), are distinguished from the economically, politically and culturally powerful groups within society and are hence potentially capable of being united – of being organised into 'the people versus the power bloc' – if their separate struggles are connected (Bennett, 1986: 20).

This is of course to make popular culture a profoundly political concept.

> Popular culture is a site where the construction of everyday life may be examined. The point of doing this is not only academic – that is, as an attempt to understand a process or practice – it is also political, to examine the power relations that constitute this form of everyday life and thus reveal the configurations of interests its construction serves (Turner, 2003: 6).

In Chapter 12, I will consider John Fiske's 'semiotic' use of Gramsci's concept of hegemony. Fiske argues, as does Paul Willis from a slightly different perspective (also discussed in Chapter 12), that popular culture is what people make from the products of the culture industries – mass culture is the repertoire, popular culture is what people actively make from it, actually do with the commodities and commodified practices they consume.

A sixth definition of popular culture is one informed by recent thinking around the debate on postmodernism. This will be the subject of Chapter 10. All I want to do now is to draw attention to some of the basic points in the debate about the relationship between postmodernism and popular culture. The main point to insist on here is the claim that postmodern culture is a culture that no longer recognizes the distinction between high and popular culture. As we shall see, for some this is a reason to celebrate an end to an elitism constructed on arbitrary distinctions of culture; for others it is a reason to despair at the final victory of commerce over culture. An example of the supposed interpenetration of commerce and culture (the postmodern blurring of the distinction between 'authentic' and 'commercial' culture) can be found in the relationship between television commercials and pop music. For example, there is a growing list of artists who have had hit records as a result of their songs appearing in television commercials. One of the questions this relationship raises is: 'What is being sold: song or product?' I suppose the obvious answer is both. Moreover, it is now possible to buy CDs that consist of the songs that have become successful, or have become successful again, as a result of being used in advertisements. There is a wonderful circularity to this: songs are used to sell products and the fact that they do this successfully is then used to sell the songs. For those with little sympathy for either postmodernism or the celebratory theorizing of some postmodernists, the real question is: 'What is such a relationship doing to culture?' Those on the political left might worry about its effect on the oppositional possibilities of popular culture. Those on the political right might worry about what it is doing to the status of real culture. This has resulted in a sustained debate in cultural studies. The significance of popular culture is central to this debate. This, and other questions, will be explored in Chapter 10. The chapter will also address, from the perspective of the student of popular culture, the question: 'What is postmodernism?'

Finally, what all these definitions have in common is the insistence that whatever else popular culture is, it is definitely a culture that only emerged following industrialization and urbanization. As Williams (1963) argues in the Foreword to *Culture and Society*, 'The organising principle of this book is the discovery that the idea of culture, and the word itself in its general modern uses, came into English thinking in the period which we commonly describe as that of the Industrial Revolution' (11). It is a definition of culture and popular culture that depends on there being in place a capitalist market economy. This of course makes Britain the first country to produce popular culture defined in this historically restricted way. There are other ways to define popular culture, which do not depend on this particular history or these particular circumstances, but they are definitions that fall outside the range of the cultural theorists and the cultural theory discussed in this book. The argument, which underpins this particular periodization of popular culture, is that the experience of industrialization and urbanization changed fundamentally the cultural relations within the landscape of popular culture. Before industrialization and urbanization, Britain had two cultures: a common culture that was shared, more or less, by all classes, and a separate elite culture produced and consumed by a section of the dominant classes in society (see Burke, 1994; Storey,

2003). As a result of industrialization and urbanization, three things happened, which together had the effect of redrawing the cultural map. First of all, industrialization changed the relations between employees and employers. This involved a shift from a relationship based on mutual obligation to one based solely on the demands of what Thomas Carlyle calls the 'cash nexus' (quoted in Morris, 1979: 22). Second, urbanization produced a residential separation of classes. For the first time in British history there were whole sections of towns and cities inhabited only by working men and women. Third, the panic engendered by the French Revolution – the fear that it might be imported into Britain – encouraged successive governments to enact a variety of repressive measures aimed at defeating radicalism. Political radicalism and trade unionism were not destroyed, but driven underground to organize beyond the influence of middle-class interference and control. These three factors combined to produce a cultural space outside of the paternalist considerations of the earlier common culture. The result was the production of a cultural space for the generation of a popular culture more or less outside the controlling influence of the dominant classes. How this space was filled was a subject of some controversy for the founding fathers of culturalism (see Chapter 3). Whatever we decide was its content, the anxieties engendered by the new cultural space were directly responsible for the emergence of the 'culture and civilization' approach to popular culture (see Chapter 2).

Popular culture as *other*

What should be clear by now is that the term 'popular culture' is not as definitionally obvious as we might have first thought. A great deal of the difficulty arises from the *absent other* which always haunts any definition we might use. It is never enough to speak of popular culture; we have always to acknowledge that with which it is being contrasted. And whichever of popular culture's others we employ – mass culture, high culture, working-class culture, folk culture, etc. – it will carry into the definition of popular culture a specific theoretical and political inflection. 'There is', as Bennett (1982a) indicates, 'no single or "correct" way of resolving these problems; only a series of different solutions which have different implications and effects' (86). The main purpose of this book is to chart the many problems encountered, and the many solutions suggested, in cultural theory's complex engagement with popular culture. As we shall discover, there is a lot of ground between Arnold's view of popular culture as 'anarchy' and Dick Hebdige's (1988) claim that, 'In the West popular culture is no longer marginal, still less subterranean. Most of the time and for most people it simply is culture.' Or, as Geoffrey Nowell-Smith (1987) notes, 'popular cultural forms have moved so far towards centre stage in British cultural life that the separate existence of a distinctive popular culture in an oppositional relation to high culture is now in question' (80). This of course makes an understanding of the range of ways of theorizing popular culture all the more important.

This book, then, is about the theorizing that has brought us to our present state of thinking on popular culture. It is about how the changing terrain of popular culture has been explored and mapped by different cultural theorists and different theoretical approaches. It is upon their shoulders that we stand when we think critically about popular culture. The aim of this book is to introduce readers to the different ways in which popular culture has been analysed and the different popular cultures that have been articulated as a result of the process of analysis. For it must be remembered that popular culture is not a historically fixed set of popular texts and practices, nor is it a historically fixed conceptual category. The object under theoretical scrutiny is both historically variable, and always in part constructed by the very act of theoretical engagement. This is further complicated by the fact that different theoretical perspectives have tended to focus on particular areas of the popular cultural landscape. The most common division is between the study of texts (popular fiction, television, pop music, etc.) and lived cultures or practices (seaside holidays, youth subcultures, the celebration of Christmas, etc.). The aim of this book, therefore, is to provide readers with a map of the terrain to enable them to begin their own explorations, to begin their own mapping of the main theoretical and political debates that have characterized the study of popular culture.

The contextuality of meaning

At the beginning of this chapter, in the initial discussion of the difficulties involved in defining popular culture, I said 'The main argument that I suspect readers will take from this book is that popular culture is in effect an *empty* conceptual category, one that can be filled in a wide variety of often conflicting ways, depending on the context of use'. As the claim suggests, context is always crucial to an understanding of what something means. But what is a context? The word context comes into English in the late fifteenth century. It derives from the Latin words *contextus*, meaning to join together, and *contexere*, meaning to weave together. Knowing its origins helps us to understand its current use.

First, contexts are the other texts that make a particular text fully meaningful. These other texts *join together* with the text in question to produce meaning. If, in the course of a conversation, you use the word 'it', your meaning will only become clear if you provide a context that indicates to what it refers. When a student tells me, 'It is a difficult book', it only becomes fully meaningful if she explains that she is talking about Karl Marx's *Capital* – it and *Capital* join together to make her meaning clear. However, we should not think of contexts as only texts being joined with other texts. When we try to make sense of a text we always bring to it a set of presuppositions, which provide a framework for our analysis. These assumptions help construct a specific context for our understanding of the text – these are *woven together* around the text to be analysed. For example, to understand Bram Stoker's novel *Dracula* (1897) in terms of the 'New Woman' we have to situate the book in the historical context of its first publication.

Establishing this context allows us to read the novel in a very particular way. However, if we use psychoanalysis or feminism to interpret the novel, it is this mode of analysis that produces the context for our understanding of the novel. In these examples *Dracula* is articulated (i.e. made to mean) in relation to other texts supplied by a particular historical or theoretical perspective. In other words, the novel will seem very different if the context of our analysis is the theoretical presuppositions of feminism or psychoanalysis or our assumptions about the historical moment of the book's first publication. In these ways, then, contexts are both the co-texts of a text (the texts we join to a particular text) and the inter-texts brought to the text by a reader (the texts we weave around a particular text in order to fully understand it). The first is an extension of the text in question and the second is something that helps to construct a new understanding of the text. For example, Marx's *Capital* is a co-text that completes the meaning of what the student is telling me, whereas feminism is a body of inter-texts that can be used as a frame for producing a particular understanding of *Dracula*.

Another way of saying everything I have said about texts and contexts is simply to say texts do not have intrinsic meanings; meaning is something that a text acquires in a particular context. In other words, there is no 'text in itself' untroubled by context and reader activity: texts are always read and understood in relation to other texts. But a context is only ever a temporary fixing of meaning, as contexts change meaning changes. We might use the word 'it' many times during the course of a day and on each occasion what it refers to – what it is joined with – might be different. The student who told me, 'It is a difficult book' would change the meaning of 'it' by telling me she was talking about *Marxism and Literature* by Raymond Williams or Pierre Macherey's *A Theory of Literary Production*. In each case 'it' will mean something quite different. Take, for example, the Union Jack, the national flag of the UK. It can signify different things in a variety of contexts. Flying over a colonial outpost it may signify either imperialism or a civilizing mission; over the casket of a dead soldier it may signify honour and bravery or a pointless loss of life; as worn by Mods and post-Mods and those associated with BritPop it signifies 'cool Britannia'; displayed at a political rally it usually signifies right-wing politics; worn over the shoulders of a British athlete after winning an Olympic medal it signifies national sporting achievement; burned in another country it signifies opposition to British foreign policy. The meaning of the flag is always contextual – its meaning changes as it is situated in different contexts.

The texts that establish contexts can be anything that enables and constrains meaning. For example, watching television is rarely like reading a book. Whereas we tend to read in silence as we concentrate on the words on the page, eating, drinking, chatting, playing with children, tidying up, and a whole range of other activities, often accompany watching television. This is the context for most television viewing and unless we take it seriously we will not understand what we call 'watching television'. We should not of course think of a context as something stable and fixed, waiting passively for the inclusion of a particular text. Just as a context enables and constrains the meaning of a text, a text constrains and enables the meaning of a context – it is an active and interactive relationship. For example, feminism's encounter with *Dracula* changed the meaning of the novel, but working on the novel changes what counts as feminism.

Similarly, situating *Dracula* in its original historical moment of emergence changes how we see this particular historical period. And watching television changes how we eat, drink, chat, play with children or tidy up. A door can be both an exit and an entrance; although the materiality of the door remains the same, what it signifies depends on the context in which we view it.

To conclude this brief discussion of contextuality, we understand things in contexts; we also create contexts by our modes of understanding, and contexts change as a consequence of our inclusion of a particular text. Possible contexts for a text are almost endless. The chapters that follow will offer many examples of contextual analysis.

Notes

1. For an excellent discussion of Shakespeare as popular culture in nineteenth-century America, see Lawrence Levine (1988).
2. Slavoj Žižek (1992) identifies the retroactive evaluation that fixed film noir's current status: 'It started to exist only when it was discovered by French critics in the '50s (it is no accident that even in English, the term used to designate this genre is French: *film noir*). What was, in America itself, a series of low-budget B-productions of little critical prestige, was miraculously transformed, through the intervention of the French gaze, into a sublime object of art, a kind of film pendant to philosophical existentialism. Directors who had in America the status of skilled craftsmen, at best, became *auteurs*, each of them staging in his films a unique tragic vision of the universe' (112).
3. For a discussion of opera in popular culture, see Storey, 2002a, 2003, 2006 and 2010a.
4. See Storey, 2003 and 2005.

Further reading

Storey, John (ed.), *Cultural Theory and Popular Culture: A Reader*, 4th edn, Harlow: Pearson Education, 2009. This is the companion volume to the previous edition of this book. A fully updated 5th edition containing further readings is due for publication in 2018. An interactive website is also available (www.routledge.com/cw/storey), which contains helpful student resources and a glossary of terms for each chapter.

Agger, Ben, *Cultural Studies as Cultural Theory*, London: Falmer Press, 1992. As the title implies, this is a book about cultural studies written from a perspective sympathetic to the Frankfurt School. It offers some useful commentary on popular culture, especially Chapter 2: 'Popular culture as serious business'.

Allen, Robert C. (ed.), *Channels of Discourse, Reassembled*, London: Routledge, 1992. Although this collection is specifically focused on television, it contains some excellent essays of general interest to the student of popular culture.

Bennett, Tony, Colin Mercer and Janet Woollacott (eds), *Popular Culture and Social Relations*, Milton Keynes: Open University Press, 1986. An interesting collection of essays, covering both theory and analysis.

Brooker, Peter, *A Concise Glossary of Cultural Theory*, London: Edward Arnold, 1999. A brilliant glossary of the key terms in cultural theory.

Day, Gary (ed.), *Readings in Popular Culture*, London: Macmillan, 1990. A mixed collection of essays, some interesting and useful, others too unsure about how seriously to take popular culture.

Du Gay, Paul, Stuart Hall, Linda Janes, Hugh Mackay and Keith Negus, *Doing Cultural Studies: The Story of the Sony Walkman*, London: Sage, 1997. An excellent introduction to some of the key issues in cultural studies. Certainly worth reading for the explanation of 'the circuit of culture'.

Fiske, John, *Reading the Popular*, London: Unwin Hyman, 1989. A collection of essays analysing different examples of popular culture.

Fiske, John, *Understanding Popular Culture*, London: Unwin Hyman, 1989. A clear presentation of his particular approach to the study of popular culture.

Goodall, Peter, *High Culture, Popular Culture: The Long Debate*, St Leonards: Allen & Unwin, 1995. The book traces the debate between high and popular culture, with particular, but not exclusive, reference to the Australian experience, from the eighteenth century to the present day.

Milner, Andrew, *Contemporary Cultural Studies*, 2nd edn, London: UCL Press, 1994. A useful introduction to contemporary cultural theory.

Mukerji, Chandra and Michael Schudson (eds), *Rethinking Popular Culture*, Berkeley: University of California Press, 1991. A collection of essays, with an informed and interesting introduction. The book is helpfully divided into sections on different approaches to popular culture: historical, anthropological, sociological and cultural.

Naremore, James and Patrick Brantlinger, *Modernity and Mass Culture*, Bloomington and Indianapolis: Indiana University Press, 1991. A useful and interesting collection of essays on cultural theory and popular culture.

Storey, John, *Inventing Popular Culture*, Malden, MA: Blackwell, 2003. An historical account of the concept of popular culture.

Storey, John, *Culture and Power in Cultural Studies: The Politics of Signification*, Edinburgh: Edinburgh University Press, 2010. Extends many of the arguments in this book into more detailed areas of research.

Storey, John (ed.), *The Making of English popular Culture*, Abingdon: Routledge, 2016. An excellent collection of essays on the historical development of English popular culture.

Strinati, Dominic, *An Introduction to Theories of Popular Culture*, London: Routledge, 1995. A clear and comprehensive introduction to theories of popular culture.

Tolson, Andrew, *Mediations: Text and Discourse in Media Studies*, London: Edward Arnold, 1996. An excellent introduction to the study of popular media culture.

Turner, Graeme, *British Cultural Studies*, 3rd edn, London: Routledge, 2003. Still the best introduction to British cultural studies.

Walton, David, *Introducing Cultural Studies: Learning Through Practice*, London: Sage, 2008. Another excellent introduction to cultural studies: useful, informative and funny.

2 The 'culture and civilization' tradition

The popular culture of the majority has always been a concern of powerful minorities. Those with political power have always thought it necessary to police the culture of those without political power, reading it 'symptomatically' (see Chapter 6) for signs of political unrest; reshaping it continually through patronage and direct intervention. In the nineteenth century, however, there is a fundamental change in this relationship. Those with power lose, for a crucial period, the means to control the culture of the subordinate classes. When they begin to recover control, it is culture itself, and not culture as a symptom or sign of something else, that becomes, really for the first time, the actual focus of concern. As we noted at the end of Chapter 1, two factors are crucial to an understanding of these changes: industrialization and urbanization. Together they produce other changes that contribute to the making of a popular culture that marks a decisive break with the cultural relationships of the past.

If we take early nineteenth-century Manchester as our example of the new industrial urban civilization, certain points become clear. First of all, the town evolved clear lines of class segregation; second, residential separation was compounded by the new work relations of industrial capitalism. Third, on the basis of changes in living and working relations, there developed cultural changes. Put very simply, the Manchester working class was given space to develop an independent culture at some remove from the direct intervention of the dominant classes. Industrialization and urbanization had redrawn the cultural map. No longer was there a shared common culture, with an additional culture of the powerful. Now, for the first time in history, there was a separate culture of the subordinate classes of the urban and industrial centres. It was a culture of two main sources: (i) a culture offered for profit by the new cultural entrepreneurs, and (ii) a culture made by and for the political agitation of radical artisans, the new urban working-class and middle-class reformers, all described so well by E.P. Thompson in *The Making of the English Working Class* (see Chapter 3). Each of these developments in different ways threatened traditional notions of cultural cohesion and social stability. One threatened to weaken authority through the commercial dismantling of cultural cohesion; the other offered a direct challenge to all forms of political and cultural authority.

These were not developments guaranteed to hearten those who feared for the continuation of a social order based on power and privilege. Such developments, it was argued, could only mean a weakening of social stability, a destabilizing of the social order. It marked the beginning of what Benjamin Disraeli would call the 'two nations' (Disraeli, 1980), and it eventually gave birth to the first political and cultural movement of the new urban working class – Chartism. It is out of this context, and its continuing aftermath, that the *political* study of popular culture first emerges.

Matthew Arnold

The study of popular culture in the modern age can be said to begin with the work of Matthew Arnold. In some ways this is surprising, as he had very little to say directly about popular culture. Arnold's significance is that he inaugurates a tradition, a particular way of seeing popular culture, a particular way of placing popular culture within the general field of culture. The tradition has come to be known as the 'culture and civilization' tradition. My discussion of Arnold's contribution to the study of popular culture will focus mainly (but not exclusively) on *Culture and Anarchy* (1867–9), the work that secured, and continues to sustain, his reputation as a cultural critic. Arnold established a cultural agenda that remained dominant in debate from the 1860s until the 1950s. His significance, therefore, lies not with any body of empirical work, but with the enormous influence of his general perspective – the Arnoldian perspective – on popular culture.

For Arnold (1960), culture begins by meaning two things. First and foremost, it is a body of knowledge: in Arnold's famous phrase, 'the best that has been thought and said in the world' (6). Second, culture is concerned 'to make reason and the will of God prevail' (42). It is in the 'sweetness and light' of the second claim that 'the moral, social, and beneficial character of culture becomes manifest' (46). That is, 'culture . . . is a study of perfection . . . perfection which consists in becoming something rather than in having something, in an inward condition of the mind and spirit, not in an outward set of circumstances' (48). In other words, culture is the endeavour to know the best and to make this knowledge prevail for the good of all humankind. But how is culture to be attained? According to Arnold, we shall attain it by 'the disinterested and active use of reading, reflection, and observation, in the endeavour to know the best that can be known' (179). Culture, therefore, no longer consists in two things, but in three. Culture is now the means to know the best that has been thought and said, as well as that body of knowledge and the application of that knowledge to the 'inward condition of the mind and spirit' (31). There is, however, a fourth aspect to consider: Arnold insists that culture seeks 'to minister to the diseased spirit of our time' (163). This would appear to be an example of culture's third aspect. However, we are quickly told that culture will play its part 'not so much by lending a hand to our friends and countrymen in their *actual operations* for the removal of certain definite evils, but rather in getting our countrymen to seek culture' (163–4; my italics). This is Arnold's fourth and final definition: culture is the seeking of culture, what Arnold calls 'cultivated inaction' (163). For Arnold, then, culture is: (i) the ability to know what is best;

(ii) what is best; (iii) the mental and spiritual application of what is best, and (iv) the pursuit of what is best.

Popular culture is never actually defined. However, it becomes clear when reading through Arnold's work that the term 'anarchy' operates in part as a synonym for popular culture. Specifically, anarchy/popular culture is used to refer to Arnold's conception of the supposedly disruptive nature of working-class lived culture: the political dangers that he believes to be inevitably concomitant with the entry of the male urban working class into formal politics in 1867. The upshot of this is that anarchy and culture are for Arnold deeply political concepts. The social function of culture is to police this disruptive presence: the 'raw and uncultivated . . . masses' (176); 'the raw and unkindled masses' (69); 'our masses . . . quite as raw and uncultivated as the French' (76); 'those vast, miserable unmanageable masses of sunken people' (193). The problem is working-class lived culture: 'The rough [i.e. a working-class political protester] . . . asserting his personal liberty a little, going where he likes, assembling where he likes, bawling as he likes, hustling as he likes' (80–1). Again:

> the working class . . . raw and half developed . . . long lain half hidden amidst its poverty and squalor . . . now issuing from its hiding place to assert an Englishman's heaven born privilege of doing as he likes, and beginning to perplex *us* by marching where it likes, meeting where it likes, bawling what it likes, breaking what it likes (105; my italics).

The context of all this is the suffrage agitation of 1866–67. Arnold's employment of the phrase 'beginning to perplex us' is a clear indication of the class nature of his discourse. His division of society into Barbarians (aristocracy), Philistines (middle class) and Populace (working class) would seem at first sight to defuse the class nature of this discourse. This seems to be supported by his claim that under all 'our class divisions, there is a common basis of human nature' (ibid.). However, if we examine what Arnold means by a common basis, we are forced to a different conclusion. If we imagine the human race existing on an evolutionary continuum with itself at one end and a common ancestor shared with the ape at the other, what Arnold seems to be suggesting is that the aristocracy and middle class are further along the evolutionary continuum than the working class. This is shown quite clearly in his example of the common basis of our human nature. He claims that

> every time that we snatch up a vehement opinion in ignorance and passion, every time that we long to crush an adversary by sheer violence, every time that we are envious, every time that we are brutal, every time that we adore mere power or success, every time that we add our voice to swell a blind clamour against some unpopular personage, every time that we trample savagely on the fallen [we have] found in our own bosom the eternal spirit of the Populace (107).

According to Arnold, it takes only a little help from 'circumstances' to make this 'eternal spirit' triumph in both Barbarian and Philistine. Culture has two functions in this scenario. First, it must carefully guide the aristocracy and the middle class from such circumstances. Second, it must bring to the working class, the class in which this so-called human nature is said to reside, 'a much wanted principle . . . of authority, to counteract the tendency to anarchy that seems to be threatening us' (82). The principle of authority, as we shall see, is to be found in a strong centralized State.

Against such 'anarchy', culture recommends the State: 'We want an authority . . . culture suggests the idea of the State' (96). Two factors make the State necessary: first, the decline of the aristocracy as a centre of authority; second, the rise of democracy. Together they create a terrain favourable to anarchy. The solution is to occupy this terrain with a mixture of culture and coercion. Arnold's cultured State is to function to control and curtail the social, economic and cultural aspirations of the working class until the middle class is sufficiently cultured to take on this function itself. The State will operate in two ways: (i) through coercion to ensure no more Hyde Park riots, and (ii) through the instilling of the 'sweetness and light' of culture.

Why did Arnold think like this? The answer has a great deal to do with the historical changes witnessed by the nineteenth century. When he recommends culture 'as the great help out of our present difficulties' (6), it is these changes he has in mind. The 'present difficulties' have a double context. On the one hand, they are the immediate 'problems' raised by the granting of the franchise to the male urban working class. On the other, they are recognition of a historical process that had been in play from at least the eighteenth century (the development of industrial capitalism). Arnold believed that the franchise had given power to men as yet uneducated for power. A working class which has lost 'the strong feudal habits of subordination and deference' (76) is a very dangerous working class. It is the function of education to restore a sense of subordination and deference to this class. In short, education would bring to the working class a 'culture' that would in turn remove the temptations of trade unionism, political agitation and cheap entertainment. In short, culture would remove popular culture.

Culture and Anarchy informs its reader that 'education is the road to culture' (209). It is, therefore, worth looking briefly at his vision of education. Arnold does not envisage working-class, middle-class and aristocratic students all walking down the same road to culture. For the aristocracy, education is to accustom it to decline, to banish it as a class to history. For the working class, education is to civilize it for subordination, deference and exploitation. Arnold saw working-class schools (primary and elementary) as little more than outposts of civilization in a dark continent of working-class barbarism: 'they civilize the neighbourhood where they are placed' (1973: 39). According to Arnold, working-class children had to be civilized before they could be instructed. In a letter to his mother, written in 1862, he writes: 'the State has an interest in the primary school as a civilizing agent, even prior to its interest in it as an instructing agent' (1896: 187). It was culture's task to accomplish this. For the middle class, education was something quite different. Its essential function is to prepare middle-class children for the power that is to be theirs. Its aim is to convert 'a middle class, narrow, ungenial, and unattractive [into] a cultured, liberalised, ennobled, transformed middle class, [one to which the working class] may with joy direct its aspirations' (1954: 343).

Arnold (1960) called his various proposals, quoting the Duke of Wellington, 'a revolution by due course of law' (97). What it amounts to is a revolution from above, a revolution to prevent popular revolution from below. It works on the principle that a reform given is always better than a reform taken, forced or won. Popular demands are met, but in such a way as to weaken claims for further demands. It is not that Arnold did not desire a better society, one with less squalor, less poverty, less ignorance, etc., but that a better society could never be envisaged as other than a society in which the new urban middle class were 'hegemonic' (see Chapter 4).

Most of what I have said is a roundabout way of saying that the first grand theorist of popular culture had in fact very little to say about popular culture, except, that is, to say that it is symptomatic of a profound political disorder. Culture is not the main concern of Arnold's work; rather the main concern is social order, social authority, won through cultural subordination and deference. Working-class culture is significant to the extent that it signals evidence of social and cultural disorder and decline – a breakdown in social and cultural authority. The fact that working-class culture exists at all is evidence enough of decline and disorder. Working-class 'anarchy' is to be suppressed by the harmonious influences of culture – 'the best that has been thought and said in the world'.

Many of Arnold's ideas are derived from the Romantic critique of industrialism (see Williams, 1963). One writer in particular seems especially relevant: Samuel Taylor Coleridge. Coleridge (1972) distinguishes between 'civilisation' ('a mixed good, if not far more a corrupting influence') and 'cultivation' ('the harmonious development of those qualities and faculties which characterise our humanity') (33). To simplify, Coleridge suggests that civilization refers to the nation as a whole; cultivation is the property of a small minority, whom he calls the 'clerisy'. It is the function of the cultivated clerisy to guide the progress of civilization:

> the objects and final intention of the whole order being these – preserve the stores, and to guard the treasures, of past civilisation, and thus to bind the present to the past; to perfect and add to the same, and thus to connect the present with the future; but especially to diffuse through the whole community, and to every native entitled to its laws and rights, that quantity and quality of knowledge which was indispensable both for understanding of those rights, and for the performance of the duties correspondent (34).

Arnold builds on Coleridge's ideas. Instead of a clerisy, he writes of 'aliens' or 'the remnant'. But the purpose is essentially the same: the mobilization of culture to police the unruly forces of mass society. According to Arnold, history shows that societies have always been destroyed by 'the moral failure of the unsound majority' (1954: 640). Such a reading of history is hardly likely to inspire much confidence in democracy – let alone in popular culture. Arnold's vision is based on a curious paradox: the men and women of culture know the best that has been thought and said, but for whom are they preserving these treasures when the majority is unsound and has always been, and always will be, unsound? The inescapable answer seems to be: for themselves, a self-perpetuating cultural elite. All that is required from the rest of us is to recognize our cultural differ-ence and acknowledge our cultural deference. Arnold is clear on this point:

> The mass of mankind will never have any ardent zeal for seeing things as they are; very inadequate ideas will always satisfy them. On these inadequate ideas reposes, and must repose, the general practice of the world. That is as much as saying that whoever sets himself to see things as they are will find himself one of a very small circle; but it is only by this small circle resolutely doing its own work that adequate ideas will ever get current at all (364–5).

And again,

> The highly instructed few, and not the scantily instructed many, will ever be the organ to the human race of knowledge and truth. Knowledge and truth in the full sense of the words, are not attainable by the great mass of the human race at all (Arnold, 1960–77: 591).

These are very revealing statements. If the mass of humankind is to be always satisfied with inadequate ideas, never able to attain truth and knowledge, for whom are the small circle working? And what of the adequate ideas they will make current – current for whom? For other small circles of elites? Arnold's small circle would appear to be little more than a self-perpetuating intellectual elite. If they are never to engage in practical politics, and never to have any real influence on the mass of humankind, what is the purpose of all the grand humanistic claims to be found scattered throughout Arnold's work? It would appear that Arnold has been ensnared by his own elitism: and the working class are destined to remain to wallow in 'their beer, their gin, and their fun' (1954: 591). However, Arnold does not so much reject practical politics, as leave them in the safe hands of established authority. Therefore, the only politics that are being rejected are the politics of protest, the politics of opposition. This is a very stale defence of the dominant order. Despite this, or perhaps because of it, his influence has been enormous in that the Arnoldian perspective virtually mapped out the way of thinking about popular culture and cultural politics that dominated the field until the late 1950s.

Leavisism

> For Matthew Arnold it was in some ways less difficult. I am thinking of the so much more desperate plight of culture today (Leavis, 2009: 12).

The influence of Arnold on F.R. Leavis is there for all to see. Leavis takes Arnold's cul-tural politics and applies them to the supposed 'cultural crisis' of the 1930s. According to Leavis and the Leavisites, the twentieth century is marked by an increasing cultural decline. What had been identified by Arnold as a feature of the nineteenth century, it is argued, had continued and been compounded in the twentieth: that is, the increasing spread of a culture of 'standardisation and levelling down' (Leavis and Thompson, 1977: 3). It is against this process and its results that 'the citizen . . . must be trained to discriminate and to resist' (5).

The work of Leavisism spans a period of some forty years. However, the Leavisite attitude to popular culture was formed in the early 1930s with the publication of three texts: *Mass Civilisation and Minority Culture*, by F.R. Leavis, *Fiction and the Reading Public*, by Q.D. Leavis and *Culture and Environment*, by F.R. Leavis and Denys Thompson. Together these form the basis of the Leavisite response to popular culture.

Leavisism is based on the assumption that 'culture has always been in minority keeping' (Leavis and Thompson, 1977: 3):

> Upon the minority depends our power of profiting by the finest human experience of the past; they keep alive the subtlest and most perishable parts of tradition. Upon them depend the implicit standards that order the finer living of an age, the sense that this is worth more than that, this rather than that is the direction in which to go, that the centre is here rather than there (5).

What has changed is the status of this minority. No longer can it command cultural deference, no longer is its cultural authority unchallenged. Q.D. Leavis (1978) refers to a situation in which 'the minority, who had hitherto set the standard of taste without any serious challenge' have experienced a 'collapse of authority' (185, 187). Just as Arnold regretted the passing of 'the strong feudal habits of subordination and deference' (see previous section), Q.D. Leavis is nostalgic for a time when the masses exhibited an 'unquestioning assent to authority' (191).[1] She quotes Edmund Gosse to confirm the seriousness of the situation:

> One danger which I have long foreseen from the spread of the democratic sentiment, is that of the traditions of literary taste, the canons of literature, being reversed with success by a popular vote. Up to the present time, in all parts of the world, the masses of uneducated or semieducated persons, who form the vast majority of readers, though they cannot and do not appreciate the classics of their race, have been content to acknowledge their traditional supremacy. Of late there have seemed to me to be certain signs, especially in America, of a revolt of the mob against our literary masters. . . . If literature is to be judged by a plebiscite and if the plebs recognises its power, it will certainly by degrees cease to support reputations which give it no pleasure and which it cannot comprehend. The revolution against taste, once begun, will land us in irreparable chaos (190).

According to Leavis and Thompson, what Gosse had only feared had now come to pass:

> culture has always been in minority keeping. But the minority now is made conscious, not merely of an uncongenial, but of a hostile environment. . . . 'Civilisation'

and 'culture' are coming to be antithetical terms. It is not merely that the power and the sense of authority are now divorced from culture, but that some of the most disinterested solicitude for civilisation is apt to be, consciously or unconsciously, inimical to culture (1977: 26).

Mass civilization and its mass culture pose a subversive front, threatening 'to land us in irreparable chaos'. It is against this threat that Leavisism writes its manifestoes, and proposes 'to introduce into schools a training in resistance [to mass culture]' (Leavis, 1933: 188–9); and outside schools, to promote a 'conscious and directed effort . . . [to] take the form of resistance by an armed and active minority' (Q.D. Leavis, 1978: 270). The threat of democracy in matters both cultural and political is a terrifying thought for Leavisism. Moreover, according to Q.D. Leavis, 'The people with power no longer represent intellectual authority and culture' (191). Like Arnold, she sees the collapse of traditional authority coming at the same time as the rise of mass democracy. Together they squeeze the cultured minority and produce a terrain favourable for 'anarchy'.

Leavisism isolates certain key aspects of mass culture for special discussion. Popular fiction, for example, is condemned for offering addictive forms of 'compensation' and 'distraction':

> This form of compensation . . . is the very reverse of recreation, in that it tends, not to strengthen and refresh the addict for living, but to increase his unfitness by habituating him to weak evasions, to the refusal to face reality at all (Leavis and Thompson, 1977: 100).

Q.D. Leavis (1978) refers to such reading as 'a drug addiction to fiction' (152), and for those readers of romantic fiction it can lead to 'a habit of fantasying [which] will lead to maladjustment in actual life' (54). Self-abuse is one thing, but there is worse: their addiction 'helps to make a social atmosphere unfavourable to the aspirations of the minority. They actually get in the way of genuine feeling and responsible thinking' (74). For those not addicted to popular fiction, there is always the danger of cinema. Its popularity makes it a very dangerous source of pleasure indeed: 'they [films] involve surrender, under conditions of hypnotic receptivity, to the cheapest emotional appeals, appeals the more insidious because they are associated with a compellingly vivid illusion of actual life' (Leavis, 2009: 14). For Q.D. Leavis (1978), Hollywood films are 'largely masturbatory' (165). Although the popular press is described as 'the most powerful and pervasive de-educator of the public mind' (Leavis and Thompson, 1977: 138), and radio is claimed to be putting an end to critical thought (Leavis, 2009), it is for advertising, with its 'unremitting, pervasive, masturbatory manipulations' (Leavis and Thompson, 1977: 139), that Leavisism saves its most condemnatory tone.

Advertising, and how it is consumed, is for Leavisism the main symptom of cultural decline. To understand why, we must understand Leavisism's attitude to language. In *Culture and Environment*, Leavis and Thompson state: 'it should be brought home to learners that this debasement of language is not merely a matter of words; it is a debasement of emotional life, and the quality of living' (1977: 4). Advertising, therefore, is not just blamed for debasing the language, but condemned for debasing the emotional life of the whole language community, reducing 'the standard of living'. They provide examples for analysis (mostly written by F.R. Leavis himself). The questions they pose are very revealing of Leavisism's general attitude. Here is a typical example, an advert for 'Two Quakers' tobacco:

THE TOBACCO OF TYPICAL TWIST
'Yes, it's the best I've ever smoked. But it's deuced expensive.' 'What's the tuppence extra? And anyway, you get it back an' more. Burns clean and slow that's the typical twist, gives it the odd look. Cute scientific dodge. You see, they experimented. . . .' 'Oh! cut the cackle, and give us another fill. You talk like an advertisement.' Thereafter peace and a pipe of Two Quakers.

They then suggest the following questions for school students in the fifth and sixth forms:

1 Describe the type of person represented.
2 How are you expected to feel towards him?
3 What do you think his attitude would be towards us? How would he behave in situations where mob passions run high? (16–17)

Two things are remarkable about these questions. First of all, the connection that is made between the advertisement and so-called mob passions. This is an unusual question, even for students of cultural studies. Second, notice the exclusive 'us'; and note also how the pronoun attempts to construct membership of a small educated elite. Other questions operate in much the same way. Here are a few examples:

Describe the kind of reader this passage would please, and say why it would please him. What kind of person can you imagine responding to such an appeal as this last? What acquaintance would you expect them to have of Shakespeare's work and what capacity for appreciating it? (40).

Pupils can be asked to recall their own observations of the kind of people they may have seen visiting 'shrines' (51).

In the light of the 'Gresham Law', what kind of influence do you expect the cinema to have on general taste and mentality? (114).

What kind of standards are implied here? What would you judge to be the quality of the 'literature' he reads, and the reading he devotes to it? (119).

Why do we wince at the mentality that uses this idiom? (121).

[After describing the cinema as 'cheapening, debasing, distorting']: Develop the discussion of the educational value of cinema as suggested here (144).

It is difficult to see how such questions, rather than encouraging 'discrimination and resistance', would invite anything other than a critically debilitating and self-confirming snobbery.

In a temporary escape from the 'irreparable chaos' of the present, Leavisism looks back longingly to a cultural golden age, a mythic rural past, when there existed a shared culture uncorrupted by commercial interests. The Elizabethan period of Shakespeare's theatre is often cited as a time of cultural coherence before the cultural disintegration of the nineteenth and twentieth centuries. F.R. Leavis (1933) writes of Shakespeare belonging 'to a genuinely national culture, to a community in which it was possible for the theatre to appeal to the cultivated and the populace at the same time' (216). Q.D. Leavis (1978), in *Fiction and the Reading Public*, has charted this supposed decline. Her account of the organic relations between populace and cultivated are very revealing: 'the masses were receiving their amusement from above. . . . They had to take the same amusements as their betters. . . . Happily, they had no choice' (85). According to Q.D. Leavis,

> the spectator of Elizabethan drama, though he might not be able to follow the 'thought' minutely in the great tragedies, was getting his amusement from the mind and sensibility that produced those passages, from an artist and not from one of his own class. There was then no such complete separation as we have . . . between the life of the cultivated and the life of the generality (264).

What is interesting about their account of the past is what it reveals about their ideal future. The golden age was marked not just by cultural coherence, but happily for the Leavisites, by a cultural coherence based on authoritarian and hierarchical principles. It was a common culture that gave intellectual stimulation at one end, and affective pleasure at the other. This was a mythic world in which everyone knew their place, knew their station in life. F.R. Leavis (1984) is insistent 'that there was in the seventeenth century, a real culture of the people . . . a rich traditional culture . . . a positive culture which has disappeared' (188–9). Most of this culture was, according to Leavisism, destroyed by the changes brought about by the Industrial Revolution. The last remnants of the organic community, however, could still be found in rural communities in nineteenth-century England. He cites the works of George Bourne, *Change in the Village* and *The Wheelwright's Shop*, as evidence of this.[2] In the opening pages of *Culture and Environment*, F.R. Leavis and Thompson (1977) offer a reminder of what had been lost:

> What we have lost is the organic community with the living culture it embodied. Folk songs, folk dances, Cotswold cottages and handicraft products are signs and expressions of something more: an art of life, a way of living, ordered and patterned, involving social arts, codes of intercourse and a responsive adjustment, growing out of immemorial experience, to the natural environment and the rhythm of the year (1–2).

They also claim that the quality of work has also deteriorated with the loss of the organic community. The growing importance placed on leisure is seen as a sign of this loss. While in the past a worker lived in his or her work, he or she now works in order to live outside his or her work. But as a result of industrialization, the experience of work has deteriorated to such an extent that workers are actually 'incapacitated by their work' (69). Therefore, instead of recreation (re-creating what is lost in work), leisure provides workers with only 'decreation' (a compounding of the loss experienced through work). Given such a situation, it is little wonder that people turn to mass culture for compensation and passive distraction; the drug habit develops and they become junkies addicted to 'substitute living' (see Chapter 4 for a similar argument made from the perspective of Marxism). A world of rural rhythms had been lost to the monotony and mediocrity of 'suburbanism' (99). While in the organic community everyday culture was a constant support to the health of the individual, in mass civilization one must make a conscious and directed effort to avoid the unhealthy influence of everyday culture. The Leavisites fail to mention, as Williams (1963) remarks, 'the penury, the petty tyranny, the disease and mortality, the ignorance and frustrated intelligence which were also among its ingredients' (253). What we are presented with is not a historical account, but a literary myth to draw attention to the nature of our supposed loss: 'the memory of the old order must be the chief incitement towards a new' (Leavis and Thompson, 1977: 97).

Although the organic community is lost, it is still possible to get access to its values and standards by reading works of great literature. Literature is a treasury embodying all that is to be valued in human experience. Unfortunately, literature as the jewel in the crown of culture, has, like culture itself, lost its authority. Leavisism, as noted earlier, made plans to remedy this by dispatching cultural missionaries, a small select band of literary intellectuals, to establish outposts of culture within universities to maintain the literary/cultural tradition and encourage its 'continuous collaborative renewal' (Leavis, 1972: 27); and into schools to arm students to wage war against the general barbarism of mass culture and mass civilization. The re-establishment of literature's authority would not of course herald the return of the organic community, but it would keep under control the expansion of the influence of mass culture and thus preserve and maintain the continuity of England's cultural tradition. In short, it would help maintain and produce an 'educated public', who would continue the Arnoldian project of keeping in circulation 'the best that has been thought and said' (now more or less reduced to the reading of works of great literature).

It is very easy to be critical of the Leavisite approach to popular culture. But, as Bennett (1982b) points out, with perhaps a little too much generosity,

> Even as late as the mid fifties . . . 'Leavisism' [provided] the only developed intellectual terrain on which it was possible to engage with the study of popular culture. Historically, of course, the work produced by the 'Leavisites' was of seminal importance, constituting the first attempt to apply to popular forms techniques of literary analysis previously reserved for 'serious' works. . . . Perhaps more importantly, the general impact of 'Leavisism' at least as scathing in its criticisms of established 'high' and 'middle brow' culture as of popular forms tended to unsettle the prevailing canons of aesthetic judgement and evaluation with, in the long term, quite radical and often unforeseen consequences (5–6).

In Chapter 3 we shall begin to consider some of these radical and often unforeseen consequences as they appear in the work of Richard Hoggart, Raymond Williams and the early work of Stuart Hall.

Mass culture in America: the post-war debate

In the first fifteen or so years following the end of the Second World War, American intellectuals engaged in a debate about so-called mass culture. Andrew Ross (1989) sees 'mass' as 'one of the key terms that governs the official distinction between American/UnAmerican' (42). He argues that, '[t]he history behind this official distinction is in many ways the history of the formation of the modern national culture' (ibid.). Following the Second World War, America experienced the temporary success of a cultural and political consensus – supposedly based on liberalism, pluralism and classlessness. Until its collapse in the agitation for black civil rights, the formation of the counterculture, the opposition to America's war in Vietnam, the women's liberation movement and the campaign for gay and lesbian rights, it was a consensus dependent to a large extent on the cultural authority of American intellectuals. As Ross points out: 'For perhaps the first time in American history, intellectuals, as a social grouping, had the opportunity to recognize themselves as national agents of cultural, moral, and political leadership' (43). This newly found significance was in part due to 'the intense, and quite public, debate about "mass culture" that occupied intellectuals for almost fifteen years, until the late fifties' (ibid.). Ross spends most of his time relating the debate to the Cold War ideology of 'containment': the need to maintain a healthy body politic both within (from the dangers of cultural impoverishment) and without (from the dangers of Soviet communism). He identifies three positions in the debate:

1. An aesthetic–liberal position that bemoans the fact that given the choice the majority of the population choose so-called second- and third-rate cultural texts and practices in preference to the texts and practices of high culture.
2. The corporate–liberal or progressive–evolutionist position that claims that popular culture serves a benign function of socializing people into the pleasures of consumption in the new capitalist–consumerist society.
3. The radical or socialist position which views mass culture as a form of, or means to, social control.

Towards the end of the 1950s, the debate became increasingly dominated by the first two positions. This reflected in part the growing McCarthyite pressure to renounce anything resembling a socialist analysis. Given limited space, I will focus only on the debate about the health of the body politic within. In order to understand the debate one publication is essential reading – the anthology *Mass Culture: The Popular Arts in America*, published in 1957. Reading the many contributions, one quickly gets a sense of the parameters of the debate – what is at stake in the debate, and who are the principal participants.

Bernard Rosenberg (co-editor with David Manning White) argues that the material wealth and well-being of American society are being undermined by the dehumanizing effects of mass culture. His greatest anxiety is that, 'At worst, mass culture threatens not merely to cretinize our taste, but to brutalize our senses while paving the way to totalitarianism' (1957: 9). He claims that mass culture is not American by nature, or by example, nor is it the inevitable culture of democracy. Mass culture, according to Rosenberg, is nowhere more widespread than in the Soviet Union. Its author is not capitalism, but technology. Therefore America cannot be held responsible for its emergence or for its persistence.

White (1957) makes a similar point but for a different purpose. 'The critics of mass culture' (13), White observes, 'take an exceedingly dim view of contemporary American society' (14). His defence of American (mass) culture is to compare it with aspects of the popular culture of the past. He maintains that critics romanticize the past in order to castigate the present. He condemns those 'who discuss American culture as if they were holding a dead vermin in their hands' (ibid.), and yet forget the sadistic and brutal reality of animal baiting that was the everyday culture in which Shakespeare's plays first appeared. His point is that every period in history has produced 'men who preyed upon the ignorance and insecurities of the largest part of the populace . . . and therefore we need not be so shocked that such men exist today' (ibid.). The second part of his defence consists of cataloguing the extent to which high culture flourishes in America: for example, Shakespeare on TV, record figures for book borrowing from libraries, a successful tour by the Sadler's Wells Ballet, the fact that more people attend classical music events than attend baseball games, the increasing number of symphony orchestras.

A key figure in the debate is Dwight Macdonald. In a very influential essay, 'A theory of mass culture', he attacks mass culture on a number of fronts. First of all, mass culture undermines the vitality of high culture. It is a parasitic culture, feeding on high culture, while offering nothing in return.

> Folk art grew from below. It was a spontaneous, autochthonous expression of the people, shaped by themselves, pretty much without the benefit of High Culture, to suit their own needs. Mass Culture is imposed from above. It is fabricated by technicians hired by businessmen; its audience are passive consumers, their partici-pation limited to the choice between buying and not buying. The Lords of kitsch, in short, exploit the cultural needs of the masses in order to make a profit and/or to maintain their class-rule . . . in Communist countries, only the second purpose obtains. Folk art was the people's own institution, their private little garden walled off from the great formal park of their masters' High Culture. But Mass Culture breaks down the wall, integrating the masses into a debased form of High Culture and thus becoming an instrument of political domination (1998: 23).

Like other contributors to the debate, Macdonald is quick to deny the claim that America is the land of mass culture: 'the fact is that the U.S.S.R. is even more a land of

Mass Culture than is the U.S.A' (ibid.). This fact, he claims, is often missed by critics who focus only on the 'form' of mass culture in the Soviet Union. But it is mass culture (not folk culture: the expression of the people; nor high culture: the expression of the individual artist); and it differs from American mass culture in that 'its quality is even lower', and in that 'it exploits rather than satisfies the cultural needs of the masses . . . for political rather than commercial reasons' (24). In spite of its superiority to Soviet mass culture, American mass culture still represents a problem ('acute in the United States'): 'The eruption of the masses onto the political stage [produced] . . . disastrous cultural results' (ibid.). This problem has been compounded by the absence of 'a clearly defined cultural elite' (ibid.). If one existed, the masses could have mass culture and the elite could have high culture. However, without a cultural elite, America is under threat from a Gresham's Law of culture: the bad will drive out the good; the result will be not just a homogeneous culture but a 'homogenized culture . . . that threatens to engulf everything in its spreading ooze' (27), dispersing the cream from the top and turning the American people into infantile masses. His conclusions are very pessimistic to say the least: 'far from Mass Culture getting better, we will be lucky if it doesn't get worse' (29).

The analysis changes again as we move from the disillusioned ex-Trotskyism of Macdonald to the liberalism of Ernest van den Haag (1957), who suggests that mass culture is the inevitable outcome of mass society and mass production:

> The mass produced article need not aim low, but it must aim at an average of tastes. In satisfying all (or at least many) individual tastes in some respects, it violates each in other respects. For there are so far no average persons having average tastes. Averages are but statistical composites. A mass produced article, while reflecting nearly everybody's taste to some extent, is unlikely to embody anybody's taste fully. This is one source of the sense of violation which is rationalized vaguely in theories about deliberate debasement of taste (512).

He also suggests another reason: the temptations offered by mass culture to high culture. Two factors must be particularly tempting: (i) the financial rewards of mass culture, and (ii) the potentially enormous audience. He uses the famous Italian poet Dante Alighieri (1265–1321) as an illustration. Although Dante may have suffered religious and political pressures, he was not tempted to shape his work to make it appeal to an average of tastes. Had he been 'tempted to write for *Sports Illustrated*' or had he been asked 'to condense his work for *Reader's Digest*' or had he been given a contract 'to adapt it for the movies', would he have been able to maintain his aesthetic and moral standards? Dante was fortunate; his talent was never really tempted to stray from the true path of creativity: 'there were no alternatives to being as good a writer as his talent permitted' (521).

It is not so much that mass taste has deteriorated, van den Haag argues, but that mass taste has become more important to the cultural producers in Western societies. Like White, he notes the plurality of cultural texts and practices consumed in America. However, he also notes the way in which high culture and folk culture are absorbed into mass culture, and are consequently consumed as mass culture: 'it is not new nor disastrous that few people read classics. It is new that so many people misread them' (528). He cannot help in the end declaring that mass culture is a drug that 'lessens people's capacity to experience life itself' (529). Mass culture is ultimately a sign of impoverishment. It marks the de-individualization of life: an endless search after what Sigmund Freud calls 'substitute gratifications'.[3] The trouble with substitute gratifications, according to the mass culture critique, is that they shut out 'real gratifications' (532–5). This leads van den Haag to suggest that the consumption of mass culture is a form of repression; the empty texts and practices of mass culture are consumed to fill an emptiness within, which grows ever more empty the more the empty texts and practices of mass culture are consumed. The operation of this cycle of repression makes it increasingly impossible to experience 'real gratification'. The result is a nightmare in which the cultural 'masturbator' or the 'addict' of mass culture is trapped in a cycle of non-fulfilment, moving aimlessly between boredom and distraction:

> Though the bored person hungers for things to happen to him, the disheartening fact is that when they do he empties them of the very meaning he unconsciously yearns for by using them as distractions. In popular culture even the second coming would become just another 'barren' thrill to be watched on television till Milton Berle comes on (535).

Van den Haag differs from the 'cultural nostalgics', who use romanticized versions of the past to condemn the present, in his uncertainty about the past. He knows that 'popular culture impoverishes life without leading to contentment. But whether "the mass of men" felt better or worse without mass production techniques of which popular culture is an ineluctable part, we shall never know' (536).

Edward Shils (1978) has none of van den Haag's uncertainty. Moreover, he knows that when van den Haag says that industry has impoverished life he is talking nonsense:

> The present pleasures of the working and lower middle class are not worthy of profound aesthetic, moral or intellectual esteem but they are surely not inferior to the villainous things which gave pleasure to their European ancestors from the Middle Ages to the nineteenth century (35).

Shils rejects completely

> the utterly erroneous idea that the twentieth century is a period of severe intellectual deterioration and that this alleged deterioration is a product of a mass culture. . . . Indeed, it would be far more correct to assert that mass culture is now less damaging to the lower classes than the dismal and harsh existence of earlier centuries had ever been (36).

As far as Shils can see the problem is not mass culture, but the response of intellectuals to mass culture. In similar fashion, D.W. Brogan (1978), whilst in agreement with much of Macdonald's argument, remains more optimistic. He believes that Macdonald, in being 'so grimly critical of the present America, is too kind to the past in America and to the past and present in Europe' (191). In this way, Macdonald's pessimism about the present is only sustained by his overly optimistic view of the past. In short, he 'exaggerates . . . the bad eminence of the United States' (193).

In 'The middle against both ends', Leslie Fiedler (1957), unlike most other contributors to the debate, claims that mass culture

> is a peculiarly American phenomenon. . . . I do not mean . . . that it is found only in the United States, but that wherever it is found, it comes first from us, and is still to be discovered in fully developed form only among us. Our experience along these lines is, in this sense, a preview for the rest of the world of what must follow the inevitable dissolution of the older aristocratic cultures (539).

For Fiedler, mass culture is popular culture that 'refuses to know its place'. As he explains,

> contemporary vulgar culture is brutal and disturbing: the quasi spontaneous expression of the uprooted and culturally dispossessed inhabitants of anonymous cities, contriving mythologies which reduce to manageable form the threat of science, the horror of unlimited war, the general spread of corruption in a world where the social bases of old loyalties and heroisms have long been destroyed (540).

Fiedler poses the question: what is wrong with American mass culture? He knows that for some critics, at home and abroad, the fact that it is American is enough reason to condemn it. But, for Fiedler, the inevitability of the American experience makes the argument meaningless; that is, unless those who support the argument are also against industrialization, mass education and democracy. He sees America 'in the midst of a strange two-front class war'. In the centre is 'the genteel middling mind', at the top is 'the ironical-aristocratic sensibility', and at the bottom is 'the brutal-populist mentality' (545). The attack on popular culture is a symptom of timidity and an expression of conformity in matters of culture: 'the fear of the vulgar is the obverse of the fear of excellence, and both are aspects of the fear of difference: symptoms of a drive for conformity on the level of the timid, sentimental, mindless-bodiless genteel' (547). The genteel middling mind wants cultural equality on its own terms. This is not the Leavisite demand for cultural deference, but an insistence on an end to cultural difference. Therefore, Fiedler sees American mass culture as hierarchical and pluralist, rather than homogenized and levelling. Moreover, he celebrates it as such.

Shils (1978) suggests a similar model – American culture is divided into three cultural 'classes', each embodying different versions of the cultural: '"superior" or "refined" culture' at the top, '"mediocre" culture' in the middle, and '"brutal" culture' at the bottom (206). Mass society has changed the cultural map, reducing the significance of 'superior or refined culture', and increasing the importance of both 'mediocre' and 'brutal' (209). However, Shils does not see this as a totally negative development: 'It is an indication of a crude aesthetic awakening in classes which previously accepted what was handed down to them or who had practically no aesthetic expression and reception' (ibid.). Like Fiedler, Shils does not shy away from the claim that America is the home of mass culture. He calls America 'that most massive of all mass societies' (218). But he remains optimistic: 'As a matter of fact, the vitality, the individuality, which may re-habilitate our intellectual public will probably be the fruits of the liberation of powers and possibilities inherent in mass societies' (226). As Ross (1989) suggests, in Fiedler's essay, and in the work of other writers in the 1950s and early 1960s,

> the concept of 'class' makes a conditional return after its years in the intellectual wilderness. This time, however, class analysis returns not to draw attention to conflicts and contradictions, as had been the case in the thirties, but rather to serve a hegemonic moment in which a consensus was being established about the non-antagonistic coexistence of different political conceptions of the world. Cultural classes could exist as long as they kept themselves to themselves (58).

Cultural choice and consumption become both the sign of class belonging and the mark of class difference. However, instead of class antagonism, there is only plurality of consumer choice within a general consensus of the dangers within and the dangers without. In short, the debate about mass culture had become the terrain on which to construct the Cold War ideology of containment. After all, as Melvin Tumin (1957) points out, 'America and Americans have available to them the resources, both of mind and matter, to build and support the finest culture the world has ever known' (550). The fact that this has not yet occurred does not dismay Tumin; for him it simply prompts the question: how do we make it happen? For the answer, he looks to American intellectuals, who 'never before have . . . been so well placed in situations where they can function as intellectuals' (ibid.), through the debate on mass culture, to take the lead in helping to build the finest *popular culture* the world has ever known.

The culture of other people

It is easy to be critical of the 'culture and civilization' tradition's approach to popular culture. Given the recent developments in the field of cultural theory, it is almost enough to present a narrative of its approach to condemn it to populist disapproval. However, it must be remembered that from a historical point of view, the tradition's work is absolutely foundational to the project of the study of popular culture in British cultural studies. Furthermore, the impact of the tradition is difficult to overestimate: for more than a century it was undoubtedly the dominant paradigm in cultural analysis. Indeed, it could be argued that it still forms a kind of repressed 'common sense' in certain areas of British and American academic and non-academic life.

Although the 'culture and civilization' tradition, especially in its Leavisite form, created an educational space for the study of popular culture, there is also a real sense in which this approach to popular culture 'actively impeded its development as an area of study' (Bennett, 1982b: 6). The principal problem is its working assumption that popular culture always represents little more than an example of cultural decline and potential political disorder. Given this assumption, theoretical research and empirical investigation continued to confirm what it always expected to find.

> It was an assumption of the theory that there was something wrong with popular culture and, of course, once that assumption had been made, all the rest followed: one found what one was looking for – signs of decay and deterioration – precisely because the theory required that these be found. In short, the only role offered to the products of popular culture was that of fall guy (ibid.).

As we have noted, popular culture is condemned for many things. However, as Bennett points out, the 'culture and civilization' tradition is not noted for its detailed analyses of the texts and practices of popular culture. Instead, it looked down from the splendid heights of high culture to what it saw as the commercial wastelands of popular culture, seeking only confirmation of cultural decline, cultural difference, and the need for cultural deference, regulation and control. It

> was very much a discourse of the 'cultured' about the culture of those without 'culture'. . . . In short, popular culture was approached from a distance and gingerly, held at arm's length by outsiders who clearly lacked any sense of fondness for or participation in the forms they were studying. It was always the culture of 'other people' that was at issue (ibid.).

The anxieties of the 'culture and civilization' tradition are anxieties about social and cultural extension: how to deal with challenges to cultural and social exclusivity. As the nineteenth century receded, and those traditionally outside 'culture' and 'society' demanded inclusion, strategies were adopted to incorporate and to exclude. Acceptance brought into being 'high society' and 'high culture', to be distinguished from society and culture or, better still, mass society and mass culture. In short, it is a tradition that demanded, and expected, two responses from the 'masses' (see Photo 2.1) – cultural and social difference and cultural and social deference. As we shall see (in Chapters 10 and 12), some of the debates around postmodernism may be in part little more than the latest struggle for inclusion in, and exclusion from, Culture (with a capital C), which ultimately is less about texts, and much more about people and their everyday lived cultures.

Photo 2.1   A day trip to Blackpool in the early 1950s. 'There are . . . no masses; there are only ways of seeing [other] people as masses' (Raymond Williams, 1963: 289).

Notes

1. John Docker (1994) refers to her as 'an old-style colonialist ethnographer, staring with distaste at the barbaric ways of strange and unknown people' (25).
2. It is not just that F.R. Leavis offers us an idealized account of the past, which he does; he actually idealizes Bourne's own account, failing to mention his criticisms of rural life.
3. It should be noted that, contrary to van den Haag, Freud is referring to all art, and not just popular culture.

Further reading

Storey, John (ed.), *Cultural Theory and Popular Culture: A Reader*, 4th edn, Harlow: Pearson Education, 2009. This is the companion volume to the previous edition of this book. A fully updated 5th edition containing further readings is due for publication in 2018. An interactive website is also available (www.routledge.com/cw/storey), which contains helpful student resources and a glossary of terms for each chapter.

Baldick, Chris, *The Social Mission of English 1848–1932*, Oxford: Clarendon Press, 1983. Contains interesting and informed chapters on Arnold and Leavisism.

Bilan, R.P., *The Literary Criticism of F.R. Leavis*, Cambridge: Cambridge University Press, 1979. Although mostly on Leavis as a literary critic, it contains some useful material on his attitude to high and popular culture.

Bramson, Leon, *The Political Context of Sociology*, Princeton, NJ: Princeton University Press, 1961. Contains an illuminating chapter on the mass culture debate in America.

Gans, Herbert J., *Popular Culture and High Culture: An Analysis and Evaluation of Taste*, New York: Basic Books, 1974. The book is a late contribution to the mass culture debate in America. It presents a compelling argument in defence of cultural pluralism.

Johnson, Lesley, *The Cultural Critics*, London: Routledge & Kegan Paul, 1979. Contains useful chapters on Arnold and on F.R. Leavis.

Mulhern, Francis, *The Moment of Scrutiny*, London: New Left Books, 1979. Perhaps the classic account of Leavisism.

Ross, Andrew, *No Respect: Intellectuals and Popular Culture*, London: Routledge, 1989. An interesting book, with a useful chapter on the mass culture debate in America.

Trilling, Lionel, *Matthew Arnold*, London: Unwin University Press, 1949. Still the best introduction to Arnold.

Waites, Bernard, Tony Bennett and Graham Martin (eds), *Popular Culture: Past and Present*, London: Croom Helm, 1982. A collection of essays on different examples of popular culture. Chapters 1, 4 and 6 address popular culture and the historical context that gave rise to the anxieties of the 'culture and civilization' tradition.

Williams, Raymond, *Culture and Society*, Harmondsworth: Penguin, 1963. The seminal book on the 'culture and civilization' tradition: includes chapters on Arnold and F.R. Leavis.

3 Culturalism

In this chapter I shall consider the work produced in the late 1950s and early 1960s by Richard Hoggart, Raymond Williams, E.P. Thompson, and Stuart Hall and Paddy Whannel. This body of work, despite certain differences between its authors, constitutes the founding texts of culturalism. As Hall (1978) was later to observe, 'Within cultural studies in Britain, "culturalism" has been the most vigorous, indigenous strand' (19). The chapter will end with a brief discussion of the institutionalization of culturalism at the Centre for Contemporary Cultural Studies.

Both Hoggart and Williams develop positions in response to Leavisism. As we noted in Chapter 2, the Leavisites opened up an educational space in Britain for the study of popular culture. Hoggart and Williams occupy this space in ways that challenge many of the basic assumptions of Leavisism, whilst also sharing some of these assumptions. It is this contradictory mixture – looking back to the 'culture and civilization' tradition, whilst at the same time moving forward to culturalism and the foundations of the cultural studies approach to popular culture – that has led *The Uses of Literacy, Culture and Society* and *The Long Revolution* to be called both texts of the 'break' and examples of 'left-Leavisism' (Hall, 1996a).

Thompson, on the other hand, would describe his work, then and always, as Marxist. The term 'culturalism' was coined to describe his work, and the work of Hoggart and Williams, by one of the former directors of the Centre for Contemporary Cultural Studies, Richard Johnson (1979). Johnson uses the term to indicate the presence of a body of theoretical concerns connecting the work of the three theorists. Each, in his different way, breaks with key aspects of the tradition he inherits. Hoggart and Williams break with Leavisism; Thompson breaks with mechanistic and economistic versions of Marxism. What unites them is an approach which insists that by analysing the culture of a society – the textual forms and documented practices of a culture – it is possible to reconstitute the patterned behaviour and constellations of ideas shared by the men and women who produce and consume the texts and practices of that society. It is a perspective that stresses 'human agency', the active production of culture, rather than its passive consumption. Although not usually included in accounts of the formation of culturalism out of left-Leavisism, Hall and Whannel's *The Popular Arts* is included here because of its classic left-Leavisite focus on popular culture. Taken together as a body of work, the contributions of Hoggart, Williams, Thompson, and Hall and Whannel clearly mark the emergence of what is now known as the cultural studies approach to popular culture. The institutional home of these developments was, especially in the 1970s and early 1980s, the Centre for Contemporary Cultural Studies at the University of Birmingham (see Green, 1996).

Richard Hoggart: *The Uses of Literacy*

The Uses of Literacy is divided into two parts: 'An "older" order', describing the working-class culture of Hoggart's childhood in the 1930s; and 'Yielding place to new', describing a traditional working-class culture under threat from the new forms of mass entertainment of the 1950s. Dividing the book in this way in itself speaks volumes about the perspective taken and the conclusions expected. On the one hand, we have the traditional 'lived culture' of the 1930s. On the other, we have the cultural decline of the 1950s. Hoggart is in fact aware that during the course of writing the book, 'nostalgia was colouring the material in advance: I have done what I could to remove its effects' (1990: 17). He is also aware that the division he makes between the 'older' and the 'new', underplays the amount of continuity between the two. It should also be noted that his evidence for the 'older' depends not on 'invoking some rather mistily conceived pastoral tradition the better to assault the present, [but] to a large extent on memories of my childhood about twenty years ago' (23, 24). His evidence for the cultural decline represented by the popular culture of the 1950s is material gathered as a university lecturer and researcher. In short, the 'older' is based on personal experience; the 'new' on academic research. This is a significant and informing distinction.

It is also worth noting something about Hoggart's project that is often misunderstood. What he attacks is not a 'moral' decline in the working class as such, but what he perceives as a decline in the 'moral seriousness' of the culture provided for the working class. He repeats on a number of occasions his confidence in the working class's ability to resist many of the manipulations of mass culture: 'This is not simply a power of passive resistance, but something which, though not articulate, is positive. The working classes have a strong natural ability to survive change by adapting or assimilating what they want in the new and ignoring the rest' (32). His confidence stems from his belief that their response to mass culture is always partial: 'with a large part of themselves they are just "not there", are living elsewhere, living intuitively, habitually, verbally, drawing on myth, aphorism, and ritual. This saves them from some of the worst effects' (33).

According to Hoggart,

> working class people have traditionally, or at least for several generations, regarded art as escape, as something enjoyed but not assumed to have much connexion with the matter of daily life. Art is marginal, 'fun' . . . 'real' life goes on elsewhere. . . . Art is for you to use (238).

He describes the aesthetic of the working class as an 'overriding interest in the close detail' of the everyday; a profound interest in the already known; a taste for culture that 'shows' rather than 'explores'. The working-class consumer, according to Hoggart's account, therefore seeks not 'an escape from ordinary life', but its intensification, in the embodied belief 'that ordinary life is intrinsically interesting' (120). The new mass entertainment of the 1950s is said to undermine this aesthetic:

> Most mass entertainments are in the end what D.H. Lawrence described as 'anti-life'. They are full of a corrupt brightness, of improper appeals and moral evasions . . . they offer nothing which can really grip the brain or heart. They assist a gradual drying up of the more positive, the fuller, the more cooperative kinds of enjoyment, in which one gains much by giving much (340).

It is not just that the pleasures of mass entertainment are 'irresponsible' and 'vicarious' (ibid.); they are also destroying the very fabric of an older, healthier, working-class culture. He is adamant that (in the 1950s)

> we are moving towards the creation of a mass culture; that the remnants of what was at least in parts an urban culture 'of the people' are being destroyed; and that the new mass culture is in some important ways less healthy than the often crude culture it is replacing (24).

He claims that the working-class culture of the 1930s expressed what he calls 'The rich full life', marked by a strong sense of community. This is a culture that is by and large made by the people. Here is a fairly well-known example of what he means – his description of a typical day at the seaside:

> the 'charas' go rolling out across the moors for the sea, past the road houses which turn up their noses at coach parties, to one the driver knows where there is coffee and biscuits or perhaps a full egg and bacon breakfast. Then on to a substantial lunch on arrival, and after that a fanning out in groups. But rarely far from one another, because they know their part of the town and their bit of beach, where they feel at home. . . . They have a nice walk past the shops; perhaps a drink; a sit in a deck chair eating an ice cream or sucking mint humbugs; a great deal of loud laughter – at Mrs Johnson insisting on a paddle with her dress tucked in her bloomers, at Mrs Henderson pretending she has 'got off' with the deck chair attendant, or in the queue at the ladies lavatory. Then there is the buying of presents for the family, a big meat tea, and the journey home with a stop for drinks on the way. If the men are there, and certainly if it is a men's outing, there will probably be several stops and a crate or two of beer in the back for drinking on the move. Somewhere in the middle of the moors the men's parties all tumble out, with much horseplay and noisy jokes about bladder capacity. The driver knows exactly what is expected of him as he steers his warm, fuggy, and singing community back to the town; for his part he gets a very large tip, collected during the run through the last few miles of the town streets (147–8).

This is a popular culture that is communal and self-made. Hoggart can be criticized for his romanticism, but we should also recognize here, in the passage's utopian energy, an example of Hoggart's struggle to establish a working distinction between a culture 'of the people' and a 'world where things are done for the people' (151).

The first half of *The Uses of Literacy* consists mostly of examples of communal and self-made entertainment. The analysis is often in considerable advance of Leavisism. For example, he defends working-class appreciation of popular song against the dismissive hostility of Cecil Sharp's (Leavisesque) longing for the 'purity' of folk music (see Storey, 2003 and 2016) in terms that were soon to become central to the project of cultural studies. Songs succeed, he argues, 'no matter how much Tin Pan Alley plugs them' (159), only if they can be *made to* meet the emotional requirements of their popular audience. As he says of the popular appropriation of 'After the Ball is Over', 'they have taken it on their own terms, and so it is not for them as poor a thing as it might have been' (162).

The idea of an audience appropriating for its own purposes – on its own terms – the commodities offered to it by the culture industries is never fully explored. But the idea is there in Hoggart, again indicating the underexploited sophistication of *parts* of *The Uses of Literacy* – too often dismissed as a rather unacademic, and nostalgic, semi-autobiography. The real weakness of the book is its inability to carry forward the insights from its treatment of the popular culture of the 1930s into its treatment of the so-called mass culture of the 1950s. If it had done, it would have, for example, quickly found totally inadequate the contrasting descriptive titles, 'The full rich life' and 'Invitations to a candy-floss world'.

It is worth noting at this point that it is not necessary to say that Hoggart's picture of the 1930s is romanticized in order to prove that his picture of the 1950s is exaggeratedly pessimistic and overdrawn; he does not have to be proved wrong about the 1930s, as some critics seem to think, in order to be proved wrong about the 1950s. It is possible that he is right about the 1930s, whilst being wrong about the 1950s. Like many intellectuals whose origins are working class, he is perhaps prone to bracket off his own working-class experience against the real and imagined condescension of his new middle-class colleagues: 'I know the contemporary working class is deplorable, but *mine* was different.' Although I would not wish to overstress this motivation, it does get some support in Williams's (1957) review of *The Uses of Literacy*, when he comments on 'lucky Hoggart's' account of the scholarship boy: 'which I think', Williams observes, 'has been well received by some readers (and why not? it is much what they wanted to hear, and now an actual scholarship boy is saying it)' (426–7). Again, in a discussion of the 'strange allies' dominant groups often attract, Williams (1965) makes a similar, but more general point:

> In our own generation we have a new class of the same kind: the young men and women who have benefited by the extension of public education and who, in surprising numbers, identify with the world into which they have been admitted, and spend much of their time, to the applause of their new peers, expounding and

documenting the hopeless vulgarity of the people they have left: the one thing that is necessary now, to weaken belief in the practicability of further educational extension (377–8).

When, in the second part of his study, Hoggart turns to consider 'some features of contemporary life' (169), the self-making aspect of working-class culture is mostly kept from view. The popular aesthetic, so important for an understanding of the working-class pleasure on show in the 1930s, is now forgotten in the rush to condemn the popular culture of the 1950s. The success of 'the radio "soap operas", with working class women . . . is due to the consummateness of their attention . . . to their remarkably sustained presentation of the perfectly ordinary and unremarkable' (181). This is repeated in newspaper cartoons featuring such figures as 'the "little man" worrying for days on end about his daughter's chances in the school cookery competition . . . a daily exercise in spinning out the unimportant and insignificant' (ibid.). What has happened to the intrinsic significance of the everyday? Instead of talk of a popular aesthetic, we are invited on a tour of the manipulative power of the culture industries. The popular culture of the 1950s, as described by Hoggart, no longer offers the possibility of a full rich life; everything is now far too thin and insipid. The power of 'commercial culture' has grown, relentless in its attack on the old (traditional working-class culture) in the name of the new, the 'shiny barbarism' (193) of mass culture. This is a world in which 'To be "old fashioned" is to be condemned' (192). It is a condition to which the young are particularly vulnerable. These 'barbarians in wonderland' (193) demand more, and are given more, than their parents and their grandparents had or expected to have. But such supposedly mindless hedonism, fed by thin and insipid fare, leads only to debilitating excess.

> 'Having a good time' may be made to seem so important as to override almost all other claims; yet when it has been allowed to do so, having a good time becomes largely a matter of routine. The strongest argument against modern mass entertainments is not that they debase taste – debasement can be alive and active – but that they over excite it, eventually dull it, and finally kill it. . . . They kill it at the nerve, and yet so bemuse and persuade their audience that the audience is almost entirely unable to look up and say, 'But in fact this cake is made of sawdust' (196–7).

Although (in the late 1950s) that stage had not yet been reached, all the signs, according to Hoggart, indicate that this is the way in which the world is travelling. But even in this 'candy-floss world' (206) there are still signs of resistance. For example, although mass culture may produce some awful popular songs,

> people do not have to sing or listen to these songs, and many do not: and those who do, often make the songs better than they really are . . . people often read them in their own way. So that even there they are less affected than the extent of their purchases would seem to indicate (231).

Again, this reminds us that Hoggart's target is (mostly) the producers of the commodities from which popular culture is made and not those who make these commodities (or not) into popular culture. Although he offers many examples of 'proof' of cultural decline, popular fiction is arguably his key example of deterioration. He compares a piece of contemporary writing (in fact it is an imitation written by himself) with an extract from *East Lynne* and an extract from *Adam Bede*. He concludes that in comparison the contemporary extract is thin and insipid: a 'trickle of tinned milk and water which staves off the pangs of a positive hunger and denies the satisfactions of a solidly filling meal' (237). Leaving aside the fact that the contemporary extract is an imitation (as are all his contemporary examples), Hoggart argues that its inferiority is due to the fact that it lacks the 'moral tone' (236) of the other two extracts. This may be true, but what is also significant is the way in which the other two extracts are *full* of 'moral tone' in a quite definite sense: they attempt to tell the reader what to think; they are, as he admits, 'oratory' (235). The contemporary extract is similarly thin in a quite definite sense: it does not tell the reader what to think. Therefore, although there may be various grounds on which we might wish to rank the three extracts, with *Adam Bede* at the top and the contemporary extract at the bottom, 'moral tone' (meaning fiction should tell people what to think) seems to lead us nowhere but back to the rather bogus certainties of Leavisism. Moreover, we can easily reverse the judgement: the contemporary extract is to be valued for its elliptic and interrogative qualities; it invites us to think by not thinking for us; this is not to be dismissed as an absence of thought (or 'moral tone' for that matter), but as an absence full of potential presence, which the reader is invited to *actively* produce.

One supposedly striking portent of the journey into the candy-floss world is the habitual visitor to the new milk bars, 'the juke box boy' (247) – his term for the Teddy boy. Milk bars are themselves symptomatic: they 'indicate at once, in the nastiness of their modernistic knick-knacks, their glaring showiness, an aesthetic breakdown so complete' (ibid.). Patrons are mostly 'boys between fifteen and twenty, with drape suits, picture ties, and an American slouch' (248). Their main reason for being there is to 'put copper after copper into the mechanical record player' (ibid.). The music 'is allowed to blare out so that the noise would be sufficient to fill a good sized ballroom' (ibid.). Listening to the music, 'The young men waggle one shoulder or stare, as desperately as Humphrey Bogart, across the tubular chairs' (ibid.).

> Compared even with the pub around the corner, this is all a peculiarly thin and pallid form of dissipation, a sort of spiritual dry-rot amid the odour of boiled milk. Many of the customers – their clothes, their hair styles, their facial expressions all indicate – are living to a large extent in a myth world compounded of a few simple elements which they take to be those of American life (ibid.).

According to Hoggart,

> They are a depressing group . . . perhaps most of them are rather less intelligent than the average [working-class youth], and are therefore even more exposed than

others to the debilitating mass trends of the day . . . they have no responsibilities, and little sense of responsibilities, to themselves or to others (248–9).

Although 'they are not typical', they are an ominous sign of things to come:

> these are the figures some important contemporary forces are tending to create, the directionless and tamed helots of a machine-minding class. . . . The hedonistic but passive barbarian who rides in a fifty-horse-power bus for threepence, to see a five-million-dollar film for one-and-eightpence, is not simply a social oddity; he is a portent (250).

The juke-box boy symptomatically bears the prediction of a society in which 'the larger part of the population is reduced to a condition of obediently receptive passivity, their eyes glued to television sets, pin ups, and cinema screens' (316).

Hoggart, however, does not totally despair at the march of mass culture. He knows, for instance, that the working class 'are not living lives which are imaginatively as poor as a mere reading of their literature would suggest' (324). The old communal and self-made popular culture still remains in working-class ways of speaking, in 'the Working-Men's Clubs, the styles of singing, the brass bands, the older types of magazines, the close group games like darts and dominoes' (ibid.). Moreover, he trusts their 'considerable moral resources' (325) to allow them, and to encourage them, to continue to adapt for their own purposes the commodities and commodified practices of the culture industries. In short, they 'are a good deal less affected than they might well be. The question, of course, is how long this stock of moral capital will last, and whether it is being renewed' (ibid.). For all his guarded optimism, he warns that it is a 'form of democratic self-indulgence to over-stress this resilience' in the face of the 'increasingly dangerous pressures' (330) of mass culture, with all its undermining of genuine community with an increasingly 'hollow . . . invitation to share in a kind of palliness' (340). His ultimate fear is that 'competitive commerce' (243) may have totalitarian designs:

> Inhibited now from ensuring the 'degradation' of the masses economically . . . competitive commerce . . . becomes a new and stronger form of subjection; this subjection promises to be stronger than the old because the chains of cultural subordination are both easier to wear and harder to strike away than those of economic subordination (243–4).

Hoggart's approach to popular culture has much in common with the approach of Leavisism (this is most noticeable in the analysis of popular culture in the second part of the book); both operate with a notion of cultural decline; both see education in discrimination as a means to resist the manipulative appeal of mass culture. However, what makes his approach different from that of Leavisism is his detailed preoccupation with, and, above all, his clear commitment to, working-class culture. His distance from Leavisism is most evident in the content of his own 'good past/bad present' binary opposition: instead of the organic community of the seventeenth century, his 'good past' is the working-class culture of the 1930s. What Hoggart celebrates from the 1930s is, significantly, the very culture that the Leavisites were armed to resist. This alone makes his approach an implicit critique of, and an academic advance on, Leavisism. But, as Hall (1980b) points out, although Hoggart 'refused many of [F.R.] Leavis's embedded cultural judgements', he nevertheless, in his use of Leavisite literary methodology, 'continued "a tradition" while seeking, in practice, to transform it' (18).

Raymond Williams: 'The analysis of culture'

Raymond Williams's influence on cultural studies has been enormous. The range of his work alone is formidable. He has made significant contributions to our understanding of cultural theory, cultural history, television, the press, radio and advertising. Alan O'Connor's (1989) bibliography of Williams's published work runs to thirty-nine pages. His contribution is all the more remarkable when one considers his origins in the Welsh working class (his father was a railway signalman), and that as an academic he was professor of drama at Cambridge University. In this section, I will comment only on his contribution to the founding of culturalism and its contribution to the study of popular culture.

In 'The analysis of culture', Williams (2009) outlines the 'three general categories in the definition of culture' (32). First, there is 'the "ideal", in which culture is a state or process of human perfection, in terms of certain absolute or universal values' (ibid.). The role of cultural analysis, using this definition, 'is essentially the discovery and description, in lives and works, of those values which can be seen to compose a timeless order, or to have permanent reference to the universal human condition' (ibid.). This is the definition inherited from Arnold and used by Leavisism: what he calls, in *Culture and Society*, culture as an ultimate 'court of human appeal, to be set over the processes of practical social judgement and yet to offer itself as a mitigating and rallying alternative' (Williams, 1963: 17).

Second, there is the 'documentary' record: the surviving texts and practices of a culture. In this definition, 'culture is the body of intellectual and imaginative work, in which, in a detailed way, human thought and experience are variously recorded' (Williams, 2009: 32). The purpose of cultural analysis, using this definition, is one of critical assessment. This can take a form of analysis similar to that adopted with regard to the 'ideal'; an act of critical sifting until the discovery of what Arnold calls 'the best that has been thought and said' (see Chapter 2). It can also involve a less exalted practice: the cultural as the critical object of interpretative description and evaluation (literary studies is the obvious example of this practice). Finally, it can also involve a more historical, less literary evaluative function: an act of critical reading to measure its significance as a 'historical document' (historical studies is the obvious example of this practice).

Third, 'there is the "social" definition of culture, in which culture is a description of a particular way of life' (ibid.). The 'social' definition of culture is crucial to the founding of culturalism. This definition introduces three new ways of thinking about culture: first, the 'anthropological' position, which sees culture as a description of a particular way of life; second, the proposition that culture 'expresses certain meanings and values' (ibid.); third, the claim that the work of cultural analysis should be the 'clarification of the meanings and values implicit and explicit in a particular way of life, a particular culture' (ibid.). Williams is aware that the kind of analysis the 'social' definition of culture demands will often 'involve analysis of elements in the way of life that to followers of the other definitions are not "culture" at all' (ibid.). Moreover, while such analysis might still operate modes of evaluation of the 'ideal' and the 'documentary' type, it will also extend

> to an emphasis which, from studying particular meanings and values, seeks not so much to compare these, as a way of establishing a scale, but by studying their modes of change to discover certain general 'laws' or 'trends', by which social and cultural development as a whole can be better understood (32–3).

Taken together, the three points embodied in the 'social' definition of culture – culture as a particular way of life, culture as expression of a particular way of life, and cultural analysis as a method of reconstituting a particular way of life – establish both the general perspective and the basic procedures of culturalism.

Williams, however, is reluctant to remove from analysis any of the three ways of understanding culture: 'there is a significant reference in each . . . and, if this is so, it is the relations between them that should claim our attention' (33). He describes as 'inadequate' and 'unacceptable' any definition that fails to include the other definitions: 'However difficult it may be in practice, we have to try to see the process as a whole, and to relate our particular studies, if not explicitly at least by ultimate reference, to the actual and complex organization' (34). As he explains,

> I would then define the theory of culture as the study of relationships between elements in a whole way of life. The analysis of culture is the attempt to discover the nature of the organization which is the complex of these relationships. Analysis of particular works or institutions is, in this context, analysis of their essential kind of organization, the relationships which works or institutions embody as parts of the organization as a whole (35).

In addressing the 'complex organization' of culture as a particular way of life, the purpose of cultural analysis is always to understand what a culture is expressing: 'the actual experience through which a culture was lived'; the 'important common element'; 'a particular community of experience' (36). In short, it aims to reconstitute what Williams calls 'the structure of feeling' (ibid.). By structure of feeling, he means the shared values of a particular group, class or society. The term is used to describe a discursive structure that is a cross between a collective cultural unconscious and an ideology. He uses, for example, the term to explain the way in which many nineteenth-century novels employ 'magic solutions' to close the gap in that society between 'the ethic and the experience'. He gives examples of how men and women are released from loveless marriages as a result of the convenient death or the insanity of their partners; legacies turn up unexpectedly to overcome reverses in fortune; villains are lost in the Empire; poor men return from the Empire bearing great riches; and those whose aspirations could not be met by prevailing social arrangements are put on a boat to make their dreams come true elsewhere. All these (and more) are presented as examples of a shared structure of feeling, the unconscious and conscious working out in fictional texts of the contradictions of nineteenth-century society. The purpose of cultural analysis is to read the structure of feeling through the documentary record, 'from poems to buildings and dress-fashions' (37). As he makes clear,

> What we are looking for, always, is the actual life that the whole organization is there to express. The significance of documentary culture is that, more clearly than anything else, it expresses that life to us in direct terms, when the living witnesses are silent (ibid.).

The situation is complicated by the fact that culture always exists on three levels:

> We need to distinguish three levels of culture, even in its most general definition. There is the lived culture of a particular time and place, only fully accessible to those living in that time and place. There is the recorded culture, of every kind, from art to the most everyday facts: the culture of a period. There is also, as the factor connecting lived culture and period cultures, the culture of the selective tradition (37).

Lived culture is culture as experienced by people in their day-to-day existence in a particular place and at a particular moment in time; the only people who have full access to this culture are those who actually lived its structure of feeling. Once the historical moment is gone the structure of feeling begins to fragment. Cultural analysis has access only through the documentary record of the culture. But the documentary record itself fragments under the processes of 'the selective tradition' (ibid.). Between a lived culture and its reconstitution in cultural analysis, clearly, a great deal of detail is lost. For example, as Williams points out, nobody can claim to have read all the novels of the nineteenth century. Instead, what we have is the specialist who can claim perhaps to have read many hundreds; the interested academic who has read somewhat fewer; the 'educated reader' who has read fewer again. This quite clear process of selectivity does not prevent the three groups of readers from sharing a sense of the nature of *the* nineteenth-century novel. Williams is of course aware that no nineteenth-century reader would in fact have read *all* the novels of the nineteenth century. His point, however, is that the nineteenth-century reader 'had something which . . . no later individual can wholly recover: that sense of the life within which the novels were written, and which we now approach through our selection' (38). For Williams, it is crucial to understand the selectivity of cultural traditions. It always (inevitably) produces a cultural record, a cultural tradition, marked by 'a rejection of considerable areas of what was once a living culture' (38). Furthermore, as he explains in *Culture and Society*, 'there will always be a tendency for this process of selection to be related to and even governed by the interests of the class that is dominant' (1963: 313).

> Within a given society, selection will be governed by many kinds of special interests, including class interests. Just as the actual social situation will largely govern contemporary selection, so the development of the society, the process of historical change, will largely determine the selective tradition. The traditional culture of a society will always tend to correspond to its contemporary system of interests and values, for it is not an absolute body of work but a continual selection and interpretation (2009: 38–9).

This has quite profound ramifications for the student of popular culture. Given that selection is invariably made on the basis of 'contemporary interests', and given the incidence of many 'reversals and rediscoveries', it follows that 'the relevance of past work, in any future situation, is unforeseeable' (39). If this is the case, it also follows that absolute judgements about what is good and what is bad, about what is high and what is low, in contemporary culture, should be made with a great deal less certainty, open as they are to historical realignment in a potential whirlpool of historical contingency. Williams advocates, as already noted, a form of cultural analysis that is conscious that 'the cultural tradition is not only a selection but also an interpretation' (ibid.). Although cultural analysis cannot reverse this, it can, by returning a text or practice to its historical moment, show other 'historical alternatives' to contemporary interpretation and 'the particular contemporary values on which it rests' (ibid.). In this way, we are able to make clear distinctions between 'the whole historical organization within which it was expressed' and 'the contemporary organization within which it is used' (ibid.). By working in this way, 'real cultural processes will emerge' (ibid.).

Williams's analysis breaks with Leavisism in a number of ways. First, there is no special place for art – it is a human activity alongside other human activities: 'art is there, as an activity, with the production, the trading, the politics, the raising of families' (34). Williams presses the case for a democratic account of culture: culture as a particular way of life. In *Culture and Society*, he distinguishes between middle-class culture as 'the basic individualist idea and the institutions, manners, habits of thought, and intentions which proceed from that' and working-class culture as 'the basic collective idea, and the institutions, manners, habits of thought, and intentions which proceed from this' (1963: 313). He then gives this account of the achievements of working-class culture:

> The working class, because of its position, has not, since the Industrial Revolution, produced a culture in the narrower sense. The culture which it has produced, and which it is important to recognise, is the collective democratic institution, whether

in the trade unions, the cooperative movement, or a political party. Working-class culture, in the stage through which it has been passing, is primarily social (in that it has created institutions) rather than individual (in particular intellectual or imaginative work). When it is considered in context, it can be seen as a very remarkable creative achievement (314).

It is when Williams insists on culture as a definition of the 'lived experience' of 'ordinary' men and women, made in their daily interaction with the texts and practices of everyday life, that he finally breaks decisively with Leavisism. Here is the basis for a democratic definition of culture. He takes seriously Leavis's call for a common culture. But the difference between Leavisism and Williams on this point is that Williams does want a common culture, whilst Leavisism wants only a hierarchical culture of difference and deference. Williams's review of *The Uses of Literacy* indicates some of the key differences between his own position and the traditions of Leavisism (in which he partly locates Hoggart):

> The analysis of Sunday newspapers and crime stories and romances is . . . familiar, but, when you have come yourself from their apparent public, when you recognise in yourself the ties that still bind, you cannot be satisfied with the older formula: enlightened minority, degraded mass. You know how bad most 'popular culture' is, but you know also that the irruption of the 'swinish multitude', which Burke had prophesied would trample down light and learning, is the coming to relative power and relative justice of your own people, whom you could not if you tried desert (1957: 424–5).

Although he still claims to recognize 'how bad most "popular culture" is', this is no longer a judgement made from within an enchanted circle of certainty, policed by 'the older formula: enlightened minority, degraded mass'. Moreover, Williams is insistent that we distinguish between the commodities made available by the culture industries and what people make of these commodities. He identifies what he calls

> the extremely damaging and quite untrue identification of 'popular culture' (commercial newspapers, magazines, entertainments, etc.) with 'working-class culture'. In fact the main source of this 'popular culture' lies outside the working class altogether, for it is instituted, financed and operated by the commercial bourgeoisie, and remains typically capitalist in its methods of production and distribution. That working-class people form perhaps a majority of the consumers of this material . . . does not, as a fact, justify this facile identification (425).

In other words, people are not reducible to the commodities they consume. Hoggart's problem, according to Williams, is that he 'has taken over too many of the formulas', from 'Matthew Arnold' to 'contemporary conservative ideas of the decay of politics in the working class'; the result is an argument in need of 'radical revision' (ibid.). The publication of 'The analysis of culture', together with the other chapters in *The Long*

Revolution, has been described by Hall (1980b) as 'a seminal event in English post-war intellectual life' (19), which did much to provide the radical revision necessary to lay the basis for a non-Leavisite study of popular culture.

E.P. Thompson: *The Making of the English Working Class*

In the Preface to *The Making of the English Working Class*, E.P. Thompson states:

> This book has a clumsy title, but it is one which meets its purpose. Making, because it is a study in an active process, which owes as much to agency as conditioning. The working class did not rise like the sun at an appointed time. It was present at its own making (1980: 8).

The English working class, like any class, is for Thompson 'a *historical* phenomenon' (original emphasis); it is not a 'structure' or a 'category', but the coming together of 'a number of disparate and seemingly unconnected events, both in the raw material of experience and in consciousness'; it is 'something which in fact happens (and can be shown to happen) in human relationships' (ibid.). Moreover, class is not a 'thing'; it is always a historical relationship of unity and difference: uniting one class as against another class or classes. As he explains: 'class happens when some men, as a result of common experiences (inherited or shared), feel and articulate the identity of their interests as between themselves, and as against other men whose interests are different from (and usually opposed to) theirs' (8–9). The common experience of class 'is largely determined by the productive relations into which men are born – or enter involuntarily' (9). However, the consciousness of class, the translation of experience into culture, 'is defined by men as they live their own history, and, in the end, this is its only definition' (10). Class is for Thompson, then, 'a social and cultural formation, arising from processes which can be studied as they work themselves out over a considerable historical period' (11).

The Making of the English Working Class details the political and cultural formation of the English working class by approaching its subject from three different but related perspectives. First, it reconstructs the political and cultural traditions of English radicalism in the late eighteenth century: religious dissent, popular discontent, and the influence of the French Revolution. Second, it focuses on the social and cultural experience of the Industrial Revolution as it was lived by different working groups: weavers, field labourers, cotton spinners, artisans, etc. Finally, it analyses the growth of working-class consciousness evidenced in the corresponding growth in a range of political, social and cultural 'strongly based and self conscious working-class institutions' (212–13). As he insists: 'The working class made itself as much as it was made' (213). He draws two conclusions from his research. First, 'when every caution has been made, the outstanding fact of the period between 1790 and 1830 is the formation of "the working class"' (212). Second, he claims that 'this was, perhaps, the most distinguished popular culture England has known' (914).

The Making of the English Working Class is the classic example of 'history from below'. Thompson's aim is to place the 'experience' of the English working class as central to any understanding of the formation of an industrial capitalist society in the decades leading up to the 1830s. It is a history from below in the double sense suggested by Gregor McLellan (1982): a history from below in that it seeks to reintroduce working-class experience into the historical process; and a history from below in that it insists that the working class were the conscious agents of their own making.[1] Thompson is working with Marx's (1977) famous claim about the way in which men and women make history: 'Men make their own history, but they do not make it just as they please; they do not make it under circumstances chosen by themselves, but under circumstances directly encountered, given and transmitted from the past' (10). What Thompson does is to emphasize the first part of Marx's claim (human agency) against what he considers to have been an overemphasis by Marxist historians on the second part (structural determinants). Paradoxically, or perhaps not so, he has himself been criticized for overstressing the role of human agency – human experiences, human values – at the expense of structural factors (see Anderson, 1980).

The Making of the English Working Class is in so many ways a monumental contribution to social history (in size alone: the Penguin edition runs to over nine hundred pages). What makes it significant for the student of popular culture is the nature of its historical account. Thompson's history is not one of abstract economic and political processes, nor is it an account of the doings of the great and the worthy. The book is about 'ordinary' men and women, their experiences, their values, their ideas, their actions, their desires: in short, popular culture as a site of resistance to those in whose interests the Industrial Revolution was made. Hall (1980b) calls it 'the most seminal work of social history of the post-war period', pointing to the way it challenges 'the narrow, elitist conception of "culture" enshrined in the Leavisite tradition, as well as the rather evolutionary approach which sometimes marked Williams's *The Long Revolution*' (19–20).

In an interview a decade or so after the publication of the book, Thompson (1976) commented on his historical method as follows: 'If you want a generalization I would have to say that the historian has got to be listening all the time' (15). He is by no means the only historian who listens; the conservative historian G.M. Young also listens, if in a rather more selective fashion: 'history is [he claims] the conversation of people who counted' (quoted in McLellan, 1982: 107). What makes Thompson's listening radically different is the people to whom he listens. As he explains in a famous passage from the Preface to *The Making of the English Working Class*:

> I am seeking to rescue the poor stockinger, the Luddite cropper, the 'obsolete' hand loom weaver, the 'utopian' artisan, and even the deluded follower of Joanna Southcott, from the enormous condescension of posterity. Their crafts and traditions

may have been dying. Their hostility to the new industrialism may have been backward looking. Their communitarian ideals may have been fantasies. Their insurrectionary conspiracies may have been foolhardy. But they lived through these times of acute social disturbance, and we did not. Their aspirations were valid in terms of their own experience; and, if they were casualties of history, they remain, condemned in their own lives, as casualties (1980: 12).

Before concluding this brief account of Thompson's contribution to the study of popular culture, it should be noted that he himself does not accept the term 'culturalism' as a description of his work. This and other related points was the subject of a heated 'History Workshop' debate between Richard Johnson, Stuart Hall and Thompson himself (see Samuel, 1981). One of the difficulties when reading the contributions to the debate is the way that culturalism is made to carry two quite different meanings. On the one hand, it is employed as a description of a particular methodology (this is how I am using it here). On the other, it is used as a term of critique (usually from a more 'traditional' Marxist position or from the perspective of Marxist structuralism). This is a complex issue, but as a coda to this discussion of Hoggart, Williams and Thompson, here is a very simplified clarification: positively, culturalism is a methodology that stresses culture (human agency, human values, human experience) as being of crucial importance for a full sociological and historical understanding of a given social formation; negatively, culturalism is used to suggest the employment of such assumptions without full recognition and acknowledgement that culture is the effect of structures beyond itself, and that these have the effect of ultimately determining, constraining and, finally, producing, culture (human agency, human values and human experience). Thompson disagrees strongly with the second proposition, and rejects totally any suggestion that culturalism, regardless of the definition, can be applied to his own work.

Stuart Hall and Paddy Whannel: *The Popular Arts*

The 'main thesis' of *The Popular Arts* is that 'in terms of actual quality . . . the struggle between what is good and worthwhile and what is shoddy and debased is not a struggle *against* the modern forms of communication, but a conflict *within* these media' (Hall and Whannel, 1964: 15). Hall and Whannel's concern is with the difficulty of making these distinctions. They set themselves the task to develop 'a critical method for handling . . . problems of value and evaluation' (ibid.) in the study of popular culture. In this task they pay specific thanks to the work of Hoggart and Williams, and passing thanks to the key figures of Leavisism.

The book was written against a background of concern about the influence of popular culture in the school classroom. In 1960 the National Union of Teachers (NUT) Annual Conference passed a resolution that read in part:

Conference believes that a determined effort must be made to counteract the debasement of standards which result from the misuse of press, radio, cinema and television. . . . It calls especially upon those who use and control the media of mass communication, and upon parents, to support the efforts of teachers in an attempt to prevent the conflict which too often arises between the values inculcated in the classroom and those encountered by young people in the world outside (quoted in Hall and Whannel, 1964: 23).

The resolution led to the NUT Special Conference, 'Popular culture and personal responsibility'. One speaker at the conference, the composer Malcolm Arnold, said: 'Nobody is in any way a better person morally or in any other way for liking Beethoven more than Adam Faith. . . . Of course the person who likes both is in a very happy position since he is able to enjoy much more in his life than a lot of other people' (ibid.: 27). Although Hall and Whannel (1964) recognize 'the honest intention' in Arnold's remarks, they question what they call 'the random use of Adam Faith as an example' because, as they claim, 'as a singer of popular songs he is by any serious standards far down the list'. Moreover, as they explain, 'By serious standards we mean those that might be legitimately applied to popular music – the standards set, for example, by Frank Sinatra or Ray Charles' (28). What Hall and Whannel are doing here is rejecting the arguments of both Leavisism and the (mostly American) mass culture critique, which claims that all high culture is good and that all popular culture is bad, for an argument that says, on the one hand, that most high culture is good, and on the other, contrary to Leavisism and the mass culture critique, that some popular culture is also good – it is ultimately a question of popular discrimination.

Part of the aim of *The Popular Arts*, then, is to replace the 'misleading generalizations' of earlier attacks on popular culture by helping to facilitate popular discrimination within and across the range of popular culture itself. Instead of worrying about the 'effects' of popular culture, 'we should be seeking to train a more demanding audience' (35). A more demanding audience, according to Hall and Whannel, is one that prefers jazz to pop, Miles Davis to Liberace, Frank Sinatra to Adam Faith, Polish films to mainstream Hollywood, *L'Année Dernière à Marienbad* to *South Pacific*; and knows intuitively and instinctively that high culture ('Shakespeare, Dickens and Lawrence') is usually always best. They take from Clement Greenberg (who took it from Theodor Adorno) the idea that mass culture is always 'pre-digested' (our responses are predetermined rather than the result of a genuine interaction with the text or practice), and use the idea as a means not just to discriminate between good and bad popular culture, but to suggest that it can also be applied to examples of high culture: 'The important point about such a definition [culture as "pre-digested"] is that it cuts across the commonplace distinctions. It applies to films but not all, to some TV but not all. It covers segments of the traditional as well as the popular culture' (36).

Their approach leads them to reject two common teaching strategies often encountered when popular culture is introduced into the classroom. First, there is the defensive strategy that introduces popular culture in order to condemn it as second-rate culture. Second, there is the 'opportunist' strategy that embraces the popular tastes of students in the hope of eventually leading them to better things. 'In neither case', they contend, 'is there a genuine response, nor any basis for real judgements' (37). Neither would lead to what they insist is necessary: 'a training in discrimination' (ibid.). This is not (to repeat a point made earlier) the classic discrimination of Leavisism, defending the 'good' high culture against the encroachments of the 'bad' popular culture, but discrimination within and not just against popular culture: sifting the 'good' popular culture from the 'bad' popular culture. However, although they do not believe in introducing the texts and practices of popular culture into education 'as steppingstones in a hierarchy of taste' leading ultimately to *real* culture,[2] they still insist (as do Hoggart and Williams) that there is a fundamental categorical difference – a difference of value – between high and popular culture. Nevertheless, the difference is not necessarily a question of superiority/inferiority; it is more about different kinds of satisfaction: it is not useful to say that the music of Cole Porter is inferior to that of Beethoven. The music of Porter and Beethoven is not of equal value, but Porter was not making an unsuccessful attempt to create music comparable to Beethoven's (39).

Not unequal, but of different value, is a very difficult distinction to unload. What it seems to suggest is that we must judge texts and practices on their own terms: 'recognise different aims . . . assess varying achievements with defined limits' (38). Such a strategy will open up discrimination to a whole range of cultural activity and prevent the defensive ghettoization of high against the rest. Although they acknowledge the 'immense debt' they owe to the 'pioneers' of Leavisism, and accept more or less the Leavisite view (modified by a reading of William Morris) of the organic culture of the past, they nevertheless, in a classic left-Leavisite move, reject the conservatism and pessimism of Leavisism, and insist, against calls for 'resistance by an armed and conscious minority' to the culture of the present (Q.D. Leavis), that 'if we wish to re-create a genuine popular culture we must seek out the points of growth within the society that now exists' (39). They claim that by adopting 'a critical and evaluative attitude' (46) and an awareness that it is 'foolish to make large claims for this popular culture' (40), it is possible 'to break with the false distinction . . . between the "serious" and the "popular" and between "entertainment" and "values"' (47).

This leads Hall and Whannel to what we might call the second part of their thesis: the necessity to recognize within popular culture a distinct category they call 'popular art'. Popular art is not art that has attempted and failed to be 'real' art, but art that operates within the confines of the popular. Using the best of music hall, especially Marie Lloyd, as an example (but also thinking of the early Charlie Chaplin, *The Goon Show* and jazz musicians), they offer this definition:

> while retaining much in common with folk art, it became an individual art, existing within a literate commercial culture. Certain 'folk' elements were carried through, even though the artist replaced the anonymous folk artist, and the 'style' was that of the performer rather than a communal style. The relationships here are more complex – the art is no longer simply created by the people from below – yet the interaction, by way of the conventions of presentation and feeling, re-establishes the rapport. Although this art is no longer directly the product of the 'way of life'

of an 'organic community', and is not 'made by the people', it is still, in a manner not applicable to the high arts, a popular art, for the people (59).

According to this argument, good popular culture ('popular art') is able to re-establish the relationship ('rapport') between performer and audience that was lost with the advent of industrialization and urbanization. As they explain:

> Popular art . . . is essentially a conventional art which re-states, in an intense form, values and attitudes already known; which measures and reaffirms, but brings to this something of the surprise of art as well as the shock of recognition. Such art has in common with folk art the genuine contact between audience and performer: but it differs from folk art in that it is an individualised art, the art of the known performer. The audience as community has come to depend on the performer's skills, and on the force of a personal style, to articulate its common values and interpret its experiences (66).

One problem with their distinction between art and popular art is that it depends for its clarity on art as 'surprise', but this is art as defined in modernist terms. Before the modernist revolution in art, everything here claimed for popular art could equally have been claimed for art in general. They make a further distinction to include 'mass art'. There is popular art (good and bad), and there is art (good and not so good), and there is mass art. Mass art is a 'corrupt' version of popular art; here they adopt uncritically the standard criticisms made of mass culture: it is formulaic, escapist, aesthetically worthless, emotionally unrewarding.

Rather than confront the mass culture critique, they seek to privilege certain of the texts and practices of popular culture and thus remove them from the condemnation of the critics of mass culture. In order to do this they introduce a new category – the popular arts. Popular art is mass culture that has risen above its origins. Unlike 'average films or pop music [which] are processed mass art', popular art is, for example, the 'best cinema', the 'most advanced jazz' (78). They claim that, 'Once the distinction between popular and mass art has been made, we find we have by-passed the cruder generalizations about "mass culture", and are faced with the full range of material offered by the media' (ibid.).

The main focus of *The Popular Arts* is on the textual qualities of popular culture. However, when Hall and Whannel turn to questions of youth culture they find it necessary to discuss the interaction between text and audience. Moreover, they recognize that to do full justice to this relationship, they have to include other aspects of teenage life: 'work, politics, the relation to the family, social and moral beliefs and so on' (269). This of course invites the question why this is not also necessary when other aspects of popular culture are discussed. Pop music culture – songs, magazines, concerts, festivals, comics, interviews with pop stars, films, etc. – helps to establish a sense of identity among youth:

> The culture provided by the commercial entertainment market . . . plays a crucial role. It mirrors attitudes and sentiments which are already there, and at the same

time provides an expressive field and a set of symbols through which these attitudes can be projected (276).

Moreover, pop songs

reflect adolescent difficulties in dealing with a tangle of emotional and sexual problems. They invoke the need to experience life directly and intensely. They express the drive for security in an uncertain and changeable emotional world. The fact that they are produced for a commercial market means that the songs and settings lack a certain authenticity. Yet they dramatize authentic feelings. They express vividly the adolescent emotional dilemma (280).

Pop music exhibits a kind of emotional realism; young men and women 'identify with these collective representations and . . . use them as guiding fictions. Such symbolic fictions are the folklore by means of which the teenager, in part, shapes and composes his mental picture of the world' (281). Hall and Whannel also identify the way in which teenagers use particular ways of talking, particular places to go, particular ways of dancing, and particular ways of dressing, to establish distance from the world of adults. They describe dress style, for example, as 'a minor popular art . . . used to express certain contemporary attitudes . . . for example, a strong current of social non-conformity and rebelliousness' (282). This line of investigation would come to full fruition in the work of the Centre for Contemporary Cultural Studies, carried out during the 1970s, under the directorship of Hall himself. But here Hall and Whannel draw back from the full force of the possibilities opened up by their enquiries; anxious that an 'anthropological . . . slack relativism', with its focus on the functionality of pop music culture, would prevent them from posing questions of value and quality, about likes ('are those likes enough?') and needs ('are the needs healthy ones?') and taste ('perhaps tastes can be extended') (296).

In their discussion of pop music culture, they concede that the claim that 'the picture of young people as innocents exploited' by the pop music industry 'is over-simplified' (ibid.). Against this, they argue that there is very often conflict between the use made of a text, or a commodity that is turned into a text (see discussion of the difference in Chapter 12) by an audience, and the use intended by the producers. Significantly, they observe, 'This conflict is particularly marked in the field of teenage entertainments . . . [although] it is to some extent common to the whole area of mass entertainment in a commercial setting' (270). The recognition of the potential conflict between commodities and their use leads Hall and Whannel to a formulation that is remarkably similar to the cultural studies appropriation (led by Hall himself) of Gramsci's concept of hegemony (see Chapter 4): 'Teenage culture is a contradictory mixture of the authentic and manufactured: it is an area of self-expression for the young and a lush grazing pasture for the commercial providers' (276).

As we noted earlier, Hall and Whannel compare pop music unfavourably with jazz. They claim that jazz is 'infinitely richer . . . both aesthetically and emotionally' (311). They also claim that the comparison is 'much more rewarding' than the more usual comparison between pop music and classical music, as both jazz and pop are popular musics. Now all this may be true, but what is the ultimate purpose of the comparison? In the case of classical against pop music, it is always to show the banality of pop music and to say something about those who consume it. Is Hall and Whannel's comparison fundamentally any different? Here is their justification for the comparison:

> The point behind such comparisons ought not to be simply to wean teenagers away from the juke-box heroes, but to alert them to the severe limitations and ephemeral quality of music which is so formula dominated and so directly attuned to the standards set by the commercial market. It is a genuine widening of sensibility and emotional range which we should be working for – an extension of tastes which might lead to an extension of pleasure. The worst thing which we would say of pop music is not that it is vulgar, or morally wicked, but, more simply, that much of it is not very good (311–12).

Despite the theoretical suggestiveness of much of their analysis (especially their identification of the contradictions of youth culture), and despite their protests to the contrary, their position on pop music culture is a position still struggling to free itself from the theoretical constraints of Leavisism: teenagers should be persuaded that their taste is deplorable and that by listening to jazz instead of pop music they might break out of imposed and self-imposed limitations, widen their sensibilities, broaden their emotional range and perhaps even increase their pleasure. In the end, Hall and Whannel's position seems to drift very close to the teaching strategy they condemn as 'opportunist', in that they seem to suggest that because most school students do not have access, for a variety of reasons, to the best that has been thought and said, they can instead be given critical access to the best that has been thought and said within the popular arts of the new mass media: jazz and good films will make up for the absence of Beethoven and Shakespeare. As they explain,

> This process – the practical exclusion of groups and classes in society from the selective tradition of the best that has been and is being produced in the culture – is especially damaging in a democratic society, and applies to both the traditional and new forms of high art. However, the very existence of this problem makes it even more important that some of the media which are capable of communicating work of a serious and significant kind should remain open and available, and that the quality of popular work transmitted there should be of the highest order possible, on its own terms (75).

Where they do break significantly with Leavisism is in advocating training in critical awareness, not as a means of defence *against* popular culture, but as a means to discriminate between what is good and what is bad *within* popular culture. It is a move that was to lead to a decisive break with Leavisism when the ideas of Hall and Whannel, and those of Hoggart, Williams and Thompson, were brought together under the banner of culturalism at the Birmingham University Centre for Contemporary Cultural Studies.

The Centre for Contemporary Cultural Studies

In the introduction to *The Long Revolution*, Williams (1965) regrets the fact that 'there is no academic subject within which the questions I am interested in can be followed through; I hope one day there might be' (10). Three years after the publication of these comments, Hoggart established the Centre for Contemporary Cultural Studies at the University of Birmingham. In the inaugural lecture, 'Schools of English and contemporary society', establishing the Centre, Hoggart (1970) states: 'It is hard to listen to a programme of pop songs . . . without feeling a complex mixture of attraction and repulsion' (258). Once the work of the Centre began its transition, as Michael Green[3] (1996) describes it, 'from Hoggart to Gramsci' (49), especially under the directorship of Hall, we find emerging a very different attitude towards pop music culture, and popular culture in general. Many of the researchers who followed Hoggart into the Centre (including myself) did not find pop music in the least repulsive; on the contrary, we found it profoundly attractive. We focused on a different Hoggart, one critical of taking what is said at face value, a critic who proposed a procedure that would eventually resonate through the reading practices of cultural studies:

> we have to try and see beyond the habits to what the habits stand for, to see through the statements to what the statements really mean (which may be the opposite of the statements themselves), to detect the differing pressures of emotion behind idiomatic phrases and ritualistic observances. . . . [And to see the way] mass publications [for example] connect with commonly accepted attitudes, how they are altering those attitudes, and how they are meeting resistance (1990: 17–19).

Culturalists study cultural texts and practices in order to reconstitute or reconstruct the experiences, values, etc. – the 'structure of feeling' of particular groups or classes or whole societies, in order to better understand the lives of those who lived the culture. In different ways Hoggart's example, Williams's social definition of culture, Thompson's act of historical rescue, Hall and Whannel's 'democratic' extension of Leavisism – each contribution discussed here argues that popular culture (defined as the lived culture of ordinary men and women) is worth studying. It is on the basis of these and other assumptions of culturalism, channelled through the traditions of English, sociology and history, that British cultural studies began. However, research at the Centre quickly brought culturalism into complex and often contradictory and conflictual relations with imports of French structuralism (see Chapter 6), in turn bringing the two approaches into critical dialogue with developments in 'Western Marxism', especially the work of Louis Althusser and Antonio Gramsci (see Chapter 4). It is from this complex and critical mixture that the 'post-disciplinary' field of British cultural studies was born.

Notes

1. For another excellent example of 'history from below', see Chauncey (1994). As Chauncey explains, 'As my focus on street-level policing of gender suggests, another of the underlying arguments of this book is that histories of homosexuality – and sex and sexuality more generally – have suffered from their overreliance on the discourse of the elite. The most powerful elements of American society devised the official maps of the culture. . . . While this book pays those maps their due, it is more interested in reconstructing the maps etched in the city streets by daily habit, the paths that guided men's practices even if they were never published or otherwise formalized. . . . This book seeks to analyze . . . the changing representation of homosexuality in popular culture and the street-level social practices and dynamics that shaped the ways homosexually active men were labeled, understood themselves, and interacted with others' (26–7).

2. I remember at school a teacher who encouraged us to bring to music lessons our records by the Beatles, Dylan and the Stones. The class would always end the same way (as would his liberalism) – he would try to convince us of the fundamental error of our adolescent musical taste.

3. Michael died in December 2010. He was my supervisor at the Centre for Contemporary Cultural Studies, University of Birmingham. His contribution to my academic development (at the CCCS and after) was enormous; I could never thank him enough.

Further reading

Storey, John (ed.), *Cultural Theory and Popular Culture: A Reader*, 4th edn, Harlow: Pearson Education, 2009. This is the companion volume to the previous edition of this book. A fully updated 5th edition containing further readings is due for publication in 2018. An interactive website is also available (www.routledge.com/cw/storey), which contains helpful student resources and a glossary of terms for each chapter.

Chambers, Iain, *Popular Culture: The Metropolitan Experience*, London: Routledge, 1986. An interesting and informed survey – mostly from the perspective of culturalism – of the rise of urban popular culture since the 1880s.

Clarke, John, Chas Critcher and Richard Johnson (eds), *Working Class Culture: Studies in History and Theory*, London: Hutchinson, 1979. Some good essays from a culturalist perspective. See especially Richard Johnson's 'Three problematics: elements of a theory of working class culture'.

Eagleton, Terry (ed.), *Raymond Williams: Critical Perspectives*, Cambridge: Polity Press, 1989. Essays in critical appreciation of the work of Raymond Williams.

Hall, Stuart and Tony Jefferson (eds), *Resistance Through Rituals*, London: Hutchinson, 1976. The Centre for Contemporary Cultural Studies' seminal account of youth subcultures. Chapter 1 provides a classic statement of the CCCS's version of culturalism.

Hall, Stuart, Dorothy Hobson, Andrew Lowe and Paul Willis (eds), *Culture, Media, Language*, London: Hutchinson, 1980. A selection of essays covering almost the first ten years of the CCCS's published work. See especially Chapter 1, Stuart Hall's important account of the theoretical development of work at the CCCS: 'Cultural studies and the Centre: some problematics and problems'.

Jones, Paul, *Raymond Williams's Sociology of Culture: A Critical Reconstruction*, Basingstoke: Palgrave, 2004. An interesting account, but its relentless insistence on claiming Williams for sociology distorts his place in cultural studies.

Kaye, Harvey J. and Keith McClelland (eds), *E.P. Thompson: Critical Perspectives*, Oxford: Polity Press, 1990. A collection of critical essays on different aspects of Thompson's contribution to the study of history; some useful references to *The Making of the English Working Class*.

O'Connor, Alan (ed.), *Raymond Williams: Writing, Culture, Politics*, Oxford: Basil Blackwell, 1989. Provides a critical survey of Williams's work. Excellent bibliography.

4 Marxisms

✳

Classical Marxism

Marxism is a difficult and contentious body of work. But it is also *more* than this: it is a body of revolutionary theory with the purpose of changing the world. As Marx (1976b) famously said: 'The philosophers have only *interpreted* the world, in various ways; the point is to change it' (65). This makes Marxist analysis political in a quite specific way. But this is not to suggest that other methods and approaches are apolitical; on the contrary, Marxism insists that all are ultimately political. As the American Marxist cultural critic Fredric Jameson (1981) puts it, 'the political perspective [is] the absolute horizon of all reading and all interpretation' (17).

The Marxist approach to culture insists that texts and practices must be analysed in relation to their historical conditions of production (and in some versions, the changing conditions of their consumption and reception). What makes the Marxist methodology different from other 'historical' approaches to culture is the Marxist conception of history. The fullest statement of the Marxist approach to history is contained in the Preface and Introduction to *A Contribution to the Critique of Political Economy*. Here Marx outlines the now famous 'base/superstructure' account of social and historical development. In Chapter 1, I discussed this formulation briefly in relation to different concepts of ideology. I shall now explain the formulation in more detail and demonstrate how it might be used to understand the 'determinations' that influence the production and consumption of popular culture.

Marx argues that each significant period in history is constructed around a particular 'mode of production': that is, the way in which a society is organized (i.e. slave, feudal, capitalist) to produce the material necessaries of life – food, shelter, etc. In general terms, each mode of production produces: (i) specific ways of obtaining the necessaries of life; (ii) specific social relationships between workers and those who control the mode of production, and (iii) specific social institutions (including cultural ones). At the heart of this analysis is the claim that how a society produces its means of existence (its particular 'mode of production') ultimately determines the political, social and cultural shape of that society and its possible future development. As Marx explains, 'The mode of production of material life conditions the social, political and intellectual life process in general' (1976a: 3). This claim is based on certain assumptions about the relationship between 'base' and 'superstructure'. It is on this relationship – between 'base' and 'superstructure' – that the classical Marxist account of culture rests.

The 'base' consists of a combination of the 'forces of production' and the 'relations of production'. The forces of production refer to the raw materials, the tools, the technology, the workers and their skills, etc. The relations of production refer to the class relations of those engaged in production. That is, each mode of production, besides being different, say, in terms of its basis in agrarian or industrial production, is also different in that it produces particular relations of production: the slave mode produces master/slave relations; the feudal mode produces lord/peasant relations; the capitalist mode produces bourgeois/proletariat relations. It is in this sense that one's class position is determined by one's relationship to the mode of production.

The 'superstructure' (which develops in conjunction with a specific mode of production) consists of institutions (political, legal, educational, cultural, etc.), and 'definite forms of social consciousness' (political, religious, ethical, philosophical, aesthetic, cultural, etc.) generated by these institutions. The relationship between base and superstructure is twofold. On the one hand, the superstructure both legitimates and challenges the base. On the other, the base is said to 'condition' or 'determine' the limits of the content and form of the superstructure. This relationship can be understood in a range of different ways. It can be seen as a mechanical relationship ('economic determinism') of cause and effect: what happens in the superstructure is a passive reflection of what is happening in the base. This often results in a vulgar Marxist 'reflection theory' of culture, in which the politics of a text or practice are read off from, or reduced to, the material conditions of its production. The relationship can also be seen as the setting of limits, the providing of a specific framework in which some developments are probable and others unlikely. However we view the relationship, we will not fully understand it if we reduce the base to an economic monolith (a static economic institution) and forget that for Marx the base also include social relations and class antagonisms.

After Marx's death in 1883, Frederick Engels, friend and collaborator, found himself having to explain, through a series of letters, many of the subtleties of Marxism to younger Marxists who, in their revolutionary enthusiasm, threatened to reduce it to a form of economic determinism. Here is part of his famous letter to Joseph Bloch:

> According to the materialist conception of history [Marxism], the ultimately determining element in history is the production and reproduction of real life. Neither Marx nor I have ever asserted more than this. Therefore if somebody twists this into saying that the economic factor is the only determining one, he is transforming that proposition into a meaningless, abstract, absurd phrase. The economic situation is the basis, but the various components of the superstructure . . . also exercise their influence upon the course of the historical struggles and in many cases determine their form. . . . We make our own history, but, first of all, under very definite assumptions and conditions. Among these the economic ones are ultimately decisive. But the political ones, etc., and indeed even the traditions which haunt human minds also play a part, although not the decisive one (2009: 61).

What Engels claims is that the base produces the superstructural terrain (this terrain and not that), but that the form of activity that takes place there is determined not just by the fact that the terrain was produced and is reproduced by the base (although this clearly sets limits and influences outcomes), but by the interaction of the institutions and the participants as they occupy the terrain. Therefore, although texts and practices are never the 'primary force' in history, they can be active agents in historical change or the servants of social stability.

A brief discussion of ideology should make the relationship between base and superstructure a little clearer. Marx and Engels (2009) claim that, 'The ideas of the ruling class are in every epoch the ruling ideas, i.e. the class which is the ruling *material* force in society, is at the same time its ruling *intellectual* force' (58). What they mean by this is that the dominant class, on the basis of its ownership of, and control over, the means of material production (the mode of production), is virtually guaranteed to have control over the means of intellectual production. However, this does not mean that the ideas of the ruling class are simply imposed on subordinate classes. A ruling class is 'compelled . . . to represent its interest as the common interest of all the members of society . . . to give its ideas the form of universality, and represent them as the only rational, universally valid ones' (59). Unless we include both formulations (ruling ideas and compulsion, and especially the way the second qualifies the first), we arrive at a very simplified notion of power: one in which class struggle is replaced by social control; where power is simply something imposed rather than something for which men and women have to struggle. During periods of social transformation ideological struggle becomes chronic: as Marx (1976a) points out, it is in the 'ideological forms' of the superstructure (which include the texts and practices of popular culture) that men and women 'become conscious of . . . conflict and fight it out' (4).

A classical Marxist approach to popular culture would above all else insist that to understand and explain a text or practice it must always be situated in its historical moment of production, analysed in terms of the historical conditions that produced it. There are dangers here: historical conditions are reduced to the mode of production and the superstructural becomes a passive reflection of the base. It is crucial, as Engels and Marx warn, and, as Thompson demonstrates (see Chapter 3), to keep in play a subtle dialectic between 'agency' and 'structure'. For example, a full analysis of nineteenth-century stage melodrama (one of the first culture industries) would have to weave together into focus both the changes in the mode of production that made stage melodrama's audience a possibility and the theatrical traditions that generated its form. The same also holds true for a full analysis of music hall (another early culture industry). Although in neither instance should performance be reduced to changes in the material forces of production, what would be insisted on is that a full analysis of stage melodrama or music hall would not be possible without reference to the changes in theatre attendance brought about by changes in the mode of production. It is these changes, a Marxist analysis would argue, that ultimately produced the conditions of possibility for the performance of a play like *My Poll* and *My Partner Joe*[1] and for the emergence and success of a music hall performer like Marie Lloyd. In this way, then, a Marxist analysis would insist that ultimately, however indirectly, there is nevertheless a real and fundamental relationship between the emergence of stage melodrama and music hall and changes that took place in the capitalist mode of production. I have made a similar argument about the invention of the 'traditional' English Christmas in the nineteenth century (Storey, 2008, 2010a, 2016).

The English Marxism of William Morris

William Morris, according to E.P. Thompson (1976), is the first English Marxist. Although best known as a designer and poet, Morris was, in his later life, also a revolutionary socialist. He joined the first British Marxist party, the Democratic Federation, in 1883. The following year he formed the Socialist League (other founding members included Eleanor Marx, the youngest daughter of Karl Marx). His commitment to the cause was total, and he involved himself in all aspects of its work, from political campaigns to editing and selling its newspaper, *The Commonweal*. Morris's contribution to Marxist thought is extensive. Here I shall discuss only one aspect, his critique of capitalist society in terms of art and alienation and how this provides an implicit commentary on what is popular culture.

Like Marx and Engels, Morris argued that creative labour is not just an activity to be enjoyed or avoided: it is an essential part of what makes us human. Industrial capitalism, with its repetition, its long hours and its denial of creativity, engenders what Marx called the alienation of labour. As Marx explained, the worker 'does not fulfil himself in his work . . . does not develop freely a physical and mental energy, but is physically exhausted and mentally debased' (1963: 177). This situation is compounded by the fact that work 'is not the satisfaction of a need, but only a *means* for satisfying other needs' (177; original emphasis). Lacking the ability to find herself (i.e. express her natural creativity) in her work, she is forced to seek it outside her work. 'The worker therefore feels himself at home only during his leisure, whereas at work he feels homeless' (177). In other words, she works to earn money in order to express her natural creativity (denied to her in industrial work) in patterns of consumption (see Storey 2017).

On the basis of this analysis, making art is seen as an ideal model of how work should be experienced. Accordingly, Morris's definition of art is not the narrow definition as, for example, used in traditional forms of art history; for Morris it includes all creative human production. 'I use the word *art* in a wider sense than is commonly used. . . . To a Socialist a house, a knife, a cup, a steam engine, or . . . anything . . . that is made by man and has form, must either be a work of art or destructive to art' (1979: 84). Ultimately, for Morris, art is 'the expression of pleasure in the labour of production' (84). Under the conditions of industrial capitalism, 'founded on the art-lacking or unhappy labour of the greater part of men' (85), only the artist can achieve such pleasure. A fundamental part of the promise of socialism is that it will extend this pleasure to all humankind. Rejecting assembly line methods of production ('Fordism'), labour under socialism will use 'the whole of a man for the production of a piece of goods, and not small portions of many men' (87). Art, therefore, is not for Morris an ornamental addition to everyday life; it is the very substance of what makes us truly human.

In a non-alienated world of communist social relations, the worker is returned to herself (i.e. to an ability to express his natural creativity in his labour). Like Morris, Marx and Engels understand this in terms of popular art: 'The exclusive concentration of artistic talent in particular individuals, and its suppression in the broad mass which is bound up with this, is a consequence of division of labour. . . . In a communist society there are no painters but at most people who engage in painting among other activities' (1974: 109). The end of capitalism means the end of the division of labour. 'In communist society . . . nobody has an exclusive area of activity and each can train himself in any branch he wishes . . . making it possible for me to do one thing today and another tomorrow, to hunt in the morning, fish in the afternoon, breed cattle in the evening, criticise after dinner, just as I like without ever becoming a hunter, a fisherman, a herdsman, or a critic' (quoted in McLellan, 1982: 36).

In other words, in a non-alienated, communist society all men and women will work like artists: all work will in effect produce popular art, because all work will be creative. As Morris insisted, 'What business have we with art at all unless all can share it? (1986: 139). Moreover, 'The absence of popular art from modern times is more disquieting and grievous to bear for this reason than for any other, that it betokens that fatal division of men into the cultivated and the degraded classes which competitive commerce [capitalism] has bred and fosters' (139). The end of alienation will mean the end of the distinction between culture and popular culture.

Morris's (2003) [1890] novel *News From Nowhere* describes a twenty-first-century, post-revolutionary England. Guest, the novel's main character, falls asleep in the 1880s and wakes up in the twenty first century to discover that England has undergone a revolution in 1952–54 and is now a non-alienated, communist society. Goods made to sell for profit have been replaced by goods produced to the satisfaction of the worker and to meet the needs of the community. In similar fashion, private ownership has been replaced by common use. Moreover, art as a separate category has disappeared, as art and creativity are now fully integrated into the routines of everyday life.

The novel should not be read as a literal picture of a future society. Rather, it should be read as a political incitement to make the society Guest finds in twenty-first-century England. The aim of the novel is 'the education of desire' (Thompson, 1976): that is, to make men and women aware of the possibility of a non-alienated society and to educate their desire to make such a society. As Morris observed, capitalism 'has reduced the workman to such a skinny and pitiful existence, that he scarcely knows how to frame a desire for any life much better than that which he now endures' (1986: 37). Morris wishes to educate the desire for a 'life much better', hoping that to allow men and women to think of such a life is to create the desire for them to make such a life (see Storey 2018).

News From Nowhere provides a beautiful example of what Morris, Marx and Engels had in mind when they envisaged a non-alienated, communist society. The novel depicts a world a million miles away from the authoritarian horrors of the Stalinism of the Soviet Union; moreover, it is a society in which the distinction between culture and popular culture, and the corresponding divisions of social class, no longer exist.

The Frankfurt School

The Frankfurt School is the name given to a group of German intellectuals associated with the Institute for Social Research at the University of Frankfurt. The Institute was established in 1923. Following the coming to power of Adolf Hitler and the Nazi Party in 1933, it moved to New York, attaching itself to the University of Columbia. In 1949 it moved back to Germany. 'Critical Theory' is the name given to the Institute's critical mix of Marxism and psychoanalysis. The Institute's work on popular culture is mostly associated with the writings of Theodor Adorno, Walter Benjamin, Max Horkheimer, Leo Lowenthal and Herbert Marcuse.

In 1944 Theodor Adorno and Max Horkheimer (1979) coined the term 'culture industry' to designate the products and processes of mass culture. The products of the culture industry, they claim, are marked by two features: homogeneity, 'film, radio and magazines make up a system which is uniform as a whole and in every part . . . all mass culture is identical' (120–1); and predictability:

> As soon as the film begins, it is quite clear how it will end, and who will be rewarded, punished, or forgotten. In light music [popular music], once the trained ear has heard the first notes of the hit song, it can guess what is coming and feel flattered when it does come. . . . The result is a constant reproduction of the same thing (125, 134).

While Arnold and Leavisism had worried that popular culture represented a threat to cultural and social authority, the Frankfurt School argue that it actually produces the opposite effect: it maintains cultural and social authority. Where Arnold and Leavis saw 'anarchy', the Frankfurt School see only 'conformity': a situation in which 'the deceived masses' (133) are caught in a 'circle of manipulation and retroactive need in which the unity of the system grows ever stronger' (121). Here is Adorno reading an American situation comedy about a young schoolteacher who is both underpaid (some things do not change), and continually fined by her school principal. As a result, she is without money and therefore without food. The humour of the storyline consists in her various attempts to secure a meal at the expense of friends and acquaintances. In his reading of this situation comedy, Adorno is guided by the assumption that while it is always difficult, if not impossible, to establish the unmistakable 'message' of a work of 'authentic' culture, the 'hidden message' of a piece of mass culture is not at all difficult to discern. According to Adorno (1991a), 'the script implies' that:

> If you are humorous, good natured, quick witted, and charming as she is, do not worry about being paid a starvation wage. . . . In other words, the script is a shrewd method of promoting adjustment to humiliating conditions by presenting them as objectively comical and by giving a picture of a person who experiences even her own inadequate position as an object of fun apparently free of any resentment (143–4).

This is one way of reading this TV comedy. But it is by no means the only way. The German Marxist playwright Bertolt Brecht might have offered another way of reading, one that implies a less passive audience. Discussing his own play, *Mother Courage and Her Children*, Brecht (1978) suggests, 'Even if Courage learns nothing else at least the audience can, in my view, learn something by observing her' (229). The same point can be made against Adorno with reference to the schoolteacher's behaviour. It is only by starting with the assumption that the text dictates its meaning to a passive audience that he can be so certain about the meaning of the TV comedy.

Leo Lowenthal (1961) contends that the culture industry, by producing a culture marked by 'standardisation, stereotype, conservatism, mendacity, manipulated consumer goods' (11), has worked to depoliticize the working class – limiting its horizon to political and economic goals that could be realized within the oppressive and exploitative framework of capitalist society. He maintains that, 'Whenever revolutionary tendencies show a timid head, they are mitigated and cut short by a false fulfilment of wish-dreams, like wealth, adventure, passionate love, power and sensationalism in general' (ibid.). In short, the culture industry discourages the 'masses' from thinking beyond the confines of the present. As Herbert Marcuse (1968a) claims in *One Dimensional Man*:

> the irresistible output of the entertainment and information industry [the culture industry] carry with them prescribed attitudes and habits, certain intellectual and emotional reactions which bind the consumers more or less pleasantly to the producers and, through the latter, to the whole. The products indoctrinate and manipulate; they promote a false consciousness which is immune against its falsehood . . . it becomes a way of life. It is a good way of life – much better than before – and as a good way of life, it militates against qualitative change. Thus emerges a pattern of one-dimensional thought and behaviour in which ideas, aspirations, and objectives that, by their content, transcend the established universe of discourse and action are either repelled or reduced to terms of this universe (26–7).

In other words, by supplying the means to the satisfaction of certain needs, capitalism is able to prevent the formation of more fundamental desires. The culture industry thus stunts the political imagination.

As with Arnold and Leavisism, art or high culture is seen to be working differently. It embodies ideals denied by capitalism. As such it offers an implicit critique of capitalist society, an alternative, utopian vision. 'Authentic' culture, according to Horkheimer (1978), has taken over the utopian function of religion: to keep alive the human desire for a better world beyond the confines of the present. It carries the key to unlock the prison-house established by the development of mass culture by the capitalist culture industry (5). But increasingly the processes of the culture industry threaten the radical potential of 'authentic' culture. The culture industry increasingly flattens out what remains of

> the antagonism between culture and social reality through the obliteration of the oppositional, alien, and transcendent elements in the higher culture by virtue of

which it constituted another dimension of reality. This liquidation of two-dimensional culture takes place not through the denial and rejection of the 'cultural values', but through their wholesale incorporation into the established order, through their reproduction and display on a massive scale (Marcuse, 1968a: 58).

Therefore, the better future promised by 'authentic' culture is no longer in contradiction with the unhappy present – a spur to make the better future; culture now confirms that this is the better future – here and now – the only better future. It offers 'fulfilment' instead of the promotion of 'desire'. Marcuse holds to the hope that the 'most advanced images and positions' of 'authentic' culture may still resist 'absorption' and 'continue to haunt the consciousness with the possibility of their rebirth' in a better tomorrow (60). He also hopes that one day those on the margins of society, 'the outcasts and outsiders' (61), who are out of reach of the full grasp of the culture industry, will undo the defeats, fulfil the hopes, and make capitalism keep all its promises in a world beyond capitalism. Or, as Horkheimer (1978) observes,

> One day we may learn that in the depths of their hearts, the masses . . . secretly knew the truth and disbelieved the lie, like catatonic patients who make known only at the end of their trance that nothing had escaped them. Therefore it may not be entirely senseless to continue speaking a language that is not easily understood (17).

But, as Adorno (1991b) points out, mass culture is a difficult system to challenge:

> Today anyone who is incapable of talking in the prescribed fashion, that is of effortlessly reproducing the formulas, conventions and judgments of mass culture as if they were his own, is threatened in his very existence, suspected of being an idiot or an intellectual (79).

The culture industry, in its search for profits and cultural homogeneity, deprives 'authentic' culture of its critical function, its mode of negation – '[its] Great Refusal' (Marcuse, 1968a: 63). Commodification (sometimes understood by other critics as 'commercialization') devalues 'authentic' culture, making it too accessible by turning it into yet another saleable commodity.

> The neo-conservative critics of leftist critics of mass culture ridicule the protest against Bach as background music in the kitchen, against Plato and Hegel, Shelley and Baudelaire, Marx and Freud in the drugstore. Instead, they insist on recognition of the fact that the classics have left the mausoleum and come to life again, that people are just so much more educated. True, but coming to life as classics, they come to life as other than themselves; they are deprived of their antagonistic force, of the estrangement which was the very dimension of their truth. The intent and function of these works have thus fundamentally changed. If they once stood in contradiction to the status quo, this contradiction is now flattened out (63–4).

It is not difficult to think of examples of this process (whether or not we read them in quite the same way, leftist or neo-conservative). In the 1960s, a bedsit without a poster of Che Guevara was hardly furnished at all. Was the poster a sign of a commitment to revolutionary politics or a commitment to the latest fashion (or was it a complicated mixture of both)? Bennett (1977) provides a telling example of an advertisement inserted in *The Times* in 1974:

> an advertisement which consisted of a full page colour reproduction of Matisse's *Le Pont*, below which there appeared the legend: 'Business is our life, but life isn't all business.' Profoundly contradictory, what was ostensibly opposed to economic life was made to become a part of it, what was separate became assimilated since any critical dimension which might have pertained to Matisse's painting was eclipsed by its new and unsolicited function as an advertisement for the wares of finance capital (45).

We might also think of the way opera and classical music are used to sell anything from bread to expensive motorcars (for examples see Table 4.1). Is it possible, for instance, to hear the second movement from Antonin Leopold Dvořák's *New World Symphony* without conjuring up an image of Hovis bread?

It is not that Marcuse or the other members of the Frankfurt School object to the 'democratization' of culture, only that they believe that the culture industry's 'assimilation is historically premature; it establishes cultural equality while preserving domination' (Marcuse, 1968a: 64). In short, the democratization of culture results in the blocking of the demand for full democracy; it stabilizes the prevailing social order.

According to the Frankfurt School, work and leisure under capitalism form a compelling relationship: the effects of the culture industry are guaranteed by the nature of work; the work process secures the effects of the culture industry. The function of the culture industry is therefore, ultimately, to organize leisure time in the same way as industrialization has organized work time. Work under capitalism stunts the senses; the culture industry continues the process: 'The escape from everyday drudgery which the whole culture industry promises . . . [is a] paradise . . . [of] the same old drudgery . . . escape . . . [is] predesigned to lead back to the starting point. Pleasure promotes the resignation which it ought to help to forget' (Adorno and Horkheimer, 1979: 142). In short, work leads to mass culture; mass culture leads back to work. Similarly, art or 'authentic' culture circulated by the culture industry operates in the same way. Only 'authentic' culture operating outside the confines of the culture industry could ever hope to break the cycle.

To make more concrete these general points, I shall now examine a specific example of the Frankfurt School's approach to popular culture – Adorno's (2009) essay, 'On popular music'. In the essay he makes three specific claims about popular music. First, he claims that it is 'standardized'. 'Standardization', according to Adorno, 'extends from the most general features to the most specific ones' (64). Once a musical and/or lyrical pattern has proved successful it is exploited to commercial exhaustion, culminating in 'the crystallisation of standards' (ibid.). Moreover, details from one popular song can

Table 4.1 Depriving 'authentic' culture of its critical function.

The use of opera and classical music in advertisements	
Bach: Suite No. 3 in D – Hamlet cigars	Offenbach: Tales of Hoffmann – Bailey's Irish Cream
Bach: Sleepers Awake! – Lloyds Bank	Offenbach: Orpheus in the Underworld – Bio Speed Weed
Bach: Harpsichord Concerto in F minor – NASDAQ	Orff: Carmina Burana – Old Spice/Carling Black Label/Fiat Marea
Beethoven: Symphony No. 6 in F – Blueband margarine	Pachelbel: Canon in D – Thresher wines
Beethoven: Für Elise – Heinz spaghetti/Uncle Ben's rice	Prokofiev: Peter and the Wolf – Vauxhall Astra
Bellini: Norma – Ford Mondeo	Prokofiev: Romeo and Juliet – Chanel L'Egoiste
Boccherini: Minuet – Save and Prosper building society	Puccini: Madama Butterfly – Twinings tea/Del Monte orange juice
Britten: Simple Symphony Opus 4 – Royal Bank of Scotland	Puccini: Gianni Schicchi – Philips DCC
Debussy: Suite Bergamasque – Boursin cheese	Puccini: La Bohème – Sony Walkman
Delibes: Lakmé – British Airways/basmati rice/Ryvita/IBM computers/Kleenex tissues	Puccini: Tosca – FreeServe
Delibes: Coppelia – Jus-Rol pastry	Ravel: Boléro – Ryvita
Dukas: The Sorcerer's Apprentice – Fiesta kitchen towels/Sun Liquid/Royal Bank of Scotland/Philips DCC	Rimsky-Korsakov: Tsar Saltan – Black and Decker
Dvořák: New World Symphony – Hovis bread	Rossini: The Barber of Seville – Ragu pasta sauce/Fiat Strada/Braun cordless shavers
Fauré: Requiem Opus 48 – Lurpak butter	Saint-Saëns: Carnival of the Animals – Tesco
Gluck: Orfeo ed Euridice – Comfort fabric softener	Satie: Gymnopédie No. 3 – Bournville chocolate/Strepsils lozenges
Grieg: Peer Gynt – Nescafé/AEG/Alton Towers	Schumann: Scenes from Childhood – Chocolate Break
Handel: Serse – Rover cars	Smetana: Má Vlast – Peugeot 605
Handel: Solomon – Woolworths	J. Strauss: Morning Papers Waltz – TSB
Holst: The Planet Suite – Dulux Weathershield	Tchaikovsky: The Nutcracker Suite – Reactolite sunglasses/Cadbury's Fruit and Nut/Hellmann's mayonnaise
Khachaturian: Spartacus – Nescafé	Verdi: Aida – Diet Pepsi/Michelob/Egypt
Mascagni: Cavalleria rusticana – Kleenex tissues/Stella Artois/Baci chocolates	Verdi: Il Trovatore – Ragu pasta sauce
Mozart: Piano Concerto No. 21 – Aer Lingus	Verdi: La Forza del Destino – Stella Artois
Mozart: The Marriage of Figaro – Citroën ZX	Verdi: Nabucco – British Airways
Mozart: Cosí Fan Tutte – Mercedes-Benz	Verdi: Rigoletto – Ragu pasta sauce/Little Caesar's pizza
Mozart: Horn Concerto No. 4 – Vauxhall Carlton	Vivaldi: The Four Seasons – Chanel No. 19 perfume/Kingsmill bread/Citroën BX/Braun
Mussorgsky: Night on a Bare Mountain – Maxell tapes	

be interchanged with details from another. Unlike the organic structure of 'serious music', where each detail expresses the whole, popular music is mechanical in the sense that a given detail can be shifted from one song to another without any real effect on the structure as a whole. In order to conceal standardization, the music industry engages in what Adorno calls 'pseudo-individualization': 'Standardisation of song hits keeps the customers in line by doing their listening for them, as it were. Pseudo-individualization, for its part, keeps them in line by making them forget that what they listen to is already listened to for them, or "pre-digested" ' (69).

Adorno's second claim is that popular music promotes passive listening. As already noted, work under capitalism is dull and therefore promotes the search for escape, but, because it is also dulling, it leaves little energy for real escape – the demands of 'authentic' culture. Instead refuge is sought in forms such as popular music – the consumption of which is always passive, and endlessly repetitive, confirming *the world as it is*. While 'serious' music (Beethoven, for example) plays to the pleasure of the imagination, offering an engagement with *the world as it could be*, popular music is the 'non-productive correlate' (70) to life in the office or on the factory floor. The 'strain and boredom' of work lead men and women to the 'avoidance of effort' in their leisure time (ibid.). Adorno makes it all sound like the hopeless ritual of a heroin addict (as taken from the detective genre he detested so much). Denied 'novelty' in their work time, and too exhausted for it in their leisure time, 'they crave a stimulant' – popular music satisfies the craving.

> Its stimulations are met with the inability to vest effort in the ever-identical. This means boredom again. It is a circle which makes escape impossible. The impossibility of escape causes the widespread attitude of inattention toward popular music. The moment of recognition is that of effortless sensation. The sudden attention attached to this moment burns itself out instanter and relegates the listener to a realm of inattention and distraction (71).

Popular music operates in a kind of blurred dialectic: to consume it demands inattention and distraction, while its consumption produces in the consumer inattention and distraction.

Adorno's third point is the claim that popular music operates as 'social cement' (72). Its 'socio-psychological function' is to achieve in the consumers of popular music 'psychical adjustment' to the needs of the prevailing structure of power (ibid.). This 'adjustment' manifests itself in 'two major socio-psychological types of mass behaviour . . . the "rhythmically" obedient type and the "emotional" type' (ibid.). The first type of listener dances in distraction to the rhythm of his or her own exploitation and oppression. The second type wallows in sentimental misery, oblivious to the real conditions of existence.

There are a number of points to be made about Adorno's analysis. First, we must acknowledge that he is writing in 1941. Popular music has changed a great deal since then. However, having said that, Adorno never thought to change his analysis following the changes that occurred in popular music up until his death in 1969. Is popular music as monolithic as he would have us believe? For example, does pseudo-individualization really explain the advent of rock'n'roll in 1956, the emergence of the Beatles in 1962, the music of the counterculture in 1965? Does it explain punk rock and Rock Against Racism in the 1970s, acid house and indie pop in the 1980s, rave and hip hop in the 1990s?

Moreover, is the consumption of popular music as passive as Adorno claims? Simon Frith (1983) provides sales figures that suggest not: 'despite the difficulties of the calculations . . . most business commentators agree that about 10 per cent of all records released (a little less for singles, a little more for LPs) make money' (147). In addition to this, only about another 10 per cent cover their costs (ibid.). This means that about 80 per cent of records actually lose money. Moreover, Paul Hirsch has calculated that at least 60 per cent of singles released are never played by anyone (cited in Frith, 1983: 147). This does not suggest the workings of an all-powerful culture industry, easily able to manipulate its consumers. It sounds more like a culture industry trying desperately to sell records to a critical and discriminating public. Such figures certainly imply that consumption is rather more active than Adorno's argument suggests. Subcultural use of music is clearly at the leading edge of such active discrimination, but is by no means the only example.

Finally, does popular music really function as social cement? Subcultures or music taste cultures, for instance, would appear to consume popular music in a way not too dissimilar to Adorno's ideal mode for the consumption of 'serious music'. Richard Dyer (1990) argues that this is certainly the case with regard to the gay consumption of disco. He detects a certain romanticism in disco that keeps alive a way of being that is always in conflict with the mundane and the everyday. As he explains, 'Romanticism asserts that the limits of work and domesticity are not the limits of experience' (417).

The analysis offered by the majority of the Frankfurt School works with a series of binary oppositions held in place by the supposed fundamental difference between culture and mass culture (Table 4.2).

Walter Benjamin's (1973) essay 'The work of art in the age of mechanical reproduction' is much more optimistic about the possibility of a revolutionary transformation of capitalism. He claims that capitalism will 'ultimately . . . create conditions which would make it possible to abolish capitalism itself' (219). Benjamin believes that changes in the technological reproduction of culture are changing the function of culture in society: 'technical reproduction can put the copy of the original into situations which would be out of reach for the original itself' (222). Reproduction thus challenges what Benjamin calls the 'aura' of texts and practices.

Table 4.2 'Culture' and 'mass culture' according to the Frankfurt School.

Culture	Mass culture
Real	False
European	American
Multi-dimensional	One-dimensional
Active consumption	Passive consumption
Individual creation	Mass production
Imagination	Distraction
Negation	Social cement

> One might generalise by saying: the technique of reproduction detaches the reproduced object from the domain of tradition. By making many reproductions it substitutes a plurality of copies for a unique existence. And in permitting the reproduction to meet the beholder or listener in his own particular situation, it reactivates the object reproduced. These two processes lead to a tremendous shattering of tradition . . . Their most powerful agent is film. Its social significance, particularly in its most positive form, is inconceivable without its destructive, cathartic aspect, that is, the liquidation of the traditional value of the cultural heritage (223).

The 'aura' of a text or practice is its sense of 'authenticity', 'authority', 'autonomy' and 'distance'. The decay of the aura detaches the text or practice from the authority and rituals of tradition. It opens them to a plurality of reinterpretation, freeing them to be used in other contexts, for other purposes. No longer embedded in tradition, significance is now open to dispute; meaning becomes a question of consumption, an active (political), rather than a passive (for Adorno: psychological) event. Technological reproduction changes production: 'To an ever greater degree the work of art reproduced becomes the work of art designed for reproducibility' (226). Consumption is also changed: from its location in religious ritual to its location in the rituals of aesthetics, consumption is now based on the practice of politics. Culture may have become mass culture, but consumption has not become mass consumption.

> Mechanical reproduction of art changes the reaction of the masses toward art. The reactionary attitude toward a Picasso painting changes into the progressive reaction toward a Chaplin movie. The progressive reaction is characterised by the direct, intimate fusion of visual and emotional enjoyment with the orientation of the expert (236).

Questions of meaning and consumption shift from passive contemplation to active political struggle. Benjamin's celebration of the positive potential of 'mechanical reproduction', his view that it begins the process of a move from an 'auratic' culture to a 'democratic' culture in which meaning is seen no longer as unique, but as open to question, open to use and mobilization, has had a profound (if often unacknowledged) influence on cultural theory and popular culture. Susan Willis (1991) describes Benjamin's essay thus: 'This may well be the single most important essay in the development of Marxist popular culture criticism' (10). While Adorno locates meaning in the mode of production (how a cultural text is produced determines its consumption and significance), Benjamin suggests that meaning is produced at the moment of consumption; significance is determined by the process of consumption, regardless of the mode of production. As Frith points out, the 'debate'[2] between Adorno and Benjamin – between a socio-psychological account of consumption combined with an insistence on the determining power of production, against the argument that consumption is a matter of politics – continues to be argued in contemporary accounts of popular music: 'Out of Adorno have come analyses of the economics of entertainment . . . [and the] ideological effects of commercial music making. . . . From Benjamin have come subcultural theories, descriptions of the struggle . . . to make their own meanings in their acts of consumption' (57).

Despite its Marxist sophistication and admirable political intent, the approach of the Frankfurt School to popular culture (with the exception of Benjamin) would in some respects fit easily into the 'culture and civilization' tradition discussed in Chapter 2. Like the perspective developed by Arnold, Leavisism and some of the American mass culture theorists, the Frankfurt School perspective on popular culture is essentially a discourse from above on the culture of other people (a discourse of 'us' and 'them'). It is true that the Frankfurt School are very critical of conservative cultural critics who bemoaned the passing of, or threat to, a 'pure' autonomous culture for its own sake. Adorno, as J.M. Bernstein (1978) points out, 'regards the conservative defence of high culture as reflecting an unreflective hypostatization of culture that protects the economic status quo' (15). Nevertheless, it remains the case that there are certain similarities between the focus of the 'culture and civilization' tradition and that of the Frankfurt School. They condemn the same things, but for different reasons. The 'culture and civilization' tradition attack mass culture because it threatens cultural standards and social authority, the Frankfurt School attack mass culture because it threatens cultural standards and depoliticizes the working class, and thus maintains the iron grip of social authority: 'obedience to the rhythm of the iron system . . . the *absolute* power of capitalism' (Adorno and Horkheimer, 1979: 120; my italics). It is very difficult to imagine the possibility of political agency in a situation of absolute power.

Althusserianism

The ideas of Louis Althusser have had an enormous influence on cultural theory and popular culture. As Hall (1978) suggests, 'Althusser's interventions and their consequent development are enormously formative for the field of cultural studies' (21). Althusser's most significant contribution to the field is his different attempts to theorize the concept of ideology. I shall therefore restrict discussion to this aspect of his work.

Althusser begins by rejecting mechanistic interpretation of the base/superstructure formulation, insisting instead on the concept of the social formation. According to Althusser (1969), a social formation consists of three practices: the economic, the political and the ideological. The relationship between the base and the superstructure is not one of expression, i.e. the superstructure being an expression or passive reflection of the base, but rather the superstructure is seen as necessary to the existence of the base. The model allows for the relative autonomy of the superstructure. Determination remains, but it is determination in 'the last instance'. This operates through what he calls the 'structure in dominance'; that is, although the economic is always ultimately 'determinant', this does not mean that in a particular historical conjuncture it will necessarily be dominant. Under feudalism, for example, the political was the dominant level. Nevertheless, the practice that is dominant in a particular social formation will depend on the specific form of economic production. What he means by this is that the economic contradictions of capitalism never take a pure form: 'the lonely hour of the last instance never comes' (113). The economic is determinant in the last instance, not because the other instances are its epiphenomena, but because it determines which practice is dominant. In volume one of *Capital*, Marx (1976c) makes a similar point in response to criticisms suggesting definite limits to the critical reach of Marxist analysis:

> [Marxism, so its critics say,] is all very true for our own time, in which material interests are preponderant, but not for the Middle Ages, dominated by Catholicism, nor for Athens and Rome, dominated by politics. . . . One thing is clear: the Middle Ages could not live on Catholicism, nor could the ancient world on politics. On the contrary, it is the manner in which they gained their livelihood which explains why in one case politics, in the other case Catholicism, played the chief part. . . . And then there is Don Quixote, who long ago paid the penalty for wrongly imagining that knight errantry was compatible with all economic forms of society (176).

Althusser produced three definitions of ideology, two of which have proved particularly fruitful for the student of popular culture. The first definition, which overlaps in some ways with the second, is the claim that ideology – 'a system (with its own logic and rigour) of representations (images, myths, ideas or concepts)' (1969: 231) – is a 'practice' through which men and women live their relations to the real conditions of existence. 'By practice . . . I . . . mean any process of transformation of a determinate given raw material into a determinate product, a transformation effected by a determinate human labour, using determinate means (of "production")' (166). Therefore, as the economic, the historically specific mode of production, transforms certain raw materials into products by determinate means of production, involving determinate relations of production, so ideological practice shapes an individual's lived relations to the social formation. In this way, ideology dispels contradictions in lived experience. It accomplishes this by offering false, but seemingly true, resolutions to real problems. This is not a 'conscious' process; ideology 'is profoundly unconscious' (233) in its mode of operation.

> In ideology men . . . express, not the relation between them and their conditions of existence, but the way they live the relation between them and their conditions of existence: this presupposes both a real relation and an 'imaginary', 'lived' relation. Ideology . . . is the expression of the relation between men and their 'world', that is, the (overdetermined) unity of the real relation and the imaginary relation between them and their real conditions of existence (233–4).

The relationship is both real and imaginary in the sense that ideology is the way we live our relationship to the real conditions of existence at the level of representations (myths, concepts, ideas, images, discourses): there are real conditions and there are the ways in which we represent these conditions to ourselves and to others. This applies to both dominant and subordinate classes; ideologies do not just convince oppressed groups that all is well with the world, they also convince ruling groups that exploitation and oppression are really something quite different: acts of universal necessity. Only a 'scientific' discourse (Althusser's Marxism) can see through ideology to the real conditions of existence.

Because ideology is for Althusser a closed system, it can only ever set itself such problems as it can answer; that is, to remain within its boundaries (a mythic realm without contradictions), it must stay silent on questions that threaten to take it beyond these boundaries. This formulation leads Althusser to the concept of the 'problematic'. He first uses the concept to explain the 'epistemological break' that he claims occurs in Marx's work in 1845. Marx's problematic, 'the objective internal reference system . . . the system of questions commanding the answers given' (67), determines not only the questions and answers he is able to bring into play, but also the absence of problems and concepts in his work.

According to Althusser a problematic consists of the assumptions, motivations, underlying ideas, etc., from which a text (say, an advert) is made. In this way, it is argued, a text is structured as much by what is absent (what is not said) as by what is present (what is said). Althusser argues that if we are to fully understand the meaning of a text, we have to be aware of not only what is in a text but also the assumptions that inform it (which may not appear in the text itself in any straightforward way but exist only in the text's problematic). One way in which a text's problematic is supposedly revealed is in the way a text may appear to answer questions it has not formally posed. Such questions, it is argued, have been posed in the text's problematic. The task of an Althusserian critical practice is to deconstruct the text to reveal the problematic. To do this is to perform what Althusser calls a 'symptomatic reading'.

In *Reading Capital*, Althusser characterizes Marx's method of reading the work of Adam Smith as 'symptomatic' in that

> it divulges the undivulged event in the text it reads, and in the same movement relates it to a different text, present as a necessary absence in the first. Like his first reading, Marx's second reading presupposes the existence of two texts, and the measurement of the first against the second. But what distinguishes this new reading from the old is the fact that in the new one the second text is articulated with the lapses in the first text (Althusser and Balibar, 1979: 67).

Through a symptomatic reading of Smith, Marx is able to construct for analysis 'the problematic initially visible in his writings against the invisible problematic contained in the paradox of *an answer which does not correspond to any question posed*' (28). Marx (1951) himself says this of Smith, 'Adam Smith's contradictions are of significance because they contain problems which it is true he does not solve, but which he reveals by contradicting himself' (146).

To read a text symptomatically, therefore, is to perform a double reading: reading first the manifest text, and then, through the lapses, distortions, silences and absences (the 'symptoms' of a problem struggling to be posed) in the manifest text, to produce and read the latent text. For example, a symptomatic reading of the film *Taxi Driver* would reveal a problematic in which answers are posed to questions it can hardly name: 'How does the veteran return home to America after the imperial horrors of Vietnam?' At the heart of the film's problematic are questions relating to real historical problems, albeit deformed and transformed into a fantasy quest and a bloody resolution. A symptomatic reading of *Taxi Driver*, reading the 'symptoms' for evidence of an underlying *disease*, would construct from the film's contradictions, its evasions, its silences, its inexplicable violence, its fairy-tale ending, the central and structuring absence – America's war in Vietnam.

Another example can be seen in the number of recent car advertisements that situate vehicles isolated in nature (for example, see Photo 4.1). This mode of advertising, I would argue, is a response to the growing body of negative publicity that car ownership has attracted (especially in terms of pollution and road congestion). To prevent this publicity having an adverse effect on car sales these criticisms have to be countered. To confront them in a direct way would always run the risk of allowing the criticisms to come between the car being advertised and any potential buyer. Therefore, showing cars in both nature (unpolluted) and space (uncongested) confronts the claims without the risk of giving them a dangerous and unnecessary visibility. In this way, the criticisms are answered without the questions themselves having been formally posed. The emphasis placed on nature and space is, therefore, a response to the twin questions (which remain unasked in the advertisements themselves but exist in the assumptions that organize the adverts – in the text's 'problematic'): does buying a car increase both pollution and road congestion? The answer given, without the question being asked, is that these cars, as if by magic, neither pollute nor contribute to, or experience, road congestion.

Pierre Macherey's (1978) *A Theory of Literary Production* is undoubtedly the most sustained attempt to apply the technique of the Althusserian symptomatic reading to cultural texts. Although, as the book's title implies, Macherey's main focus is on literary production, the approach developed in the book is of great interest to the student of popular culture.

In his elaboration of Althusser's method of symptomatic reading, he rejects what he calls 'the interpretative fallacy': the view that a text has a single meaning, which it is the task of criticism to uncover. For him the text is not a puzzle that conceals a meaning; it is a construction with a multiplicity of meanings. To 'explain' a text is to recognize this. To do so it is necessary to break with the idea that a text is a harmonious unity, spiralling forth from a moment of overwhelming intentionality. Against this, he claims that the literary text is 'decentred'; it is incomplete in itself. To say this does not mean that something needs to be added in order to make it whole. His point is that all literary texts are 'decentred' (not centred on an authorial intention) in the specific sense that they consist of a confrontation between several discourses: explicit, implicit, present and absent. The task of critical practice is not, therefore, the attempt to measure and evaluate a text's coherence, its harmonious totality, its aesthetic unity, but instead to explain the disparities in the text that point to a conflict of meanings.

Photo 4.1   Advertising as an example of the 'problematic'.

Source: Image courtesy of The Advertising Archives

This conflict is not the sign of an imperfection; it reveals the inscription of an otherness in the work, through which it maintains a relationship with that which it is not, that which happens at its margins. To explain the work is to show that, contrary to appearances, it is not independent, but bears in its material substance the imprint of *a determinate absence* which is also the principle of its identity. The book is furrowed by the allusive presence of those other books against which it is elaborated; it circles about the absence of that which it cannot say, haunted by the absence of certain repressed words which make their return. The book is not the extension of a meaning; it is generated from the incompatibility of several meanings, the strongest bond by which it is attached to reality, in a tense and ever renewed confrontation (79–80; my italics).

A text may seek to control the production of meaning, but there is always a surplus of signification; that is, other meanings threatening to dislodge the authority of the primary meaning. It is this conflict of several meanings that structures a text: it displays this conflict but cannot speak it – its determinate absence. Traditionally, criticism has seen its role as making explicit what is implicit in the text, to make audible that which is merely a whisper (i.e. a single meaning). For Macherey, it is not a question of making what is there speak with more clarity so as to be finally sure of the text's meaning. Because a text's meanings are 'both interior and absent' (78), to simply repeat the text's self-knowledge is to fail to really explain the text. The task of a fully competent critical practice is not to make a whisper audible, nor to complete what the text leaves unsaid, but to produce a new knowledge of the text: one that explains the ideological necessity of its silences, its absences, its structuring incompleteness – the *staging* of that which it cannot speak.

> The act of knowing is not like listening to a discourse already constituted, a mere fiction which we have simply to translate. It is rather the elaboration of a new discourse, the articulation of a silence. Knowledge is not the discovery or reconstruction of a latent meaning, forgotten or concealed. It is something newly raised up, an addition to the reality from which it begins (6).

Borrowing from Sigmund Freud's work on dreams (see Chapter 5), Macherey contends that in order for something to be said, other things must be left unsaid. It is the reason(s) for these absences, these silences, within a text that must be interrogated. 'What is important in the work is what it does not say' (87). Again, as with Freud, who believed that the meanings of his patients' problems were not hidden in their conscious discourse, but repressed in the turbulent discourse of the unconscious, necessitating a subtle form of analysis acute to the difference between what is said and what is shown, Macherey's approach dances between the different nuances of *telling* and *showing*. This leads him to the claim that there is a 'gap', an 'internal distanciation', between what a text wants to say and what a text actually says. To explain a text it is necessary to go beyond it, to understand what it 'is compelled to say in order to say what it wants to say' (94). It is here that the text's 'unconscious' (Macherey's term for Althusser's problematic) is constituted. And it is in a text's unconscious that its relationship to the ideological and historical conditions of its existence is revealed. It is in the absent centre, hollowed out by conflicting discourses, that the text is related to history – to a particular moment in history and to the specific ideological discourses that circulate in that moment. The text's unconscious does not reflect historical contradictions; rather, it evokes, stages and displays them, allowing us not a 'scientific' knowledge of ideology, but an awareness of 'ideology in contradiction with itself'; breaking down before questions it cannot answer, failing to do what ideology is supposed to do: 'ideology exists precisely in order to efface all trace of contradiction' (130).

In a formal sense, a text always begins by posing a problem that is to be solved. The text then exists as a process of unfolding: the narrative movement to the final resolution of the problem. Macherey contends that between the problem posed and the resolution offered, rather than continuity, there is always a rupture. It is by examining this rupture that we discover the text's relationship with ideology and history: 'We always eventually find, at the edge of the text, the language of ideology, momentarily hidden, but eloquent by its very absence' (60).

All narratives contain an ideological project: that is, they promise to tell the 'truth' about something. Information is initially withheld on the promise that it will be revealed. Narrative constitutes a movement towards disclosure. It begins with a truth promised and ends with a truth revealed. To be rather schematic, Macherey divides the text into three instances: the ideological project (the 'truth' promised), the realization (the 'truth' revealed), and the unconscious of the text (produced by an act of symptomatic reading): the return of the repressed historical 'truth'. 'Science', he claims, 'does away with ideology, obliterates it; literature challenges ideology by using it. If ideology is thought of as a non-systematic ensemble of significations, the work proposes a *reading* of these significations, by combining them as signs. Criticism teaches us to read these signs' (133). In this way, Machereyan critical practice seeks to explain the way in which, by giving ideology form, the text displays ideology in contradiction with itself.

In a discussion of the work of the French science fiction writer Jules Verne, he demonstrates how Verne's work stages the contradictions of late nineteenth-century French imperialism. He argues that the ideological project of Verne's work is the *fantastic* staging of the adventures of French imperialism: its colonizing conquest of the earth. Each adventure concerns the hero's conquest of nature (a mysterious island, the moon, the bottom of the sea, the centre of the earth). In telling these stories, Verne is 'compelled' to tell another: each voyage of conquest becomes a voyage of rediscovery, as Verne's heroes discover that either others have been there before or are there already. The significance of this, for Macherey, lies in the disparity he perceives between 'representation' (what is intended: the subject of the narrative) and 'figuration' (how it is realized: its inscription in narrative): Verne 'represents' the ideology of French imperialism, while at the same time, through the act of 'figuration' (making material in *the form* of a fiction), undermines one of its central *myths* in the continual staging of the fact that the lands are always already occupied (similarly, the first edition of this book was written in the middle of a discursive avalanche of media – and other – claims that America was *discovered* in 1492, ignoring the fact that people had lived there for more than 15,000 years.). 'In the passage from the level of representation to that of figuration, ideology undergoes a complete *modification* . . . perhaps because no ideology is sufficiently consistent to survive the test of figuration' (194–5). Thus by giving fictional form to the ideology of imperialism, Verne's work – 'to read it against the grain of its intended meaning' (230) – stages the contradictions between the myth and the reality of imperialism. The stories do not provide us with a 'scientific' denunciation ('a knowledge in the strict sense') of imperialism, but by an act of symptomatic reading 'which dislodges the work internally', they 'make us see', 'make us perceive', 'make us feel', the terrible contradictions of the ideological discourses from which each text is constituted: 'from which it is born, in which it bathes, from which it detaches itself . . . and to which it alludes' (Althusser, 1971: 222). Verne's science fiction, then, can be made to reveal to us – though not in the ways intended – the ideological and historical conditions of its emergence.

In the nineteenth century there were a great number of books written to advise young women on appropriate conduct. Here, for example, is an extract from Thomas Broadhurst's *Advice to Young Ladies on the Improvement of the Mind and Conduct of Life* (1810):

> She who is faithfully employed in discharging the various duties of a wife and daughter, a mother and a friend, is far more usefully occupied than one who, to the culpable neglect of the most important obligations, is daily absorbed by philosophic and literary speculations, or soaring aloft amidst the enchanted regions of fiction and romance (quoted in Mills, 2004: 80).

Rather than see this as a straightforward sign of women's oppression, a Machereyan analysis would interrogate the extent to which this text is also an indication of the refusal of women to occupy positions traditionally demanded of them. In other words, if women were not engaging in philosophic and literary speculation, there would be no need to advise them against it. Women actually engaging in literary and philosophic speculation (and probably so much more) is, therefore, the determinate absence of the text. Similarly, Sara Mills (2004) points out how women's travel writing in the nineteenth century had to continually address a discourse of femininity that suggested that travel was something beyond a woman's strength and commitment. For example, in Alexandra David-Neel's account of her travels in Tibet we read, 'For nineteen hours we had been walking. Strangely enough, I did not feel tired' (quoted in Mills, 2004: 90). It is the phrase 'strangely enough' that points to a determinate absence: a masculine discourse of disbelief that haunts the unconscious of the text.

Finally, Photo 4.2 shows two figures on an otherwise empty beach; they look cold and uncomfortable. When trying to decide what this photograph signifies, it is very likely that our understanding may well be organized and shaped by a historically specific determinate absence: a normative expectation of a beach as a place of holiday-makers, relaxed and enjoying themselves. It is this determinate absence that locates the 'meaning' of the photograph in a specific historical moment: before the rise of the seaside holiday in the 1840s, this normative expectation would have been unavailable as an interpretative framework. In other words, the meaning we make is both historical and structured by absence.

In Althusser's second formulation, ideology is still a representation of the imaginary relationship of individuals to the real conditions of existence, only now ideology is seen no longer as only a body of ideas, but as a lived, material practice – rituals, customs, patterns of behaviour, ways of thinking taking practical form – reproduced through the practices and productions of the Ideological State Apparatuses (ISAs): education, organized religion, the family, organized politics, the media, the culture industries, etc. According to this second definition, 'all ideology has the function (which defines it) of "constructing" concrete individuals as subjects' (2009: 309). Ideological subjects are produced by acts of 'hailing' or 'interpellation'. Althusser uses the analogy of a police

Photo 4.2 Two figures on a beach.

officer hailing an individual: 'Hey, you there!' When the individual hailed turns in response, he or she has been interpellated; has become a subject of the police officer's discourse. In this way, ideology is a material practice that creates subjects who are in turn subjected to its specific patterns of thought and modes of behaviour.

This definition of ideology has had a significant effect on the field of cultural studies and the study of popular culture. Judith Williamson (1978), for example, deploys Althusser's second definition of ideology in her influential study of advertising, *Decoding Advertisements*. She argues that advertising is ideological in the sense that it represents an imaginary relationship to our real conditions of existence. Instead of class distinctions based on our role in the process of production, advertising continually suggests that what really matters are distinctions based on the consumption of particular goods. Thus social identity becomes a question of what we consume rather than what we produce. Like all ideology, advertising functions by interpellation: it creates subjects who in turn are subjected to its meanings and its patterns of consumption. The consumer is interpellated to make meaning and ultimately to purchase and consume and purchase and consume again. For example, when I am addressed in terms such as 'people like you' are turning to this or that product, I am interpellated as one of a group, but more importantly as an individual 'you' of that group. I am addressed as an individual who can recognize myself in the imaginary space opened up by the pronoun 'you'. Thus I am invited to become the imaginary 'you' spoken to in the advertisement. But such a process is for Althusser an act of ideological 'misrecognition': first, in the sense that in order for the advert to work it must attract many others who also recognize themselves in the 'you' (each one thinking they are the real 'you' of its discourse). Second, it is misrecognition in another sense: the 'you' I recognize in the advert is in fact a 'you' created by the advertisement. As Slavoj Žižek (1992) points out, interpellation works like this: 'I don't recognise myself in it because I'm its addressee, I become its addressee the moment I recognise myself in it' (12). Advertising, then, according to this perspective, flatters us into thinking we are the special 'you' of its discourse and in so doing we become subjects of and subjected to its material practices: acts of consumption. Advertising is thus ideological both in the way it functions and in the effects it produces.

One of the problems with Althusser's second model of ideology, and its application in cultural theory, is that it seems to work too well. Men and women are always successfully reproduced with all the necessary ideological habits required by the capitalist mode of production; there is no sense of failure, let alone any notion of conflict, struggle or resistance. In terms of popular culture, do advertisements, for example, always successfully interpellate us as consuming subjects? Moreover, even if interpellation works, previous interpellations may get in the way of current interpellations (contradict and prevent from working). Put simply, if I know that racism is wrong, a racist joke will fail to interpellate me. It was against this background of concerns that many working within the field of cultural studies turned to the work of the Italian Marxist Antonio Gramsci.

Hegemony

Central to the cultural studies appropriation of Gramsci is the concept of hegemony. Hegemony is for Gramsci a political concept developed to explain (given the exploitative and oppressive nature of capitalism) the absence of socialist revolutions in the Western capitalist democracies. The concept of hegemony is used by Gramsci (2009) to refer to a *condition in process* in which a dominant class (in alliance with other classes or class fractions) does not merely *rule* a society but *leads* it through the exercise of 'intellectual and moral leadership' (75). Hegemony involves a specific kind of consensus: a social group seeks to present its own particular interests as the general interests of the society as a whole. In this sense, the concept is used to suggest a society in which, despite oppression and exploitation, there is a high degree of consensus, a large measure of social stability; a society in which subordinate groups and classes appear to actively support and subscribe to values, ideals, objectives, cultural and political meanings, which bind them to, and 'incorporate' them into, the prevailing structures of power. For example, throughout most of the course of the twentieth century, general elections in Britain were contested by what are now the two main political parties, Labour and

Conservative. On each occasion the contest circled around the question, who best can administer capitalism (usually referred to by the less politically charged term 'the economy') – less public ownership, more public ownership, less taxation, more taxation, etc. And on each occasion, the mainstream media concurred. In this sense, the parameters of the election debate are ultimately dictated by the particular needs and interests of capitalism, presented as the interests and needs of society as a whole. Once the election is won the new prime minister will be accompanied on all official overseas visits by a large group of capitalists, each hoping that new business opportunities will be forthcoming. Similarly, new government policies will be justified and scrutinized in terms of how 'the markets' (i.e. capitalism in general) will respond. This is clearly an example of a situation in which the interests of one powerful section of society have been 'universalized' as the interests of the society as a whole. The situation seems perfectly 'natural', virtually beyond serious contention. But it was not always like this. Capitalism's hegemony is the result of profound political, social, cultural and economic changes that have taken place over a period of around 500 years. Until as late as the second part of the nineteenth century, capitalism's position was still uncertain.[3] It is only in the twenty-first century that the system seems to have won, or at least to be winning, especially with the political and economic collapse of the Soviet Union and Eastern Europe, and the introduction of the 'Open Door' policy and 'market socialism' in China. Capitalism is now, more or less, internationally hegemonic.

Although hegemony implies a society with a high degree of consensus, it should not be understood to refer to a society in which all conflict has been removed. What the concept is meant to suggest is a society in which conflict is contained and channelled into ideologically safe harbours; that is, hegemony is maintained (and must be continually maintained: it is an ongoing process) by dominant groups and classes 'negotiating' with, and making concessions to, subordinate groups and classes. For example, consider the historical case of British hegemony in the Caribbean. One of the ways in which Britain attempted to secure its control over the indigenous population, and the African men, women and children it had transported there as slaves, was by means of the imposition of a version of British culture (a standard practice for colonial regimes everywhere): part of the process was to institute English as the official language. In linguistic terms, the result was not the imposition of English, but, for the majority of the population, the creation of a new language. The dominant element of this new language is English, but the language itself is not simply English. What emerged was a transformed English, with new stresses and new rhythms, with some words dropped and new words introduced (from African languages and elsewhere). The new language is the result of a 'negotiation' between dominant and subordinate cultures, a language marked by both 'resistance' and 'incorporation': that is, not a language imposed from above, nor a language that had spontaneously arisen from below, but a language that is the result of a hegemonic struggle between two language cultures – a dominant language culture and a mix of subordinate language cultures, involving both 'resistance' and 'incorporation'.

Hegemony is never simply power imposed from above: it is always the result of 'negotiations' between dominant and subordinate groups, a process marked by both 'resistance' and 'incorporation'. There are of course limits to such negotiations and concessions. As Gramsci makes clear, they can never be allowed to challenge the economic fundamentals of class power. Moreover, in times of crisis, when moral and intellectual leadership is not enough to secure continued authority, the processes of hegemony are replaced, temporarily, by the coercive power of the 'repressive state apparatus': the army, the police, the prison system, etc.

Hegemony is 'organized' by those whom Gramsci designates 'organic intellectuals'. According to Gramsci, intellectuals are distinguished by their social function. That is to say, all men and women have the capacity for intellectual endeavour, but only certain men and women have in society the function of intellectuals. Each class, as Gramsci explains, creates 'organically' its own intellectuals:

> one or more strata of intellectuals which give it homogeneity and an awareness of its own function not only in the economic sphere but also in the social and political fields. The capitalist entrepreneur [for example] creates alongside himself the industrial technician, the specialist in political economy, the organisers of a new culture, of a new legal system, etc. (2009: 77).

Organic intellectuals function as class organizers (in the broadest sense of the term). It is their task to shape and to organize the reform of moral and intellectual life. I have argued elsewhere[4] that Matthew Arnold is best understood as an organic intellectual, what Gramsci identifies as one of 'an elite of men of culture, who have the function of providing leadership of a cultural and general ideological nature' (Storey, 1985: 217; Storey, 2010a). Gramsci tends to speak of organic intellectuals as individuals, but the way the concept has been mobilized in cultural studies, following Althusser's barely acknowledged borrowings from Gramsci, is in terms of *collective* organic intellectuals – the so-called 'ideological state apparatuses' of the family, television, the press, education, organized religion, the culture industries, etc.

Using hegemony theory, popular culture is what men and women make from their active consumption of the texts and practices of the culture industries. Youth subcultures are perhaps the most spectacular example of this process. Dick Hebdige (1979) offers a clear and convincing explanation of the process ('bricolage') by which youth subcultures appropriate for their own purposes and meanings the commodities commercially provided. Products are combined or transformed in ways not intended by their producers; commodities are re-articulated to produce 'oppositional' meanings. In this way, and through patterns of behaviour, ways of speaking, taste in music, etc., youth subcultures engage in symbolic forms of resistance to both dominant and parent cultures. Youth cultures, according to this model, always move from originality and opposition to commercial incorporation and ideological diffusion as the culture industries eventually succeed in marketing subcultural resistance for general consumption and profit. As Hebdige explains: 'Youth cultural styles may begin by issuing symbolic challenges, but they must end by establishing new sets of conventions; by creating new commodities, new industries or rejuvenating old ones' (96).

The concept of hegemony allows students of popular culture to free themselves from the disabling analysis of many of the previous approaches to the subject. Popular culture is no longer a history-stopping, imposed culture of political manipulation (the Frankfurt School); nor is it the sign of social decline and decay (the 'culture and civilization' tradition); nor is it something emerging spontaneously from below (some versions of culturalism); nor is it a meaning-machine imposing subjectivities on passive subjects (some versions of structuralism). Instead of these and other approaches, hegemony theory allows us to think of popular culture as a 'negotiated' mix of what is made both from 'above' and from 'below', both 'commercial' and 'authentic'; a shifting balance of forces between resistance and incorporation. This can be analysed in many different configurations: class, gender, generation, ethnicity, 'race', region, religion, disability, sexuality, etc. From this perspective, popular culture is a contradictory mix of competing interests and values: neither middle nor working class, neither racist nor non-racist, neither sexist nor non-sexist, neither homophobic nor homophilic ... but always a shifting balance between the two – what Gramsci calls 'a compromise equilibrium' (2009: 76). The commercially provided culture of the culture industries is redefined, reshaped and redirected in tactical acts of selective consumption and productive acts of reading and articulation, often in ways not intended or even foreseen by its producers.

Post-Marxism and cultural studies

As Angela McRobbie (1992) observes, Marxism is no longer as influential in cultural studies as it has been in the past:

> Marxism, a major point of reference for the whole cultural studies project in the UK, has been undermined not just from the viewpoint of the postmodern critics who attack its teleological propositions, its meta-narrative status, its essentialism, economism, Eurocentrism, and its place within the whole Enlightenment project, but also, of course, as a result of the events in Eastern Europe, with the discrediting of much of the socialist project (719).

What is certain, as she explains, is that 'the return to a pre-postmodern Marxism as marked out by critics like Fredric Jameson (1984) and David Harvey (1989) is untenable because the terms of that return are predicated on prioritizing economic relations and economic determinations over cultural and political relations by positioning these latter in a mechanical and reflectionist role' (ibid.). But more than this, there is a real sense in which cultural studies was always-already post-Marxist. As Hall (1992) points out,

> There was never a prior moment when cultural studies and Marxism represented a perfect theoretical fit. From the beginning ... there was always-already the

question of the great inadequacies, theoretically and politically, the resounding silences, the great evasions of Marxism – the things that Marx did not talk about or seem to understand which were our privileged object of study: culture, ideology, language, the symbolic. These were always-already, instead, the things which had imprisoned Marxism as a mode of thought, as an activity of critical practice – its orthodoxy, its doctrinal character, its determinism, its reductionism, its immutable law of history, its status as a metanarrative. That is to say, the encounter between British cultural studies and Marxism has first to be understood as the engagement with a problem – not a theory, not even a problematic (279).

Post-Marxism can mean at least two things. As Ernesto Laclau and Chantal Mouffe (2001) point out in their deeply influential contribution to post-Marxism, *Hegemony and Socialist Strategy: Towards a Radical Democratic Politics*, 'if our intellectual project in this book is *post*-Marxist, it is evidently also post-*Marxist*' (4). To be *post*-Marxist is to leave behind Marxism for something better, whereas to be post-*Marxist* is to seek to transform Marxism, by adding to it recent theoretical developments from, especially, feminism, postmodernism, post-structuralism and Lacanian psychoanalysis. Laclau and Mouffe are more post-*Marxist* than they are *post*-Marxist. They envisage a partnership between Marxism and the 'new feminism, the protest movements of ethnic, national and sexual minorities, the anti-institutional ecology struggles waged by marginalized layers of the population, the anti-nuclear movement, the atypical forms of social struggle in countries on the capitalist periphery' (1). In my view, cultural studies is post-Marxist in the positive sense advocated by Laclau and Mouffe.

The concept of discourse is central to the development of post-Marxism. As Laclau (1993) explains, 'The basic hypothesis of a discursive approach is that the very possibility of perception, thought and action depends on the structuration of a certain meaningful field which pre-exists any factual immediacy' (431). To explain what they mean by discourse Laclau and Mouffe (2009) give an example of two people building a wall. The first person asks the second to pass him/her a brick. On receiving the brick, the second person adds it to the wall. The totality of this operation consists in a linguistic moment (the request for a brick) and a non-linguistic moment (adding the brick to the wall). Discourse, according to Laclau and Mouffe, consists in the totality of the linguistic and non-linguistic. In other words, they use the term discourse 'to emphasize the fact that every social configuration is *meaningful*. If I kick a spherical object in the street or if I kick a ball in a football match, the *physical* fact is the same, but its *meaning* is different. The object is a football only to the extent that it establishes a system of relations with other objects, and these relations are not given by the mere referential materiality of the objects, but are, rather, socially constructed. This systematic set of relations is what we call discourse' (159).

Moreover,

the discursive character of an object does not, by any means, imply putting its existence into question. The fact that a football is only a football as long as it is integrated within a system of socially constructed rules does not mean that it ceases to be a physical object. . . . For the same reason it is the discourse which constitutes the subject position of the social agent, and not, therefore, the social agent which is the origin of discourse – the same system of rules that makes that spherical object into a football, makes me a player (159).

To understand this we have to differentiate between objectivity (the supposed ability to judge without context or interest) and the objective world, which exists independent of our experiences of it or our thoughts about it. In other words, objects exist independently of their discursive articulation, but it is only within discourse that they can exist as meaningful objects. For example, earthquakes exist in the real world, but whether they are

constructed in terms of 'natural phenomena' or 'expressions of the wrath of God', depends upon the structuring of a discursive field. What is denied is not that such objects exist externally to thought, but the rather different assertion that they could constitute themselves as objects outside any discursive condition of emergence (Laclau and Mouffe, 2001: 108).

As Gramsci (2007) points out, 'East and West . . . never cease to be "objectively real" even though when analysed they turn out to be nothing more than a "historical" or "conventional construct"' (175).

It is obvious that East and West are arbitrary and conventional (historical) constructions, since every spot on the earth is simultaneously East and West. Japan is probably the Far East not only for the European but also for the American from California and even for the Japanese himself, who, through English political culture might call Egypt the Near East. . . . Yet these references are real, they correspond to real facts, they allow one to travel by land and by sea and to arrive at the predetermined destination (176).

In other words, East and West are historical constructions, directly connected to the imperial power of the West. However, they are forms of signification that have been realized and embedded in social practice: cultural constructs they may be, but they do designate real geographic locations and guide real human movement.

As Gramsci's example makes clear, meanings produced in discourse inform and organize social action. It is only in discourse, for example, that 'a relation of subordination' can become 'a relation of oppression', and thereby constitute itself as a site of struggle (Laclau and Mouffe 153). Someone may be 'objectively' oppressed but unless they recognize their subordination as oppression, it is unlikely that this relation will ever become antagonistic and therefore open to the possibility of change. Hegemony works, as Laclau (1993) explains, by the transformation of antagonism into simple difference.

A class is hegemonic not so much to the extent that it is able to impose a uniform conception of the world on the rest of society, but to the extent that it can articulate different visions of the world in such a way that their potential antagonism is neutralised. The English bourgeoisie of the 19th century was transformed into a hegemonic class not through the imposition of a uniform ideology upon other classes, but to the extent that it succeeded in articulating different ideologies to its hegemonic project by an elimination of their antagonistic character (161–2).

'Articulation' is a key term in post-Marxist cultural studies. 'The practice of articulation', as Laclau and Mouffe (2001) explain, 'consists in the . . . partial fix[ing] of meaning' (113). Hall (1996b) has developed the concept to explain the ways in which culture is a terrain of ideological struggle. Like Laclau and Mouffe, he argues that texts and practices are not inscribed with meaning; meaning is always the result of an act of articulation. As he points out, 'Meaning is a social production, a practice. The world has to be *made to mean*' (2009a: 121). He also draws on the work of the Russian theorist Valentin Volosinov (1973). Volosinov argues that texts and practices are 'multi-accentual': that is, they can be 'spoken' with different 'accents' by different people in different discourses and different social contexts for different politics. When, for example, a black performer uses the word 'nigger' to attack institutional racism, it is 'spoken' with an 'accent' very different from the 'accent' given the word in, say, the racist discourse of a neo-Nazi. This is, of course, not simply a question of linguistic struggle – a conflict over semantics – but a sign of political struggle about who can claim the power and the authority to (partially) fix the meaning of social reality.

An interesting example of the processes of articulation is the reggae music of Rastafarian culture. Bob Marley, for example, had international success with songs articulating the values and beliefs of Rastafari. This success can be viewed in two ways. On the one hand, it signals the circulation of the 'message' of his religious convictions to an enormous audience worldwide; undoubtedly for many of his audience the music had the effect of enlightenment, understanding and perhaps even conversion to, and bonding for those already convinced of, the principles of the faith. On the other hand, the music has made and continues to make enormous profits for the music industry (promoters, Island Records, etc.). What we have is a paradox in which the anti-capitalist politics of Rastafari are being articulated in the economic interests of capitalism: the music is helping to reproduce the very system it seeks to condemn; that is, the politics of Rastafari are being expressed in a form that is ultimately of financial benefit to the dominant culture (i.e. as a commodity that circulates for profit). Nevertheless, the music *is* an expression of an oppositional (religious) politics, and it may circulate as such, and it may produce certain political and cultural effects. Therefore, Rastafarian reggae is a force for change that paradoxically stabilizes (at least economically) the very forces of power it seeks to overthrow.

Another example, in some ways more compelling than that of reggae, is the music of the American counterculture. It inspired people to resist the draft and to organize against *Amerika*'s (spelling used by political sections of the counterculture, intended to imply, by use of the Germanic 'k', that the USA was fascist) war in Vietnam; yet, at the same time, its music made profits (over which it had no control) that could then be used to support the war effort in Vietnam. The more Jefferson Airplane sang 'All your private property/Is target for your enemy/And your enemy/Is *We*',[5] the more money RCA Records made. The proliferation of Jefferson Airplane's anti-capitalist politics increased the profits of their capitalist record company. Again, this is an example of the process of articulation: the way in which dominant groups in society attempt to 'negotiate' oppositional voices on to a terrain which secures for the dominant groups a continued position of leadership. The music of the counterculture was not denied expression (and there can be little doubt that this music produced particular cultural and political effects), but what is also true is that this music was also articulated in the economic interests of the war-supporting capitalist music industry.[6] As Keith Richards of the Rolling Stones discovered,

> We found out, and it wasn't for years that we did, that all the bread we made for Decca was going into making black boxes that go into American Air Force bombers to bomb fucking North Vietnam. They took the bread we made for them and put it into the radar section of their business. When we found that out, it blew our minds. That was it. Goddam, you find out you've helped kill God knows how many thousands of people without really knowing it (quoted in Storey, 2010a: 28–9).

In Chapter 3 we examined Williams's (2009) social definition of culture. We discussed it in terms of how it broadens the definition of culture: instead of culture being defined as only the 'elite' texts and practices (ballet, opera, the novel, poetry), Williams redefined culture to include *as* culture, for example, pop music, television, cinema, advertising, going on holiday, etc. However, another aspect of Williams's social definition of culture has proved even more important for cultural studies, especially post-Marxist cultural studies – the connection he makes between meaning and culture.

> There is the 'social' definition of culture, in which culture is a description of a particular way of life, *which expresses certain meanings and values* not only in art and learning but also in institutions and ordinary behaviour. The analysis of culture, from such a definition, is *the clarification of the meanings and values* implicit in a particular way of life (32; my italics).

The importance of a particular way of life is that it 'expresses certain meanings and values'. Cultural analysis from the perspective of this definition of culture 'is the clarification of the meanings and values implicit in a particular way of life'. Moreover, culture as a signifying system is not reducible to 'a particular way of life'; rather, it is fundamental to the shaping and holding together of a particular way of life. This is not to reduce everything 'upwards' to culture as a signifying system, but it is to insist that culture, defined in this way, should be understood 'as essentially involved in all forms of social activity' (Williams, 1981: 13). While there is more to life than signifying systems, it is nevertheless the case that 'it would . . . be wrong to suppose that we can ever usefully discuss a social system without including, as a central part of its practice, its signifying systems, on which, as a system, it fundamentally depends' (207).

Following this definition, and the discourse theory of Laclau and Mouffe, post-Marxist cultural studies defines culture as the production, circulation and consumption of meanings. As Hall (1997a), for example, explains, 'Culture . . . is not so much a set of things – novels and paintings or TV programmes and comics – as a process, a set of practices. Primarily, culture is concerned with the production and exchange of meanings – the giving and taking of meaning' (2). According to this definition, cultures do not so much consist of, say, books; cultures are the shifting networks of signification in which, say, books are *made* to signify as meaningful objects. For example, if I pass a business card to someone in China, the polite way to do it is with two hands. If I pass it with one hand I may cause offence. This is clearly a matter of culture. However, the 'culture' is not simply in the social act, nor is it just in the materiality of the card; it is in the 'realized' meaning of both act and card. In other words, there is nothing essentially polite about using two hands; using two hands has been made to signify politeness. Nevertheless, signification has become embodied in a material practice, which may, in turn, produce material effects (I shall say more about this in Chapter 11). Similarly, as Marx (1976c) observed, 'one man is king only because other men stand in the relation of subjects to him. They, on the contrary, imagine that they are subjects because he is king' (149). This relationship works because they share a culture in which such relations are meaningful. Outside such a culture this relationship would seem meaningless. Being a king, therefore, is not a gift of nature but something constructed in culture. It is culture and not nature that gives the relation meaning.

To share a culture, therefore, is to interpret the world – make it meaningful and experience it as meaningful – in recognizably similar ways. So-called 'culture shock' happens when we encounter radically different networks of meaning: when our 'natural' or our 'common sense' is confronted by someone else's 'natural' or 'common sense'. However, cultures are never simply shifting networks of shared meanings. On the contrary, cultures are always both shared and contested networks of meanings: culture is where we share and contest meanings of ourselves, of each other and of the social worlds in which we live.

Post-Marxist cultural studies draws two conclusions from this way of thinking about culture. First, although the world exists in all its enabling and constraining materiality outside culture, it is only in culture that the world *can be made to mean*. In other words, culture constructs the realities it appears only to describe. Second, because different meanings can be ascribed to the same 'text' (anything that can be made to signify), meaning making (i.e. the making of culture) is always a potential site of struggle and/or negotiation. For example, masculinity has real material conditions of existence, which we think of as 'biological', but there are different ways of representing masculinity in culture, different ways of 'being masculine'. Moreover, these different ways do not all carry the same claims to 'authenticity' and 'normality'. Masculinity, therefore, may depend on biological conditions of existence, but what it *means*, and the struggle over what it *means*, always takes place *in* culture. This is not a question of semantic difference – a simple question of interpreting the world differently – it is about relations of culture and power; about who can claim the power and authority to define social reality; to *make the world (and the things in it) mean* in particular ways.

Culture and power is the primary object of study in post-Marxist cultural studies. As Hall (1997a: 4) explains, 'Meanings [i.e. cultures] . . . regulate and organize our conduct and practices – they help to set the rules, norms and conventions by which social life is ordered and governed. They are . . . , therefore, what those who wish to govern and regulate the conduct and ideas of others seek to structure and shape.' Meanings have a 'material' existence, in that they help organize practice; they establish norms of behaviour, as we recognized in the examples of different masculinities and the passing of a business card in China.

In other words, then, dominant ways of making the world meaningful, produced by those with the power to make their meanings circulate in the world, can generate the 'hegemonic discourses', which may come to assume an authority over the ways in which we see, think, communicate and act in the world and become the 'common sense' which directs our actions or become that against which our actions are directed. However, although post-Marxist cultural studies recognizes that the culture industries are a major site of ideological production, constructing powerful images, descriptions, definitions, frames of reference for understanding the world, it rejects the view that 'the people' who consume these productions are 'cultural dupes', victims of 'an up-dated form of the opium of the people'. As Hall (2009b) insists,

> That judgment may make us feel right, decent and self-satisfied about our denunciations of the agents of mass manipulation and deception – the capitalist cultural industries: but I don't know that it is a view which can survive for long as an adequate account of cultural relationships; and even less as a socialist perspective on the culture and nature of the working class. Ultimately, the notion of the people as a purely passive, outline force is a deeply unsocialist perspective (512).

Post-Marxist cultural studies is informed by the proposition that people *make* popular culture from the repertoire of commodities supplied by the culture industries. *Making* popular culture ('production in use') can be empowering to subordinate and resistant to dominant understandings of the world. But this is not to say that popular culture is always empowering and resistant. To deny the passivity of consumption is not to deny that sometimes consumption is passive; to deny that consumers are cultural dupes is not to deny that the culture industries seek to manipulate. But it is to deny that popular culture is little more than a degraded landscape of commercial and ideological manipulation, imposed from above in order to make profit and secure social control. Post-Marxist cultural studies insists that to decide these matters requires vigilance and attention to the details of the production, distribution and consumption of the commodities from which people may or may not make popular culture. These are not matters that can be decided once and for all (outside the contingencies of history and politics) with an elitist glance and a condescending sneer. Nor can they be read off from the moment of production (locating meaning, pleasure, ideological effect, the probability of incorporation, the possibility of resistance, in, variously, the intention, the means of production or the production itself): these are only aspects of the contexts for 'production in use';

and it is, ultimately, in 'production in use' that questions of meaning, pleasure, ideological effect, incorporation or resistance can be (contingently) decided.

Notes

1. See Storey 1992 and 2010a.
2. See *New Left Review* (1977).
3. See Stedman Jones (1998).
4. See Storey (1985 and 2010a).
5. 'We Can Be Together', from the album *Volunteers* (1969).
6. See Storey (2010a and 2009).

Further reading

Storey, John (ed.), *Cultural Theory and Popular Culture: A Reader*, 4th edn, Harlow: Pearson Education, 2009. This is the companion volume to the previous edition of this book. A fully updated 5th edition containing further readings is due for publication in 2018. An interactive website is also available (www.routledge.com/cw/storey), which contains helpful student resources and a glossary of terms for each chapter.

Barrett, Michele, *The Politics of Truth: From Marx to Foucault*, Cambridge: Polity Press, 1991. An interesting introduction to 'post Marxism'.
Bennett, Tony, *Formalism and Marxism*, London: Methuen, 1979. Contains helpful chapters on Althusser and Macherey.
Bennett, Tony, Colin Mercer and Janet Woollacott (eds), *Culture, Ideology and Social Process*, London: Batsford, 1981. Section 4 consists of extracts from Gramsci and three essays informed by hegemony theory. The book also contains similar sections on culturalism and structuralism.
Hebdige, Dick, *Subculture: The Meaning of Style*, London: Methuen, 1979. The seminal account of youth subcultures: an excellent introduction to hegemony theory and popular culture.
Laing, Dave, *The Marxist Theory of Art: An Introductory Survey*, Hemel Hempstead: Harvester Wheatsheaf, 1978. A very readable introduction to Marxist theories of culture. Contains an interesting section on popular culture.
Marx, Karl and Frederick Engels, *On Literature and Art*, St Louis: Telos, 1973. A useful selection of the writings by Marx and Engels on matters cultural.
Nelson, Cary and Lawrence Grossberg (eds), *Marxism and the Interpretation of Culture*, London: Macmillan, 1988. An interesting collection of essays on Marxism and culture.

Showstack Sassoon, Anne (ed.), *Approaches to Gramsci*, London: Writers and Readers, 1982. A collection of essays on Gramsci. Contains a useful glossary of key terms.

Sim, Stuart (ed.), *Post-Marxism: A Reader*, Edinburgh: Edinburgh University Press, 1998. Interesting collection of essays on the question of post-Marxism.

Simon, Roger, *Gramsci's Political Thought: An Introduction*, London: Lawrence & Wishart, 1982. A very readable introduction to Gramsci.

Slater, Phil, *Origin and Significance of the Frankfurt School: A Marxist Perspective*, London: Routledge & Kegan Paul, 1977. The book provides a critical overview of the work of the Frankfurt School. Chapter 4, on the culture industry, is of particular interest to the student of popular culture.

Storey, John, *Culture and Power in Cultural Studies: The Politics of Signification*, Edinburgh: Edinburgh University Press, 2010. A collection of essays examining culture from the perspective of Gramscian cultural studies.

Storey, John, *Utopian Desire*, London: Routledge, forthcoming. The book explores radical utopianism from the perspective of a Gramscian cultural studies.

Wayne, Mike, *Marxism and Media Studies*, London: Verso. An excellent overview of what should be the focus of Marxist media studies.

5 Psychoanalysis

In this chapter I shall explore psychoanalysis as a method of reading texts and practices. This means that although I shall to a certain extent explain how psychoanalysis understands human behaviour, this will be done only as it can be extended to cultural analysis in cultural studies. Therefore, I shall be very selective in terms of which aspects of psychoanalysis I choose for discussion.

Freudian psychoanalysis

Sigmund Freud (1973a) argues that the creation of civilization has resulted in the repression of basic human instincts. Moreover, 'each individual who makes a fresh entry into human society repeats this sacrifice of instinctual satisfaction for the benefit of the whole community' (47). The most important instinctual drives are sexual. Civilization demands that these are redirected in unconscious processes of sublimation:

> that is to say, they are diverted from their sexual aims and directed to others that are socially higher and no longer sexual. But this arrangement is unstable; the sexual are imperfectly tamed, and, in the case of every individual who is supposed to join in the work of civilization, there is a risk that his sexual instincts may refuse to be put to that use. Society believes that no greater threat to its civilization could arise than if the sexual instincts were to be liberated and returned to their original aims (47–8).[1]

Fundamental to this argument is Freud's discovery of the unconscious. He first divides the psyche into two parts, the conscious and the unconscious. The conscious is the part that relates to the external world, while the unconscious is the site of instinctual drives and repressed wishes. He then adds to this binary model the preconscious. What we cannot remember at any given moment, but know we can recall with some mental effort, is recovered from the preconscious. What is in the unconscious, as a consequence of censorship and repression is only ever expressed in distorted form; we cannot, as an act of will recall material from the unconscious into the conscious.[2] Freud's final

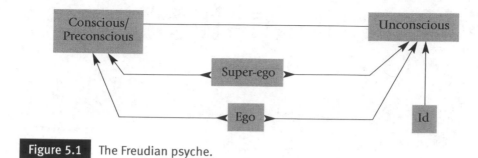

Figure 5.1   The Freudian psyche.

model of the psyche introduces three new terms: the ego, the super-ego and the id (see Figure 5.1).[3]

The id is the most primitive part of our being. It is the part of 'our nature [which] is impersonal, and, so to speak, subject to natural law' (Freud, 1984: 362); it 'is the dark, inaccessible part of our personality . . . a chaos, a cauldron full of seething excitations. . . . It is filled with energy reaching it from the instincts, but it has no organization, produces no collective will, but only a striving to bring about the satisfaction of the instinctual needs subject to the observance of the pleasure principle' (Freud, 1973b: 106).

The ego develops out of the id: 'the ego cannot exist in the individual from the start; the ego has to be developed' (1984: 69). As he further explains, the ego

> is that part of the id which has been modified by the direct influence of the external world. . . . Moreover, the ego seeks to bring the influence of the external world to bear upon the id and its tendencies, and endeavours to substitute the reality principle for the pleasure principle which reigns unrestrictedly in the id. . . . The ego represents what may be called reason and common sense, in contrast to the id, which contains the passions (363–4).

Freud (1973b) compares the relationship between the id and the ego as similar to a person riding a horse: 'The horse supplies the locomotive energy, while the rider has the privilege of deciding on the goal and of guiding the powerful animal's movement. But only too often there arises between the ego and the id the not precisely ideal situation of the rider being obliged to guide the horse along the path by which it itself wants to go' (109–10). In fact, the ego struggles to serve three masters, the 'external world', the 'libido of the id', and the 'severity of the super-ego' (1984: 397).

It is with the dissolution of the Oedipus complex (discussed later in this chapter) that the super-ego emerges. The super-ego begins as the internalization or introjection of the authority of the child's parents, especially of the father. This first authority is then overlaid with other voices of authority, producing what we think of as 'conscience'. Although the super-ego is in many ways the voice of culture, it remains in alliance with the id. Freud explains it thus: 'Whereas the ego is essentially the representative of the external world, of reality, the super-ego stands in contrast to it as the

Id ◄----------► Ego (Super-ego)
'Pleasure Principle' ◄----------► 'Reality Principle'

Figure 5.2   Freud's conflict model of the human psyche.

representative of the internal world, of the id' (366). 'Thus the super-ego is always close to the id and can act as its representative vis-à-vis the ego. It reaches deep down into the id and for that reason is farther from consciousness than the ego is' (390). Furthermore, 'Analysis eventually shows that the super-ego is being influenced by processes that have remained unknown to the ego' (392).

There are two particular things to note about Freud's model of the psyche. First, we are born with an id, while the ego develops through contact with culture, which in turn produces the super-ego. In other words, our 'nature' is governed (sometimes successfully, sometimes not) by culture. What is called 'human nature' is not something 'essentially' natural but the governance of our nature by culture. This means that human nature is not something innate and unchangeable, it is something at least in part introduced from outside. Moreover, given that culture is always historical and variable, it is itself always open to change.[4] Second, and perhaps much more fundamental to psychoanalysis, the psyche is envisaged as a site of perpetual conflict (see Figure 5.2). The most fundamental conflict is between the id and the ego. The id wants desires satisfied regardless of the claims of culture, while the ego, sometimes in loose alliance with the super-ego, is obliged to meet the claims and conventions of society. This conflict is sometimes portrayed as a struggle between the 'pleasure principle' and the 'reality principle'. For example, while the id (governed by the pleasure principle) may demand 'I want it' (whatever 'it' might be), the ego (governed by the reality principle) must defer thinking about 'it' in order to consider how to get 'it'.

'The essence of repression', according to Freud, 'lies simply in turning something away, and keeping it at a distance, from the conscious' (147). In this way, then, we could say that repression is a special form of amnesia; it removes all the things with which we cannot or will not deal. But as Freud (1985) makes clear, we may have repressed these things, but they have not really gone away: 'Actually, we never give anything up; we only exchange one thing for another. What appears to be a renunciation is really the formation of a substitute or surrogate' (133). These 'substitutive formations' make possible the 'return of the repressed' (Freud, 1984: 154). Dreams provide perhaps the most dramatic staging of the return of the repressed.[5] As Freud (1976) claims, 'The interpretation of dreams is the royal road to the unconscious' (769).

The primary function of dreams is to be 'the guardians of sleep which get rid of disturbances of sleep' (Freud, 1973a: 160). Sleep is threatened from three directions: external stimulus, recent events and 'repressed instinctual impulses which are on the watch for an opportunity of finding expression' (45). Dreams guard sleep by incorporating potential disturbances into the narrative of the dream. If, for example, a noise sounds during sleep, a dream will attempt to include the noise in its narrative organization. Similarly, when a sleeper experiences somatic disturbances (indigestion is the most obvious example), the dream will attempt to accommodate this in order not to disturb the dreamer's sleep. However, outside and inside stimulus of this sort is always transformed. As he explains, 'Dreams do not simply reproduce the stimulus; they work it over, they make allusions to it, they include it in some context, they replace it by something else' (125). An alarm clock, for example, may appear as the sound of church bells on a sunny Sunday morning or as the sound of the fire brigade rushing to the scene of a devastating fire. Therefore, although we can recognize how outside stimulation may contribute something to a dream, it does not explain why or how this something is worked over. Similarly, dreams are also informed by recent experiences, 'the day's residues' (264). These may often determine much of the content of a dream, but, as Freud insists, this, as with noise and somatic disturbances, is merely the material out of which the dream is formulated and is not the same as the unconscious wish. As he explains, the 'unconscious impulse is the true creator of the dream; it is what produces the psychical energy for the dream's construction' (1973b: 47).

Dreams, according to Freud, are always a 'compromise-structure' (48) – that is, a compromise between wishes emanating from the id and censorship enacted by the ego: 'If the meaning of our dreams usually remains obscure to us . . . it is because [they contain] wishes of which we are ashamed; these we must conceal from ourselves, and they have consequently been repressed, pushed into the unconscious. Repressed wishes of this sort and their derivatives are only allowed to come to expression in a very distorted form' (1985: 136). Censorship occurs but wishes are expressed; that is, they are coded in an attempt to elude censorship. According to Freud's (1976) famous formulation, 'a dream is a (disguised) fulfilment of a (suppressed or repressed) wish' (244).

Dreams move between two levels: the latent dream thoughts (unconscious) and the manifest content (what the dreamer remembers dreaming). Dream analysis attempts to decode the manifest content in order to discover the 'real meaning' of the dream. To do this it has to decipher the different mechanisms that have translated latent dream thoughts into manifest content. He calls these mechanisms the 'dream-work' (2009: 246). The dream-work consists of four processes: condensation, displacement, symbolization and secondary revision. Each in turn produces 'the transformation of thoughts into hallucinatory experience' (1973a: 250).

The manifest content is always smaller than the latent content. This is the result of condensation, which can work in three different ways: (i) latent elements are omitted; (ii) only part of a latent element arrives in the manifest content; and (iii) latent elements which have something in common are condensed into 'composite structures' (2009: 247). 'As a result of condensation, one element in the manifest dream may correspond to numerous elements in the latent dream-thoughts; but, conversely too, one element in the dream-thoughts may be represented by several images in [the manifest content of] the dream' (1973b: 49). Freud provides the following example:

> You will have no difficulty in recalling instances from your own dreams of different people being condensed into a single one. A compromise figure of this kind may look like A perhaps, but may be dressed like B, may do something that we remember C doing, and at the same time we may know that he is D (2009: ibid.).

Latent elements also appear in the manifest content via a chain of association or allusion Freud calls displacement. This process works in two ways:

> In the first, a latent element is replaced not by a component part of itself but by something more remote – that is, by an allusion; and in the second, the psychical accent is shifted from an important element on to another which is unimportant, so that the dream appears differently centred and strange (248).

This first aspect of displacement operates along chains of association in which what is in the manifest content alludes to something in the latent dream thoughts. If, for example, I know someone who works as a schoolteacher, she may appear in my dreams as a satchel. In this way, affect (the emotional intensity attached to the figure) is shifted from its source (she who works in a school), to something associated with her working in a school. Or if I know someone called Clarke, she may appear in my dreams as someone working in an office. Again, affect has been moved along a chain of association from the name of someone I know to an activity associated with her name. I may have a dream situated in an office, in which I observe someone working at a desk (it may not even be a woman), but the 'essence' of my dream is a woman I know called Clarke. These examples work metonymically in terms of similarity based on contraction: a part standing in for a whole. The second mechanism of displacement changes the focus of the dream. What appears in the manifest content is 'differently centred from the dream-thoughts – its content has different elements as its central point' (1976: 414). 'With the help of displacement the dream-censorship creates substitutive structures which . . . are allusions which are not easily recognizable as such, from which the path back to the genuine thing is not easily traced, and which are connected with the genuine thing by the strangest, most unusual, external associations' (1973a: 272). He illustrates this second aspect of displacement with a joke.

> There was a blacksmith in a village, who had committed a capital offence. The Court decided that the crime must be punished; but as the blacksmith was the only one in the village and was indispensable, and as on the other hand there were three tailors living there, one of them was hanged instead (2009: 249).

In this example, the chain of association and affect has shifted dramatically. To get back to the blacksmith from the fate of one of the tailors would require a great deal of analysis, but the central idea seems to be: 'Punishment must be exacted even if it does not fall upon the guilty' (1984: 386). Moreover, as he explains, 'No other part of the dream-work is so much responsible for making the dream strange and incomprehensible to the dreamer. Displacement is the principal means used in the *dream-distortion* to which the [latent] dream-thoughts must submit under the influence of the censorship' (1973b: 50).

The third aspect of the dream-work, operative in the first two, is symbolization, the 'translation of dream-thoughts into a primitive mode of expression similar to picture-writing' (1973a: 267), in which 'the latent dream-thoughts . . . are dramatized and illustrated' (1973b: 47). Symbolization transforms 'the latent [dream] thoughts which are expressed in words into sensory images, mostly of a visual sort' (1973a: 215). But as Freud makes clear, not everything is transformed in this way: certain elements exist in other forms. Nevertheless, symbols 'comprise the essence of the formation of dreams' (2009: 249). Furthermore, 'The very great majority of symbols in dreams', as Freud maintains, 'are sexual symbols' (1973a: 187). So, for example, male genitals are represented in dreams by a range of 'symbolic substitutes' that are erect such as 'sticks, umbrellas, posts, trees' and things that are able to penetrate such as 'knives, daggers, spears, sabres . . . rifles, pistols and revolvers' (188). Female genitals are represented by things that share the 'characteristic of enclosing a hollow space which can take something into itself' such as 'pits, cavities . . . hollows . . . vessels and bottles . . . receptacles, boxes, trunks, cases, chests, pockets, and so on' (189).

These symbolic substitutes are drawn from an ever-changing repertoire of symbols. He makes this clear in his discussion of the way in which objects that are able to defy the laws of gravity are used to represent the male erection. Writing in 1917, he points to the fact that the Zeppelin airship had recently joined the repertoire of such objects (1976: 188). Although these symbols are drawn from myths, religion, fairy stories, jokes and everyday language use, objects are not consciously selected from the repertoire: 'the knowledge of symbolism is unconscious to the dreamer . . . it belongs to his mental life' (1973a: 200).[6]

Freud is absolutely clear about 'the impossibility of interpreting a dream unless one has the dreamer's associations to it at one's disposal' (1973b: 36). Symbols may provide a preliminary answer to the question 'What does this dream mean?' But it is only a preliminary answer, to be confirmed, or otherwise, by an analysis of other aspects of the dream-work in conjunction with analysis of the associations brought into play by the person whose dream is being analysed. As he warns: 'I should like to utter an express warning against overestimating the importance of symbols in dream-interpretation, against restricting the work of translating dreams merely to translating symbols and against abandoning the technique of making use of the dreamer's associations' (477). Moreover, symbols 'frequently have more than one or even several meanings, and . . . the correct interpretation can only be arrived at on each occasion from the context' (1976: 470). Again, context will be something established by the dreamer.

The dream-work's final process is secondary revision. This is the narrative placed by the dreamer on the dream symbolism. It takes two forms. First, it is the verbal account of the dream: the translation of symbols into language and narrative – 'we fill in gaps and introduce connections, and in doing so are often guilty of gross misunderstandings' (1973b: 50). Second, and more importantly, secondary revision is the final policing and channelling strategy of the ego, making meaning and coherence in an act of (unconscious) censorship.

After the interpretation of dreams, Freud is perhaps best known for his theory of the Oedipus complex. Freud developed the complex from Sophocles's drama *Oedipus the King* (*c.* 427 BC). In Sophocles's play Oedipus kills his father (unaware that he is his father) and marries his mother (unaware that she is his mother). On discovering the truth, Oedipus blinds himself and goes into exile. Freud developed two versions of the Oedipus complex, one for boys and one for girls. At around the age of three to five years, the mother (or who has the symbolic role of the mother) becomes an object of the boy's desire. In the light of this desire, the father (or who has the symbolic role of the father) is seen as a rival for the mother's love and affection. As a consequence, the boy wishes for the father's death. However, the boy fears the father's power, in particular his power to castrate. So the boy abandons his desire for the mother and begins to identify with the father, fairly confident in the knowledge that one day he will have the father's power, including a wife (a substitute symbolic mother) of his own.

Freud was unsure how the Oedipus complex worked for girls: 'It must be admitted . . . that in general our insight into these developmental processes in girls is unsatisfactory, incomplete and vague' (1977: 321).[7] As a consequence, he continued to revise his thinking on this subject. One version begins with the girl desiring the father (or whoever has the symbolic role of the father). The mother (or whoever has the symbolic role of the mother) is seen as a rival for the father's love and affection. The girl wishes for the mother's death. The complex is resolved when the girl identifies with the mother, recognizing that one day she will be like her. But it is a resentful identification – the mother lacks power. In another account, he argues that the Oedipus complex 'seldom goes beyond the taking her mother's place and the adopting of a feminine attitude towards her father' (ibid.). Already aware that she has been castrated, the girl seeks compensation: 'She gives up her wish for a penis and puts in place of it a wish for a child: and *with that purpose in view* she takes her father as a love-object' (340; original emphasis). The girl's desire for her father's child gradually diminishes: 'One has the impression that the Oedipus complex is then gradually given up because the wish is never fulfilled' (321). The paradox being, 'Whereas in boys the Oedipus complex is destroyed by the castration complex, in girls it is made possible and led up to by the castration complex' (341).[8]

There are at least two ways in which Freudian psychoanalysis can be used as a method to analyse texts. The first approach is author-centred, treating the text as the equivalent to an author's dream. Freud (1985) identifies what he calls 'the class of dreams that have never been dreamt at all – dreams created by imaginative writers and ascribed to invented characters in the course of a story' (33). The surface of a text (words and images, etc.) is regarded as the manifest content, while the latent content is the author's hidden desires. Texts are read in this way to discover an author's fantasies; these are seen as the real meaning of the text. According to Freud (1973a),

An artist is . . . an introvert, not far removed from neurosis. He is oppressed by excessively powerful instinctual needs. He desires to win honour, power, wealth, and the love of women; but he lacks the means for achieving these satisfactions. Consequently, like any other unsatisfied man, he turns away from reality and transfers all his interest, and his libido too, to the wishful constructions of his life of phantasy, whence the path might lead to neurosis (423).

The artist sublimates his or her desire. In so doing, she or he makes his or her fantasies available to others, thus making 'it possible for others to share in the enjoyment of them' (423–4). He or she 'makes it possible for other people . . . to derive consolation and pleasure in their unconscious which have become inaccessible to them' (424). Texts 'allay ungratified wishes – in the first place in the creative artist himself and subsequently in his audience or spectators' (1986: 53). As he explains: 'The artist's first aim is to set himself free and, by communicating his work to other people suffering from the same arrested desires, he offers them the same liberation' (53).

The second approach is reader-centred, and derives from the secondary aspect of the author-centred approach. This approach is concerned with how texts allow readers to symbolically play out desires and fantasies in the texts they read. In this way, a text works like a substitute dream. Freud deploys the idea of 'fore-pleasure' to explain the way in which the pleasures of the text 'make possible the release of still greater pleasure arising from deeper psychical sources' (1985: 141). In other words, fictional texts stage fantasies that offer the possibility of unconscious pleasure and satisfaction. As he further explains,

> In my opinion, all the aesthetic pleasure which a creative writer affords us has the character of a fore-pleasure . . . our actual enjoyment of an imaginative work proceeds from a liberation of tensions in our minds . . . enabling us thenceforward to enjoy our day-dreams without self-reproach or shame (ibid.).

Although we may derive pleasure from the aesthetic qualities of a text, these are really only the mechanism that allows us access to the more profound pleasures of unconscious fantasy.

Little Redcape

There was once a sweet little girl who was loved by everyone who so much as looked at her, and most of all her grandmother loved her and was forever trying to think of new presents to give the child. Once she gave her a little red velvet cape, and because it suited her so well and she never again wanted to wear anything else, she was known simply as Little Redcape. One day her mother said to her: 'Come, Little Redcape, here's a piece of cake and a bottle of wine; take them out to your grandmother, she's sick and weak and she'll enjoy them very much. Set out before it gets hot, and when you're on your way watch your step like a good girl and don't stray from the path, or you'll fall and break the bottle and grandmother will get nothing. And when you go into her room, remember to say good morning and not to stare all round the room first.'

'Don't worry, I'll do everything as I should,' said Little Redcape to her mother and promised faithfully. Now her grandmother lived out in the forest, half an hour from the village. And as Little Redcape entered the forest the wolf met her. But Little Redcape didn't know what a wicked beast he was, and wasn't afraid of him. 'Good morning, Little Redcape,' he said. 'Thank you, wolf.' 'Where are you going so early, Little Redcape?' 'To my grandmother's.' 'What are you carrying under your apron?' 'Cake and wine – we were baking yesterday, and my grand-mother's ill and weak, so she's to have something nice to help her get strong again.' 'Little Redcape, where does your grandmother live?' 'A good quarter of an hour's walk further on in the forest, under the three big oak trees, that's where her house is; there are hazel hedges by it, I'm sure you know the place,' said Little Redcape. The wolf thought to itself: This delicate young thing, she'll make a plump morsel, she'll taste even better than the old woman. But I must go about it cunningly and I'll catch them both. So he walked for a while beside Little Redcape and then said: 'Little Redcape, just look at those lovely flowers growing all round us, why don't you look about you? I think you don't even notice how sweetly the birds are singing. You're walking straight ahead as if you were going to school, and yet it's such fun out here in the wood.'

Little Redcape looked up, and when she saw the sunbeams dancing to and fro between the trees and all the lovely flowers growing everywhere, she thought: If I take Grandmama a bunch of fresh flowers, that'll please her too; it's so early that I'll still get there soon enough. And she ran off the path and into the forest to look for flowers. And every time she picked one she seemed to see a prettier one grow-ing further on, and she ran to pick it and got deeper and deeper into the forest. But the wolf went straight to her grandmother's house and knocked at the door. 'Who's there?' 'Little Redcape, bringing you some cake and wine; open the door.' 'Just push down the latch,' said the grandmother, 'I'm too weak to get out of bed.' The wolf pushed down the latch, and without a word he went straight to the old woman's bed and gobbled her up. Then he put on her clothes and her nightcap and lay down in her bed and closed the curtains.

But Little Redcape had been running about picking flowers, and when she had collected so many that she couldn't carry any more she remembered her grandmother and set out again towards her house. She was surprised to find the door open, and when she went into the room everything seemed so strange that she thought: Oh my goodness, how nervous I feel today, and yet I always enjoy visiting Grandmama! She called out: 'Good morning,' but got no answer. Then she went to the bed and drew back the curtains – and there lay her grandmother with her bonnet pulled down low over her face and looking so peculiar. 'Why, Grandmama, what big ears you have!' 'The better to hear you with,' 'Why Grandmama, what big eyes you have!' 'The better to see you with.' 'Why, Grandmama, what big hands you have!' 'The better to grab you with.' 'But, Grandmama, what terrible big jaws you have!' 'The better to eat you with.' And no sooner had the wolf said that than it made one bound out of the bed and gobbled up poor Little Redcape.

Having satisfied its appetite, the wolf lay down on the bed again, went to sleep and began to snore very loudly. The huntsman was just passing the house at that moment and he thought: How the old woman is snoring; let's see if anything's the matter with her. So he came into the room, and when he got to the bed he saw the wolf lying there: 'So I've found you here, you old sinner,' he said, 'I've been looking for you for a long time.' He was just about to take aim with his gun when it occurred to him that the wolf might have swallowed the old woman and she might still be saved – so instead of firing he took a pair of scissors and began to cut open the sleeping wolf's stomach. When he had made a snip or two, he saw the bright red of the little girl's cape, and after another few snips she jumped out and cried: 'Oh, how frightened I was, how dark it was inside the wolf!' And then her old grandmother came out too, still alive though she could hardly breathe. But Little Redcape quickly fetched some big stones, and with them they filled the wolf's belly, and when he woke up he tried to run away; but the stones were so heavy that he collapsed at once and was killed by the fall.

At this all three of them were happy; the huntsman skinned the wolf and took his skin home, the grandmother ate the cake and drank the wine that Little Redcape had brought, and they made her feel much better. But Little Redcape said to herself: As long as I live I'll never again leave the path and run into the forest by myself, when my mother has said I mustn't.

The above is a folk tale collected by Jacob and Wilhelm Grimm in the early nineteenth century. A psychoanalytic approach to this story might analyse it as a substitute dream (looking for the processes of the dream-work) in which the drama of the Oedipus complex is staged. Little Redcape is the daughter who desires the father (played in the first instance by the wolf). To remove the mother (condensed into the composite figure of mother and grandmother), Little Redcape directs the wolf to her grandmother's house. In a story that is extremely elliptical, it is significant that her description of where her grandmother lives is the only real moment of detail in the whole story. Answering the wolf's question, she says, 'A good quarter of an hour's walk further on in the forest, under the three big oak trees, that's where her house is; there are hazel hedges by it, I'm sure you know the place.' The wolf eats the grandmother and then eats Little Redcape (a displacement for sexual intercourse). The story ends with the huntsman (the post-Oedipal father) delivering the (grand)mother and daughter to a post-Oedipal world, in which 'normal' family relations have been restored. The wolf is dead and Little Redcape promises never again to 'leave the path and run into the forest by myself, when mother has said I mustn't'. The final clause hints at Freud's point about a resentful identification. In addition to these examples of condensation and displacement, the story contains many instances of symbolization. Examples include the flowers, the forest, the path, the red velvet cape, the bottle of wine beneath her apron (if she leaves the path she may 'fall and break the bottle') – all of these add a definite symbolic charge to the narrative.

What Freud said about the interpretation of dreams should be borne in mind when we consider the activities of readers. As you will recall, he warned about 'the impossibility of interpreting a dream unless one has the dreamer's associations to it at one's disposal'

(1973b: 36). This raises some very interesting theoretical issues with regard to the meaning of texts. It suggests that the meaning of a text is not merely in the text itself; rather, that we need to know the associations a reader brings to bear upon the text. In other words, he is clearly pointing to the claim that the reader does not passively accept the meaning of a text: he or she actively produces its meaning, using the discourses he or she brings to the encounter with the text. My particular reading of Little Redcape is possible only because of my knowledge of Freudian psychoanalysis. Without this knowledge, my interpretation would be very different. Moreover, my analysis may say more about me than it does about this particular folk tale.

Freud's translation of psychoanalysis to textual analysis begins with a somewhat crude version of psychobiography and ends with a rather sophisticated account of how meanings are made. However, his suggestions about the real pleasures of reading may have a certain disabling effect on psychoanalytic criticism. That is, if meaning depends on the associations a reader brings to a text, what value can there be in psychoanalytic textual analysis? When a psychoanalytic critic tells us that the text really means X, the full logic of Freudian psychoanalysis is to say that this is only what it means to *you*.

Lacanian psychoanalysis

Jacques Lacan re-reads Freud using the theoretical methodology developed by structuralism. He seeks to anchor psychoanalysis firmly in culture rather than biology. As he explains, his aim is to turn 'the meaning of Freud's work away from the biological basis he would have wished for it towards the cultural references with which it is shot through' (1989: 116). He takes Freud's developmental structure and re-articulates it through a critical reading of structuralism to produce a post-structuralist psychoanalysis. Lacan's account of the development of the human 'subject' has had an enormous influence on cultural studies, especially the study of film.

According to Lacan, we are born into a condition of 'lack', and subsequently spend the rest of our lives trying to overcome this condition. 'Lack' is experienced in different ways and as different things, but it is always a non-representable expression of the fundamental condition of being human. The result is an endless quest in search of an imagined moment of plenitude. Lacan figures this as a search for what he terms l'*objet petit a* (the object small other); that which is desired but forever out of reach; a lost object, signifying an imaginary moment in time when we were whole. Unable to ever take hold of this object, we console ourselves with displacement strategies and substitute objects.

Lacan argues that we make a journey through three determining stages of development. The first is the 'mirror stage', the second is the 'fort-da' game, and the third is the 'Oedipus complex'. Our lives begin in the realm Lacan calls the Real. Here we simply are. In the Real we do not know where we end and where everything else begins. The Real is like Nature before symbolization (i.e. before cultural classification). It is both outside in what we might call 'objective reality' and inside in what Freud calls our instinctual drives. The Real is everything before it becomes mediated by the Symbolic. The Symbolic cuts up the Real into separate parts. If it were possible to get beyond the Symbolic, we would see the Real as everything merged into one mass. What we think of as a natural disaster, for example, is an irruption of the Real. However, how we categorize it is always from within the Symbolic; even when we call it a natural disaster, we have symbolized the Real. To put it another way, nature as Nature is always an articulation of culture: the Real exists, but always as a reality constituted (that is, brought into being) by culture – the Symbolic. As Lacan explains it, 'the kingdom of culture' is superimposed 'on that of nature' (73): 'the world of words . . . creates the world of things' (72).

In the realm of the Real, our union with the mother (or who is playing this symbolic role) is experienced as perfect and complete. We have no sense of a separate selfhood. Our sense of being a unique individual begins to emerge only in what Lacan (2009) calls 'the mirror stage' (see Photo 5.1). As Lacan points out, we are all born prematurely. It takes time to be able to control and coordinate our movements. This has not been fully accomplished when the infant first sees itself in a mirror (between the ages of six and eighteen months).[9] The infant, 'still sunk in his motor incapacity and nursling dependence' (256), forms an identification with the image in the mirror. The mirror suggests

Photo 5.1 The Mirror Stage.

control and coordination that as yet do not exist. Therefore, when the infant first sees itself in a mirror, it sees not only an image of its current self but also the promise of a more complete self; it is in this promise that the ego begins to emerge. According to Lacan, 'The mirror stage is a drama whose internal thrust is precipitated from insufficiency to anticipation – and which manufactures for the subject, caught up in the lure of spatial identification, the succession of phantasies that extends from a fragmented body-image to a form of its totality' (257). On the basis of this recognition or, more properly, *misrecognition* (not the self, but an image of the self), we begin to see ourselves as separate individuals: that is, as both subject (self that looks) and object (self that is looked at). The 'mirror stage' heralds the moment of entry into an order of subjectivity Lacan calls the Imaginary:

> The imaginary for Lacan is precisely this realm of images in which we make identifications, but in the very act of doing so we are led to misperceive and misrecognize ourselves. As a child grows up, it will continue to make such imaginary identifications with objects, and this is how the ego will be built up. For Lacan, the ego is just this narcissistic process whereby we bolster up a fictive sense of unitary selfhood by finding something in the world with which we can identify (Eagleton, 1983: 165).

With each new image we will attempt to return to a time before 'lack', to find ourselves in what is not ourselves; and each time we will fail. 'The subject . . . is the place of *lack*, an empty place that various attempts at identification try to fill' (Laclau, 1993: 436). In other words, desire is the desire to find that which we lack, our selves whole again, as we were before we encountered the Imaginary and the Symbolic. All our acts of identification are always acts of misidentification; it is never our selves that we recognize but only ever another potential image of our selves. '[D]esire is a metonymy' (Lacan, 1989: 193): it allows us to discover another part, but never ever the whole.

The second stage of development is the 'fort-da' game, originally named by Freud after watching his grandson throw a cotton reel away ('gone') and then pull it back again by means of an attached thread ('here'). Freud saw this as the child's way of coming to terms with its mother's absence – the reel symbolically representing the mother, over which the child is exerting mastery. In other words, the child compensates for his mother's absence by taking control of the situation: he makes her disappear (fort) and then reappear (da). Lacan rereads this as a representation of the child beginning to enter the Symbolic, and, in particular, its introduction *into* language: 'the moment when desire becomes human is also that in which the child is born into language' (113). Like the 'fort-da' game, language is 'a presence made of absence' (71). Once we enter language, the completeness of the Real is gone forever. Language introduces an alienating split between being and meaning; before language we had only being (a self-complete nature), after language we are both object and subject: this is made manifest every time I think (subject) about myself (object). In other words, 'I identify myself in language, but only by losing myself in it like an object' (94). I am 'I' when I speak to you and 'you' when you speak to me. As Lacan explains, 'It is not a question of knowing whether I speak of myself in a way that conforms to what I am, but rather of knowing whether I am the same as that of which I speak' (182). In an attempt to explain this division, Lacan rewrites René Descartes's (1993) 'I think therefore I am' as 'I think where I am not, therefore I am where I do not think' (Lacan, 1989: 183). In this formulation 'I think' is the subject of the enunciation (the Imaginary/Symbolic subject) and 'I am' is the subject of the enunciated (the Real subject). Therefore, there is always a gap between the I who speaks and the I of whom is spoken. Entry into the Symbolic results in what Lacan (2001) describes as castration: the symbolic loss of being that is necessary to enter meaning. In order to engage in culture we have given up self-identity with our nature. When 'I' speak I am always different from the 'I' of whom I speak, always sliding into difference and defeat: 'when the subject appears somewhere as meaning, he is manifested elsewhere as "fading", as disappearance' (218).

The Symbolic is an intersubjective network of meanings, which exists as a structure we must enter. As such, it is very similar to the way in which culture is understood in post-Marxist cultural studies (see Chapter 4). It is, therefore, what we experience as reality: reality being the symbolic organization of the Real. Once in the Symbolic our subjectivity is both enabled (we can do things and make meaning) and constrained (there are limits to what we can do and how we can make meaning). The Symbolic order confirms who we are. I may think I am this or that, but unless this is confirmed – unless I and others can recognize this in the Symbolic – it will not be really true. The day I was awarded my PhD I was no more intelligent than the day before, but in a symbolic sense I was: I now had a PhD and I could call myself Doctor! The Symbolic order had recognized and therefore allowed me and others to recognize my new intellectual status.

The third stage of development is the 'Oedipus complex': the encounter with sexual difference. Successful completion of the Oedipus complex enforces our transition from the Imaginary to the Symbolic. It also compounds our sense of 'lack'. The impossibility of fulfilment is now experienced as a movement from signifier to signifier, unable to fix upon a signified. For Lacan (1989), desire is the hopeless pursuit of the fixed signified (the 'other', the 'Real', the moment of plenitude, the mother's body), always forever becoming another signifier – the 'incessant sliding of the signified under the signifier' (170). Desire exists in the impossibility of closing the gap between self and other – to make good that which we 'lack'. We long for a time when we existed in 'nature' (inseparable from the mother's body), where everything was simply itself, before the mediations of language and the Symbolic. As we move forward through the narrative of our lives, we are driven by a desire to overcome the condition, and as we look back, we continue to 'believe' (this is mostly an unconscious process) that the union with the mother (or the person playing the symbolic role of the mother) was a moment of plenitude before the fall into 'lack'. The 'lesson' of the 'Oedipus complex' is that

> [t]he child must now resign itself to the fact that it can never have any direct access to . . . the prohibited body of the mother. . . . [A]fter the Oedipus crisis, we will never again be able to attain this precious object, even though we will spend all our lives hunting for it. We have to make do instead with substitute objects . . . with which we try vainly to plug the gap at the very centre of our being. We move

among substitutes for substitutes, metaphors for metaphors, never able to recover the pure (if fictive) self-identity and self-completion. . . . In Lacanian theory, it is an original lost object – the mother's body – which drives forward the narrative of our lives, impelling us to pursue substitutes for this lost paradise in the endless metonymic movement of desire (Eagleton, 1983: 167, 168, 185).

The discourse of romantic love – in which 'love' is the ultimate solution to all our problems – could be cited as an example of this endless search. What I mean by this is the way that romance as a discursive practice (see discussions of Foucault in Chapter 6 and post-Marxism in Chapter 4) holds that love makes us whole, it completes our being. Love in effect promises to return us to the Real: that blissful moment of plenitude, inseparable from the body of the mother. We can see this played out in the masculine romance of *Paris, Texas*. The film can be read as a road movie of the unconscious, a figuration of Travis Henderson's impossible struggle to return to the moment of plenitude. The film stages three attempts at return: first, Travis goes to Mexico in search of his *mother's* origins; then he goes to Paris (Texas) in search of the moment when he was conceived in his *mother's* body; finally, in an act of 'displacement', he returns Hunter to Jane (a son to his *mother*), in symbolic recognition that his own quest is doomed to failure.

Cine-psychoanalysis

Laura Mulvey's (1975) essay 'Visual pleasure and narrative cinema' is perhaps the classic statement on popular film from the perspective of feminist psychoanalysis. The essay is concerned with how popular cinema produces and reproduces what she calls the 'male gaze'. Mulvey describes her approach as 'political psychoanalysis'. Psychoanalytic theory is 'appropriated . . . as a political weapon [to demonstrate] the way the unconscious of patriarchal society has structured film form' (6).

The inscription of the image of woman in this system is twofold: (i) she is the object of male desire, and (ii) she is the signifier of the threat of castration. In order to challenge popular cinema's 'manipulation of visual pleasure', Mulvey calls for what she describes as the 'destruction of pleasure as a radical weapon' (7). She is uncompromising on this point: 'It is said that analysing pleasure, or beauty, destroys it. This is the intention of this article' (8).

So what are the pleasures that must be destroyed? She identifies two. First, there is scopophilia, the pleasure of looking. Citing Freud, she suggests that it is always more than just the pleasure of looking: scopophilia involves 'taking other people as objects, subjecting them to a controlling gaze' (ibid.). The notion of the controlling gaze is crucial to her argument. But so is sexual objectification: scopophilia is also sexual, 'using another person as an object of sexual stimulation through sight' (10). Although it clearly presents itself to be seen, Mulvey argues that the conventions of popular cinema are such as to suggest a 'hermetically sealed world which unwinds magically, indifferent to the presence of the audience' (9). The audience's 'voyeuristic fantasy' is encouraged by the contrast between the darkness of the cinema and the changing patterns of light on the screen.

Popular cinema promotes and satisfies a second pleasure: 'developing scopophilia in its narcissistic aspect' (ibid.). Here Mulvey draws on Lacan's (2009) account of the 'mirror stage' (see earlier section) to suggest that there is an analogy to be made between the constitution of a child's ego and the pleasures of cinematic identification. Just as a child recognizes and misrecognizes itself in the mirror, the spectator recognizes and misrecognizes itself on the screen. She explains it thus:

> The mirror stage occurs at a time when the child's physical ambitions outstrip his motor capacity, with the result that his recognition of himself is joyous in that he imagines his mirror image to be more complete, more perfect than he experiences his own body. Recognition is thus overlaid with misrecognition: the image recognised is conceived as the reflected body of the self, but its misrecognition as superior projects this body outside itself as an ideal ego, the alienated subject, which, re-introjected as an ego ideal, gives rise to the future generation of identification with others (9–10).

Her argument is that popular cinema produces two contradictory forms of visual pleasure. The first invites scopophilia; the second promotes narcissism. The contradiction arises because 'in film terms, one implies a separation of the erotic identity of the subject from the object on the screen (active scopophilia), the other demands identification of the ego with the object on the screen through the spectator's fascination with and recognition of his like' (10). In Freudian terms, the separation is between 'scopophilic instinct (pleasure in looking at another person as an erotic object)' and 'ego libido (forming identification processes)' (17). But in a world structured by 'sexual imbalance', the pleasure of the gaze has been separated into two distinct positions: men look and women exhibit 'to-be-looked-at-ness' – both playing to, and signifying, male desire (11). Women are therefore crucial to the pleasure of the (male) gaze.

> Traditionally, the woman displayed has functioned on two levels: as erotic object for the characters within the screen story, and as erotic object for the spectator within the auditorium, with a shifting tension between the looks on either side of the screen (11–12).

She gives the example of the showgirl who can be seen to dance for both looks. When the heroine removes her clothes, it is for the sexual gaze of both the hero in the narrative and the spectator in the auditorium. It is only when they subsequently make love that a tension arises between the two looks.

Popular cinema is structured around two moments: moments of narrative and moments of spectacle. The first is associated with the active male, the second with the passive female. The male spectator fixes his gaze on the hero ('the bearer of the look') to satisfy ego formation, and through the hero to the heroine ('the erotic look') to satisfy libido. The first look recalls the moment of recognition/misrecognition in front of the mirror. The second look confirms women as sexual objects, but it is made more complex by the claim that

> [u]ltimately, the meaning of woman is sexual difference. . . . She connotes something that the look continually circles around but disavows: her lack of a penis, implying a threat of castration and hence unpleasure. . . . Thus the woman as icon, displayed for the gaze and enjoyment of men, the active controllers of the look, always threatens to evoke the anxiety it originally signified (13).

To salvage pleasure and escape an unpleasurable re-enactment of the original castration complex, the male unconscious can take two routes to safety. The first means of escape is through detailed investigation of the original moment of trauma, usually leading to 'the devaluation, punishment or saving of the guilty object' (ibid.). She cites the narratives of film noir as typical of this method of anxiety control. The second means of escape is through 'complete disavowal of castration by the substitution of a fetish object or turning the represented figure itself into a fetish so that it becomes reassuring rather than dangerous' (13–14). She gives the example of 'the cult of the female star . . . [in which] fetishistic scopophilia builds up the physical beauty of the object, transforming it into something satisfying in itself' (14). This often leads to the erotic look of the spectator no longer being borne by the look of the male protagonist, producing moments of pure erotic spectacle as the camera holds the female body (often focusing on particular parts of the body) for the unmediated erotic look of the spectator.

Mulvey concludes her argument by suggesting that the pleasure of popular cinema must be destroyed in order to liberate women from the exploitation and oppression of being the '(passive) raw material for the (active) male gaze' (17). She proposes what amounts to a Brechtian revolution in the making of films.[10] To produce a cinema no longer 'obsessively subordinated to the neurotic needs of the male ego' (18), it is necessary to break with illusionism, making the camera material, and producing in the audience 'dialectics, passionate detachment' (ibid.). Moreover, '[w]omen, whose image has continually been stolen and used for this end [objects of the male gaze], cannot view the decline of the traditional film form with anything much more than sentimental regret' (ibid.). (For feminist criticisms of Mulvey's argument, see Chapter 8.)

Slavoj Žižek and Lacanian fantasy

Terry Eagleton describes the Slovenian critic Slavoj Žižek 'as the most formidably brilliant exponent of psychoanalysis, indeed of cultural theory in general, to have emerged in Europe for some decades (quoted in Myers, 2003: 1). Ian Parker (2004), on the other hand, claims that '[t]here is no theoretical system as such in Žižek's work, but it often seems as if there is one. . . . He does not actually add any specific concepts to those of other theorists but articulates and blends the concepts of others' (115, 157). The three main influences on Žižek's work are the philosophy of Georg Wilhelm

Friedrich Hegel, the politics of Marx and the psychoanalysis of Lacan. It is, however, the influence of Lacan that organizes the place of Marx and Hegel in his work. Whether we agree with Eagleton or Parker, what is true is that Žižek is an interesting reader of texts (see, for example, Žižek, 1991, 2009). In this short account, I shall focus almost exclusively on his elaboration of the Lacanian notion of fantasy.

Fantasy is not the same as illusion; rather, fantasy organizes how we see and understand reality. It works as a frame through which we see and make sense of the world. Our fantasies are what make us unique; they provide us with our point of view; organizing how we see and experience the world around us. When the pop musician Jarvis Cocker (former lead singer with Pulp) appeared on BBC Radio 4's long-running programme, *Desert Island Discs* (24 April 2005), he made this comment: 'It doesn't really matter where things happen, it's kinda what's going on in your head that makes life interesting.' This is an excellent example of the organizing role of fantasy.

Žižek (1989) argues that '"Reality" is a fantasy construction that enables us to mask the Real of our desire' (45). Freud (1976) gives an account of a man who dreams that his dead son came to him to complain, 'Can't you see that I am burning?' The father, Freud argues, is awoken by the overwhelming smell of burning. In other words, the outside stimulation (burning), which had been incorporated into the dream, had become too strong to be accommodated by the dream. According to Žižek (1989),

> The Lacanian reading is directly opposed to this. The subject does not awake himself when the external irritation becomes too strong; the logic of his awakening is quite different. First he constructs a dream, a story which enables him to prolong his sleep, to avoid awakening into reality. But the thing that he encounters in the dream, the reality of his desire, the Lacanian Real – in our case, the reality of the child's reproach to his father, 'Can't you see that I am burning?', implying the father's fundamental guilt – is more terrifying than so-called external reality itself, and that is why he awakens: to escape the Real of his desire, which announces itself in the terrifying dream. He escapes into so-called reality to be able to continue to sleep, to maintain his blindness, to elude awakening into the Real of his desire (45).

It is the father's guilt about not having done enough to prevent his son's death that is the Real that the dream seeks to conceal. In other words, the reality to which he awakes is less Real than that which he encountered in his dream.

Žižek (2009) provides other examples from popular culture of the fantasy construction of reality. Rather than fulfilling desire, fantasy is the staging of desire. As he explains,

> [W]hat the fantasy stages is not a scene in which our desire is fulfilled, fully satisfied, but on the contrary, a scene that realises, stages, the desire as such. The fundamental point of psychoanalysis is that desire is not something given in advance, but something that has to be constructed – and it is precisely the role of fantasy to give the coordinates of the subject's desire, to specify its object, to locate the position the subject assumes in it. It is only through fantasy that the subject is constituted as desiring: through fantasy, we learn how to desire (335).

In this way, then, 'fantasy space functions as an empty surface, a kind of screen for the projection of desires' (336). He gives as an example a short story by Patricia Highsmith, 'Black House'. In a small American town old men gather in a bar each evening to remember the past. In different ways their memories always seem to become focused on an old black house on a hill just outside town. It is in this house that each man can recall certain adventures, especially sexual, having taken place. There is now, however, a general agreement amongst the men that it would be dangerous to go back to the house. A young newcomer to the town informs the men that he is not afraid to visit the old house. When he does explore the house, he finds only ruin and decay. Returning to the bar, he informs the men that the black house is no different from any other old, decaying property. The men are outraged by this news. As he leaves, one of the men attacks him, resulting in the young newcomer's death. Why were the men so outraged by the young newcomer's behaviour? Žižek explains it thus:

> [T]he 'black house' was forbidden to the men because it functioned as an empty space wherein they could project their nostalgic desires, their distorted memories; by publicly stating that the 'black house' was nothing but an old ruin, the young intruder reduced their fantasy space to everyday, common reality. He annulled the difference between reality and fantasy space, depriving the men of the place in which they were able to articulate their desires (337).

Desire is never fulfilled or fully satisfied; it is endlessly reproduced in our fantasies. 'Anxiety is brought on by the disappearance of desire' (336). In other words, anxiety is the result of getting too close to what we desire, thus threatening to eliminate 'lack' itself and end desire. This is further complicated by the retroactive nature of desire. As Žižek observes, 'The paradox of desire is that it posits retroactively its own cause, i.e. the *objet a* [object small other] is an object that can be perceived only by a gaze "distorted" by desire, an object that does not exist for an "objective" gaze' (339). In other words, what I desire is organized by processes of fantasy that fix on an object and generate a desire which appears to have drawn me to the object but which in fact did not exist until I first fixed upon the object: what appears to be a forward movement is always retroactive.

Notes

1. The film *Human Nature* presents a very funny staging of this idea. Freud (1985) uses the volcanic eruption at Pompeii in AD 79 as a means to explain repression and how to undo its work: 'There is, in fact, no better analogy for repression, by which something in the mind is at once made inaccessible and preserved, than burial of the sort to which Pompeii fell a victim and from which it could emerge once more through the work of spades' (65).

2. Another way to think of this is as the difference between repression and suppression: the former is when something is blocked from consciousness, whereas the second is a conscious effort not to think about something.

3. In the original German, ego, super-ego and id are *Ich* (I), *über-Ich* (over-I) and *es* (it).

4. Freud's idea of human nature is similar to that developed by Karl Marx. In volume 1 of *Capital* Marx distinguishes between 'human nature in general' and 'human nature as historically modified in each historical epoch' (1976c: 759). Human nature in general consists of certain needs and capacities. These can be divided into those that are 'natural' and those that belong to our 'species being'. Our 'natural' needs and capacities we share with other animals (food, shelter, reproduction, etc.), those of our 'species being' are unique to us as humans and are historically and socially variable in their concrete manifestation. In other words, and contrary to many conservative accounts, human nature is not fixed and unchanging; it is not something set, but always in a state of becoming. What it means to be human in the contemporary world is very different from what it was 5,000 or 10,000 years ago. It will be different again in the future.

5. Parapraxes offer the other main means of access to the repressed. See Freud, 1975 and Storey, 2014.

6. Another example of the play of culture in psychoanalysis is language. The associations a patient may bring to something will be enabled and constrained by the language(s) he or she may speak. Moreover, the various examples that Freud (1976) provides of words standing in for something other than their literal meaning are also limited to the language(s) the patient understands.

7. The manner in which Freud discusses the girl's experience of the Oedipus complex, especially the language he uses, seems to suggest that a real understanding of the process was not very important to him.

8. It should also be noted that Freud (1977) believed there were two ways to navigate the Oedipus complex: 'positive', which resulted in heterosexuality, and 'negative', which produces homosexuality. A boy may 'take the place of his mother and be loved by his father' (318).

9. 'As a witty poet remarks so rightly, the mirror would do well to reflect a little more before returning our image to us' (Lacan, 1989: 152).

10. For Brechtian aesthetics, see Brecht (1978).

Further reading

Storey, John (ed.), *Cultural Theory and Popular Culture: A Reader*, 4th edn, Harlow: Pearson Education, 2009. This is the companion volume to the previous edition of this book. A fully updated 5th edition containing further readings is due for publication in 2018. An interactive website is also available (www.routledge.com/cw/storey), which contains helpful student resources and a glossary of terms for each chapter.

Belsey, Catherine, *Culture and the Real*, London: Routledge, 2005. A very clear account of Lacan and Žižek.

Easthope, Antony, *The Unconscious*, London: Routledge, 1999. An excellent introduction to psychoanalysis. Highly recommended.

Evans, Dylan, *An Introductory Dictionary of Lacanian Psychoanalysis*, London: Routledge, 1996. Indispensable for understanding Lacan.

Frosh, Stephen, *Key Concepts in Psychoanalysis*, London: British Library, 2002. An excellent introduction.

Kay, Sarah, *Žižek: A Critical Introduction*, Cambridge: Polity Press, 2003. An excellent introduction. I particularly like the way she acknowledges that sometimes she just does not understand what Žižek is saying.

Laplanche, J. and J.-B. Pontalis, *The Language of Psychoanalysis*, London: Karnac Books, 1988. A brilliant glossary of concepts.

Mitchell, Juliet, *Psychoanalysis and Feminism*, Harmondsworth: Pelican, 1974. A classic and groundbreaking account of how feminism can use psychoanalysis to undermine patriarchy. As she claims, 'psychoanalysis is not a recommendation for a patriarchal society, but an analysis of one'.

Myers, Tony, *Slavoj Žižek*, London: Routledge, 2003. A very accessible introduction to Žižek's work.

Parker, Ian, *Slavoj Žižek: A Critical Introduction*, London: Pluto, 2004. Another very good account of Žižek's work. The most critical of the recent introductions.

Wright, Elizabeth, *Psychoanalytic Criticism*, London: Methuen, 1984. A very good introduction to psychoanalytic criticism.

Žižek, Slavoj, *Looking Awry: An Introduction to Jacques Lacan through Popular Culture*, Cambridge, MA: MIT Press, 1991. An excellent introduction to Žižek and popular culture.

6 Structuralism and post-structuralism

Structuralism, unlike the other approaches discussed here, is, as Terry Eagleton (1983) points out, 'quite indifferent to the cultural value of its object: anything from *War and Peace* to *The War Cry* will do. The method is analytical, not evaluative' (96). Structuralism is a way of approaching texts and practices that is derived from the theoretical work of the Swiss linguist Ferdinand de Saussure. Its principal exponents are French: Louis Althusser in Marxist theory, Roland Barthes in literary and cultural studies, Michel Foucault in philosophy and history, Jacques Lacan in psychoanalysis, Claude Lévi-Strauss in anthropology and Pierre Macherey in literary theory. Their work is often very different, and at times very difficult. What unites these authors is the influence of Saussure, and the use of a particular vocabulary drawn from his work. It is as well, then, to start our exploration with a consideration of his work in linguistics. This is best approached by examining a number of key concepts.

Ferdinand de Saussure

Saussure divides language into two component parts. When I write the word 'cat' it produces the inscription 'cat', but also the concept or mental image of a cat: a four-legged feline creature. He calls the first the 'signifier', and the second the 'signified'. Together (like two sides of a coin or a sheet of paper) they make up the 'sign'. He then goes on to argue that the relationship between signifier and signified is completely arbitrary. The word 'cat', for example, has no cat-like qualities; there is no reason why the signifier 'cat' should produce the signified 'cat': four-legged feline creature (other languages have different signifiers to produce the same signified). The relationship between the two is simply the result of convention – of cultural agreement (see Table 6.1). The signifier 'cat' could just as easily produce the signified 'dog': four-legged canine creature.

On the basis of this claim, he suggests that meaning is not the result of an essential correspondence between signifiers and signifieds; it is rather the result of difference and relationship. In other words, Saussure's is a relational theory of language. Meaning is produced not through a one-to-one relation to things in the world, but by establishing difference. For example, 'mother' has meaning in relation to 'father', 'daughter', 'son',

Table 6.1 Words for 'cat', various languages.

Chinese	mao
English	cat
French	chat
German	katze
Japanese	neiko
Spanish	gato
Russian	koska

etc. Traffic lights operate within a system of four signs: red = stop, green = go, amber = prepare for red, amber and red = prepare for green. The relationship between the signifier 'green' and the signified 'go' is arbitrary; there is nothing in the colour green that naturally attaches it to the verb 'go'. Traffic lights would work equally well if red signified 'go' and green signified 'stop'.

The system works not by expressing a *natural* meaning but by marking a difference, a distinction within a system of difference and relationships. To make the point about meaning being relational rather than substantial, Saussure gives the example of train systems. The 12.11 from Bochum to Bremen, for instance, runs every day at the same time. To each of these trains we assign the same identity ('the 12.11 from Bochum to Bremen'). However, we know that the locomotive, the carriages, the staff, are unlikely to be the same each day. The identity of the train is fixed not by its substance, but by its relational distinction from other trains, running at other times, on other routes. Saussure's other example is the game of chess. A knight, for example, could be represented in any way a designer thought desirable, provided that how it was represented marked it as different from the other chess pieces.

According to Saussure, meaning is also made in a process of combination and selection, horizontally along the syntagmatic axis, and vertically along the paradigmatic axis. For example, the sentence, 'Miriam made chicken broth today', is meaningful through the accumulation of its different parts: Miriam/made/chicken broth/today. Its meaning is complete only once the final word is spoken or inscribed. Saussure calls this process the syntagmatic axis of language. One can add other parts to extend its meaningfulness: 'Miriam made chicken broth today while dreaming about her lover.' Meaning is thus accumulated along the syntagmatic axis of language. This is perfectly clear when a sentence is interrupted. For example, 'I was going to say that . . .'; 'It is clear to me that David should . . .'; 'You promised to tell me about . . .'.

Substituting certain parts of the sentence for new parts can also change meaning. For example, I could write, 'Miriam made salad today while dreaming about her lover' or 'Miriam made chicken broth today while dreaming about her new car'. Such substitutions are said to be operating along the paradigmatic axis of language. Let us consider a more politically charged example. 'Terrorists carried out an attack on an army base today.' Substitutions from the paradigmatic axis could alter the meaning of this sentence considerably. If we substitute 'freedom fighters' or 'anti-imperialist volunteers' for the word 'terrorists' we would have a sentence meaningful in quite a different way. This would be achieved without any reference to a corresponding reality outside of the sentence itself. The meaning of the sentence is produced through a process of selection and combination. This is because the relationship between 'sign' and 'referent' (in our earlier example, real cats in the real world) is also conventional. It follows, therefore, that the language we speak does not simply *reflect* the material reality of the world; rather, by providing us with a conceptual map with which to impose a certain order on what we see and experience, the language we speak plays a significant role in *shaping what constitutes* for us the reality of the material world.

Structuralists argue that language organizes and constructs our sense of reality – different languages in effect produce different mappings of the real. When, for example, a European gazes at a snowscape, he or she sees snow. An Inuit, with over thirty words to describe snow and ice, looking at the same snowscape would presumably see so much more. Therefore an Inuit and a European standing together surveying the snowscape would in fact be seeing two quite different conceptual scenes. Similarly, Australian Aborigines have many words to describe the desert. What these examples demonstrate to a structuralist is that the way we conceptualize the world is ultimately dependent on the language we speak. And by analogy, it will depend on the culture we inhabit. The meanings made possible by language are thus the result of the interplay of a network of relationships between combination and selection, similarity and difference. Meaning cannot be accounted for by reference to an extra-linguistic reality. As Saussure (1974) insists, 'in language there are only differences *without positive terms* . . . [L]anguage has neither ideas nor sounds that existed before the linguistic system, but only conceptual and phonic differences that have issued from the system' (120; original emphasis). We might want to query this assumption by noting that Inuits name the snowscape differently because of the material bearing it has on their day-to-day existence. It could also be objected that substituting 'terrorists' for 'freedom fighters' produces meanings not accounted for purely by the linguistic system (see Chapter 4).

Saussure makes another distinction that has proved essential to the development of structuralism. This is the division of language into *langue* and *parole*. *Langue* refers to the system of language, the rules and conventions that organize it. This is language as a social institution, and as Roland Barthes (1967) points out, 'it is essentially a collective contract which one must accept in its entirety if one wishes to communicate' (14). *Parole* refers to the individual utterance, the individual use of language. To clarify this point, Saussure compares language to the game of chess. Here we can distinguish between the rules of the game and an actual game of chess. Without the body of rules there could be no actual game, but it is only in an actual game that these rules are made manifest. Therefore, there is *langue* and *parole*, structure and performance. It is the homogeneity of the structure that makes the heterogeneity of the performance possible.

Finally, Saussure distinguishes between two theoretical approaches to linguistics: the diachronic approach, which studies the historical development of a given language, and the synchronic approach, which studies a given language in one particular moment in time. He argues that in order to found a science of linguistics it is necessary to adopt a synchronic approach. Structuralists have, generally speaking, taken the synchronic approach to the study of texts or practices. They argue that in order to really understand a text or practice it is necessary to focus exclusively on its structural properties. This of course allows critics hostile to structuralism to criticize it for its ahistorical approach to culture.

Structuralism takes two basic ideas from Saussure's work: first, a concern with the underlying relations of texts and practices, the 'grammar' that makes meaning possible; second, the view that meaning is always the result of the interplay of relationships of selection and combination made possible by the underlying structure. In other words, texts and practices are studied as analogous to language. Imagine, for example, that aliens from outer space had landed in Barcelona in May 1999, and as an earthly display of welcome they were invited to attend the Champions League Final between Manchester United and Bayern Munich. What would they witness? Two groups of men in different coloured costumes, one red, the other in silver and maroon, moving at different speeds, in different directions, across a green surface, marked with white lines. They would notice that a white spherical projectile appeared to have some influence on the various patterns of cooperation and competition. They would notice a man dressed in dark green, with a whistle that he blew to stop and start the combinations of play. They would also note that he appeared to be supported by two other men also dressed in dark green, one on either side of the main activity, each using a flag to support the limited authority of the man with the whistle. Finally, they would note the presence of two men, one at each end of the playing area, standing in front of partly netted structures. They would see that periodically these men engaged in acrobatic routines that involved contact with the white projectile. The visiting aliens could observe the occasion and describe what they saw to each other, but unless someone explained to them the rules of association football, its *structure*, the Champions League Final, in which Manchester United became the first English team in history to win the 'treble' of Champions League, Premier League and FA Cup, would make very little sense to them at all. It is the underlying rules of cultural texts and practices that interest structuralists. It is structure that makes meaning possible. The task of structuralism, therefore, is to make explicit the rules and conventions (the structure) that govern the production of meaning (acts of *parole*).

Claude Lévi-Strauss, Will Wright and the American Western

Claude Lévi-Strauss (1968) uses Saussure to help him discover the 'unconscious foundations' (18) of the culture of so-called 'primitive' societies. He analyses cooking, manners, modes of dress, aesthetic activity and other forms of cultural and social practices as analogous to systems of language; each in its different way is a mode of communication, a form of expression. As Terence Hawkes (1977) points out, 'His quarry, in short, is the *langue* of the whole culture; its system and its general laws: he stalks it through the particular varieties of its *parole*' (39). In pursuit of his quarry, Lévi-Strauss investigates a number of 'systems'. It is, however, his analysis of myth that is of central interest to the student of popular culture. He claims that beneath the vast heterogeneity of myths, there can be discovered an homogeneous structure. In short, he argues that individual myths are examples of *parole*, articulations of an underlying structure or *langue*. By understanding this structure we should be able to truly understand the meaning – 'operational value' (Lévi-Strauss, 1968: 209) – of particular myths.

Myths, Lévi-Strauss argues, work like language: they comprise individual 'mythemes', analogous to individual units of language, 'morphemes' and 'phonemes'. Like morphemes and phonemes, mythemes take on meaning only when combined in particular patterns. Seen in this way, the anthropologists' task is to discover the underlying 'grammar': the rules and regulations that make it possible for myths to be meaningful. He also observes that myths are structured in terms of 'binary oppositions'. Dividing the world into mutually exclusive categories produces meaning: culture/nature, man/woman, black/white, good/bad, us/them, for example. Drawing on Saussure, he sees meaning as a result of the interplay between a process of similarity and difference. For example, in order to say what is bad we must have some notion of what is good. In the same way, what it means to be a man is defined against what it means to be a woman.

Lévi-Strauss claims that all myths have a similar structure. Moreover, he also claims – although this is by no means his primary focus – that all myths have a similar socio-cultural function within society. That is, the purpose of myth is to make the world explicable, to magically resolve its problems and contradictions. As he contends, 'mythical thought always progresses from the awareness of oppositions toward their resolution. . . . The purpose of myth is to provide a logical model capable of overcoming a contradiction' (224, 229). Myths are stories we tell ourselves as a culture in order to banish contradictions and make the world understandable and therefore habitable; they attempt to put us at peace with ourselves and our existence.

In *Sixguns and Society*, Will Wright (1975) uses Lévi-Strauss's structuralist methodology to analyse the Hollywood Western. He argues that much of the narrative power of the Western is derived from its structure of binary oppositions. However, Wright differs from Lévi-Strauss in that his concern 'is not to reveal a mental structure but to show how the myths of a society, through their structure, communicate a conceptual order to the members of that society' (17). In short, while Lévi-Strauss's primary concern is the structure of the human mind, Wright's focus is on the way the Western 'presents a symbolically simple but remarkably deep conceptualisation of American social beliefs' (23). He contends that the Western has evolved through three stages: 'classic' (including a variation he calls 'vengeance'), 'transition theme' and 'professional'. Despite the genre's different types, he identifies a basic set of structuring oppositions, shown in Table 6.2. But, as he insists (taking him beyond Lévi-Strauss), in order to fully understand the social meaning of a myth, it is necessary to analyse not only its binary structure but its narrative structure – 'the progression of events and the resolution of conflicts' (24). The 'classic' Western, according to Wright, is divided into sixteen narrative 'functions' (see Propp, 1968).

Table 6.2 Structuring oppositions in the Western.

Inside society	Outside society
Good	Bad
Strong	Weak
Civilization	Wilderness (49)

1. The hero enters a social group.
2. The hero is unknown to the society.
3. The hero is revealed to have an exceptional ability.
4. The society recognizes a difference between themselves and the hero; the hero is given a special status.
5. The society does not completely accept the hero.
6. There is a conflict of interests between the villains and the society.
7. The villains are stronger than the society; the society is weak.
8. There is a strong friendship or respect between the hero and a villain.
9. The villains threaten the society.
10. The hero avoids involvement in the conflict.
11. The villains endanger a friend of the hero.
12. The hero fights the villains.
13. The hero defeats the villains.
14. The society is safe.
15. The society accepts the hero.
16. The hero loses or gives up his special status (165).

Shane (1953) is perhaps the best example of the classic Western: the story of a stranger who rides out of the wilderness and helps a group of farmers defeat a powerful rancher, and then rides away again, back into the wilderness. In the classic Western the hero and society are (temporarily) aligned in opposition to the villains who remain outside society.

In the 'transition theme' Western, which Wright claims provides a bridge between the classic Western, the form that dominated the 1930s, the 1940s and most of the 1950s, and the professional Western, the form that dominated the 1960s and 1970s, the binary oppositions are reversed, and we see the hero outside society struggling against a strong, but corrupt and corrupting, civilization (Table 6.3). Many of the narrative functions are also inverted. Instead of being outside the society, the hero begins as a valued member of the society. But the society is revealed to be the real 'villain' in opposition to the hero and those outside society and civilization. In his support for, and eventual alignment with, those outside society and civilization, he himself crosses from inside to outside and from civilization to wilderness. But in the end the society is too strong for those outside it, who are ultimately powerless against its force. The best they can do is escape to the wilderness.

Table 6.3 Structuring oppositions in the 'professional' Western.

Hero	Society
Outside society	Inside society
Good	Bad
Weak	Strong
Wilderness	Civilization (48–9)

Although, according to Wright, the last 'transition theme' Western was *Johnny Guitar* in 1954, it appears clear, using his own binary oppositions and narrative functions, that *Dances with Wolves*, made in 1990, is a perfect example of the form. A cavalry officer, decorated for bravery, rejects the East ('civilization') and requests a posting to the West ('wilderness') – as the film publicity puts it, 'in 1864 one man went in search of the frontier and found himself'. He also found *society* among the Sioux. The film tells the story of how 'he is drawn into the loving and honourable folds of a Sioux tribe . . . and ultimately, the crucial decision he must make as white settlers continue their violent and ruthless journey into the lands of the Native Americans' (Guild Home Video, 1991). His decision is to fight on the side of the Sioux against the 'civilization' he has rejected. Finally, considered a traitor by the cavalry, he decides to leave the Sioux, so as not to give the cavalry an excuse to butcher them. The final scene, however, shows his departure as, unbeknown to him or the Sioux, the cavalry close in for what is undoubtedly to be the massacre of the tribe.

If we accept *Dances with Wolves* as a 'transition theme' Western, it raises some interesting questions about the film as myth. Wright (1975) claims that each type of Western 'corresponds' to a different moment in the recent economic development of the United States:

> the classic Western plot corresponds to the individualistic conception of society underlying a market economy. . . . [T]he vengeance plot is a variation that begins to reflect changes in the market economy. . . . [T]he professional plot reveals a new conception of society corresponding to the values and attitudes inherent in a planned, corporate economy (15).

Each type in turn articulates its own mythic version of how to achieve the *American Dream*:

> The classical plot shows that the way to achieve such human rewards as friendship, respect, and dignity is to separate yourself from others and use your strength as an autonomous individual to succor them. . . . The vengeance variation . . . weakens the compatibility of the individual and society by showing that the path to respect and love is to separate yourself from others, struggling individually against your many and strong enemies but striving to remember and return to the softer values of marriage and humility. The transition theme, anticipating new social values, argues

that love and companionship are available at the cost of becoming a social outcast to the individual who stands firmly and righteously against the intolerance and ignorance of society. Finally, the professional plot . . . argues that companionship and respect are to be achieved only by becoming a skilled technician, who joins an elite group of professionals, accepts any job that is offered, and has loyalty only to the integrity of the team, not to any competing social or community values (186–7).

Given the critical and financial success of *Dances with Wolves* (winner of seven Oscars; fifth most successful film in both the UK and the USA, grossing £10.9 million and $122.5 million in the first year of release in the UK and USA respectively), it may well (if we accept Wright's rather reductive correspondence theory) represent a 'transition theme' Western that marks the beginning of a reverse transition, back to a time of less mercenary social and community values – back in fact to a time of *society* and *community*.

Roland Barthes: *Mythologies*

Roland Barthes's early work on popular culture is concerned with the processes of signification, the mechanisms by which meanings are produced and put into circulation. *Mythologies* (1973) is a collection of essays on French popular culture. In it he discusses, among many things, wrestling, soap powders and detergents, toys, steak and chips, tourism and popular attitudes towards science. His guiding principle is always to interrogate 'the falsely obvious' (11), to make explicit what too often remains implicit in the texts and practices of popular culture. His purpose is political; his target is what he calls the 'bourgeois norm' (9). As he states in the 'Preface' to the 1957 edition, 'I resented seeing Nature and History confused at every turn, and I wanted to track down, in the decorative display of *what goes-without-saying*, the ideological abuse which, in my view, is hidden there' (11). *Mythologies* is the most significant attempt to bring the methodology of semiology to bear on popular culture. The possibility of semiology was first posited by Saussure (1974):

Language is a system of signs that express ideas, and is therefore comparable to a system of writing, the alphabet of deaf mutes, symbolic rites, polite formulas, military signals, etc. . . . A science that studies the life of signs within society is conceivable . . . I shall call it semiology (16).

Mythologies concludes with the important theoretical essay, 'Myth today'.[1] In the essay Barthes outlines a semiological model for reading popular culture. He takes Saussure's schema of signifier/signified = sign and adds to it a second level of signification.

As we noted earlier, the signifier 'cat' produces the signified 'cat': a four-legged feline creature. Barthes argues that this indicates only primary signification. The sign 'cat' produced at the primary level of signification is available to become the signifier

1. signifier > signified = sign
         \
                2. signifier > signified = sign

(1. Primary signification or denotation)
(2. Secondary signification or connotation)

Figure 6.1   Signification.

'cat' at a second level of signification. This may then produce at the secondary level the signified 'cat': someone cool and hip. As illustrated in Figure 6.1, the sign of primary signification becomes the signifier in a process of secondary signification. In *Elements of Semiology*, Barthes (1967) substitutes the more familiar terms 'denotation' (primary signification) and 'connotation' (secondary signification): 'the first system [denotation] becomes the plane of expression or signifier of the second system [connotation]. . . . The signifiers of connotation . . . are made up of signs (signifiers and signifieds united) of the denoted system' (89–91).

He claims that it is at the level of secondary signification or connotation that myth is produced for consumption. By myth he means ideology understood as a body of ideas and practices, which, by actively promoting the values and interests of dominant groups in society, defend the prevailing structures of power. To understand this aspect of his argument, we need to understand the polysemic nature of signs – that is, that they have the potential to signify multiple meanings. An example might make the point clearer. I discussed in Chapter 1 how the Conservative Party presented a party political broadcast that concluded with the word 'socialism' being transposed into red prison bars. This was undoubtedly an attempt to fix the secondary signification or connotations of the word 'socialism' to mean restrictive, imprisoning, against freedom. Barthes would see this as an example of the fixing of new connotations in the production of myth – the production of ideology. He argues that all forms of signification can be shown to operate in this way. His most famous example of the workings of secondary signification (see Photo 6.1) is taken from the cover of the French magazine *Paris Match* (1955). He begins his analysis by establishing that the primary level of signification consists of a signifier: patches of colour and figuration. This produces the signified: 'a black soldier saluting the French flag'. Together they form the primary sign. The primary sign then becomes the signifier 'black soldier saluting the French flag', producing, at the level of secondary signification, the signified 'French imperiality'. Here is his account of his encounter with the cover of the magazine:

> I am at the barber's, and a copy of Paris Match is offered to me. On the cover, a young Negro in a French uniform is saluting, with his eyes uplifted, probably fixed on the fold of the tricolour. All this is the meaning of the picture. But, whether naively or not, I see very well what it signifies to me: that France is a great Empire, that all her sons, without colour discrimination, faithfully serve under her flag, and that there is no better answer to the detractors of an alleged colonialism than the

Photo 6.1 Black soldier saluting the flag.

Source: IZIS/Paris Match Archive/Getty Images

zeal shown by this Negro in serving his so called oppressors. I am therefore faced with a greater semiological system: there is a signifier, itself already formed with a previous system (a black soldier is giving the French salute); there is a signified (it is a purposeful mixture of Frenchness and militariness); finally there is a presence of the signified through the signifier (2009: 265).

At the first level: black soldier saluting the French flag; at the second level: a positive image of French imperialism. The cover illustration is therefore seen to represent *Paris Match*'s attempt to produce a positive image of French imperialism. Following the defeat in Vietnam (1946–54), and the then current war in Algeria (1954–62), such an image would seem to many to be of some political urgency. And as Barthes suggests, 'myth has . . . a double function: it points out and it notifies, it makes us understand something and it imposes it on us' (265). What makes this a possibility are the shared cultural codes on which both Barthes and the readership of *Paris Match* are able to draw. Connotations are therefore not simply produced by the makers of the image, but activated from an already existing cultural repertoire. In other words, the image both draws from the cultural repertoire and at the same time adds to it. Moreover, the cultural repertoire does not form a homogeneous block. Myth is continually confronted by counter-myth. For example, an image containing references to pop music culture might be seen by a young audience as an index of freedom and heterogeneity, while to an older audience it might signal manipulation and homogeneity. Which codes are mobilized will largely depend on the triple context of the location of the text, the historical moment and the cultural formation of the reader.

In 'The photographic message' Barthes (1977a: 26) introduces a number of further considerations. Context of publication is important, as I have already said. If the photograph of the black soldier saluting the flag had appeared on the cover of the *Socialist Review*, its connotative meaning(s) would have been very different. Readers would have looked for irony. Rather than being read as a positive image of French imperialism, it would have been seen as a sign of imperial exploitation and manipulation. In addition to this, a socialist reading the original *Paris Match* would have seen the image not as a positive image of French imperialism, but as a desperate attempt to project such an image given the general historical context of France's defeat in Vietnam and its pending defeat in Algeria. But despite all this the intention behind the image is clear:

> Myth has an imperative, buttonholing character . . . [it arrests] in both the physical and the legal sense of the term: French imperialism condemns the saluting Negro to be nothing more than an instrumental signifier, the Negro suddenly hails me in the name of French imperiality; but at the same moment the Negro's salute thickens, becomes vitrified, freezes into an eternal reference meant to establish French imperiality (2009: 265–6).[2]

This is not the only way French imperialism might be given positive connotations. Barthes suggests other mythical signifiers the press might use: 'I can very well give to French imperiality many other signifiers beside a Negro's salute: a French general pins a decoration on a one-armed Senegalese, a nun hands a cup of tea to a bed ridden Arab, a white schoolmaster teaches attentive piccaninnies' (266).

Barthes envisages three possible reading positions from which the image could be read. The first would simply see the black soldier saluting the flag as an 'example' of French imperiality, a 'symbol' for it. This is the position of those who produce such myths. The second would see the image as an 'alibi' for French imperiality. This is the position of the socialist reader discussed above. The final reading position is that of the 'myth-consumer' (268). He or she reads the image not as an example or as a symbol, nor as an alibi: the black soldier saluting the flag 'is the very *presence* of French imperiality' (267; original emphasis); that is, the black soldier saluting the flag is seen as *naturally* conjuring up the concept of French imperiality. There is not anything to discuss: it is obvious that one implies the presence of the other. The relationship between the black soldier saluting the flag and French imperiality has been 'naturalized'. As Barthes explains:

> what allows the reader to consume myth innocently is that he does not see it as a semiological system but as an inductive one. Where there is only equivalence, he sees a kind of causal process: the signifier and the signified have, in his eyes, a natural relationship. This confusion can be expressed otherwise: any semiological system is a system of values; now the myth-consumer takes the signification for a system of facts: myth is read as a factual system, whereas it is but a semiological system (268).

There is of course a fourth reading position, that of Barthes himself the mythologist. This reading produces what he calls a 'structural description'. It is a reading position that seeks to determine the means of ideological production of the image, its transformation of history into nature. According to Barthes, 'Semiology has taught us that myth has the task of giving an historical intention a natural justification, and making contingency appear eternal. Now this process is exactly that of bourgeois ideology' (ibid.). His argument is that 'myth is constituted by the loss of the historical quality of things: in it, things lose the memory that they once were made' (ibid.). It is what he calls 'depoliticized speech'.

> In the case of the soldier Negro . . . what is got rid of is certainly not French imperiality (on the contrary, since what must be actualised is its presence); it is the contingent, historical, in one word: fabricated, quality of colonialism. Myth does not deny things, on the contrary, its function is to talk about them; simply, it purifies them, it makes them innocent, it gives them a natural and eternal justification, it gives them a clarity which is not that of an explanation but that of a statement of fact. If I state the fact of French imperiality without explaining it, I am very near to finding that it is natural and goes without saying. . . . In passing from history to nature, myth acts economically: it abolishes the complexity of human acts . . . it organises a world which is without contradictions because it is without depth, a world wide open and wallowing in the evident, it establishes a blissful clarity: things appear to mean something by themselves (269).[3]

Images rarely appear without the accompaniment of a linguistic text of one kind or another. A newspaper photograph, for example, will be surrounded by a title, a caption, a story and the general layout of the page. It will also, as we have already noted, be situated within the context of a particular newspaper or magazine. The context provided by the *Daily Telegraph* (readership and reader expectation) is very different from that provided by the *Socialist Worker*. The accompanying text controls the production of connotations in the image.

> Formerly, the image illustrated the text (made it clearer); today, the text loads the image, burdening it with culture, a moral, an imagination. Formerly, there was reduction from text to image; today, there is amplification from one to the other. The connotation is now experienced only as the natural resonance of the fundamental denotation constituted by the photographic analogy and we are thus confronted with a typical process of naturalisation of the cultural (Barthes, 1977a: 26).

In other words, image does not illustrate text, it is the text which amplifies the connotative potential of the image. He refers to this process as 'relay'. The relationship can of course work in other ways. For example, rather than 'amplifying a set of connotations already given in the photograph . . . the text produces (invents) an entirely new signified which is retroactively projected into the image, so much so as to appear denoted there' (27). An example might be a photograph taken in 2016 (see Photo 6.2) of a rock star looking reflective, and originally used to promote a love song: 'My baby done me wrong'. In late 2017 the photograph is reused to accompany a newspaper account of the death by a drug overdose of one of the rock star's closest friends. The photograph is recaptioned: 'Drugs killed my best friend' (see Photo 6.3). The caption would feed into the image producing (inventing) connotations of loss, despair, and a certain thoughtfulness about the role of drugs in rock music culture. Barthes refers to this process as 'anchorage'. What this example of the different meanings made of the same photograph of the rock star reveals, as noted earlier, is the polysemic nature of all signs:

 Rock-a-day Johnny 'My baby done me wrong' from the album *Dogbucket Days.*

Photo 6.3   Rock-a-day Johnny 'Drugs killed my best friend'.

that is, their potential for multiple signification. Without the addition of a linguistic text the meaning of the image is very difficult to pin down. The linguistic message works in two ways. It helps the reader to identify the denotative meaning of the image: this is a rock star looking reflective. Second, it limits the potential proliferation of the connotations of the image: the rock star is reflective because of the drug overdose by one of his closest friends. Therefore, the rock star is contemplating the role of drugs in rock music culture. Moreover, it tries to make the reader believe that the connotative meaning is actually present at the level of denotation.

What makes the move from denotation to connotation possible is the store of social knowledge (a cultural repertoire) upon which the reader is able to draw when he or she reads the image. Without access to this shared code (conscious or unconscious) the operations of connotation would not be possible. And of course such knowledge is always both historical and cultural. That is to say, it might differ from one culture to another, and from one historical moment to another. Cultural difference might also be marked by differences of class, ethnicity, gender, generation or sexuality. As Barthes points out,

> reading closely depends on my culture, on my knowledge of the world, and it is probable that a good press photograph (and they are all good, being selected) makes ready play with the supposed knowledge of its readers, those prints being chosen which comprise the greatest possible quantity of information of this kind in such a way as to render the reading fully satisfying (29).

Again, as he explains, 'the variation in readings is not, however, anarchic; it depends on the different kinds of knowledge – practical, national, cultural, aesthetic – invested in the image [by the reader]' (Barthes, 1977b: 46). Here we see once again the analogy with language. The individual image is an example of *parole*, and the shared code (cultural repertoire) is an example of *langue*. The best way to draw together the different elements of this model of reading is to demonstrate it.

ONE GIRL WANTS TO GO TO UNIVERSITY.
THE OTHER WANTS TO LEAVE AT 16.
HOW DO YOU KEEP THEM BOTH INTERESTED?

Jackie on the right is motivated to learn at school by her long-term goals. However, contrary to appearances, Susan on the left may see little point in paying attention at all.

MUSIC, clothes and boys are the sort of things 14 year olds like Susan are usually most interested in.

Electromagnetism, genetics and Charles Dickens, unfortunately, are not. Unless, of course, the teacher makes them interesting.

If you think that sounds difficult, you're right.

The trick is to make whatever you're teaching relevant to the interests of less motivated pupils and, most important of all, make it enjoyable.

Remembering at the same time you have to keep your lessons stimulating and challenging for the keener ones.

This is where a strong imagination and a sense of humour come in handy. (And of course these days, there are all sorts of interesting teaching aids to help you as well, many of which you will learn about in your training).

You'll also need a lot of energy, as any teacher will tell you, but it is rewarding when you see all your efforts pay off. For example, when pupils like Jackie go on to do well in higher education (especially if they choose to pursue their subject).

And equally when pupils like Susan go on to do well at work. Or better still, decide not to leave at 16 after all.

But is it rewarding when it comes to the end of the month? Well, you may be surprised to learn that teachers' starting salaries now compare well with those of graduates in general.

From December, teachers in inner London with a good honours degree will start on around £14,000 (including inner London supplement and allowance).

And if you make it to the top of your profession as a Head teacher of a large secondary school in

inner London, you could earn up to £48,000.

Interested? For more information, fill in the coupon or call 0345 300121, quoting the department code xxxxxx.

Teaching brings out the best in people.

Photo 6.4   Advertising for teachers.

Source: Department of Education, Crown copyright material is reproduced with the permission of the Controller, Office of Public Sector Information (OPSI)

In 1991 the Department of Education and Science (DES) produced an advertisement that they placed in the popular film magazine *Empire* (see Photo 6.4). The image shows two 14-year-old schoolgirls: Jackie intends to go to university; Susan intends to leave school at 16. The poster's aim is to attract men and women to the teaching profession. It operates a double bluff. That is, we see the two girls, read the caption and decide which girl wants to go to university, which girl wants to leave at 16. The double bluff is that the girl who wants to leave is the one convention – those without the required cultural competence to teach – would consider studious. It is a double bluff because we are not intended to be taken in by the operation. We can congratulate ourselves on our perspicacity. We, unlike others, have not been taken in – we have the necessary cultural competence. Therefore we are excellent teacher material. The advertisement plays with the knowledge necessary to be a teacher and allows us to recognize that knowledge in ourselves: it provides us with a position from which to say: 'Yes, I should be a teacher.'

Post-structuralism

Post-structuralists reject the idea of an underlying structure upon which meaning can rest secure and guaranteed. Meaning is always in process. What we call the 'meaning' of a text is only ever a momentary stop in a continuing flow of interpretations following interpretations. Saussure, as we have noted, posited language as consisting of the relationship between the signifier, the signified and the sign. The theorists of post-structuralism suggest that the situation is more complex than this: signifiers do not produce signifieds, they produce more signifiers. Meaning as a result is a very unstable thing. In 'The death of the author', the now post-structuralist Barthes (1977c) insists that a text is 'a multi-dimensional space in which a variety of writings, none of them original, blend and clash. The text is a tissue of quotations drawn from the innumerable centres of culture' (146). Only a reader can bring a temporary unity to a text. Unlike the work that can be seen lying in apparent completion on library shelves and in bookshops, the text 'is experienced only in an activity of production' (157). A text is a work seen as inseparable from the active process of its many readings.

Jacques Derrida

Post-structuralism is virtually synonymous with the work of Jacques Derrida. The sign, as we have noted already, is for Saussure made meaningful by its location in a system of differences. Derrida adds to this the notion that meaning is also always deferred, never fully present, always both absent and present (see discussion of defining popular culture in Chapter 1). Derrida (1973) has invented a new word to describe the divided nature of the sign: *différance*, meaning both to defer and to differ.

Saussure's model of difference is spatial, in which meaning is made in the relations between signs that are locked together in a self-regulating structure. Derrida's model of *différance*, however, is both structural and temporal; meaning depends on structural difference but also on temporal relations of before and after.

For example, if we track the meaning of a word through a dictionary we encounter a relentless deferment of meaning. If we look up the signifier 'letter' in the *Collins*

Pocket Dictionary of the English Language, we discover that it has five possible signifieds: a written or printed message, a character of the alphabet, the strict meaning of an agreement, precisely (as in 'to the letter') and to write or mark letters on a sign. If we then look up one of these, the signified '[a written or printed] message', we find that it too is a signifier producing four more signifieds: a communication from one person or group to another, an implicit meaning, as in a work of art, a religious or political belief that some-one attempts to communicate to others, and to understand (as in 'to get the message').

Tracking through the dictionary in this way confirms a relentless intertextual defer-ment of meaning, 'the indefinite referral of signifier to signifier . . . wh i ch gives the signified meaning no respite . . . so that it always signifies again' (1978a: 25). It is only when located in a discourse and read in a context that there is a temporary halt to the endless play of signifier to signifier. For example, if we read or hear the words 'nothing was delivered', they would mean something quite different depending on whether they were the opening words of a novel, a line from a poem, an excuse, a jotting in a shopkeeper's notebook, a line from a song, an example from a phrase book, part of a monologue in a play, part of a speech in a film, an illustration in an explanation of *différance*. But even context cannot fully control the relentless, intertextual deferment of meaning: the phrase 'nothing was delivered' will carry with it the 'trace' of meanings from other contexts. If I know the line is from a song by Bob Dylan, this will resonate across the words as I read them in a shopkeeper's notebook.

For Derrida, the binary opposition, so important to structuralism, is never a simple structural relation; it is always a relation of power, in which one term is in a position of dominance with regard to the other. Moreover, the dominance of one over the other (a matter of, say, priority or privilege) is not something that arises 'naturally' out of the relationship, but something that is produced in the way the relationship is constructed. Black and white, it could be argued, exist in a binary opposition, one always existing as the absent other when one of the terms is defined. But it is not difficult to see how in many powerful discourses, white is the positive term, holding priority and privilege over black. For example, television historian David Starkey's comments on BBC 2's *Newsnight* programme (13 August 2011) about the riots in English cities in 2011 articu-lates this logic. When condemning what had happened, he said, 'The whites have become black', further compounding this logic by adding, 'Listen to David Lammy [Labour MP for Tottenham], an archetypal successful black man. If you turn the screen off, so you were listening to him on radio, you would think he was white.' In both cases, white is positive, black is negative. Even leaving aside racism, there is a long history of black connoting negatively and white connoting positively (see further discussion in Chapter 9).

The DES advertisement I discussed earlier contains what Derrida (1978b) would call a 'violent hierarchy' (41) in its couplet: 'good' girl, who is interested in electromagne-tism, genetics and Charles Dickens; and 'bad' girl, who prefers music, clothes and boys. We noted also in Chapter 1 how high culture has often depended on popular culture to give it definitional solidity. Derrida's critique alerts us to the way in which one side in such couplets is always privileged over the other; one side always claims a position of status (of pure presence) over the other. Moreover, as Derrida also points out, they are not pure opposites – each is *motivated* by the other, ultimately dependent on the absent other for its own presence and meaning. There is no naturally 'good' girl who stays on at school, who can be opposed to a naturally 'bad' girl who wants to leave at 16. Simply to reverse the binary opposition would be to keep in place the assumptions already constructed by the opposition. We must do more than 'simply . . . neutralise the binary oppositions. . . . One of the two terms controls the other . . . holds the superior position. To deconstruct the opposition [we must] . . . overthrow the hierarchy' (1978b: 41). Instead of accepting the double bluff of the DES advertisement, a 'deconstructive' reading would wish to dismantle the couplet to demonstrate that it can only be held in place by a certain 'violence' – a certain set of dubious assumptions about gender and sexuality.

A deconstructive reading could also be made of *Dances with Wolves* (discussed earlier in this chapter): instead of the film being seen to invert the binary oppositions and narrative functions of Wright's model, we might perhaps consider the way the film challenges the hierarchy implicit in the model. As Derrida (1976) points out:

> [A deconstructive] reading must always aim at a certain relationship, unperceived by the writer, between what he commands and what he does not command of the patterns of language that he uses. This relationship is . . . a signifying structure that critical [i.e. deconstructive] reading should produce. . . . [That is, a] production [which] attempts to make the not seen accessible to sight (158, 163).[4]

Discourse and power: Michel Foucault

One of the primary concerns of Michel Foucault is the relationship between knowledge and power and how this relationship operates within discourses and discursive formations. Foucault's concept of discourse is similar to Althusser's idea of the 'problematic'; that is, both are organized and organizing bodies of knowledge, with rules and regulations that govern particular practices (ways of speaking, thinking and acting).

Discourses work in three ways: they enable, they constrain, and they constitute. As Foucault (1989) explains, discourses are 'practices that systematically form the objects of which they speak' (49). Language, for example, is a discourse: it *enables* me to speak, it *constrains* what I can say; it *constitutes* me as a speaking subject (i.e. it situates and produces my subjectivity: I know myself in language; I think in language; I talk to myself in language). Academic disciplines are also discourses: like languages, they enable, constrain and constitute. Table 6.5 outlines the different ways film may be studied. Each discipline speaks about film in a particular way and in so doing it enables and constrains what can be said about film. But they do not just speak about film; by constructing film as a particular object of study, they constitute film as a specific reality ('the real meaning of film'). The game of netball is also a discourse: to play netball (regardless of individual talent), you must be familiar with the rules of the game; these

Table 6.5 Film as an object of study.

Economics	= commodity
Literary studies	= artistic text similar to literary text
History	= historical document
Art history	= example of visual culture
Cultural studies	= example of popular culture
Film studies	= textual object of study
Media studies	= particular type of media

both enable and constrain your performance. But they also constitute you as a netball player. In other words, you are a netball player only if you play netball. Being a netball player is not a 'given' (i.e. expression of 'nature'): it is enabled, constrained and constituted in discourse (i.e. a product of 'culture').

In these ways, discourses produce subject positions we are invited to occupy (member of a language community; student of film; netball player). Discourses, therefore, are social practices in which we engage; they are like social 'scripts' we perform (consciously and unconsciously). What we think of as 'experience' is always experience in or of a particular discourse. Moreover, what we think of as our 'selves' is the internalization of a multiplicity of discourses. In other words, all the things we are, are enabled, constrained and constituted in discourses.

Discursive formations consist of the hierarchical criss-crossing of particular discourses. The different ways to study film discussed earlier produce a discursive formation. In *The History of Sexuality*, Foucault (1981) charts the development of the discursive formation of sexuality. In doing this, he rejects what he calls 'the repressive hypothesis' (10); that is, the idea of sexuality as something 'essential' that the Victorians repressed. Instead he follows a different set of questions:

> Why has sexuality been so widely discussed and what has been said about it? What were the effects of power generated by what was said? What are the links between these discourses, these effects of power, and the pleasures that were invested by them? What knowledge (savoir) was formed as a result of this linkage? (11)

He tracks the discourse of sexuality through a series of discursive domains: medicine, demography, psychiatry, pedagogy, social work, criminology, governmental. Rather than the silence of repression, he encounters 'a political, economic and technical incitement to talk about sex' (22–3). He argues that the different discourses on sexuality are not *about* sexuality, they actually *constitute* the reality of sexuality. In other words, the Victorians did not repress sexuality, they actually invented it. This is not to say that sexuality does not exist non-discursively, but to claim that our 'knowledge' of sexuality and the 'power–knowledge' relations of sexuality are discursive.

Discourses produce knowledge and knowledge is always a weapon of power: 'it is in discourse that power and knowledge are joined together' (Foucault, 2009: 318). The Victorian invention of sexuality did not just produce knowledge about sexuality, it sought to produce power over sexuality; this was knowledge that could be deployed to categorize and to organize behaviour; divide it into the 'normal' and the unacceptable. In this way, then, 'power produces knowledge . . . power and knowledge directly imply one another . . . there is no power relation without the correlative constitution of a field of knowledge, nor any knowledge that does not presuppose and constitute at the same time power relations' (1979: 27). Power, however, should not be thought of as a negative force, something that denies, represses, negates; power is productive.

> We must cease once and for all to describe the effects of power in negative terms: it 'excludes', it 'represses', it 'censors', it 'abstracts', it 'masks', it 'conceals'. In fact, power produces; it produces reality; it produces domains of objects and rituals of truth (194).

Power produces reality; through discourses it produces the 'truths' we live by: 'Each society has its own regime of truth, its "general politics" of truth – that is, the types of discourse it accepts and makes function as true' (Foucault, 2002a: 131). One of his central aims, therefore, is to discover 'how men [and women] govern (themselves and others) by the production of truth (. . . the establishment of domains in which the practice of true and false can be made at once ordered and pertinent)' (2002b: 230).

What Foucault calls 'regimes of truth' do not have to be 'true'; they have only to be thought of as 'true' and acted on as if 'true'. If ideas are believed, they establish and legitimate particular regimes of truth. For example, as late as the seventeenth century the prevailing regime of truth placed the earth at the centre of the universe. In 1632 Galileo Galilei (1564–1642) was charged with heresy for his support of the theory of Nicolaus Copernicus (1473–1543) that the earth moves around the sun, eventually being sentenced to life imprisonment for something that is now taught to school children as an obvious fact of nature. In Chapter 9 we will examine Orientalism as a powerful regime of truth.

Discourse, however, is not just about the imposition of power. As Foucault (2009) points out, 'Where there is power there is resistance' (315).

> Discourses are not once and for all subservient to power or raised up against it, any more than silences are. We must make allowances for the complex and unstable process whereby discourse can be both an instrument and an effect of power, but also an hindrance, a stumbling block, a point of resistance and a starting point for an opposing strategy. Discourse transmits and produces power; it reinforces it, but also undermines it and exposes it, renders it fragile and makes it possible to thwart it (318).

The panoptic machine

The panopticon is a type of prison building designed by Jeremy Bentham in 1787 (see Photo 6.5). At the centre of the building is a tower that allows the governor to observe

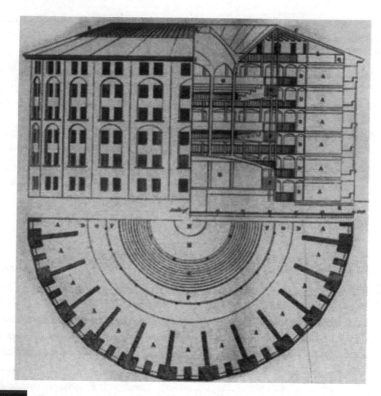

Photo 6.5 The panoptic machine.

all the prisoners in the surrounding cells without the prisoners knowing whether or not they are in fact being observed. According to Bentham, the panopticon is 'A new mode of obtaining power of mind over mind, in a quantity hitherto without example: and that, to a degree equally without example' (Bentham, 1995: 31). He also believed that the panopticon design might also be used in 'any sort of establishment, in which persons of any description are to be kept under inspection, [including] poor-houses, lazarettos, houses of industry, manufactories, hospitals, work-houses, mad-houses, and schools' (29).

According to Foucault (1979),

> the major effect of the Panopticon [is] to induce in the inmate a state of conscious and permanent visibility that assures the automatic functioning of power. . . . [S]urveillance is permanent in its effects, even if it is discontinuous in its action; that the perfection of power should tend to render its actual exercise unnecessary. . . . [T]he inmates . . . [are] caught up in a power situation of which they are themselves the bearers. . . . He who is subjected to a field of visibility, and who knows it, assumes responsibility for the constraints of power; he makes them play spontaneously upon himself; he inscribes in himself the power relation

in which he simultaneously plays both roles; he becomes the principle of his own subjection (201, 202–3).

In other words, inmates do not know whether or not they are actually being watched. Therefore, they learn to behave as if they are always being watched. This is the power of the panopticon. Panopticism is the extension of this system of surveillance to society as a whole.

Bentham's panopticon is, therefore, profoundly symptomatic of a historical shift, from the eighteenth century onwards, in methods of social control. This is, according to Foucault, a movement from punishment (enforcing norms of behaviour through spectacular displays of power: public hangings and torture, etc.) to discipline (enforcing norms of behaviour through surveillance); a shift from 'exceptional discipline to one of generalised surveillance . . . the formation of what might be called in general the disciplinary society' (209). As Foucault explains, the panopticon is 'a generalizable model [for] . . . defining power relations in terms of the everyday life. . . . [I]t is a diagram of a mechanism of power reduced to its ideal form' (205). The movement from spectacle to surveillance turns 'the whole social body into a field of perception' (214). The intersecting gazes of power criss-cross the social body, drawing more and more aspects of human existence into its field of vision. But it is not simply that power catches us in its gaze, rather power works when we recognize its gaze. As Foucault makes clear, using a theatre metaphor, 'We are neither in the amphitheatre, nor on the stage, but in the panoptic machine, invested by its effects of power, which we bring to ourselves since we are part of the mechanism' (217). In this way, then, he argues, surveillance has become the dominant mode of the operation of power. 'Panopticism is a form of power . . . organised around the norm, in terms of what [is] normal or not, correct or not, in terms of what one must do or not do' (2002c, 58–9). It is a fundamental aspect of what he calls 'normalisation' (79).

An obvious confirmation of his claim is the widespread use of surveillance technologies in contemporary society. For example, it was claimed in 2013 that there are six million CCTV cameras in the UK; roughly one for every eleven people.[5] This stands in direct relation to Bentham's panopticon. But the discipline of surveillance has also had a profound influence on popular culture. I can think of at least four examples of surveillance media. Perhaps the most obvious examples are television programmes such as *Big Brother* and *I'm a Celebrity, Get me Out of Here* – surveillance is a fundamental aspect of how these programmes work. In many ways *Big Brother* is panopticon television in its most visible form. Undoubtedly, part of its appeal is that it appears to enable us to assume the role of Bentham's imaginary governor, as we take pleasure in the ability to observe without being observed, to be involved without being involved, and to judge without being judged. However, in the light of Foucault's point about the production of regimes of truth, we should not assume that we are really outside the reach of the standards and norms that *Big Brother* promotes and legitimates. In other words, it might be possible to argue that the gaze of *Big Brother* is reciprocal; it disciplines us as much as the contestants we watch being disciplined: we are in the cells and not in the governor's tower.

The increasing number of celebrity surveillance magazines, such as *Reveal*, *Closer*, *Heat* and *New*, work in a similar way. Celebrities are monitored and scrutinized, especially in terms of body size and sexual and social behaviour, for our supposedly anonymous pleasure and entertainment. But again, the norms and standards that are used to criticize and ridicule celebrities are the same norms and standards that can be used to discipline us. Similarly, in 'make-over' and 'talk-show' surveillance programmes such as the *Jerry Springer Show* and the *Jeremy Kyle Show*, and *What Not To Wear* and *Ten Years Younger*, advice is freely combined with abuse and ridicule, as subjects are encouraged, often aggressively and to the smug self-satisfaction of the presenters, to embrace self-discipline in order to comply with currently accepted standards of aesthetic and behavioural normality.[6] The fact that we are on the other side of the screen does not mean that we are safe from the demand to conform, or safely outside of the panoptic machine.

Notes

1. Barthes's 'Myth today' and Williams's 'The analysis of culture' are two of the founding texts of British cultural studies.
2. Barthes's formulation is remarkably similar to the concept of 'interpellation' developed, some years later, by Louis Althusser (see discussion in Chapter 4).
3. Myth works in much the same way as Foucault's concept of power; it is productive rather than repressive (see later in this chapter).
4. This is very similar to the argument made by Pierre Macherey (see Chapter 4).
5. These figures were broadcast on the BBC programme Sunday Morning Live (21 July 2013).
6. If you enter Jeremy Kyle/Jon Culshaw in the search engine on YouTube you will find Jon Culshaw's wonderful parody of Jeremy Kyle. Culshaw quite brilliantly captures the aggression, the discourse of social class and the smug self-satisfaction of this type of programme.

Further reading

Storey, John (ed.), *Cultural Theory and Popular Culture: A Reader*, 4th edn, Harlow: Pearson Education, 2009. This is the companion volume to the previous edition of this book. A fully updated 5th edition containing further readings is due for publication in 2018. An interactive website is also available (www.routledge.com/cw/storey), which contains helpful student resources and a glossary of terms for each chapter.

During, Simon, *Foucault and Literature: Towards a Genealogy of Writing*, London: Routledge, 1992. Although the focus is on literature, this is nevertheless a very useful introduction to Foucault.

Eagleton, Terry, *Literary Theory: An Introduction*, Oxford: Basil Blackwell, 1983. Contains an excellent chapter on post-structuralism.

Easthope, Antony, *British Post-Structuralism*, London: Routledge, 1988. An ambitious attempt to map the field. Useful chapters on film theory, cultural studies, deconstruction and historical studies.

Hawkes, Terence, *Structuralism and Semiotics*, London: Methuen, 1977. A useful introduction to the subject.

McNay, Lois, *Foucault: A Critical Introduction*, Cambridge: Polity Press, 1994. An excellent introduction to Foucault's work.

Norris, Christopher, *Derrida*, London: Fontana, 1987. A clear and interesting introduction to Derrida.

Sarup, Madan, *An Introductory Guide to Post-Structuralism and Postmodernism*, 2nd edn, Harlow: Prentice Hall, 1993. An excellent introduction to post-structuralism.

Sheridan, Alan, *Michel Foucault: The Will to Truth*, London: Tavistock, 1980. Still the most readable introduction to Foucault.

Silverman, Kaja, *The Subject of Semiotics*, Oxford: Oxford University Press, 1983. An interesting and accessible account of structuralism, semiotics, psychoanalysis, feminism and post-structuralism. Especially useful on Barthes.

Sturrock, John (ed.), *Structuralism and Since: From Lévi-Strauss to Derrida*, Oxford: Oxford University Press, 1979. Contains good introductory essays on Lévi-Strauss, Barthes, Foucault and Derrida.

Thwaites, Tony, Lloyd Davis and Mules Warwick, *Tools for Cultural Studies: An Introduction*, Melbourne: Macmillan, 1994. Presents an informed account of the place of semiotics in the field of cultural studies.

Weedon, Chris, *Feminist Practice and Poststructuralist Theory*, Oxford: Basil Blackwell, 1987. An interesting introduction to post-structuralism from a feminist perspective. Helpful chapter on Foucault.

7 Class and class struggle

Class and popular culture

In a book on cultural theory and popular culture why concern ourselves with social class? One answer is to say that class has always been a concern of this book; what has changed is that it now has its own chapter. Another is to say that although it is an 'economic' category, it is always lived culturally and one of the places where we recognize its existence is popular culture. Put simply, popular culture is a key site for the recognition and self-recognition of class. Class is everywhere in popular culture. It can be found quite clearly in dramas such as *Downton Abbey* and in documentaries like *Benefits Street*. It would be impossible to understand either television programme without including a critical attention to representations of class. We see it explicitly in all sorts of other things: styles of dress, holiday destinations, the books and newspapers we read, the food we eat, the music we like, how we talk to each other, where we live, our dreams and hopes for the future. We also find it implicitly in the judgements that are made about how people dress and speak, where they take their holidays, the books and newspapers they read, the music they like, where they live, and how they imagine the future. In other words, class is there in the assumptions made about what is a good or bad lifestyle.

The chapter will begin with an account of the importance of class in the work of the founding fathers of cultural studies – Raymond Williams, Richard Hoggart, and EP Thompson. This will be followed by a discussion of two theories of class that have been enormously influential in cultural studies, derived from the work of Karl Marx and Pierre Bourdieu. This will be followed by a case study that highlights the relationship between class and popular culture. The chapter will conclude with a discussion of an idea that is often deployed as a means to dismiss class as an explanatory concept – 'meritocracy'.

Class in cultural studies

Until recently there was an argument that suggested that class should no longer be a central category in cultural studies. This can be illustrated by the experience of Anita Biressi and Heather Nunn. As they point out in the Preface to the paperback edition of their excellent book on culture and class:

For at least a decade or more before the publication of *Class and Contemporary British Culture* we had been experimenting with rudimentary drafts of a book manuscript on class and culture, none of which appealed to reviewers whose view was that scholarship on social class, especially in British cultural studies, was somewhat passé (Biressi and Nunn 2016: ix).

The experience of Biressi and Nunn might seem strange given the centrality of class in the emergence of British cultural studies, but there is no doubt that under the pressure of postmodernism, it had become a somewhat unfashionable concept. However, in recent times it has once again emerged as a concept that is indispensable when attempting to think critically about culture, whether our object of study is high or popular, production or consumption. While postmodernism had made class seem like an old-fashioned concept, and deindustrialization had made it less visible, and the ideology of neoliberalism had made it less available as a positive identity, the financial crash of 2008 and the politics of austerity that followed changed all this, making class suddenly very visible as a lived identity and giving the concept a new explanatory power.

Despite it going in and out of academic fashion, class was fundamental to the founding of cultural studies. Its interest in youth subcultures, resistance, hegemony and popular culture, all derived from a concern with class. The early work of three of its founding figures, Richard Hoggart, EP Thompson, and Raymond Williams is unthinkable without the concept of class. The point is obvious in the title of Thompson's *The Making of the English Working Class* (1980). The Preface to Hoggart's *The Uses of Literacy* (1957) begins with 'This book is about changes in working-class culture' (Hoggart 1990: 9). In *Culture and Society*, Williams (1963) argues that through the course of the Industrial Revolution a number of important words entered common usage or, where they had already existed, they acquired new meanings. Class was one of these words. As Williams (1983) points out, 'Development of class in its modern sense, with relatively fixed names for particular classes (lower class, middle class, upper class, working class and so on), belongs essentially to the period between 1770 and 1840, which is also the period of the Industrial Revolution and its decisive reorganisation of society' (Reader 61). Before this period, it was usual to describe social division with words such as rank, order, estate or degree. What these terms had in common was the implication that social division was 'natural' and had little to do with human actions. As Williams points out, 'the history of class, as a word which would supersede older terms for social division, relates to the increasing consciousness that social position is made rather than merely inherited' (ibid.). Moreover, it included the growing recognition that 'a particular social system . . . actually created social divisions' (Reader 62). In other words, the introduction of class is also an introduction of the idea that social division is humanly made and relates explicitly to how a society is organised. The person most associated with this idea is Karl Marx.

Class struggle

Margaret Thatcher, who did more than most in recent times to rebalance class struggle in favour of the rich and powerful, once claimed that 'Class is a communist concept' (quoted in Biressi and Nunn 2016: 202). Unlike many things she claimed, this is not entirely without foundation. Although, as we have seen, the concept of class predates Marx, it is certainly true that it was his work that gave it conceptual solidity.

As we saw in chapter 4, Marx defines class as a relationship to the prevailing mode of production. He argues that each significant period in history is constructed around a particular mode of production: that is, the way in which a society is organized (i.e. slave, feudal, capitalist) to produce the material necessaries of life – food, shelter, etc.[1] In general terms, each mode of production produces: (i) specific ways of obtaining the necessaries of life; (ii) specific social relationships between workers and those who control the mode of production, and (iii) specific social institutions (including cultural ones). At the heart of this analysis is the claim that how a society produces its means of existence (its 'base') ultimately determines the political, social and cultural shape of that society – its 'superstructure'. As Marx explains, 'The mode of production of material life conditions the social, political and intellectual life process in general' (1976a: 3).

The 'base' consists of a combination of the 'forces of production' and the 'relations of production'. The forces of production refer to the raw materials, the tools, the technology, the workers and their skills, etc. The relations of production refer to the class relations of those engaged in production. It is in this sense that one's class position is determined by one's relationship to the mode of production. Therefore, each mode of production, besides being different, say, in terms of its basis in agrarian or industrial production, with corresponding tools and technologies, is also different in that it produces particular relations of production; that is, antagonistic class relations: the slave mode produces master/slave relations; the feudal mode produces lord/peasant relations; the capitalist mode produces capitalist/worker relations. The names change but the fundamental relationship remains much the same. In this way, then, class exists objectively in the 'base' as an economic relationship and subjectively in the 'superstructure' as a form of consciousness and lived practice.

According to this model all other class divisions are direct or indirect expressions of this fundamental binary relationship. Under the capitalist mode of production, there is division between those who own the means of production and those who have only their labour power to sell. This is the fundamental division that divides capitalist society. However, when we look at contemporary capitalist society it looks so much more complicated than this, and of course it is, but all the complications lead back to this foundational division. For example, senior managers may not be capitalist themselves, but the role they are employed to play is above all to manage the fortunes of capital and thus they are ideologically and materially working in the interest of capital. There are also residual and emergent class formations. For example, the landed aristocracy are what remains of the class structure of the feudal mode of production. Although economically and politically marginalized, they serve as a kind of decorative smokescreen, hiding the real basis of power in capitalist society. The self-employed (what Marx called the petite bourgeoisie) are another exception – they own the means of production but are capitalists without anyone to exploit. But again, as a class they are marginal to the main class division in capitalist society. Marx's point is that these other divisions do not undermine the central division because they are related to it and are in many ways subservient to it. Therefore, while there can be no doubt that class appears more complicated in the twenty-first century than it did when Marx was writing in the nineteenth, the different contemporary ways of describing the class structure often seem little more than ways of talking about social difference. For Marx class is not just a marker of social difference, it is a fundamental relationship based on the dominant mode of production. To discover endless gradations in this fundamental relationship does not in any way invalidate Marx's model of class and class struggle.

For Marx, recorded human history has been a history of class conflicts. The opening words of the *Communist Manifesto* (Marx and Engels, 1998) make this very clear:

> The [written] history of all hitherto existing societies is the history of class struggles [in which] oppressor and oppressed, stood in constant opposition to one another, carried on an uninterrupted, now hidden, now open fight, a fight that each time ended, either in a revolutionary reconstitution of society at large, or in the common ruin of the contending classes (Reader 1998: 5).

If class was simply an economic category derived from a relationship with the prevailing mode of production, the idea of class consciousness and class struggle would have no meaning. While it is true that class is first and foremost an economic category, how it is lived and experienced is cultural. In this way, as we have already noted, class is always both objective and subjective, straddling both the base and the superstructure. It is founded on a particular relationship with the prevailing mode of production, but it only finds full expression when it defines itself against another class. The terms to mark this distinction are *class in itself* (objective category) and *class for itself* (subjective category). The first points to an economic relationship, the second is a form of consciousness and lived practice. As Ernst Fischer explains it, 'A class is born in the class struggle. Only through such struggle does it develop into a social and historical force' (1973: 73). As Marx explains, in a discussion of the nineteenth-century French peasantry, 'In so far as millions of families live under economic conditions of existence that separate their mode of life, their interests and their culture from those of the other classes, and put them in hostile opposition to the latter, they form a class. In so far as there is merely a local interconnection among these small-holding peasants, and the identity of their interests begets no community, no national bond and no political organization among them, they do not form a class' (1977: 106).

In other words, class is an objective category, in that it is a result of a relationship to the prevailing mode of production, and a subjective category to the extent that it produces a consciousness of this relationship. It is always what EP Thompson calls 'a historical phenomenon' (1980: 212). The common experience of class 'is largely determined by the productive relations into which men [and women] are born – or enter involuntarily' (9). However, the consciousness of class, the translation of experience into culture, 'is defined by men [and women] as they live their own history' (10). Therefore, it is not a 'thing', it is always a historical relationship of unity and difference: uniting one class as against another class or classes. As he explains, 'class happens when some men [and women], as a result of common experiences (inherited or shared), feel and articulate the identity of their interests as between themselves, and as against other men [and women] whose interests are different from (and usually opposed to) theirs' (8–9). Gramsci makes a similar point, a class always exhibits a certain 'homogeneity, self-awareness and organisation' (1971: 181). A class first constitutes itself on the basis of certain common economic interests. An awareness of these interests, gives rise to an awareness of the general economic interests of the class as a whole. This is followed by the establishment of an awareness of the unity of the economic, political, and cultural needs of the class. What the accounts of Marx, Thompson, Gramsci, and other Marxists share is an insistence that class is always both objective (based on an economic relationship) and subjective (it manifests itself in a particular way of seeing and being in the world).

Consumption as class distinction

Perhaps the most interesting development in the study of class since Marx, certainly in terms of its influence on cultural theory and popular culture, is the work of Pierre Bourdieu. According to Bourdieu, as Nicholas Garnham and Raymond Williams explain,

> all societies are characterised by a struggle between groups and/or classes and class fractions to maximise their interests in order to ensure their reproduction. The social formation is seen as a hierarchically organised series of fields within which human agents are engaged in specific struggles to maximise their control over the social resources specific to that field, the intellectual field, the educational field, the economic field etc. . . . The fields are hierarchically organised in a structure over-determined by the field of class struggle over the production and distribution of material resources and each subordinate field reproduces within its own structural logic, the logic of the field of class struggle (1980: 215).

Bourdieu argues that class manifests itself in three forms of 'capital', economic, cultural and social. The first of these capitals connects most directly with Marx's theory of class. However, how class is lived and experienced tends to be a result of the articulation of cultural and social capital. Bourdieu demonstrates, for example, how particular patterns of consumption are ultimately about class difference and class distinction. He shows how arbitrary tastes and arbitrary ways of living are continually transmuted into legitimate taste and the only legitimate way of life. The 'illusion of "natural distinction" is ultimately based on the power of the dominant to impose, by their very existence, a definition of excellence which [is] nothing other than their own way of existing' (1992: 255). In other words, dominant classes seek to impose their own tastes as if these were in fact universal tastes.

Bourdieu's interest is in the processes by which patterns of consumption help to secure and legitimate forms of power and domination that are ultimately rooted in economic inequality. He argues that although class rule is ultimately economic, the form it takes is cultural; patterns of consumption are used to secure social distinction, the making, marking and maintaining of social difference. The source of social difference and social power is thus symbolically shifted from the economic field to the field of consumption, making social power appear to be the result of a specific disposition. In this way, the production and reproduction of cultural space helps produce and reproduce social space, social power and class difference. In other words, what people consume does not simply reflect distinctions and differences embedded elsewhere, that consumption makes visible, rather consumption is the means by which difference and distinction are articulated, maintained and reproduced.

Bourdieu's purpose is not to prove the self-evident, that different classes have different patterns of consumption, but to show how consumption (from high art to food on the table) forms a distinct pattern of social distinction, and to identify and interrogate the processes by which the making and maintaining of these distinctions secures and legitimates forms of class power and control rooted ultimately in economic inequalities. He is interested not so much in the actual differences, but in how these differences are used by dominant classes as a means of social reproduction.

Bourdieu insists that taste is always more than an aesthetic category. As he points out, 'taste classifies, and it classifies the classifier' (6). We are classified by our classifications and classify others by theirs. In this way, he would argue that similar things are happening when I 'value' a holiday destination or a particular mode of dress, as are happening when I 'value' a poem by William Blake or a song by Bob Dylan or a play by Bertolt Brecht. Such valuations are never a simple matter of individual taste, consumption operates both to identify and to mark social distinction and to sustain social difference. While such strategies of classification do not in themselves produce social inequalities, the making, marking and maintaining of them functions to legitimate such inequalities. In this way, taste is a profoundly ideological discourse; it operates as a marker of 'class' (using the term in the double sense to mean both economic category and a particular level of quality). He argues that consumption is, ultimately, 'predisposed . . . to fulfil a social function of legitimating social difference' (7).

Bourdieu's work on consumption is underpinned by his view of education. Rather than being a means to lessen inequality, it functions to legitimate it. He argues that the education system fulfils a quite specific social and political function: that is, to legitimate social inequalities which exist prior to its operations. It achieves this by transforming social differences into academic differences, and presenting these differences as if they were 'grounded in nature' (387). The cultural tastes of dominant classes are given institutional form, and then, with deft ideological sleight of hand, their taste for this institutionalized culture (i.e. their own) is held up as evidence of their cultural, and, ultimately, their social, superiority. In this way, social distinction is generated by learned patterns of consumption that are internalized as 'natural' cultural preferences and interpreted and mobilized as evidence of 'natural' cultural competences, which are, ultimately, used to justify forms of class domination. Cultural and social capital is able to conceal and legitimate economic domination by reproducing it in the form of cultural and social hierarchies.

Sociologists often present Bourdieu's work on class as a theoretical advance on Marx, but in my view what Bourdieu offers is an elaboration of Marx and one that fundamentally depends on Marx for its coherence. In other words, his analysis is built on foundations laid by Marx. Beneath the very interesting concepts of cultural and social capital is economic capital, which is in part what Marx means by class as an economic category. But of course, as we have seen, Marx does not stop there, he goes on to suggest that class as an economic category is always articulated socially and culturally. Class may ultimately relate to one's place in the relations of production, but it is a position that requires a great deal of cultural and social work for it to appear 'natural'. What Bourdieu does, and does brilliantly, is show one of the significant ways in which class as an economic relationship works culturally – how it manifests itself in everyday lived experience.

Class and popular culture

We can explore the entanglement of class and popular culture through many different examples. I am sure that readers of this book will not find it difficult to make the connection. I recently discussed (Storey 2016) it in relation to the invention of the traditional English Christmas, the Folk Revival, and the development of association football. In each entanglement, we find the middle class, like any other dominant class, being 'compelled . . . to represent its interests as the common interest of all members of society . . . to give its ideas the form of universality, and represent them as the only rational, universally valid ones' (Marx and Engels 2009: 59). This attempt to build a cultural consensus based on relations of domination and subordination is part of what Gramsci (1971, 2009) would later define as hegemony. In each case, we see the playing-out of hegemony, as the middle class seek to establish a consensus which secures for itself a leading position in relation to the working class. In other words, to return to the quotation from Marx and Engels, we have in each example the playing out of the middle class's need to 'represent its interests as the common interest of all'.

Traditional histories of football present the development of the game as passing through four stages (Dunning 1971). In its first stage, from the fourteenth to the nineteenth century, it existed as a wild and unruly game played by all social classes. The term 'football' referred to ball games that involved both kicking and handling, and may even have been used to distinguish ball games played on foot rather than on horseback. What these games had in common was a ball and the idea of getting the ball to a 'goal', but the rules were oral and various. Teams could be any size from 20 up to 2,000, and the playing area could be the whole village, or the space between two villages. A game could last all day and was often played during village celebrations (Shrove Tuesday, village fairs and feasts, etc.).

In the second stage, from about 1750 to 1840, under the pressures of the Industrial Revolution, the game disappeared as a popular sport. That is to say, the enclosure movement and urbanisation removed areas where the game might be played, industrialisation introduced a stricter work discipline and the new policing system enforced the law more efficiently. What remained of the popular game survived, it was claimed, only in the universities and public schools. But even here the game was discouraged because like the game that had once existed outside these institutions, it was violent and unruly.

In the third stage, from about 1840 to 1860, the status of sport began to change: it was now seen as good for 'elite' males. Team sports, especially football, were character building, increased physical health, discipline and moral responsibility. The Clarendon Commission of 1864, established to investigate the public schools, was very clear on the benefits of sport:

> The cricket and football fields . . . are not merely places of amusement; they help to form some of the most valuable social qualities and manly virtues, and they hold, like the classroom and the boarding house, a distinct and important place in public school education (quoted in Walton and Walvin 1988: 299).

During this period, the game is supposedly civilised and codified by the public schools.

In the final stage, from about 1850 to 1890, ex-public schoolboys established the Football Association in 1863 and the FA Cup in 1871 and then, working like colonial missionaries, gradually introduced the new civilised and codified game to the working class. In an account of the development of the game, written in 1906, the author is quite clear of the role played by, in particular, Eton, Harrow, Westminster and Charterhouse: 'football, in its modern form, is entirely the product . . . of the various public school games' (quoted in Taylor 2013: 22). The Wanderers were the first winners of the FA Cup. The social make-up of their team tells us a great deal about the game as played in the early days of the FA. The team included four Harrow graduates, three old Etonians, and one each from Westminster, Charterhouse, Oxford and Cambridge.

Football, it seemed, was a game intended for the middle class, but despite this it very quickly grew to become what James Walvin (2000) calls the 'people's game'. The initial challenge to the hegemony of the middle class came from Blackburn, Lancashire. In 1882, Blackburn Rovers got to the FA Cup final, losing 1–0 to Old Etonians. However, the following year, Blackburn Olympic not only reached the final, they actually won the cup, beating Old Etonians 2–1. The *Blackburn Times* (1883) understood very well how Blackburn Olympic's victory was entangled with social class:

> The meeting and vanquishing, in a most severe trial of athletic skill, of a club composed of sons of some of the families of the upper class in the Kingdom . . . as the Old Etonian Club is, by a Provincial Club composed of entirely, we believe, of Lancashire Lads of the manual working-class, sons of small tradesmen, artisans, and operatives (quoted in Walton and Walvin 1988: 299).

Blackburn Olympic's team consisted of three weavers, a dental assistant, a gilder, a plumber, a clerk, a loomer, a licensed victualler and two iron-foundry workers. A team of ex-public schoolboys would never again win the FA Cup.

From the 1870s, football as a socially organised sport developed rapidly amongst the working class of the midlands and north (especially Lancashire). Football clubs were established in different ways: through existing sports clubs (for example, Burnley,

Sheffield Wednesday, Preston North End, Derby County, Notts County); promoted by religious organisations (for example, Aston Villa, Barnsley, Blackpool, Bolton Wanderers, Everton, Manchester City, Birmingham City); represented workplaces (for example, Stoke City, West Bromwich Albion, Manchester United, Coventry City, Crewe Alexandra); and by teachers and ex-pupils (for example, Blackburn Rovers, Leicester City, Sunderland).

The establishment of the Football League in 1888 was an inevitable consequence of professionalism. In order to pay wages, clubs needed reliable and regular fixtures. In 1884, Preston North End were expelled from the FA Cup because it was claimed they had used professional players. An inquiry was inconclusive, but it did discover that they had arranged jobs for players (i.e. sinecures that allowed them to be in effect full-time players). Preston got support from 40 clubs from the north and midlands. Together they threatened to form a British FA. In January 1885, professionalism was legalised. The Football League was founded three years later in 1888. Of the eleven founding teams, six were from Lancashire (Preston North End, Blackburn Rovers, Bolton Wanderers, Accrington, Everton, Burnley) and five from the midlands (Aston Villa, Wolverhampton Wanderers, Derby County, Notts County, Stoke City).

Why did the game develop so quickly in the industrial north and midlands? One compelling answer is that it had never really gone away. As we noted earlier, according to conventional accounts there was pre-industrial football, which disappeared as a popular game under the pressures of the Industrial Revolution. However, the public schools held on to the game, codified and civilised it, and introduced it to the world with the establishment of the FA and the FA Cup. But there is another possibility: it did not disappear but, as in the public schools, it continued to evolve in the new industrial towns and cities. In other words, the public-school version was just one version, but a version with the power to impose itself on the formal organisation of the game and on the writing of the game's history. But alongside this version there existed another version we might call working-class football. The existence of this second version would also help explain how what is presented as the public school game was able to develop so rapidly in the industrial north and the midlands.

An article published in 1838 in *Bell's Life in London*, at a time when the game had supposedly disappeared as a popular sport, offers evidence for the existence of a working-class version of the game:

> A match at football will be played at the cricket ground, Leicester, on Good Friday next, between eleven (principally printers) from Derby and the same number of Leicester. The winners to challenge an equal number from any town in England, for a purse not exceeding £25 (quoted in Walton and Walvin 1988: 299).

In 1842, a witness at a Parliamentary inquiry into the conditions of working-class children in the mining areas of the North of England wrote:

> Although Christmas Day and Good Friday were the only fixed holidays in the mining region of Yorkshire, children had at least one day off a week and a fair portion of time in the evening. This they could use to play sport on the considerable areas

of wasteland in the neighbourhood. Their games included cricket, nur and spell [a bat and ball game] and football (quoted in Harvey 2005: 59).

Although children working long hours in the mining industry and then playing on wasteland offers little to celebrate, it does present evidence that football had continued to exist outside the universities and public schools. Therefore, although the middle class established the FA and the FA Cup, the game's rapid development from the 1870s onwards in the industrial north and midlands suggests that the popular game had not disappeared; rather, it had simply changed in ways quite similar to what had happened to it in the public schools. Again, it is impossible to fully understand the complex history of the development of the game, and how this history has been written, without including as part of the explanation the important role played by social class.

The ideological work of meritocracy

Meritocracy is perhaps the great lie of class inequality. As Jo Littler (2013; see also Littler 2017) points out, it is 'a mechanism to both perpetuate, and create, social and cultural inequality' (Reader 53). Rather than accept it as an obvious good,

> we should pay close attention to meritocracy because it has become a key ideological means by which plutocracy – or government by a wealthy elite – perpetuates itself through neoliberal culture. It is not, in other words, merely a coincidence that the common idea that we live, or should live, in a meritocratic age co-exists with a pronounced lack of social mobility and the continuation of vested hereditary economic interests (ibid.).

Littler identifies five assumptions that underpin meritocracy. The first is that 'intelligence' and 'talent' are innate qualities. In other words, it is an argument that an expensive education makes little difference to your perceived talent and intelligence. This is then connected to a second assumption: natural intelligence and talent combined with effort is what is required to achieve success. A meritocratic society, therefore, is a society structured by only inequalities of natural talent and intelligence guided by effort. Of course, not all talented and intelligent people will make it to the top, but this is seen as acceptable because the system is competitive. So, if you are at the bottom, it is either because you do not have the necessary talent and intelligence to succeed or because you were not competitive enough to win (to have winners we must have losers). Such an assumption fits perfectly with the dominant idea of capitalism that competition is an ultimate good.

A third assumption, perhaps the key assumption, follows from and supports the first two: the idea that talent and intelligence plus effort produce merit is saying something politically even more important: circumstances of birth and social structure are irrelevant to social and economic achievement. One of the great myths of capitalist society is that everyone has the freedom to climb the ladder of success. Social mobility ensures that the best rise to the top and we end up with a hierarchy we all deserve. To dismiss the idea that individual merit alone determines social destination is not to deny that social mobility exists. But even the mobility that exists is often greatly exaggerated, often as a means to defend what is mostly a strong and stable class structure, ultimately determining where we end up regardless of talent and hard work. For example, I am a professor from a working-class background (my father was an unskilled worker and my mother a cleaner), indicating that social mobility exists, but the fact that the vast majority of professors do not come from such a background also makes clear that social mobility is in this instance very limited. So, while we can always point to examples of social mobility, its impact on class structure is often exaggerated. Moreover, if our focus is the very top and bottom, social mobility is very limited indeed (i.e. few rise from the very bottom and few fall from the very top).

A fourth assumption concerns what counts as merit. On investigation, it quickly becomes clear that merit is an outcome often determined by the so-called 'market', in which certain professions attract more money and status. This has produced a situation in which a professional footballer who entertains earns considerably more than a nurse or doctor who saves lives. The final assumption is that it is better at the top than the bottom of society. While you might say, well, of course it is, the logic behind this is to produce a validation of upper class lifestyles and a devaluation of the lives of the working class.

Together the five assumptions underpin, support and justify the idea that we live in a meritocratic society. If a society is meritocratic it means that divisions and inequalities are based on natural talent, intelligence and hard work, rather than being derived from the class structure and its reproduction of economic inequalities. The role of the meritocratic state is to reproduce the conditions which enable the 'best' to rise to the top. The problem with this is revealed when we examine the background of those who make it to the top. Only 7% of the population of the UK go to independent schools (i.e. expensive fee-paying schools)[2] and yet 71% of top judges, 62% of senior military officers, 55% of civil service permanent secretaries, and 53% of Diplomats attended such schools? (Acred 2016: 16). This hardly seems to suggest that our class position is the result of individual merit and has little to do with inherited structures of privilege and inequality. Once we consider such statistics, class position seems far more important than talent, intelligence and hard work. Now this is not to say that some at the top are not talented, intelligent and work hard, only that it was not just these supposed natural attributes and effort that got them there. Or to put it another way, if the myth were true it would mean that working-class people lack intelligence and talent and do not work hard. But it does not take too much imagination to realise that class division and inequality has kept hidden from public recognition working-class people who might have made a significant contribution to, for example, the arts, science, or politics. As Ernst Bloch put it, 'history is crammed with those unfavourable circumstances which prevented the great talent from being aware of itself, and then from developing' (1995: 460). Or as the poet Thomas Gray expressed it, 'Full many a flower is born to blush unseen/And waste its sweetness on the desert air' (1997).

Under the myth of meritocracy class difference becomes a structure in which natural abilities and hard work locate you at the top, in the middle, or at the bottom. Social inequality is a symptom of lack of natural abilities and a failure to work hard. In other words, in a meritocratic society you get what you deserve. While this might sound logical and fair, and this is often how it is seen by those born into the dominant class, it is in effect little more than an ideological screen to disguise the real causes of class division and inequality.

Notes

1. Of course, what counts as necessities is historically and socially variable.
2. The misleadingly titled public schools can be very expensive indeed. Fees at Eton, Harrow and Winchester, for example, are more than £37,000 a year. The average annual wage in the UK is around £26,500. Comparing the two tells us a great deal about the ideological work required of the concept of meritocracy.

Further reading

Storey, John (ed.), *Cultural Theory and Popular Culture: A Reader*, 4th edn, Harlow: Pearson Education, 2009. This is the companion volume to the previous edition of this book. A fully updated 5th edition containing further readings is due for publication in 2018. An interactive website is also available (www.routledge.com/cw/storey), which contains helpful student resources and a glossary of terms for each chapter.

Atkinson, Will, *Class*, Cambridge: Polity, 2015. Leaving aside the book's rather simplistic understanding of Marxism, it is nevertheless an excellent introduction to debates on class and class struggle.

Biressi, Anita, and Nunn, Heather, *Class and Contemporary British Culture*, Basingstoke: Palgrave Macmillan, 2016. An excellent account of the entanglement of class and contemporary culture.

Clarke, John, et al., *Working Class Culture*, Centre for Contemporary Cultural Studies, Hutchinson University Library: London, 1979. A collection of interesting essays on class from the institutional home of cultural studies.

Edge, Sarah, *The Extraordinary Archive of Arthur J Munby: Photography, Class and Gender in the Nineteenth Century*, London: IB Tauris, 2017. A fascinating account of the representation of class in the nineteenth century.

Littler, Jo, *Against Meritocracy*, Abingdon: Routledge, 2017. An absolutely key book for understanding the ideological work performed by the concept of meritocracy.

Munt, Sally, *Cultural Studies and the Working Class*, London: Continuum, 2000. A very clear argument why cultural studies should return to class as a primary object of study.

Skeggs, Beverley, *Formations of Class & Gender*, London: Sage, 1997. One of the most significant attempts in cultural studies to foreground class as an explanatory concept.

Storey, John (ed.), *The Making of English Popular Culture*, Abingdon: Routledge, 2016. An excellent collection of essays that use class as an explanatory concept.

8 Gender and sexuality

Feminisms

'One of the most striking changes in the humanities in the 1980s has been the rise of gender as a category of analysis' (Showalter, 1990: 1). This is the opening sentence in Elaine Showalter's introduction to a book on gender and literary studies. There can be no doubt that without the emergence of feminism (second wave) in the early 1970s this sentence could not have been written. It is feminism that has placed gender on the academic agenda. However, the nature of the agenda has provoked a vigorous debate within feminism itself – so much so that it is really no longer possible, if it ever was, to talk of feminism as a monolithic body of research, writing and activity; one should really speak of *feminisms* (including post-feminism).

There are at least four different feminisms: radical, Marxist, liberal and what Sylvia Walby (1990) calls dual-systems theory. Each responds to women's oppression in a different way, positing different causes and different solutions. Radical feminists argue that women's oppression is the result of the system of patriarchy, a system of domination in which men as a group have power over women as a group. In Marxist feminist analysis the ultimate source of oppression is capitalism. The domination of women by men is seen as a consequence of capital's domination over labour. Liberal feminism differs from both Marxist and radical feminisms in that it does not posit a system – patriarchy or capitalism – determining the oppression of women. Instead, it tends to see the problem in terms of male prejudice against women, embodied in law or expressed in the exclusion of women from particular areas of life. Dual-systems theory represents the coming together of Marxist and radical feminist analysis in the belief that women's oppression is the result of a complex articulation of both patriarchy and capitalism. There are of course other feminist perspectives. Rosemary Tong (1992), for example, lists: liberal, Marxist, radical, psychoanalytic, socialist, existentialist and postmodern.

Feminism, like Marxism (discussed in Chapter 4), is always more than a body of academic texts and practices. It is also, and perhaps more fundamentally so, a political movement concerned with women's oppression and the ways and means to empower women – what bell hooks (1989) describes as 'finding a voice'.

As a metaphor for self-transformation . . . ['finding a voice'] . . . has been especially relevant for groups of women who have previously never had a public voice, women who are speaking and writing for the first time, including many women of color. Feminist focus on finding a voice may sound clichéd at times. . . . However, for women within oppressed groups . . . coming to voice is an act of resistance. Speaking becomes both a way to engage in active self-transformation and a rite of passage where one moves from being object to being subject. Only as subjects can we speak (12).

Feminism, therefore, is not just another method of reading texts. Nevertheless, it has proved an incredibly productive way of reading. As Showalter explains,

> There is an optical illusion which can be seen as either a goblet or two profiles. The images oscillate in their tension before us, one alternately superseding the other and reducing it to meaningless background. In the purest feminist literary theory we are similarly presented with a radical alteration of our vision, a demand that we see meaning in what has previously been empty space. The orthodox plot recedes, and another plot, hitherto submerged in the anonymity of the background, stands out in bold relief like a thumb print (quoted in Modleski, 1982: 25).

What Showalter claims for feminist literary criticism can equally be claimed for feminist work on popular culture. Popular culture has been the object of a great deal of feminist analysis. As Michèle Barrett (1982) points out, 'Cultural politics are crucially important to feminism because they involve struggles over *meaning*' (37; original emphasis). Lana Rakow (2009) makes much the same point, 'Feminists approaching popular culture proceed from a variety of theoretical positions that carry with them a deeper social analysis and political agenda' (195). Moreover, as Rakow observes,

> Though contemporary feminists have taken a diversity of approaches to popular culture, they have shared two major assumptions. The first is that women have a particular relationship to popular culture that is different from men's. . . . The second assumption is that understanding how popular culture functions both for women and for a patriarchal culture is important if women are to gain control over their own identities and change both social mythologies and social relations. . . . Feminists are saying that popular culture plays a role in patriarchal society and that theoretical analysis of this role warrants a major position in ongoing discussions (186).

Women at the cinema

In Chapter 5 we discussed Mulvey's (1975) extremely influential account of the female spectator. Mulvey's analysis is impressive and telling throughout, and despite the fact that it is made in an essay of fewer than thirteen pages, its influence has been enormous.[1] However, having acknowledged the essay's power and influence, it should also be noted that Mulvey's 'solution' is somewhat less telling than her analysis of the 'problem'. As an alternative to popular cinema, she calls for an avant-garde cinema 'which is radical in both a political and an aesthetic sense and challenges the basic assumptions of the mainstream film' (7–8). Some feminists, including Lorraine Gamman and Margaret Marshment (1988), have begun to doubt the 'universal validity' (5) of Mulvey's argument, questioning whether 'the gaze is always male', or whether it is 'merely "dominant"' (ibid.) among a range of different ways of seeing, including the female gaze. Moreover, as they insist,

> It is not enough to dismiss popular culture as merely serving the complementary systems of capitalism and patriarchy, peddling 'false consciousness' to the duped masses. It can also be seen as a site where meanings are contested and where dominant ideologies can be disturbed (1).

They advocate a cultural politics of intervention: 'we cannot afford to dismiss the popular by always positioning ourselves outside it' (2). It is from popular culture

> that most people in our society get their entertainment and their information. It is here that women (and men) are offered the culture's dominant definitions of themselves. It would therefore seem crucial to explore the possibilities and pitfalls of intervention in popular forms in order to find ways of making feminist meanings a part of our pleasures (1).

Christine Gledhill (2009) makes a similar point: she advocates a feminist cultural studies 'which relates commonly derided popular forms to the condition of their consumption in the lives of sociohistorical constituted audiences' (98). 'In this respect', she observes, 'feminist analysis of the woman's film and soap opera is beginning to counter more negative cine-psychoanalytic . . . accounts of female spectatorship, suggesting colonized, alienated or masochistic positions of identification' (ibid.).

Jackie Stacey's (1994) *Star Gazing: Hollywood and Female Spectatorship* presents a clear rejection of the universalism and textual determinism of much psychoanalytic work on female audiences. Her own analysis begins with the audience in the cinema rather than the audience constructed by the text. Her approach takes her from the traditions of film studies (as informed by Mulvey's position) to the theoretical concerns of cultural studies. Table 8.1 illustrates the differences marking out the two paradigms (24).

Stacey's study is based on an analysis of responses she received from a group of white British women, mostly aged over 60, and mostly working class, who had been keen cinema-goers in the 1940s and 1950s. On the basis of letters and completed questionnaires, she organized her analysis in terms of three discourses generated by the responses themselves: *escapism, identification* and *consumption.*

Escapism is one of the most frequently cited reasons given by the women for going to the cinema. Seeking to avoid the pejorative connotations of escapism, Stacey uses

Table 8.1 Film as object of study in film studies and cultural studies.

Film studies	Cultural studies
Spectatorship positioning	Audience readings
Textual analysis	Ethnographic methods
Meaning as production-led	Meaning as consumption-led
Passive viewer	Active viewer
Unconscious	Conscious
Pessimistic	Optimistic

Table 8.2 Popular texts and utopian solutions.

Social problems	Textual solutions
Scarcity	Abundance
Exhaustion	Energy
Dreariness	Intensity
Manipulation	Transparency
Fragmentation	Community[2]

Richard Dyer's (1999) excellent argument for the utopian sensibility of much popular entertainment, to construct an account of the utopian possibilities of Hollywood cinema for British women in the 1940s and 1950s. Dyer deploys a set of binary oppositions to reveal the relationship between the social problems experienced by audiences and the textual solutions played out in the texts of popular entertainment (Table 8.2).

For Dyer, entertainment's utopian sensibility is a property of the text. Stacey extends her argument to include the social context in which entertainment is experienced. The letters and completed questionnaires by the women made it clear to her that the pleasures of cinema expressed by them were always more than the visual and aural pleasures of the cinema text – they included the ritual of attending a screening, the shared experience and imagined community of the audience, the comfort and comparative luxury of the cinema building. It was never a simple matter of enjoying the glamour of Hollywood. As Stacey (1994) explains,

> The physical space of the cinema provided a transitional space between everyday life outside the cinema and the fantasy world of the Hollywood film about to be shown. Its design and decor facilitated the processes of escapism enjoyed by these female spectators. As such, cinemas were dream palaces not only in so far as they housed the screening of Hollywood fantasies, but also because of their design and decor which provided a feminised and glamorised space suitable for the cultural consumption of Hollywood films (99).

Escapism is always a historically specific two-way event. Stacey's women, therefore, were not only escaping *into* the luxury of the cinema and the glamour of Hollywood film, they were also escaping *from* the hardships and the restrictions of wartime and post-war Britain. It is this mix of Hollywood glamour, the relative luxury of the cinema interiors, experienced in a context of war and its aftermath of shortages and sacrifice, that generates 'the multi-layered meanings of escapism' (97).

Identification is Stacey's second category of analysis. She is aware of how it often functions in psychoanalytic criticism to point to the way in which film texts are said to position female spectators in the interests of patriarchy. According to this argument, identification is the means by which women collude and become complicit in their own oppression. However, by shifting the focus from the female spectator constructed within the film text to the actual female audience in the cinema, she claims that identification can be shown often to work quite differently. Her respondents continually draw attention to the way in which stars can generate fantasies of power, control and self-confidence, fantasies that can inform the activities of everyday life.

Her third category is *consumption*. Again, she rejects the rather monolithic position that figures consumption as entangled in a relationship, always successful, of domination, exploitation and control (see Storey 2017). She insists instead that 'consumption is a site of negotiated meanings, of resistance and of appropriation as well as of subjection and exploitation' (187). Much work in film studies, she claims, has tended to be production-led, fixing its critical gaze on 'the ways in which the film industry produces cinema spectators as consumers of both the film and the [associated] products of other industries' (188). Such analysis is never able to pose theoretically (let alone discuss in concrete detail) how audiences actually use and make meanings from the commodities they consume. She argues that the women's accounts reveal a more contradictory relationship between audiences and what they consume. For example, she highlights the ways in which 'American feminine ideals are clearly remembered as transgressing restrictive British femininity and thus employed as strategies of resistance' (198). Many of the letters and completed questionnaires reveal the extent to which Hollywood stars represented an alternative femininity, exciting and transgressive. In this way, Hollywood stars, and the commodities associated with them, could be *used* as a means to negotiate with, and to extend the boundaries of, what was perceived as a socially restrictive British femininity. She is careful not to argue that these women were free to construct through consumption entirely new feminine identities. Similarly, she does not deny that such forms of consumption may pander to the patriarchal gaze. The key to her position is the question of *excess*. The transformation of self-image brought about by the consumption of Hollywood stars and other associated commodities may produce identities and practices that are in excess of the needs of patriarchal culture. She contends that,

> [p]aradoxically, whilst commodity consumption for female spectators in mid to late 1950s Britain concerns producing oneself as a desirable object, it also offers an escape from what is perceived as the drudgery of domesticity and motherhood which increasingly comes to define femininity at this time. Thus, consumption

may signify an assertion of self in opposition to the self-sacrifice associated with marriage and motherhood in 1950s Britain (238).

Stacey's work represents something of a rebuke to the universalistic claims of much cine-psychoanalysis. By studying the audience, 'female spectatorship might be seen as a process of negotiating the dominant meanings of Hollywood cinema, rather than one of being passively positioned by it' (12). From this perspective, Hollywood's patriarchal power begins to look less monolithic, less seamless, its ideological success never guaranteed.

Reading romance

In *Loving with a Vengeance*, Tania Modleski (1982) claims that women writing about 'feminine narratives' tend to adopt one of three possible positions: 'dismissiveness; hostility – tending unfortunately to be aimed at the consumers of the narratives; or, most frequently, a flippant kind of mockery' (14). Against this, she declares: 'It is time to begin a feminist reading of women's reading' (34). She argues that what she calls 'mass-produced fantasies for women' (including the romance novel) 'speak to very real problems and tensions in women's lives' (14). In spite of this, she acknowledges that the way in which these narratives resolve problems and tensions will rarely 'please modern feminists: far from it' (25). However, the reader of fantasies and the feminist reader do have something in common: dissatisfaction with women's lives. For example, she claims, referring to Harlequin Romances, 'What Marx [Marx and Engels, 1957] said of religious suffering is equally true of "romantic suffering": it is "at the same time an expression of real suffering and a *protest* against real suffering"' (47).

Modleski does not condemn the novels or the women who read them. Rather, she condemns 'the conditions which have made them necessary', concluding that 'the contradictions in women's lives are more responsible for the existence of Harlequins than Harlequins are for the contradictions' (57). She drifts towards, then draws back from, the full force of a one-sided reading of Marx's position on religion, which would leave her, despite her protests to the contrary, having come very close to the mass culture position of popular culture as opiate. Nevertheless, she notes how 'students occasionally cut their women's studies classes to find out what is going on in their favourite soap opera. When this happens, it is time for us to stop merely opposing soap operas and to start incorporating them, and other mass-produced fantasies, into our study of women' (113–14).

Rosalind Coward's (1984) *Female Desire* is about women's pleasure in popular culture. The book explores fashion, romance, pop music, horoscopes, soap operas, food, cooking, women's magazines and other texts and practices that involve women in an endless cycle of pleasure and guilt: 'guilt – it's our speciality' (14). Coward does not approach the material as an 'outsider . . . a stranger to [pleasure and] guilt. The pleasures I describe are often my pleasures. . . . I don't approach these things as a distant critic but as someone examining myself, examining my own life under a microscope' (ibid.). Her position is in marked contrast to that, say, of the 'culture and civilization' tradition or the perspective of the Frankfurt School. Popular culture is not looked down on from an Olympian height as the disappointing, but rather predictable, culture of other people. This is a discourse about 'our' culture. Furthermore, she refuses to see the practices and representations of popular culture (the discourse of 'female desire') 'as the forcible imposition of false and limiting stereotypes' (16).

> Instead I explore the desire presumed by these representations, the desire which touches feminist and non-feminist women alike. But nor do I treat female desire as something unchangeable, arising from the female condition. I see the representations of female pleasure and desire as producing and sustaining feminine positions. These positions are neither distant roles imposed on us from outside which it would be easy to kick off, nor are they the essential attributes of femininity. Feminine positions are produced as responses to the pleasures offered to us; our subjectivity and identity are formed in the definitions of desire which encircle us. These are the experiences which make change such a difficult and daunting task, for female desire is constantly lured by discourses which sustain male privilege (ibid.).

Coward's interest in romantic fiction is in part inspired by the intriguing fact that 'over the past decade [the 1970s], the rise of feminism has been paralleled almost exactly by a mushroom growth in the popularity of romantic fiction' (190).[3] She believes two things about romantic novels: first, that 'they must still satisfy some very definite needs'; and second, that they offer evidence of, and contribute to, 'a very powerful and common fantasy' (ibid.). She claims that the fantasies played out in romantic fiction are 'pre-adolescent, very nearly pre-conscious' (191–2). She believes them to be 'regressive' in two key respects. On the one hand, they adore the power of the male in ways reminiscent of the very early child–father relationship, while on the other, they are regressive because of the attitude taken to female sexual desire – passive and without guilt, as the responsibility for sexual desire is projected on to the male. In other words, sexual desire is something men have and to which women merely respond. In short, romantic fiction replays the girl's experience of the Oedipal drama; only this time without its conclusion in female powerlessness; this time she does marry the father and replace the mother. Therefore there is a trajectory from subordination to a position of power (in the symbolic position of the mother). But, as Coward points out,

> Romantic fiction is surely popular because it . . . restores the childhood world of sexual relations and suppresses criticisms of the inadequacy of men, the suffocation of the family, or the damage inflicted by patriarchal power. Yet it simultaneously manages to avoid the guilt and fear which might come from that childhood world. Sexuality is defined firmly as the father's responsibility, and fear of suffocation is overcome because women achieve a sort of power in romantic fiction. Romantic fiction promises a secure world, promises that there will be safety with dependence, that there will be power with subordination (196).

Janice Radway (1987) begins her study of romance reading with the observation that the increased popularity of the genre can be in part explained by the 'important changes in book production, distribution, advertising and marketing techniques' (13). Taking issue with earlier accounts, Radway points out that the increasing success of romances may have as much to do with the sophisticated selling techniques of publishers, making romances more visible, more available, as with any simple notion of women's increased need for romantic fantasy.

Radway's study is based on research she carried out in 'Smithton', involving a group of forty-two women romance readers (mostly married with children). The women are all regular customers at the bookshop where 'Dorothy Evans' works. It was in fact Dot's reputation that attracted Radway to Smithton. Out of her own enthusiasm for the genre, Dot publishes a newsletter ('Dorothy's diary of romance reading') in which romances are graded in terms of their romantic worth. The newsletter, and Dot's general advice to customers, has in effect created what amounts to a small but significant symbolic community of romance readers. It is this symbolic community that is the focus of Radway's research. Research material was compiled through individual questionnaires, open-ended group discussions, face-to-face interviews and some informal discussions, and by observing the interactions between Dot and her regular customers at the bookshop. Radway supplemented this by reading the titles brought to her attention by the Smithton women.

The influence of Dot's newsletter on the purchasing patterns of readers alerted Radway to the inadequacy of a methodology that attempts to draw conclusions about the genre from a sample of current titles. She discovered that in order to understand the cultural significance of romance reading, it is necessary to pay attention to popular discrimination, to the process of selection and rejection that finds some titles satisfying and others not. She also encountered the actual *extent* of romance reading. The majority of the women she interviewed read every day, spending eleven to fifteen hours a week on romance reading. At least a quarter of the women informed her that, unless prevented by domestic and family demands, they preferred to read a romance from start to finish in one sitting. Consumption varies from one to fifteen books a week. Four informants actually claimed to read between fifteen and twenty-five romances a week.[4]

According to the Smithton women, the ideal romance is one in which an intelligent and independent woman with a good sense of humour is overwhelmed, after much suspicion and distrust, and some cruelty and violence, by the love of a man, who in the course of their relationship is transformed from an emotional pre-literate to someone who can *care* for her and *nurture* her in ways that are traditionally expected only from a woman to a man. As Radway explains: 'The romantic fantasy is . . . not a fantasy about discovering a uniquely interesting life partner, but a ritual wish to be cared for, loved, and validated in a particular way' (83). It is a fantasy about reciprocation; the wish to believe that men can bestow on women the care and attention women are expected regularly to bestow on men. But the romantic fantasy offers more than this; it recalls a time when the reader was in fact the recipient of an intense 'maternal' care.

Drawing on the work of Nancy Chodorow (1978), Radway claims that romantic fantasy is a form of regression in which the reader is imaginatively and emotionally transported to a time 'when she was the center of a profoundly nurturant individual's attention' (Radway, 1987: 84). However, unlike regression centred on the father as suggested by Coward, this is regression focused on the figure of the mother. Romance reading is therefore a means by which women can vicariously – through the hero–heroine relationship – experience the emotional succour that they themselves are expected to provide to others without adequate reciprocation for themselves in their everyday existence.

She also takes from Chodorow the notion of the female self as a self-in-relation-to others, and the male self as a self autonomous and independent. Chodorow argues that this results from the different relations that girls and boys have with their mothers. Radway sees a correlation between the psychological events described by Chodorow and the narrative pattern of the ideal romance: in the journey from identity in crisis to identity restored, 'the heroine successfully establishes by the end of the ideal narrative . . . the now familiar female self, the self-in-relation' (139). Radway also takes from Chodorow the belief that women emerge from the Oedipus complex with a 'triangular psychic structure intact', which means that 'not only do they need to con-nect themselves with a member of the opposite sex, but they also continue to require an intense emotional bond with someone who is reciprocally nurturant and protective in a maternal way' (140). In order to experience this regression to maternal emotional fulfilment, she has three options: lesbianism, a relationship with a man, or to seek fulfilment by other means. The homophobic nature of our culture limits the first; the nature of masculinity limits the second; romance reading may be an example of the third. Radway suggests that

> the fantasy that generates the romance originates in the oedipal desire to love and be loved by an individual of the opposite sex and in the continuing pre-oedipal wish that is part of a woman's inner-object configuration, the wish to regain the love of the mother and all that it implies – erotic pleasure, symbiotic completion, and identity confirmation (146).

The resolution to the ideal romance provides perfect triangular satisfaction: 'fatherly protection, motherly care, and passionate adult love' (149).

The failed romance is unable to provide these satisfactions because on the one hand, it is too violent, and on the other, it concludes sadly, or with an unconvincing happy ending. This highlights in an unpleasurable way the two structuring anxieties of all romances. The first is the fear of male violence. In the ideal romance, this is contained by revealing it to be not the fearful thing it appears to be, either an illusion or benign. The second anxiety is the 'fear of an awakened female sexuality and its impact on men' (169). In the failed romance, female sexuality is not confined to a permanent and loving relationship; nor is male violence convincingly brought under control. Together they find form and expression in the violent punishment inflicted on women who are seen as sexually promiscuous. In short, the failed romance is unable to produce a read-ing experience in which emotional fulfilment is satisfied through the vicarious sharing of the heroine's journey from a crisis of identity to an identity restored in the arms of a nurturing male. Whether a romance is good or bad is ultimately determined by the kind of relationship the reader can establish with the heroine.

> If the events of the heroine's story provoke too intense feelings such as anger at men, fear of rape and violence, worry about female sexuality, or worry about the need to live with an unexciting man, that romance will be discarded as a failure or judged to be very poor. If, on the other hand, those events call forth feelings of excitement, satisfaction, contentment, self-confidence, pride, and power, it matters less what events are used or how they are marshalled. In the end, what counts most is the reader's sense that for a short time she has become other and been elsewhere. She must close that book reassured that men and marriage really do mean good things for women. She must also turn back to her daily round of duties, emotionally reconstituted and replenished, feeling confident of her worth and convinced of her ability and power to deal with the problems she knows she must confront (184).

In this way, the Smithton women 'partially reclaim the patriarchal form of the romance for their own use' (ibid.). The principal 'psychological benefits' of reading romance novels derive from 'the ritualistic repetition of a single, immutable cultural myth' (198, 199). The fact that 60 per cent of the Smithton readers find it occasionally necessary to read the ending first, to ensure that the experience of the novel will not counteract the satisfactions of the underlying myth, suggests quite strongly that it is the underlying myth of the nurturing male that is ultimately most important in the Smithton women's experience of romance reading.

Following a series of comments from the Smithton women, Radway was forced to the conclusion that if she really wished to understand their view of romance reading she must relinquish her preoccupation with the text, and consider also the very *act* of romance reading itself. In conversations it became clear that when the women used the term 'escape' to describe the pleasures of romance reading, the term was operating in a double but related sense. As we have seen, it can be used to describe the process of identification between the reader and the heroine/hero relationship. But it became clear that the term was also used 'literally to describe the act of denying the present, which they believe they accomplish each time they begin to read a book and are drawn into its story' (90). Dot revealed to Radway that the very act of women reading is often found threatening by men. Women reading is seen as time reclaimed from the demands of family and domestic duties. Many of the Smithton women describe romance reading as 'a special gift' they give themselves. To explain this, Radway cites Chodorow's view of the patriarchal family as one in which, 'There is a fundamental asymmetry in daily reproduction . . . men are socially and psychologically reproduced by women, but women are reproduced (or not) largely by themselves' (91, 94). Romance reading is therefore a small but not insignificant contribution to the emotional reproduction of the Smithton women: 'a temporary but literal denial of the demands women recognise as an integral part of their roles as nurturing wives and mothers' (97). And, as Radway suggests, 'Although this experience is vicarious, the pleasure it induces is nonetheless real' (100).

> I think it is logical to conclude that romance reading is valued by the Smithton women because the experience itself is different from ordinary existence. Not only is it a relaxing release from the tension produced by daily problems and responsibilities, but it creates a time or a space within which a woman can be entirely on her own, preoccupied with her personal needs, desires, and pleasure. It is also a means of transportation or escape to the exotic or, again, to that which is different (61).

The conclusion *Reading the Romance* finally comes to is that it is at present very difficult to draw absolute conclusions about the cultural significance of romance reading. To focus on the act of reading or to focus on the narrative fantasy of the texts produces different, contradictory answers. The first suggests that 'romance reading is oppositional because it allows the women to refuse momentarily their self-abnegating social role' (210). To focus on the second suggests that 'the romance's narrative structure embodies a simple recapitulation and recommendation of patriarchy and its constituent social practices and ideologies' (ibid.). It is this difference, 'between the meaning of the act and the meaning of the text as read' (ibid.), that must be brought into tight focus if we are to understand the full cultural significance of romance reading.

On one thing Radway is clear: women do not read romances out of a sense of contentment with patriarchy. Romance reading contains an element of utopian protest, a longing for a better world. But against this, the narrative structure of the romance appears to suggest that male violence and male indifference are really expressions of love waiting to be decoded, and made benignly manifest, by the right woman. This suggests that patriarchy is a problem only until women learn how to read it properly. It is these complexities and contradictions that Radway refuses to ignore or pretend to resolve. Her only certainty is that it is too soon to know if romance reading can be cited simply as an ideological agent of the patriarchal social order.

> I feel compelled to point out . . . that neither this study nor any other to date provides enough evidence to corroborate this argument fully. We simply do not know what practical effects the repetitive reading of romances has on the way women behave after they have closed their books and returned to their normal, ordinary round of daily activities (217).

Therefore we must continue to acknowledge the activity of readers – their selections, purchases, interpretations, appropriations, uses, etc. – as an essential part of the cultural processes and complex practices of making meaning in the lived cultures of everyday life. By paying attention in this way we increase the possibility of 'articulating the differences between the repressive imposition of ideology and oppositional practices that, though limited in their scope and effect, at least dispute or contest the control of ideological forms' (221–2). The ideological power of romances may be great, but where there is power there is always resistance. The resistance may be confined to selective acts of consumption – dissatisfactions momentarily satisfied by the articulation of limited protest and utopian longing – but as feminists

[w]e should seek it out not only to understand its origins and its utopian longing but also to learn how best to encourage it and bring it to fruition. If we do not, we have already conceded the fight and, in the case of the romance at least, admitted the impossibility of creating a world where the vicarious pleasure supplied by its reading would be unnecessary (222).

Charlotte Brunsdon (1991) calls *Reading the Romance* 'the most extensive scholarly investigation of the act of reading', crediting Radway with having installed in the classroom 'the figure of the ordinary woman' (372). In a generally sympathetic review of the British edition of *Reading the Romance*, Ien Ang (2009) makes a number of criticisms of Radway's approach. She is unhappy with the way in which Radway makes a clear distinction between feminism and romance reading: 'Radway, the researcher, is a feminist and not a romance fan, the Smithton women, the researched, are romance readers and *not* feminists' (584). Ang sees this as producing a feminist politics of 'them' and 'us' in which non-feminist women play the role of an alien 'them' to be recruited to the cause. In her view, feminists should not set themselves up as guardians of the true path. According to Ang, this is what Radway does in her insistence that '"real" social change can only be brought about . . . if romance readers would stop reading romances and become feminist activists instead' (585). As we shall see shortly, in my discussion of *Watching Dallas*, Ang does not believe that one (romance reading) excludes the other (feminism). Radway's 'vanguardist . . . feminist politics' leads only to 'a form of political moralism, propelled by a desire to make "them" more like "us"'. Ang believes that what is missing from Radway's analysis is a discussion of pleasure as pleasure. Pleasure is discussed, but always in terms of its unreality – its vicariousness, its function as compensation and its falseness. Ang's complaint is that such an approach focuses too much on the effects, rather than the mechanisms, of pleasure. Ultimately, for Radway, it always becomes a question of 'the *ideological function* of pleasure'. Against this, Ang argues for seeing pleasure as something that can 'empower' women and not as something that always works 'against their own "real" interests' (585–6). Janice Radway (1994) has reviewed this aspect of her work and concluded,

Although I tried very hard not to dismiss the activities of the Smithton women and made an effort to understand the act of romance reading as a positive response to the conditions of everyday life, my account unwittingly repeated the sexist assumption that has warranted a large portion of the commentary on romance. It was still motivated, that is, by the assumption that someone ought to worry responsibly about the effect of fantasy on women readers . . . [and therefore repeated] the familiar pattern whereby the commentator distances herself as knowing analyst from those who, engrossed and entranced by fantasy, cannot know. . . . Despite the fact that I wanted to claim the romance for feminism, this familiar opposition between blind fantasy and perspicacious knowing continued to operate within my account. Thus I would now link it [*Reading the Romance*], along with Tania Modleski's *Loving with a Vengeance*, with the first early efforts to understand the changing genre, a stage in the debate that was characterised most fundamentally, I believe, by suspicion about fantasy, daydream, and play (19).

She cites with approval Alison Light's (1984) point that feminist 'cultural politics must not become "a book-burning legislature"', nor should feminists fall into the traps of moralism or dictatorship when discussing romances. '"It is conceivable . . . that Barbara Cartland could turn you into a feminist. Reading is never simply a linear con job but a . . . process which therefore remains dynamic and open to change"' (quoted in Radway, 1994: 220).[5]

Watching Dallas

Ien Ang's *Watching Dallas* was originally published in the Netherlands in 1982. The version under discussion here is the revised edition translated into English in 1985. The context for Ang's study is the emergence, in the early 1980s, of the American 'prime time soap' *Dallas* as an international success (watched in over ninety countries). In the Netherlands, *Dallas* was regularly watched by 52 per cent of the population. With its spectacular success, *Dallas* soon gathered around itself a whole discourse of activity – from extensive coverage in the popular press to souvenir hats reading 'I Hate JR'. It also attracted critics such as Jack Lang, the French Minister of Culture, who viewed it as the latest example of 'American cultural imperialism' (quoted in Ang, 1985: 2). Whether cause of pleasure or threat to 'national identity', *Dallas* made an enormous impact worldwide in the early 1980s. It is in this context that Ang placed the following advertisement in *Viva*, a Dutch women's magazine: 'I like watching the TV serial *Dallas*, but often get odd reactions to it. Would anyone like to write and tell me why you like watching it too, or dislike it? I should like to assimilate these reactions in my university thesis. Please write to . . .' (Ang, 1985: 10).

Following the advertisement she received forty-two letters (thirty-nine from women or girls), from both lovers and haters of *Dallas*. These form the empirical basis of her study of the pleasure(s) of watching *Dallas* for its predominantly female audience. She is concerned not with pleasure understood as the satisfaction of a pre-existent need, but with 'the mechanisms by which pleasure is aroused' (9). Instead of the question 'What are the effects of pleasure?' she poses the question 'What is the mechanism of pleasure; how is it produced and how does it work?'

Ang writes as 'an intellectual and a feminist', but also as someone who has 'always particularly liked watching soap operas like *Dallas*' (12). Again, we are a long way from the *view from above* that has so often characterized the relations between cultural theory and popular culture.

> The admission of the reality of this pleasure [my own] . . . formed the starting point for this study. I wanted in the first place to understand this pleasure, without

having to pass judgment on whether *Dallas* is good or bad, from a political, social or aesthetic view. Quite the contrary; in my opinion it is important to emphasise how difficult it is to make such judgments – and hence to try to formulate the terms for a progressive cultural politics – when pleasure is at stake (ibid.).

For Ang's letter-writers the pleasures or displeasures of *Dallas* are inextricably linked with questions of 'realism'. The extent to which a letter-writer finds the programme 'good' or 'bad' is determined by whether they find it 'realistic' (good) or 'unrealistic' (bad). Critical of both 'empiricist realism' (a text is considered realistic to the extent to which it adequately reflects that which exists outside itself) (34–8) and 'classic realism' (the claim that realism is an illusion created by the extent to which a text can successfully conceal its constructedness) (38–41), she contends that *Dallas* is best understood as an example of what she calls 'emotional realism' (41–7). She connects this to the way in which *Dallas* can be read on two levels: the level of denotation and the level of connotation (see Chapter 6). The level of denotation refers to the literal content of the programme, general storyline, character interactions, etc. The level of connotation(s) refers to the associations, implications, that resonate from the storyline and character interactions, etc.

> It is striking; the same things, people, relations and situations which are regarded at the denotative level as unrealistic, and unreal, are at the connotative level apparently not seen at all as unreal, but in fact as 'recognisable'. Clearly, in the connotative reading process the denotative level of the text is put in brackets (42).

Viewing *Dallas*, like watching any other programme, is a selective process, reading across the text from denotation to connotation, weaving our sense of self in and out of the narrative. As one letter-writer says: 'Do you know why I like watching it? I think it's because those problems and intrigues, the big and little pleasures and troubles occur in our own lives too. . . . In real life I know a horror like JR, but he's just an ordinary builder' (43). It is this ability to make our own lives connect with the lives of a family of Texan millionaires that gives the programme its emotional realism. We may not be rich, but we may have other fundamental things in common: relationships and broken relationships, happiness and sadness, illness and health. Those who find it realistic shift the focus of attention from the particularity of the narrative ('denotation') to the generality of its themes ('connotation').

Ang uses the term a 'tragic structure of feeling' (46) to describe the way in which *Dallas* plays with the emotions in an endless musical chairs of happiness and misery. As one letter-writer told her: 'Sometimes I really enjoy having a good cry with them. And why not? In this way my other bottled-up emotions find an outlet' (49). Viewers who 'escape' in this way are not so much engaging in 'a denial of reality as playing with it . . . [in a] game that enables one to place the limits of the fictional and the real under discussion, to make them fluid. And in that game an imaginary participation in the fictional world is experienced as pleasurable' (ibid.).

Whatever else is involved, part of the pleasure of *Dallas* is quite clearly connected to the amount of fluidity viewers are able or willing to establish between its fictional world and the world of their day-to-day existence. In order to activate *Dallas*'s tragic structure of feeling the viewer must have the necessary cultural capital to occupy a 'reading formation'[6] informed by what she calls, following Peter Brooks (1976), the 'melodramatic imagination'. The melodramatic imagination is the articulation of a way of seeing that finds in ordinary day-to-day existence, with its pain and triumphs, its victories and defeats, a world that is as profoundly meaningful and significant as the world of classical tragedy. In a world mostly cut loose from the certainties of religion, the melodramatic imagination offers a means of organizing reality into meaningful contrasts and conflicts. As a narrative form committed to melodrama's emphatic contrasts, conflicts and emotional excess, *Dallas* is well placed to give sustenance to, and make manifest, the melodramatic imagination. For those who see the world in this way (Ang claims that it demands a cultural competence most often shared by women), 'the pleasure of *Dallas* . . . is not a *compensation* for the presumed drabness of daily life, nor a flight from it, but a *dimension* of it' (Ang, 1985: 83). The melodramatic imagination activates *Dallas*'s tragic structure of feeling, which in turn produces the pleasure of emotional realism. However, because the melodramatic imagination is an effect of a specific reading formation, it follows that not all viewers of *Dallas* will activate the text in this way.

A key concept in Ang's analysis is what she calls 'the ideology of mass culture' (15). The ideology *articulates* (in the Gramscian sense discussed in Chapter 4) the view that popular culture is the product of capitalist commodity production and is therefore subject to the laws of the capitalist market economy; the result of which is the seemingly endless circulation of degraded commodities, whose only real significance is that they manipulate consumers and make a profit for their producers. She quite rightly sees this as a distorted and one-sided version of Marx's analysis of capitalist commodity production, in that it allows 'exchange value' to completely mask 'use value' (see Chapter 12). Against this, she insists, as would Marx, that it is not possible to read off how a product might be consumed from the means by which it was produced. The ideology of mass culture, like other ideological discourses, seeks to interpellate individuals into specific subject positions (see discussion of Althusser in Chapter 4). The letters suggest four positions from which to consume *Dallas*: (i) those who hate the programme; (ii) ironical viewers; (iii) fans, and (iv) populists.

Those letter-writers who claim to hate *Dallas* draw most clearly on the ideology. They use it in two ways. The programme is identified first negatively as an example of mass culture; second, as a means to account for and support their dislike of the programme. As Ang puts it, 'their reasoning boils down to this: "*Dallas* is obviously bad because it's mass culture, and that's why I dislike it"' (95–6). In this way, the ideology both comforts and reassures: 'it makes a search for more detailed and personal explanations superfluous, because it provides a finished explanatory model that convinces, sounds logical and radiates legitimacy' (96). This is not to say that it is wrong to dislike *Dallas*, only that professions of dislike are often made without thinking, in fact with a confidence born of uncritical thought.

Viewers who occupy the second position demonstrate how it is possible to like *Dallas* and still subscribe to the ideology of mass culture. The contradiction is resolved by 'mockery and irony' (97). *Dallas* is subjected to an ironizing and mocking commentary in which it 'is transformed from a seriously intended melodrama to the reverse: a comedy to be laughed at. Ironizing viewers therefore do not take the text as it presents itself, but invert its preferred meaning through ironic commentary' (98). From this position the pleasure of *Dallas* derives from the fact that it is *bad* – pleasure and bad mass culture are reconciled in an instant. As one of the letter-writers puts it: 'Of course *Dallas* is mass culture and therefore bad, but precisely because I am so well aware of that I can really enjoy watching it and poke fun at it' (100). For both the ironizing viewer and the hater of *Dallas*, the ideology of mass culture operates as a bedrock of common sense, making judgements obvious and self-evident. Although both operate within the normative standards of the ideology, the difference between them is marked by the question of pleasure. On the one hand, the ironizers can have pleasure without guilt, in the sure and declared knowledge that they know mass culture is bad. On the other hand, the haters, although secure in the same knowledge, can, nevertheless, suffer 'a conflict of feelings if, *in spite of this*, they cannot escape its seduction' (101; original emphasis).

Third, there are the fans, those who love *Dallas*. For the viewers who occupy the previous two positions, to actually like *Dallas* without resort to irony is to be identified as someone duped by mass culture. As one letter-writer puts it: 'The aim is simply to rake in money, lots of money. And people try to do that by means of all these things – sex, beautiful people, wealth. And you always have people who fall for it' (103). The claim is presented with all the confidence of having the full weight of the ideology's discursive support. Ang analyses the different strategies that those who love *Dallas* must use to deal consciously and unconsciously with such condescension. The first strategy is to 'internalize' the ideology; to acknowledge the 'dangers' of *Dallas*, but to declare one's ability to deal with them in order to derive pleasure from the programme. It is a little like the heroin user in the early 1990s British drugs awareness campaign, who, against the warnings of impending addiction, declares: 'I can handle it.' A second strategy used by fans is to confront the ideology of mass culture as one letter-writer does: 'Many people find it worthless or without substance. But I think it does have substance' (105). But, as Ang points out, the writer remains firmly within the discursive constraints of the ideology as she attempts to relocate *Dallas* in a different relationship to the binary oppositions – with substance/without substance, good/bad. 'This letter-writer "negotiates" as it were within the discursive space created by the ideology of mass culture, she does not situate herself outside it and does not speak from an opposing ideological position' (106). A third strategy of defence deployed by fans against the normative standards of the ideology of mass culture is to use irony. These fans are different from Ang's second category of viewer, the ironist, in that the strategy involves the use of 'surface irony' to justify what is in all other respects a form of non-ironic pleasure. Irony is used to condemn the characters as 'horrible' people, while at the same time demonstrating an intimate knowledge of the programme and a great involvement in its narrative development and character interactions. The letter-writer who uses this strategy is caught between the dismissive power of the ideology and the pleasure she obviously derives from watching *Dallas*. Her letter seems to suggest that she adheres to the former when viewing with friends, and to the latter when viewing alone (and perhaps secretly when viewing with friends). As Ang explains: 'irony is here a defence mechanism with which this letter-writer tries to fulfil the social norms set by the ideology of mass culture, while secretly she "really" likes *Dallas*' (109).

As Ang shows, the fans of *Dallas* find it necessary to locate their pleasure in relation to the ideology of mass culture; they 'internalize' the ideology; they 'negotiate' with the ideology; they use 'surface irony' to defend their pleasure against the withering dismissal of the ideology. What all these strategies of defence reveal is that 'there is no clear-cut ideological alternative which can be employed against the ideology of mass culture – at least no alternative that offsets the latter in power of conviction and coherence' (109–10). The struggle therefore, as so far described, between those who like *Dallas* and those who dislike it, is an unequal struggle between those who argue from within the discursive strength and security of the ideology of mass culture, and those who resist from within (for them) its inhospitable confines. 'In short, these fans do not seem to be able to take up an effective ideological position – an identity – from which they can say in a positive way and independently of the ideology of mass culture: "I like *Dallas* because . . .".' (ibid.).

The final viewing position revealed in the letters, one that might help these fans, is a position informed by the ideology of populism. At the core of this ideology is the belief that one person's taste is of equal value to another person's taste. As one letter-writer puts it: 'I find the people who react oddly rather ludicrous – they can't do anything about someone's taste. And anyway they might find things pleasant that you just can't stand seeing or listening to' (113). The ideology of populism insists that as taste is an autonomous category, continually open to individual inflection, it is absolutely meaningless to pass aesthetic judgements on other people's preferences. Given that this would seem to be an ideal discourse from which to defend one's pleasure in *Dallas*, why do so few of the letter-writers adopt it? Ang's answer is to point to the ideology's extremely limited critical vocabulary. After one has repeated 'there's no accounting for taste' a few times, the argument begins to appear somewhat bankrupt. Compared to this, the ideology of mass culture has an extensive and elaborate range of arguments and theories. Little wonder, then, that when invited to explain why they like or dislike *Dallas*, the letter-writers find it difficult to escape the normative discourse of the ideology of mass culture.

However, according to Ang, there are ways to escape: it is the very 'theoretical' nature of the discourse which restricts its influence 'to people's opinions and rational con-sciousness, to the discourse people use when *talking* about culture. These opinions and rationalizations need not, however, necessarily prescribe people's cultural *practices*' (115). This would in part explain the contradictions experienced by some letter-writers: confronted by both 'the intellectual dominance of the ideology of mass culture and the "spontaneous", practical attraction of the populist ideology' (ibid.). The difficulty with adopting the populist ideology for a radical politics of popular culture is that it has already been appropriated by the culture industries for its own purposes of profit maximization. However, drawing on the work of Bourdieu, Ang argues that populism is related to the 'popular aesthetic', in which the moral categories of middle-class taste are replaced by an emphasis on contingency, on pluralism and, above all, on pleasure (see Chapter 12). Pleasure, for Ang, is the key term in a transformed feminist cultural politics. Feminism must break with 'the paternalism of the ideology of mass culture . . . [in which w]omen are . . . seen as the passive victims of the deceptive messages of soap operas . . . [their] pleasure . . . totally disregarded' (118–19). Even when pleasure is considered, it is there only to be condemned as an obstruction to the feminist goal of women's liberation. The question Ang poses is: can pleasure through identification with the women of 'women's weepies' or the emotionally masochistic women of soap operas, 'have a meaning for women which is relatively independent of their political attitudes'? (133). Her answer is yes: fantasy and fiction do not

> function in place of, but beside, other dimensions of life (social practice, moral or political consciousness). It . . . is a source of pleasure because it puts 'reality' in parenthesis, because it constructs imaginary solutions for real contradictions which in their fictional simplicity and their simple fictionality step outside the tedious complexity of the existing social relations of dominance and subordination (135).

Of course this does not mean that representations of women do not matter. They can still be condemned for being reactionary in an ongoing cultural politics. But to experience pleasure from them is a completely different issue: 'it need not imply that we are also bound to take up these positions and solutions in our relations to our loved ones and friends, our work, our political ideals, and so on' (ibid.).

> Fiction and fantasy, then, function by making life in the present pleasurable, or at least livable, but this does not by any means exclude radical political activity or consciousness. It does not follow that feminists must not persevere in trying to produce new fantasies and fight for a place for them. . . . It does, however, mean that, where cultural consumption is concerned, no fixed standard exists for gauging the 'progressiveness' of a fantasy. The personal may be political, but the personal and the political do not always go hand in hand (135–6).

In an unnecessarily hostile review of *Watching Dallas*, Dana Polan (1988) accuses Ang of simplifying questions of pleasure by not bringing into play psychoanalysis. He also claims that Ang's attack on the ideology of mass culture simply reverses the valuations implicit and explicit in the high culture/popular culture divide. Instead of the consumer of high culture imagining 'high taste as a kind of free expression of a full subjectivity always in danger of being debased by vulgar habits', Ang is accused of presenting 'the fan of mass culture as a free individual in danger of having his/her open access to immediate pleasure corrupted by artificial and snobbish values imposed from on high' (198). Polan claims that Ang is attacking 'an antiquarian and anachronistic approach to mass culture', and that she is out of touch with the new postmodern sensibility, still clinging instead 'to mythic notions of culture as tragedy, culture as meaning' (202). The idea that the ideology of mass culture is antiquated and anachronistic might be true in the fantasy realms of American academic psychoanalytic cultural criticism, but it is still very much alive in the conscious/unconscious world of everyday culture. Moreover, while culture might be more than meaning (see Chapter 4), it is always nonetheless about signification.

Reading women's magazines

In the Preface to *Inside Women's Magazines*, Janice Winship (1987) explains how she has been doing research on women's magazines since 1969. She also tells us that it was also around the same time that she began to regard herself as a feminist. Integrating the two, she admits, has sometimes proved difficult; often it was hinted that she should research 'something more important politically' (xiii). But she insists that the two must be integrated: 'to simply dismiss women's magazines was also to dismiss the lives of millions of women who read and enjoyed them each week. More than that, I still enjoyed them, found them useful and escaped with them. And I knew I couldn't be the only feminist who was a "closet" reader' (ibid.). As she continues, this did not mean that she was not (or is not still) critical of women's magazines; it meant what is crucial to a feminist cultural politics is this dialectic of 'attraction and rejection' (ibid.).

> Many of the guises of femininity in women's magazines contribute to the secondary status from which we still desire to free ourselves. At the same time it is the dress of femininity which is both source of the pleasure of being a woman – and not a man – and in part the raw material for a feminist vision of the future. . . . Thus for feminists one important issue women's magazines can raise is how do we take over their feminine ground to create new untrammelled images of and for ourselves? (xiii–xiv).

Part of the aim of *Inside Women's Magazines* is, 'then, to explain the appeal of the magazine formula and to critically consider its limitations and potential for change' (8).

Since their inception in the late eighteenth century, women's magazines have offered their readers a mixture of advice and entertainment. Regardless of politics, women's magazines continue to operate as survival manuals, providing their readers with practical advice on how to survive in a patriarchal culture. This might take the form of an explicit feminist politics, as in *Spare Rib*, for example; or stories of women triumphing over adversity, as, for example, in *Woman's Own*. The politics may be different, but the formula is much the same.

Women's magazines appeal to their readers by means of a combination of entertainment and useful advice. This appeal, according to Winship, is organized around a range of 'fictions'. These can be the visual fictions of advertisements, or items on fashion, cookery or family and home. They can also be actual fictions: romantic serials, five-minute stories, for example. There are also the stories of the famous and reports of events in the lives of 'ordinary' women and men. Each in its different way attempts to draw the reader into the world of the magazine, and ultimately into a world of consumption. This often leads to women 'being caught up in defining their own femininity, inextricably, through consumption' (39). But pleasure is not totally dependent on purchase. She recalls how in the hot July in which she wrote *Inside Women's Magazines*, without any intention of buying the product, she gained enormous visual pleasure from a magazine advertisement showing a woman diving into an ocean surrealistically continuous with the tap-end of a bath. As she explains,

> We recognise and relish the vocabulary of dreams in which ads deal; we become involved in the fictions they create; but we know full well that those commodities will not elicit the promised fictions. It doesn't matter. Without bothering to buy the product we can vicariously indulge in the good life through the image alone. This is the compensation for the experience you do not and cannot have (56).

Magazine advertisements, like the magazines themselves, therefore provide a terrain on which to dream. In this way, they generate a desire for fulfilment (through consumption). Paradoxically, this is deeply pleasurable *because* it also always acknowledges the existence of the labours of the everyday.

> They would not offer quite the same pleasure, however, if it were not expected of women that they perform the various labours around fashion and beauty, food and furnishing. These visuals acknowledge those labours while simultaneously enabling the reader to avoid doing them. In everyday life 'pleasure' for women can only be achieved by accomplishing these tasks; here the image offers a temporary substitute, as well as providing an (allegedly) easy, often enjoyable pathway to their accomplishment (56–7).

Desire is generated for something more than the everyday, yet it can be accomplished only by what is for most women an everyday activity – shopping. What is ultimately being sold in the fictions of women's magazines, in editorial or advertisements, fashion and home furnishing items, cookery and cosmetics, is successful and therefore *pleasurable* femininity. Follow *this* practical advice or buy *this* product and be a better lover, a better mother, a better wife and a better woman. The problem with all this from a feminist perspective is that it is always constructed around a mythical *individual* woman, situated *outside* the influence of powerful social and cultural structures and constraints.

The commitment to the 'individual solution' is often revealed by the way in which women's magazines also seek to construct 'fictional collectivities' (67) of women. This can be seen in the insistent 'we' of editorials; but it is also there in the reader/editor interactions of the letters page. Here we often find women making sense of the everyday world through a mixture of optimism and fatalism. Winship identifies these tensions as an expression of women being 'ideologically bound to the personal terrain and in a position of relative powerlessness about public events' (70). Like the so-called 'triumph over tragedy' stories, the readers' letters and editorial responses often reveal a profound commitment to the 'individual solution'. Both 'teach' the same parable: individual effort will overcome all odds. The reader is interpellated as admiring subject (see discussion of Althusser in Chapter 4), her own problems put in context, able to carry on. Short stories work in much the same way. What also links these different 'fictions' is 'that the human triumphs they detail are emotional and not material ones' (76). In many ways this is essential for the continued existence of the magazines' imagined communities; for to move from the emotional to the material is to run the risk of encountering the divisive presence of, for example, class, sexuality, disability, ethnicity and 'race'.

> Thus the 'we women' feeling magazines construct is actually comprised of different cultural groups; the very notion of 'we' and 'our world', however, constantly under-cuts those divisions to give the semblance of a unity inside magazines. Outside, when the reader closes her magazine, she is no longer 'friends' with Esther Rantzen and her ilk; but while it lasted it has been a pleasant and reassuring dream (77).

This is perhaps even more evident on the problem page. Although the problems are personal, and therefore seek personal solutions, Winship argues that 'unless women have access to knowledge which explains personal lives in social terms . . . the onus on "you" to solve "your" problem is likely to be intimidating or . . . only lead to frustrated "solutions"' (80). She gives the example of a letter about a husband (with a sexual past) who cannot forget or forgive his wife's sexual past. As Winship points out, a personal solution to this problem cannot begin to tackle the social and cultural heritage of the sexual double standard. To pretend otherwise is to seriously mislead.

> Agony aunties (and magazines) act as 'friends' to women – they bring women together in their pages and yet by not providing the knowledge to allow women to see the history of their common social condition, sadly and ironically, they come between women, expecting, and encouraging, them to do alone what they can only do together (ibid.).

At the centre of Winship's book are three chapters, which in turn discuss the individual and family values of *Woman's Own*, the (hetero)sexual liberation ideology of *Cosmopolitan* and the feminist politics of *Spare Rib*. I have space only to make one point with reference to these chapters. Discussing *Spare Rib*'s reviews of popular film and television, Winship responds with comments that echo through much recent 'post-feminist' analysis (and much of the work discussed in this chapter) on popular culture:

> These reviews . . . bolster the reviewer's position and raise feminism and feminists to the lofty pedestal of 'having seen the light', with the consequent dismissal not only of a whole range of cultural events but also of many women's pleasurable and interested experiences of them. Whether intentionally or not, feminists are setting themselves distinctly apart: 'us' who know and reject most popular cultural forms (including women's magazines), 'them' who remain in ignorance and continue to buy Woman's Own or watch Dallas. The irony, however, is that many of 'us' feel like 'them': closet readers and viewers of this fare (140).

In *Reading Women's Magazines*, Joke Hermes (1995) begins with an observation on previous feminist work on women's magazines: 'I have always felt strongly that the feminist struggle in general should be aimed at claiming respect. It is probably for that reason that I have never felt comfortable with the majority of (feminist) work that has been done on women's magazines. Almost all of these studies show *concern* rather than *respect* for those who read women's magazines' (1; original emphasis). This kind of approach (what might be called 'modernist feminism'), she maintains, generates a form of media criticism in which the feminist scholar is both 'prophet and exorcist' (ibid.). As she explains, 'Feminists using modernity discourse speak on behalf of others who are, implicitly, thought to be unable to see for themselves how bad such media texts as women's magazines are. They need to be enlightened; they need good feminist texts in order to be saved from their false consciousness and to live a life free of false depictions as mediated by women's magazines, of where a woman might find happiness' (ibid.).

Against this way of thinking and working, Hermes advocates what she calls 'a more postmodern view, in which respect rather than concern – or, for that matter, celebration, a term often seen as the hallmark of a postmodern perspective – would have a central place' (ibid.). She is aware 'that readers of all kinds (including we critics) enjoy texts in some contexts that we are critical of in other contexts' (2). The focus of her study, therefore, is to 'understand how women's magazines are read while accepting the preferences of [the women she interviewed]' (ibid.). Working from the perspective of 'a postmodern feminist position', she advocates an 'appreciation that readers are producers of meaning rather than the cultural dupes of the media institutions. Appreciation too of the local and specific meanings we give to media texts and the different identities any one person may bring to bear on living our multi faceted lives in societies saturated with media images and texts of which women's magazines are a part' (ibid.). More specifically, she seeks to situate her work in a middle ground between a focus on how meanings are made of specific texts (Ang, 1985, Radway, 1987, for example) and a focus on the contexts of media consumption (Gray, 1992, Morley, 1986, for example). In other words, rather than begin with a text and show how people appropriate it and make it meaningful, or begin with the contexts of consumption and show how these constrain the ways in which appropriation and the making of meaning can take place, she has 'tried to reconstruct the diffuse genre or set of genres that is called women's magazines and [to demonstrate] how they become meaningful exclusively through the perception of their readers' (Hermes, 1995: 6). She calls this approach 'the theorisation of meaning production in everyday contexts' (ibid.). In working in this way, she is able to avoid the deployment of textual analysis, with its implied notion of an identifiably correct meaning, or limited set of meanings, which a reader may or may not activate. 'My perspective', she explains, 'is that texts acquire meaning only in the interaction between readers and texts and that analysis of the text on its own is never enough to reconstruct these meanings' (10). To enable this way of working she introduces the concept of 'repertoires'. She explains the concept as follows: 'Repertoires are the cultural resources that speakers fall back on and refer to. Which repertoires are used depends on the cultural capital of an individual reader' (8). Moreover, 'Texts do not directly have meaning. The various repertoires readers use make texts meaningful' (40).

Hermes conducted eighty interviews with both women and men. She was initially disappointed at the fact that her interviewees seemed reluctant to talk about how they made meanings from the women's magazines they read; and when they did discuss this issue, they often suggested instead, against the 'common sense' of much media and cultural theory, that their encounters with these magazines were hardly meaningful at all. After the initial disappointment, these discussions gradually prompted Hermes to recognize what she calls 'the fallacy of meaningfulness' (16). What this phrase is intended to convey is her rejection of a way of working in media and cultural analysis that is premised on the view that the encounter between reader and text should always be understood solely in terms of the production of meaning. This general preoccupation with meaning, she claims, has resulted from an influential body of work that concentrated on fans (and, I would add, on youth subcultures), rather than on the consumption practices of ordinary people; and, moreover, it resulted from a conspicuous failure to situate consumption in the routines of everyday life. Against the influence of this body of work, she argues for a critical perspective in which 'the media text has to be displaced in favour of readers' reports of their everyday lives' (148). As she explains, 'To understand and theorize everyday media use, a more sophisticated view of meaning production is required than one that does not recognise different levels of psychological investment or emotional commitment and reflection' (16).

Through a detailed and critical analysis of recurrent themes and repeated issues that arise in the interview material she collected, Hermes attempts to reconstruct the various repertoires employed by the interviewees in the consumption of women's magazines. She identifies four repertoires: 'easily put down', 'relaxation', 'practical knowledge' and 'emotional learning and connected knowing' (31). The first of these repertoires, perhaps the most straightforward to understand, identifies women's magazines as a genre that makes limited demands on its readers. It is a genre that can be easily picked up and easily put down, and because of this, it can be easily accommodated into the routines of everyday life.

The second repertoire, clearly related to the first, and perhaps as expected as the first repertoire, identifies reading women's magazines as a form of 'relaxation'. But, as Hermes points out, relaxation (like 'escapism' discussed earlier in this chapter) should not be understood as an innocent or a self-evident term – it is, as she maintains, 'ideologically loaded' (36). On the one hand, the term can be employed simply as a valid description of a particular activity, and, on the other, it can be used as a blocking mechanism in defence against personal intrusion. Given the low cultural status of women's magazines, as Hermes reminds us, using the term 'relaxation' as a means to block further entry into a private realm is perhaps understandable. In other words, I am reading this magazine to indicate to others that I am currently not available to do other things.

The third repertoire, the repertoire of 'practical knowledge', can range from tips on cooking to film and book reviews. But its apparently secure anchorage in practical application is deceptive. The repertoire of practical knowledge may offer much more than practical hints on how to become adept at Indian cuisine or culturally knowing about which films are worth going to the cinema to see. Readers can use these practical tips, Hermes claims, to fantasize an 'ideal self . . . [who] is pragmatic and solution-oriented, and a person who can take decisions and is an emancipated consumer; but above all she is a person in control' (39).

The final repertoire, the repertoire of 'emotional learning and connected knowing', is also about learning, but rather than being about the collection of practical tips, it is learning through the recognition of oneself, one's lifestyle and one's potential problems, in the problems of others as represented in the pages of magazine stories and articles. As one interviewee told Hermes, she likes to read 'short pieces about people who have had certain problems . . . [and] how such a problem can be solved' (41). Or as another interviewee told her, 'I like to read about how people deal with things' (42). With specific reference to problem pages, another interviewee observed, 'you learn a lot from other people's problems . . . and the advice they [the magazine] give' (43). As with the repertoire of practical knowledge, the repertoire of emotional and connected learning may also involve the production of an ideal self, a self who is prepared for all the potential emotional dangers and human crises that might need to be confronted in the social practices of everyday life. As Hermes explains, 'Both the repertoire of practical knowledge and the repertoire of connected knowing may help readers to gain (an imaginary and temporary) sense of identity and confidence, of being in control or feeling at peace with life, that lasts while they are reading and dissipates quickly [unlike the practical tips] when the magazine is put down' (48).

Hermes's great originality is to have broken decisively with an approach to cultural analysis in which the researcher insists on the necessity to establish first the substantive meaning of a text or texts and then how an audience may or may not read the text to make this meaning. Against this way of working, as she observes, 'the repertoires that readers use give meaning to women's magazine genres in a way that to a quite remarkable extent is independent of the women's magazine text. Readers construct new texts in the form of fantasies and imagined "new" selves. This leads to the conclusion that a genre study can be based entirely on how women's magazines are read and that it does not need to address the (narrative) structure or content of the text itself at all' (146).

Against more celebratory accounts of women and consumption, Hermes's investigation of the role of repertoires makes her reluctant to see in the practices of women reading magazines an unproblematical form of empowerment. Instead, she argues, we should think of the consumption of women's magazines as providing only temporary 'moments of empowerment' (51).

Post-feminism

Post-feminism is a complex issue. It can be used to describe a type of feminism, a theoretical position within feminism, and a tendency in contemporary popular culture. According to Janice Winship (1987), 'if it means anything useful', post-feminism refers to the way in which the 'boundaries between feminists and non-feminists have become fuzzy' (149). This is to a large extent due to the way in which 'with the "success" of feminism some feminist ideas no longer have an oppositional charge but have become part of many people's, not just a minority's, common sense' (ibid.). Of course this does not mean that all feminist demands have been met (far from it), and that feminism is now redundant. On the contrary, 'it suggests that feminism no longer has a simple coherence around a set of easily defined principles . . . but instead is a much richer, more diverse and contradictory mix than it ever was in the 1970s' (ibid.).

Angela McRobbie (2004) is much less optimistic about the 'success' of feminism. What has really happened, she argues, is that much contemporary popular culture actively undermines the feminist gains of the 1970s and 1980s. However, this should not be understood as a straightforward 'backlash' against feminism. Rather its undermining of feminism works by acknowledging feminism while at the same time suggesting that it is no longer necessary in a world where women have the freedom to shape their own individual life courses. In post-feminist popular culture feminism features as history: aged, uncool and redundant. The acknowledging of feminism, therefore, is only to demonstrate that it is no longer relevant. In place of the feminist movement, we are given instead the successful individual woman, embodying both the redundancy of feminism and the necessity of individual effort. This dual action of acknowledgement and dismissal is found in many aspects of post-feminist popular culture. McRobbie offers the example of the advertising campaign for the Wonderbra (see Photo 8.1).

The Wonderbra advert showing the model Eva Herzigova looking down admiringly at her substantial cleavage enhanced by the lacy pyrotechnics of the Wonderbra, was through the mid-1990s positioned in major high street locations in the UK on full size billboards. The composition of the image had such a textbook 'sexist ad' dimension that one could be forgiven for supposing some familiarity with both

Photo 8.1   Post-feminism and the Wonderbra

Source: Image courtesy of The Advertising Archives

cultural studies and with feminist critiques of advertising. It was, in a sense, taking feminism into account by showing it to be a thing of the past, by provocatively 'enacting sexism' while at the same time playing with those debates in film theory about women as the object of the gaze [see discussion of Laura Mulvey in Chapter 5 and earlier in this chapter] and even female desire [see discussion of Rosalind Coward earlier in this chapter]. . . . Here is an advertisement which plays back to its viewers, well known aspects of feminist media studies. . . . At the same time the advertisement expects to provoke feminist condemnation as a means of generating publicity. Thus generational differences are also generated, the younger female viewer, along with her male counterparts, educated in irony and visually literate, is not made angry by such a repertoire. She appreciates its layers of meaning; she gets the joke (258–9).

Rather than feminism working as a critique of what would once have been seen as a sexist image, it is incorporated into the text at the cost of dismissal and de-politicization; it has been drawn into the advert as a discourse from history whose only function is to deepen the image's semiotic depth and to enable it to be seen as ironic and harmless; an advert that only a feminist puritan from the 1970s could find offensive (and the fact that some still do is part of the advert's joke). In other words, post-feminist popular culture is not a return to a pre-feminist sensibility, rather it is a response to feminism: it needs to acknowledge feminism in order to dismiss it as old and uncool and no longer relevant to the individually liberated modern women.

To really understand post-feminist popular culture it needs to be situated in relation to de-traditionalization (Giddens, 1992, Beck and Beck-Gernsheim, 2002) and to neo-liberal discourses of choice and individualism ('the market has the answer to every problem'). The first suggests that women are now freed from traditional feminine iden-tities, and thus enabled to self-reflexively invent new roles, while the second claims that the free market, with its imperative of consumer choice, is the best mechanism to fully enable new female identity constructions. However, as Vicky Ball points out, rather than a de-traditionalization, what we are really witnessing is a process of re-traditionalization, in which traditional ideas of what is natural and normal about gender are once again being reinstated (see Ball, 2012a, 2012b). This movement is captured perfectly in an interview with Kelly Reilly, who plays DC Anna Travis in Lynda La Plante's television drama *Above Suspicion*. When asked if her character is the new Jane Tennison (Detective Chief Inspector in La Plante's earlier drama *Prime Suspect*), she replied,

No, my character, DC Anna Travis, is just at the beginning of her police career; Jane Tennison had reached the upper echelons and was one of a generation of women who needed to prove that they were as good as any man. Anna resides in a more contemporary era, where it isn't about sexual politics anymore. She is strong, intuitive and overtly female (quoted in Ball, 2012b).

In a move symptomatic of the 'sensibility' that is post-feminism (Gill, 2007), Reilly's comment acknowledges feminism and then dismisses it, suggesting that feminism is a movement of the past, no longer relevant to contemporary women.

The incorporation of feminism into post-feminist popular culture is a classic example of the processes of hegemony, but it could also be understood as an example of the mechanisms Marcuse identifies as producing one-dimensionality (see Chapter 4 for discussion of both positions).

Men's studies and masculinities

Feminism has brought into being many things, but one that some feminists have already disowned is men's studies. Despite Peter Schwenger's concern that for a man 'to think about masculinity is to become less masculine oneself.... The real man thinks about practical matters rather than abstract ones and certainly does not brood upon himself or the nature of his sexuality' (quoted in Showalter, 1990: 7), many men have thought, spoken and written about masculinity. As Antony Easthope[7] (1986) writes in *What a Man's Gotta Do*, 'It is time to try to speak about masculinity, about what it is and how it works' (1). Easthope's focus is on what he calls dominant masculinity (the myth of heterosexual masculinity as something essential and self-evident, which is tough, masterful, self-possessed, knowing, always in control, etc.). He begins from the proposition that masculinity is a cultural construct; that is, it is not 'natural', 'normal' or 'universal'. He argues that dominant masculinity operates as a gender norm, and that it is against this norm that the many other different types of 'lived masculinities' (including gay masculinities) are invited to measure themselves. As part of this argument, he analyses the way dominant masculinity is represented across a range of popular cultural texts – pop songs, popular fiction, films, television and newspapers – and concludes:

> Clearly men do not passively live out the masculine myth imposed by the stories and images of the dominant culture. But neither can they live completely outside the myth, since it pervades the culture. Its coercive power is active everywhere – not just on screens, hoardings and paper, but inside our own heads (167).

From a similar perspective, Sean Nixon's (1996) examination of 'new man' masculinity explores it as 'a regime of representation', focusing on 'four key sites of cultural circulation: television advertising, press advertising, menswear shops and popular magazines for men' (4).

Although it is true that feminists have always encouraged men to examine their masculinity, many feminists are less than impressed with men's studies, as Joyce Canaan and Christine Griffin (1990) make clear:

> While feminist understandings of patriarchy would undoubtedly be wider if we had access to men's understandings of how they construct and transform this pervasive system of relationships, we nevertheless fear that such research might

distort, belittle, or deny women's experiences with men and masculinity. Feminists therefore must be even more insistent about conducting research on men and masculinity at a time when a growing number of men are beginning to conduct apparently 'comparable' research (207–8).

Queer theory

Queer theory, as Paul Burston and Colin Richardson (1995) explain, 'provides a discipline for exploring the relationships between lesbians, gay men and the culture which surrounds and (for the large part) continues to seek to exclude us' (1). Moreover, '[b]y shifting the focus away from the question of what it means to be lesbian or gay within the culture, and onto the various performances of heterosexuality created by the culture, Queer Theory seeks to locate Queerness in places that had previously been thought of as strictly for the straights' (ibid.). In this way, they contend, 'Queer Theory is no more "about" lesbians and gay men than women's studies is "about" women. Indeed, part of the project of Queer is to attack . . . the very "naturalness" of gender and, by extension, the fictions supporting compulsory heterosexuality' (ibid.).

To discuss the supposed naturalness of gender and the ideological fictions supporting compulsory heterosexuality, there is no better place to begin than with one of the founding texts of queer theory, Judith Butler's (1999) very influential book *Gender Trouble*. Butler begins from Simone de Beauvoir's (1984) observation that 'one is not born a woman, but, rather, becomes one' (12). De Beauvoir's distinction establishes an analytical difference between biological sex ('nature') and gender ('culture'), suggesting that while biological sex is stable, there will always be different and competing (historically and socially variable) 'versions' of femininity and masculinity (see Figure 8.1). Although de Beauvoir's argument has the advantage of seeing gender as something made in culture – 'the cultural meanings that the sexed body assumes' (Butler, 1999: 10) – and not something fixed by nature, the problem with this model of sex/gender, according to Butler, is that it works with the assumption that there are only two biological sexes ('male' and 'female'), which are determined by nature, and which in turn generate and guarantee the binary gender system. Against this position, she argues that biology is itself always already culturally gendered as 'male' and 'female', and, as such, already guarantees a particular version of the feminine and the masculine. Therefore, the distinction between sex and gender is not a distinction between nature and culture: 'the category of "sex" is itself a *gendered* category, fully politically invested, naturalized but not natural' (143). In other words, there is not a biological 'truth' at the heart of gender; sex and gender are both cultural categories.

Furthermore, it is not just that 'gender is not to culture as sex is to nature; gender is also the discursive/cultural means by which "sexed nature" or "a natural sex" is produced and established as "prediscursive", prior to culture, a politically neutral surface *on which* culture acts. . . . [In this way,] the internal stability and binary frame for sex is

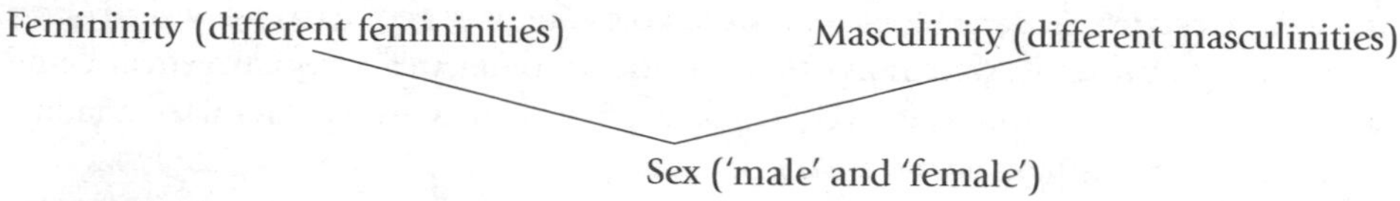

Femininity (different femininities)   Masculinity (different masculinities)

Sex ('male' and 'female')

Figure 8.1   The binary gender system.

effectively secured . . . by casting the duality of sex in a prediscursive domain' (11). As Butler explains, 'there is no reason to divide up human bodies into male and female sexes except that such a division suits the economic needs of heterosexuality and lends a naturalistic gloss to the institution of heterosexuality' (143). Therefore, as she contends, 'one is not born a woman, one becomes one; but further, one is not born female, one *becomes* female; but even more radically, one can if one chooses, become neither female nor male, woman nor man' (33).

According to Butler's argument, gender is not the expression of biological sex, it is performatively constructed in culture. In this way, 'Gender is the repeated stylization of the body, a set of repeated acts within a highly rigid regulatory frame that congeal over time to produce the appearance of substance, of a natural sort of being' (43–4). In other words, gender identities consist of the accumulation of what is outside (i.e. in culture) in the belief that they are an expression of what is inside (i.e. in nature). As a result '"persons" become intelligible only through becoming gendered in conformity with recognizable standards of intelligibility' (22).[8] Femininity and masculinity are not expressions of 'nature', they are 'cultural performances in which their "naturalness" [is] constituted through discursively constrained performative acts . . . that create the effect of the natural, the original, and the inevitable' (xxviii–xxix). However, to say that gender is a cultural construct is not to say that it constitutes the actual material body. Behind 'sex' there is always a material biology. What is constructed is not the prediscursive body, but the 'sex' of this body.

Butler's theory of performativity is a development of J.L. Austin's (1962) theory of performative language. Austin divides language into two types: constative and performative. Constative language is descriptive language. 'The sky is blue' is an example of a constative statement. Performative language, on the other hand, does not merely describe what already exists, it brings something into being. 'I now pronounce you husband and wife' is an obvious example; it does not describe something, it brings it into existence; that is, when the words are spoken by an appropriate person, they transform two single people into a married couple. Butler argues that gender works in much the same way as performative language. As she explains, 'there is no identity behind the expressions of gender; that identity is performatively constituted by the very "expressions" that are said to be its results' (Butler, 1999: 33). One of the first performative speech acts we all encounter is the pronouncement, 'It's a girl' or 'It's a boy'. The use of the noun boy or girl transforms the pre-human 'it' into a gendered subject. In this, the first of many performative acts, the body of the child is made culturally intelligible. The pronouncement, 'It's a girl' or 'It's a boy', comes with rules and regulations that pre-exist the child, which the child is expected to follow and obey: 'little boys do this, little girls don't do that', etc. In other words, what seems like an announcement of recognition is in fact a moment of constitution: the 'it' is made a subject (male or female) and thus begins a continuous process of subjectification in which the 'it' is required to conform to culturally intelligible (i.e. socially acceptable) norms of maleness or femaleness. In this way, our gender identities do not precede these moments of performativity; rather they are its result. So naming me a boy does not reveal my gender identity, it produces it – a production that maps out key aspects of my social 'destiny' – as a subject I become subjected.

However, for 'it's a girl' or 'it's a boy' to make sense it has to conform to a structure of cultural intelligibility that already exists (that is, we have to already know what it means to say 'it's a girl' or 'it's a boy'). But more than this, the structure of intelligibility demands that such a pronouncement be made: it is an act of conformity to a world that has already agreed to divide humans into male and female on the grounds of bio-logical difference. Each time this happens, the pronouncement is citing previous pro-nouncements and it is the fact that it is citing these previous pronouncements that gives it its authority and validity. There is what Butler calls a 'citational accumulation' (1993: 12).

This part of her argument draws on Jacques Derrida's extension of Austin's theory of performative language. As Derrida asks, 'Could a performative utterance succeed if its formulation did not repeat a "coded" or iterable utterance, in other words, if the for-mula I pronounce in order to open a meeting, launch a ship or a marriage were not identifiable as conforming with an iterable model?' (1982: 18). In other words, the power of each pronouncement, why it makes sense, why it has authority and validity, and why it requires conformity, is the weight of previous citations. Moreover, this first citation is the beginning of a continuous process of further citations, as the 'it' is required to conform to the social norms of its assigned gender identity. As she explains, 'In the first instance, performativity must be understood not as a singular or deliberate "act", but, rather, as the reiterative and citational practice by which discourse produces the effects that it names' (Butler 1993: 2). Our gender identity, therefore, is 'not the product of a choice, but the forcible citation of a norm, one whose complex historicity is indissociable from relations of discipline, regulation, punishment' (232). A variety of discourses, including those from parents, fashion, educational institutions, the media, will all combine to ensure our conformity to the reiteration and citation of gender norms. In this way, the performance of gender creates the illusion of an already existing gendered self (supposedly guaranteed by biology).

Butler's concept of performativity should not be confused with the idea of per-formance understood as a form of play-acting, in which a more fundamental identity remains intact beneath the theatricality of the identity on display. Gender perform-ativity is not a voluntary practice; it is a continual process of almost disciplinary reiteration: 'gender performativity cannot be theorized apart from the forcible and reiterative practice of regulatory sexual regimes . . . and in no way presupposes a choosing subject' (Butler, 1993: 15). Sarah E. Chinn (1997) provides an excellent sum-mary of the process:

While we may recognize that gender is coercive, it is familiar; it is ourselves. The naturalizing effects of gender means that gender feels natural – even the understanding that it is performative, that our subjectivities themselves are constructed through its performance, does not make it feel any the less intrinsic. Our identities depend upon successful performance of our genders, and there is an entire cultural arsenal of books, films, television, advertisements, parental injunctions and peer surveillance to make sure those performances are (ideally) unconscious and successful (306–7).

Butler (1999) chooses 'drag' as a model for explanation not, as some critics seem to think, because she thinks it is 'an example of [the] subversion [of gender]' (xxii), but because 'it dramatize[s] the signifying gestures through which gender itself is established' (xxviii). Drag exposes the assumed and apparent unity and fictional coherence of the normative heterosexual performance of gender. As Butler explains, 'In imitating gender, drag implicitly reveals the imitative structure of gender itself – as well as its contingency' (175). To be in drag is not to copy an original and natural gender identity, it is to 'imitate the myth of originality itself' (176).[9] As she explains,

If gender attributes . . . are not expressive but performative, then these attributes effectively constitute the identity they are said to express or reveal. The distinction between expression and performativeness is crucial. If gender attributes and acts, the various ways in which a body shows or produces its cultural signification, are performative, then there is no preexisting identity by which an act or attribute might be measured; there would be no true or false, real or distorted acts of gender, and the postulation of a true gender identity would be revealed as a regulatory fiction. That gender reality is created through sustained social performances means that the very notions of an essential sex and a true or abiding masculinity or femininity are also constituted as part of the strategy that conceals gender's performative character and the performative possibilities for proliferating gender configurations outside the restricting frames of masculinist domination and compulsory heterosexuality (180).[10]

Butler (2009) gives the example of Aretha Franklin singing, 'you make me feel like a natural woman':[11]

she seems at first to suggest that some natural potential of her biological sex is actualized by her participation in the cultural position of 'woman' as object of heterosexual recognition. Something in her 'sex' is thus expressed by her 'gender' which is then fully known and consecrated within the heterosexual scene. There is no breakage, no discontinuity between 'sex' as biological facticity and essence, or between gender and sexuality. Although Aretha appears to be all too glad to have her naturalness confirmed, she also seems fully and paradoxically mindful that that confirmation is never guaranteed, that the effect of naturalness is only achieved as a consequence of that moment of heterosexual recognition. After all, Aretha sings, you make me feel *like* a natural woman, suggesting that this is a kind of metaphorical substitution, an act of imposture, a kind of sublime and momentary participation in an ontological illusion produced by the mundane operation of heterosexual drag (2009: 235; italics in original).

If, as Butler (1999) maintains, 'gender reality is created through sustained social performances' (180), perhaps one of the principal theatres for its creation is consumption. Michael Warner (1993) has noted a connection between gay culture and particular patterns of consumption. Such a relationship, he argues, demands a rethinking of the political economy of culture (see Chapter 12). As he explains, there is

> the close connection between consumer culture and the most visible spaces of gay culture: bars, discos, advertising, fashion, brand-name identification, mass cultural-camp, 'promiscuity'. Gay culture in this most visible mode is anything but external to advanced capitalism and to precisely those features of advanced capitalism that many on the left are most eager to disavow. Post-Stonewall urban gay men reek of the commodity. We give off the smell of capitalism in rut, and therefore demand of theory a more dialectical view of capitalism than many people have imagination for (xxxi).

In a similar way, Corey K. Creekmur and Alexander Doty (1995) point out that 'the identity that we designate *homosexual* arose in tandem with capitalist consumer culture' (1). They draw attention to the particular relationship that gays and lesbians have often had with popular culture: 'an alternative or negotiated, if not fully subversive, reception of the products and messages of popular culture, [wondering] how they might have access to mainstream culture without denying or losing their oppositional identities, how they might participate without necessarily assimilating, how they might take pleasure in, and make affirmative meanings out of, experiences and artefacts that they have been told do not offer queer pleasures and meanings' (1–2). In other words, 'a central issue is how to be "out in culture": how to occupy a place in mass culture, yet maintain a perspective on it that does not accept its homophobic and heterocentrist definitions, images, and terms of analysis' (2).

Alexander Doty (1995) argues that 'queerness as a mass culture reception practice . . . is shared by all sorts of people in varying degrees of consistency and intensity' (73). As he explains, queer reading is not confined to gays and lesbians, 'heterosexual, straight-identifying people can experience queer moments' (ibid.). The term 'queer' is used by Doty 'to mark a flexible space for the expression of all aspects of non- (anti-, contra-) straight cultural production and reception. As such, 'this "queer space" recognizes the possibility that various and fluctuating queer positions might be occupied whenever *anyone* produces or responds to culture' (73; italics in original). The 'queer space' identified by Doty is, as he explains, best thought of as a 'contrastraight, rather than strictly antistraight, space' (83):

Queer positions, queer readings, and queer pleasures are part of a reception space that stands simultaneously beside and within that created by heterosexual and straight positions. . . . What queer reception often does, however, is stand outside the relatively clear-cut and essentializing categories of sexual identity under which most people function. You might identify yourself as a lesbian or a straight woman yet queerly experience the gay erotics of male buddy films such as *Red River* and *Butch Cassidy and the Sundance Kid*; or maybe as a gay man your cultlike devotion to *Laverne and Shirley*, *Kate and Allie*, or *The Golden Girls* has less to do with straight-defined cross-gender identification than with articulating the loving relationship between women. Queer readings aren't 'alternative' readings, wishful or wilful misreadings, or 'reading too much into things' readings. They result from the recognition and articulation of the complex range of queerness that has been in popular culture texts and their audiences all along (83–4).

Therefore, queer reading has very little to do with one's sexuality.

Notes

1. Mulvey's essay has been anthologized at least ten times.
2. Based on a diagram in Dyer (1999: 376).
3. Charlotte Lamb, originally in the *Guardian*, 13 September 1982 (quoted in Coward, 1984: 190).
4. Janice Radway finds this figure implausible.
5. In similar fashion, it may be the case that reading Enid Blyton's *Secret Seven* books as a child – with their imperative of collective action – prepared the ground for my commitment to socialism as an adult.
6. See Bennett (1983) and Storey (1992 and 2010a).
7. Antony died in December 1999. I knew him both as a teacher and as a colleague. Although I often disagreed with him, his influence on my work (and on the work of others) has been considerable. In the year Antony died I became a professor. I do not think this would have happened if, many years earlier, he had not persuaded me to write my dissertation on Pierre Macherey rather than Gerrard Winstanley.
8. Butler (1999) uses the term 'heterosexual matrix' 'to designate that grid of cultural intelligibility through which bodies, genders, and desires are naturalized. . . . [This is] a hegemonic discursive/epistemic model of gender intelligibility that assumes that for bodies to cohere and make sense there must be a stable sex expressed through a stable gender (masculine expresses male, feminine expresses female) that is oppositionally and hierarchically defined through the compulsory practice of heterosexuality' (194).
9. Esther Newton (1999), whose work on drag is used by Butler, makes the point that 'children learn sex-role identity before they learn any strictly sexual object choices. In other words, I think that children learn they are boys or girls before they are

made to understand that boys only love girls and vice versa' (108). Harold Beaver (1999) writes, 'What is "natural" is neither heterosexual nor homosexual desire but simply desire. . . . Desire is like the pull of a gravitational field, the magnet that draws body to body' (161).

10. As Newton (1972) explains, 'if sex-role behaviour can be achieved by the "wrong" sex, it logically follows that it is in reality also achieved, not inherited, by the "right" sex' (103).

11. '(You Make Me Feel Like) A Natural Woman' was written by Gerry Goffin, Carole King and Jerry Wexler. Carole King's recording of the song is on her album *Tapestry*. Aretha Franklin's version is on her *Greatest Hits* album.

Further reading

Storey, John (ed.), *Cultural Theory and Popular Culture: A Reader*, 4th edn, Harlow: Pearson Education, 2009. This is the companion volume to the previous edition of this book. A fully updated 5th edition containing further readings is due for publication in 2018. An interactive website is also available (www.routledge.com/cw/storey), which contains helpful student resources and a glossary of terms for each chapter.

Ang, Ien, *Living Room Wars: Rethinking Media Audiences for a Postmodern World*, London: Routledge, 1995. An excellent collection of essays from one of the leading intellectuals in the field.

Barrett, Michèle, *Women's Oppression Today: Problems in Marxist Feminist Analysis*, London: Verso, 1980. The book is of general interest to the student of popular culture in its attempt to synthesize Marxist and feminist modes of analysis; of particular interest is Chapter 3, 'Ideology and the cultural production of gender'.

Brunt, Rosalind and Caroline Rowan (eds), *Feminism, Culture and Politics*, London: Lawrence & Wishart, 1982. A collection of essays illustrative of feminist modes of analysis. See especially: Michèle Barrett, 'Feminism and the definition of cultural politics'.

Burston, Paul and Colin Richardson (eds), *A Queer Romance: Lesbians, Gay Men and Popular Culture*, London: Routledge, 1995. An interesting collection of essays looking at popular culture from the perspective(s) of queer theory.

Creekmur, Corey K. and Alexander Doty (eds), *Out in Culture: Gay, Lesbian, and Queer Essays on Popular Culture*, London: Cassell, 1995. An excellent collection of essays on contemporary popular culture from an anti-homophobic and antiheterocentrist perspective.

Easthope, Antony, *What a Man's Gotta Do: The Masculine Myth in Popular Culture*, London: Paladin, 1986. A useful and entertaining account of the ways in which masculinity is represented in contemporary popular culture.

Franklin, Sarah, Celia Lury and Jackie Stacey (eds), *Off Centre: Feminism and Cultural Studies*, London: HarperCollins, 1991. An excellent collection of feminist work in cultural studies.

Geraghty, Christine, *Women and Soap Opera: A Study of Prime Time Soaps*, Cambridge: Polity Press, 1991. A comprehensive introduction to feminist analysis of soap operas.

Jeffords, Susan, *The Remasculinization of America: Gender and the Vietnam War*, Bloomington and Indianapolis: Indiana University Press, 1989. The book explores representations of masculinity across a range of popular texts to argue that following the crisis of defeat in Vietnam strenuous attempts have been made to remasculinize American culture.

Macdonald, Myra, *Representing Women: Myths of Femininity in Popular Media*, London: Edward Arnold, 1995. An excellent introduction to the way women are talked about and constructed visually across a range of popular media.

McRobbie, Angela, *Feminism and Youth Culture*, London: Macmillan, 1991. A selection from the work of one of the leading figures in feminist analysis of popular culture.

Pribram, Deidre E. (ed.), *Female Spectators: Looking at Film and Television*, London: Verso, 1988. A useful collection of essays looking at different aspects of filmic and televisual popular culture.

Thornham, Sue, *Passionate Detachments: An Introduction to Feminist Film Theory*, London: Edward Arnold, 1997. An excellent introduction to the contribution of feminism to the study of film.

9 'Race', racism and representation

In this chapter I shall examine the concept of 'race' and the historical development of racism in England. I shall then explore a particular regime of racial representation, Edward Said's analysis of Orientalism. I shall use Hollywood's account of America's war in Vietnam, and its potential impact on recruitment for the first Gulf War as an example of Orientalism in popular culture. The chapter will conclude with a section on 'whiteness' and a discussion of cultural studies and anti-racism.

'Race' and racism

The first thing to insist on in discussions of 'race' is that there is just one 'race', the human race.[1] Human biology does not divide people into different 'races'; it is racism (and sometimes its counter arguments) that insists on this division. In other words, 'race' is a cultural and historical category, a way of making *difference* signify between people of a variety of skin tones. What is important is not difference as such, but how it is made to signify; how it is made meaningful in terms of a social and political hierarchy (see Chapters 4 and 6). This is not to deny that human beings come in different colours and with different physical features, but it is to insist that these differences do not issue meanings; they have to be made to mean. Moreover, there is no reason why skin colour is more significant than hair colour or the colour of a person's eyes. In other words, 'race' and racism are more about signification than about biology. As Paul Gilroy observes,

> Accepting that skin 'colour', however meaningless we know it to be, has a strictly limited basis in biology, opens up the possibility of engaging with theories of signification which can highlight the elasticity and the emptiness of 'racial' signifiers as well as the ideological work which has to be done in order to turn them into signifiers in the first place. This perspective underscores the definition of 'race' as an open political category, for it is struggle that determines which definition of 'race' will prevail and the conditions under which they will endure or wither away (2002: 36).

This should not be mistaken for a form of idealism. Whether or not they are made to signify, physical differences between human beings exist. But how they are made to signify is always a result of politics and power, rather than a question of biology. As Gilroy points out, '"Race" has to be socially and politically constructed and elaborate ideological work is done to secure and maintain the different forms of "racialization". Recognizing this makes it all the more important to compare and evaluate the different historical situations in which "race" has become politically pertinent' (35). Similarly, as Hazel Rose Markus and Paula M.L. Moya point out,

> race is not something that people or groups *have* or *are*, but rather a set of actions that people do. More specifically, race is a dynamic system of historically derived and institutionalized ideas and practices. Certainly, the process involved in doing race takes different forms in various times and places. But doing race always involves creating groups based on perceived physical and behavioral characteristics, associating differential power and privilege with these characteristics, and then justifying the resulting inequalities (2010: x).

We do race individually and institutionally. We do it every time we reduce a person to an essential, unchanging characteristic that supposedly emanates from their biology. My wife is Chinese. There is a popular stereotype that Chinese people are inscrutable (impossible to understand or interpret). To think, because she is Chinese, that inscrutability is an essential biological part of her character is to 'do race'; that is, to explain an aspect of her character and behaviour as if it were a fixed biological manifestation of her Chinese-ness.

Working from this perspective, analysis of 'race' in popular culture would be the exploration of the different ways in which it has and can be made to signify – the different ways in which individuals and institutions 'do race'.

As Stuart Hall points out, there are three key moments in the history of 'race' and racism in the West (Hall, 1997b). These occur around slavery and the slave trade, colonialism and imperialism, and 1950s immigration following decolonization. In the next section I shall focus on how slavery and the slave trade produced the first detailed public discussions around 'race' and racism. It was in these discussions that the basic assumptions and vocabulary of 'race' and racism were first formulated. It is important to understand that 'race' and racism are not natural or inevitable phenomena; they have a history and are the result of human actions and interactions. But often they are made to appear as inevitable, something grounded in nature rather than what they really are, products of human culture. Again, as Paul Gilroy observes,

> For those timid souls, it would appear that becoming resigned both to the absolute status of 'race' as a concept and to the intractability of racism as a permanent perversion akin to original sin, is easier than the creative labour involved in invisioning and producing a more just world, purged of racial hierarchy . . . Rather than accepting the power of racism as prior to politics and seeing it as an inescapable natural force that configures human consciousness and action in ways

and forms that merely political considerations simply can never match, this on-going work involves making 'race' and racism into social and political phenomena again (xx).

According to Gilroy, there needs to be a reduction in 'the exaggerated dimensions of racial difference to a liberating ordinary-ness'; he adds that '"race" is nothing special, a virtual reality given meaning only by the fact that racism endures' (xxii). In other words, without racism there would be little meaning to the concept of 'race'. It is racism that keeps the concept alive. What needs to be recognized is 'the banality of inter-mixture and the subversive ordinariness of this country's [the United Kingdom] convivial cultures in which "race" is stripped of meaning and racism just an after-effect of long gone imperial history' (xxxviii).

The ideology of racism: its historical emergence

While it is possible to argue that xenophobia, deriving from ignorance and fear, has perhaps existed as long as different ethnic groups have existed, 'race' and racism have a very particular history. Racism first develops in England as a defence of slavery and the slave trade. As Peter Fryer (1984) points out, 'Once the English slave trade, English sugar-producing plantation slavery, and English manufacturing industry had begun to operate as a trebly profitable interlocking system, the economic basis had been laid for all those ancient scraps of myth and prejudice to be woven into a more or less coherent racist ideology: a mythology of race' (134). In other words, racism first emerges as a defensive ideology, promulgated in order to defend the economic profits of slavery and the slave trade.

A key figure in the development of the ideology of racism is the planter and judge Edward Long. In his book *History of Jamaica* (1774) he popularized the idea that black people are inferior to white people, thus suggesting that slavery and the slave trade were perfectly acceptable institutions. His starting position is the assertion that there is an absolute racial division between black and white people:

> I think there are extremely potent reasons for believing, that the White and the Negroe are two distinct species. . . . When we reflect on . . . their dissimilarity to the rest of mankind, must we not conclude, that they are a different species of the same genus? . . . Nor do [orang-utans] seem at all inferior in the intellectual faculties to many of the Negroe race; with some of whom, it is credible that they have the most intimate connection and consanguinity. The amorous intercourse between them may be frequent . . . and it is certain, that both races agree perfectly well in lasciviousness of disposition (quoted in Fryer, 1984, 158–9).

Charles White, writing in 1795, made similar claims, 'The white European . . . being most removed from brute creation, may, on that account, be considered as the most beautiful of the human race. No one will doubt his superiority in intellectual powers; and I believe it will be found that his capacity is naturally superior also to that of every other man' (168).

Edward Long's own racism is clearly underpinned by sexual anxieties. In a pamphlet published in 1772, in which racism is mixed with his contempt for working-class women, he claims that

> [t]he lower class of women in England, are remarkably fond of the blacks, for reasons too brutal to mention; they would connect themselves with horses and asses if the law permitted them. By these ladies they generally have a numerous brood. Thus, in the course of a few generations more, the English blood will become so con- taminated with this mixture, and from the chances, the ups and downs of life, this alloy may spread extensively, as even to reach the middle, and then the higher orders of the people, till the whole nation resembles the Portuguese and Moriscos in complexion of skin and baseness of mind (157).

Similarly, in *Considerations on the Negroe Cause* (1772), Samuel Estwick argued that black people should be prevented from entering the country in order to 'preserve the race of Britons from stain and contamination' (156). Philip Thicknesse, writing in 1778, makes similar points:

> in the course of a few centuries they will over-run this country with a race of men of the very worst sort under heaven. . . . London abounds with an incredible number of these black men . . . and [in] every country town, nay in almost every village are to be seen a little race of mulattoes, mischievous as monkeys and infinitely more dangerous. . . . A mixture of negro blood with the natives of this country is big with great and mighty mischief (162).

Linking this concern directly to the abolition of slavery, John Scattergood, writing in 1792, argued that if slavery is allowed to end, 'the Negroes from all parts of the world will flock hither, mix with the natives, spoil the breed of our common people, increase the number of crimes and criminals, and make Britain the sink of all the earth, for mongrels, vagrants, and vagabonds' (164).

A letter published in the *London Chronicle* in 1764, which finds a dark echo in   contemporary debates on immigration (as does so much of this discourse), is concerned that too many black servants are coming into Britain:

> As they fill the places of so many of our own people, we are by this means depriving so many of them of the means of getting their bread, and thereby decreasing our native population in favour of a race, whose mixture with us is disgraceful, and whose use cannot be so various and essential as those of white people . . . They never can be considered as a part of the people, and therefore their introduction into the community can only serve to elbow as many out of it who are genuine subjects, and in every point preferable. . . . It is . . . high time that some remedy be

applied for the cure of so great an evil, which may be done by totally prohibiting the importation of any more of them (155).

Given that slavery and the slave trade were of economic benefit to many people not directly involved with its practice, the new ideology of racism spread quickly among those without a direct economic interest in slavery and the slave trade. Scottish philosopher David Hume, for example, was quite clear about the difference between whites and non-whites. Writing in 1753, he observed,

> I am apt to suspect the negroes, and in general all the other species of men (for there are four or five different kinds) to be naturally inferior to the whites. There never was a civilised nation of any other complexion than white . . . [Hume reveals here his ignorance of history]. Such a uniform and constant difference could not happen, in so many countries and ages, if nature had not made an original distinction betwixt these breeds of men. . . . In Jamaica indeed they talk of one negroe as a man of parts and learning; but 'tis likely he is admired for very slender accomplishments, like a parrot, who speaks a few words plainly (152).[2]

By the nineteenth century, it was widely taken for granted by many white Europeans that the human race was divided into superior whites and inferior others. With such natural gifts, it would seem only right that white Europeans should establish colonies across the globe. Moreover, as Fryer points out, 'racism was not confined to a handful of cranks. Virtually every scientist and intellectual in nineteenth-century Britain took it for granted that only people with white skin were capable of thinking and governing' (1984: 169). In fact, it was probably only after the Second World War that racism finally lost its scientific support.

In the nineteenth century racism could even make colonial conquest appear as if directed by God. According to Thomas Carlyle, writing in 1867, 'The Almighty Maker appointed him ["the Nigger"] to be a Servant' (quoted in Fryer, 1984: 172). Sir Harry Johnston (1899), who had worked as a colonial administrator in South Africa and Uganda, claimed that 'The negro in general is a born slave', with the natural capacity to 'toil hard under the hot sun and in unhealthy climates of the torrid zone' (173). Even if the hot sun or the unhealthy climate proved too much, the white Europeans should not overly concern themselves with possibilities of suffering and injustice. Dr Robert Knox, for example, described by Philip Curtin as 'one of the key figures in the general Western . . . pseudo-scientific racism' (1964: 377), was very reassuring on this point: 'What signify these dark races to us? . . . [T]he sooner they are put out of the way the better. . . . Destined by the nature of their race, to run, like all other animals, a certain limited course of existence, it matters little how their extinction is brought about' (quoted in Fryer, 1984: 175).

Knox is certainly extreme in his racism. A less extreme version, justifying imperialism on grounds of a supposed civilizing mission, was expressed by James Hunt. Founder of the Anthropological Society of London in 1863, Hunt argued that although 'the Negro is inferior intellectually to the European, [he or she] becomes more humanised when in his natural subordination to the European than under any other circumstances' (177). In fact, as he makes clear, 'the Negro race can only be humanised and civilised by Europeans' (ibid.).[3] Colonial secretary Joseph Chamberlain (1895) offers a wonderful summary of this argument: 'I believe that the British race is the greatest of governing races the world has ever seen. I say this not merely as an empty boast, but as proved and shown by the success which we have had in administering vast dominions . . . and I believe there are no limits accordingly to its future' (183).[4]

Orientalism

Edward Said (1985), in one of the founding texts of post-colonial theory, shows how a Western discourse on the Orient – 'Orientalism' – has constructed a 'knowledge' of the East and a body of 'power–knowledge' relations articulated in the interests of the 'power' of the West. According to Said, 'The Orient was a European invention' (1). 'Orientalism' is the term he uses to describe the relationship between Europe and the Orient, in particular, the way 'the Orient has helped to define Europe (or the West) as its contrasting image, idea, personality, experience' (1–2). He 'also tries to show that European culture gained in strength and identity by setting itself off against the Orient as a sort of surrogate and even underground self' (3).

> Orientalism can be discussed and analysed as the corporate institution for dealing with the Orient – dealing with it by making statements about it, authorising views of it, describing it, by teaching it, settling it, ruling over it: in short, Orientalism as a Western style for dominating, restructuring, and having authority over the Orient (ibid.).

In other words, Orientalism, a 'system of ideological fiction' (321), is a matter of power. It is one of the mechanisms by which the West maintained its hegemony over the Orient. This is in part achieved by an insistence on an absolute difference between the West and the Orient, in which 'the West . . . is rational, developed, humane, superior, and the Orient . . . is aberrant, undeveloped, inferior' (300).

How does all this, in more general terms, relate to the study of popular culture? It is not too difficult to see how stories of empire in imperial fictions might be better understood using the approach developed by Said. There are basically two imperial plot structures. First, there are the stories that tell of white colonizers succumbing to the primeval power of the alien colonial environment and, as the racist myth puts it, 'going native'. Kurtz in both *Heart of Darkness* and *Apocalypse Now* is such a figure. Then there are stories of whites, who because of the supposed power of their racial heredity impose themselves on the alien colonial environment and its inhabitants. 'Tarzan' (novels, films and *myth*) is the classic representation of this imperial fiction. From the perspective of Orientalism both narratives tell us a great deal more about the desires and anxieties of the culture of imperialism than they can ever tell us about the people and places of colonial conquest. What the approach does is to shift the focus of attention away from what and where the narratives are about to the 'function' that they may serve for the producers and consumers of such fictions. It prevents us from slipping into a form of naive realism: that is, away from a focus on what the stories tell us about the colonies or the colonized, to what such representations tell us about European and American imperialism. In effect, it shifts our concern from 'how' the story is told to 'why', and from those whom the story is about to those who tell and consume the story.

Hollywood's Vietnam, the way it tells the story of America's war in Vietnam, is in many ways a classic example of a particular form of Orientalism. Rather than the silence of defeat, there has been a veritable 'incitement' to talk about Vietnam. America's most unpopular war has become its most popular when measured in discursive and commercial terms. Although America no longer has 'authority over' Vietnam, it continues to hold authority over Western accounts of America's war in Vietnam. Hollywood as a 'corporate institution' deals with Vietnam 'by making statements about it, authorising views of it, describing it, by teaching it'. Hollywood has 'invented' Vietnam as a 'contrasting image' and a 'surrogate and . . . underground self' of America. In this way Hollywood – together with other discursive practices, such as songs, novels, TV serials, etc. – has succeeded in producing a very powerful discourse on Vietnam: telling America and the world that what happened there, happened because Vietnam is like that. These different discourses are not just *about* Vietnam; they may increasingly *constitute* for many Americans the *experience* of Vietnam. They may become in effect the war itself.

From the perspective of Orientalism it does not really matter whether Hollywood's representations are 'true' or 'false' (historically accurate or not); what matters is the 'regime of truth' (Michel Foucault; discussed in Chapter 6) they put into circulation. From this perspective, Hollywood's power is not a negative force, something that denies, represses, negates. On the contrary, it is productive. Foucault's general point about power is also true with regard to Hollywood's power:

> We must cease once and for all to describe the effects of power in negative terms: it 'excludes', it 'represses', it 'censors', it 'abstracts', it 'masks', it 'conceals'. In fact, power produces; it produces reality; it produces domains of objects and rituals of truth (1979: 194).

Moreover, as he also points out, 'Each society has its own regime of truth, its "general politics" of truth – that is, the types of discourse it accepts and makes function as true' (2002a: 131). On the basis of this, I want now to briefly describe three narrative paradigms, models for understanding, or 'regimes of truth', which featured strongly in Hollywood's Vietnam in the 1980s.[5]

The first narrative paradigm, as I shall call it, is 'the war as betrayal'. This is first of all a discourse about bad leaders. In *Uncommon Valor, Missing in Action I, Missing in Action II: The Beginning, Braddock: Missing in Action III* and *Rambo: First Blood Part II*, for example, politicians are blamed for America's defeat in Vietnam. When John Rambo

(Sylvester Stallone) is asked to return to Vietnam in search of American soldiers missing in action, he asks, with great bitterness: 'Do we get to win this time?' In other words, will the politicians let them win?

Second, it is a discourse about weak military leadership in the field. In *Platoon* and *Casualties of War*, for example, defeat, it is suggested, is the result of an incompetent military command. Third, it is also a discourse about civilian betrayal. Both *Cutter's Way* and *First Blood* suggest that the war effort was betrayed back home in America. Again John Rambo's comments are symptomatic. When he is told by Colonel Trautman, 'It's over Johnny', he responds,

> Nothing is over. You don't just turn it off. It wasn't my war. You asked me, and I did what I had to do to win, but somebody wouldn't let us win.

Interestingly, all the films in this category are structured around loss. In *Uncommon Valor*, *Missing in Action I, II* and *III*, *Rambo: First Blood Part II* and *POW: The Escape*, it is lost prisoners; in *Cutter's Way*, *First Blood* and *Born on the Fourth of July*, it is lost pride; in *Platoon* and *Casualties of War* it is lost innocence. It seems clear that the different versions of what is lost are symptomatic of a displacement of a greater loss: the displacement of that which can barely be named, America's defeat in Vietnam. The use of American POWs is undoubtedly the most ideologically charged of these displacement strategies. It seems to offer the possibility of three powerful political effects. First, to accept the myth that there are Americans still being held in Vietnam is to begin to retrospectively justify the original intervention. If the Vietnamese are so barbaric as to still hold prisoners decades after the conclusion of the conflict, then there is no need to feel guilty about the war, as they surely deserved the full force of American military intervention. Second, Susan Jeffords identifies a process she calls the 'femininization of loss' (1989: 145). That is, those blamed for America's defeat, whether they are unpatriotic protesters, an uncaring government, a weak and incompetent military command or corrupt politicians, are always represented as stereotypically feminine: 'the stereotyped characteristics associated with the feminine in dominant U.S. culture – weakness, indecisiveness, dependence, emotion, nonviolence, negotiation, unpredictability, deception' (145). Jeffords's argument is illustrated perfectly in the MIA (missing in action) cycle of films in which the 'feminine' negotiating stance of the politicians is played out against the 'masculine', no-nonsense approach of the returning veterans. The implication is that 'masculine' strength and single-mindedness would have won the war, while 'feminine' weakness and duplicity lost it. Third, perhaps most important of all is how these films turned what was thought to be lost into something that was only missing. Defeat is displaced by the 'victory' of finding and recovering American POWs. Puzzled by the unexpected success of *Uncommon Valor* in 1983, the *New York Times* sent a journalist to interview the film's 'audience'. One moviegoer was quite clear why the film was such a box-office success: 'We get to win the Vietnam War' (quoted in H. Bruce Franklin, 1993: 141).

The second narrative paradigm, again as I shall call it, is 'the inverted firepower syndrome'. This is a narrative device in which the United States's massive techno-military advantage is inverted. Instead of scenes of the massive destructive power of American military force, we are shown countless narratives of individual Americans fighting the numberless (and often invisible) forces of the North Vietnamese Army and/or the sinister and shadowy men and women of the National Liberation Front ('Viet Cong'). *Missing In Action I, II* and *III, Rambo: First Blood Part II* and *Platoon* all contain scenes of lone Americans struggling against overwhelming odds. John Rambo, armed only with a bow and arrow, is perhaps the most ridiculous example. *Platoon*, however, takes this narrative strategy on to another plane altogether. In a key scene, 'good' Sergeant Elias is pursued by a countless number of North Vietnamese soldiers. He is shot continually until he falls to his knees, spreading his arms out in a Christ-like gesture of agony and betrayal. The camera pans slowly to emphasize the pathos of his death throes. In Britain the film was promoted with a poster showing Elias in the full pain of his 'crucifixion'. Above the image is written the legend: 'The First Casualty of War is Innocence'. Loss of innocence is presented both as a realization of the realities of modern warfare and as a result of America playing fair against a brutal and ruthless enemy. The ideological implication is clear: if America lost by playing the good guy, it is 'obvious' that it will be necessary in all future conflicts to play the tough guy in order to win.

The third narrative paradigm I have called 'the Americanization of the war'. What I want to indicate by this term is the way in which the fundamental *meaning* of the Vietnam War has become in Hollywood's Vietnam (and elsewhere in US cultural production) an absolutely American phenomenon. This is an example of what we might call 'imperial narcissism', in which the United States is centred and Vietnam and the Vietnamese exist only to provide a context for an American tragedy, whose ultimate brutality is the loss of American innocence. And like any good tragedy, it was doomed from the beginning to follow the dictates of fate. It was something that just happened. Hollywood's Vietnam exhibits what Linda Dittmar and Gene Michaud call a 'mystique of unintelligibility' (1990: 13). Perhaps the most compelling example of the mystique of unintelligibility is the opening sequence in the American video version of *Platoon*. It begins with a few words of endorsement from the then chairman of the Chrysler Corporation. We see him moving through a clearing in a wood towards a jeep. He stops at the jeep, and resting against it, addresses the camera,

> This jeep is a museum piece, a relic of war. Normandy, Anzio, Guadalcanal, Korea, Vietnam. I hope we will never have to build another jeep for war. This film *Platoon* is a memorial not to war but to all the men and women who fought in a time and in a place *nobody really understood*, who knew only one thing: they were called and they went. It was the same from the first musket fired at Concord to the rice paddies of the Mekong Delta: they were called and they went. That in the truest sense is the spirit of America. The more we understand it, the more we honor those who kept it alive [my italics] (quoted in Harry W. Haines, 1990: 81).

This is a discourse in which there is nothing to explain but American survival. Getting 'Back to the World' is everything it is about. It is an American tragedy and America and Americans are its *only* victims. The myth is expressed with numbing precision in Chris Taylor's (Charlie Sheen) narration at the end of *Platoon*. Taylor looks back from the deck of a rising helicopter on the dead and dying of the battlefield below. Samuel Barber's mournful and very beautiful *Adagio for Strings* seems to dictate the cadence and rhythm of his voice as he speaks these words of psychobabble, about a war in which more than two million Vietnamese were killed, 'I think now looking back, we did not fight the enemy, we fought ourselves. The enemy was in us.' *Time Magazine*'s (26 January 1987) review of the film echoes and elaborates this theme:

> Welcome back to the war that, just 20 years ago, turned America schizophrenic. Suddenly we were a nation split between left and right, black and white, hip and square, mothers and fathers, parents and children. For a nation whose war history had read like a John Wayne war movie – where good guys finished first by being tough and playing fair – the polarisation was soul-souring. Americans were fighting themselves, and both sides lost.

Platoon's function in this scenario is to heal the schizophrenia of the American body politic. The film's rewriting of the war not only excludes the Vietnamese, it also rewrites the anti-war movement. Pro-war and anti-war politics are re-enacted as different positions in a debate on how best to fight and win the war. One group (led by the 'good' Sergeant Elias, who listens to Jefferson Airplane's 'White Rabbit' and smokes marijuana) wants to fight the war with honour and dignity, while the other (led by the 'bad' Sergeant Barnes, who listens to Merle Haggard's 'Okie from Muskogee' and drinks beer) wants to fight the war in any way that will win it. We are asked to believe that this was the essential conflict that tore America apart – the anti-war movement, dissolved into a conflict on how best to fight and win the war. As Michael Klein contends, 'the war is decontextualized, mystified as a tragic mistake, an existential adventure, or a rite of passage through which the White American Hero discovers his identity' (1990: 10).

Although I have outlined three of the dominant narrative paradigms in Hollywood's Vietnam, I do not want to suggest that these were or are unproblematically consumed by its American audiences (or any other audience). My claim is only that Hollywood produced a particular regime of truth. But film (like any other cultural text or practice) has to be *made* to mean (see Chapter 12). To really discover the extent to which Hollywood's Vietnam has made its 'truth' tell requires a consideration of consumption. This will take us beyond a focus on the *meaning* of a text, to a focus on the meanings that can be made in the encounter between the discourses of the text and the discourses of the 'consumer', as it is never a matter of verifying (with an 'audience') the *real meaning* of, say, *Platoon*. The focus on consumption (understood as 'production in use') is to explore the political effectivity (or otherwise) of, say, *Platoon*. If a cultural text is to become effective (politically or otherwise), it must be made to connect with people's lives – become part of their 'lived culture'. Formal analysis of Hollywood's Vietnam may point to how the industry has articulated the war as an American tragedy of bravery and betrayal, but this does not tell us that it has been consumed as a war of bravery and betrayal.

In the absence of ethnographic work on the audience for Hollywood's Vietnam, I want to point to two pieces of evidence that may provide us with clues to the circulation and effectivity of Hollywood's articulation of the war. The first consists of speeches made by President George Bush in the build-up to the first Gulf War, and the second are comments made by American Vietnam veterans about Hollywood and other representations of the war. But, to be absolutely clear, these factors, however compelling they may be in themselves, do not provide conclusive proof that Hollywood's account of the war has become hegemonic where it matters – in the lived practices of everyday life.

In the weeks leading up to the first Gulf War, *Newsweek* (10 December 1990) featured a cover showing a photograph of a serious-looking George Bush senior. Above the photograph was the banner headline, 'This will not be another Vietnam'. The headline was taken from a speech made by Bush in which he said, 'In our country, I know that there are fears of another Vietnam. Let me assure you . . . this will not be another Vietnam.' In another speech, Bush again assured his American audience that, 'This will not be another Vietnam'. But this time he explained why: 'Our troops will have the best possible support in the entire world. They will not be asked to fight with one hand tied behind their backs' (quoted in the *Daily Telegraph*, January 1991).

In these speeches, Bush was seeking to put to rest a spectre that had come to haunt America's political and military self-image, what former President Richard Nixon had called the 'Vietnam Syndrome' (1986). The debate over American foreign policy had, according to Nixon, been 'grotesquely distorted' by reluctance 'to use power to defend national interests' (13). Fear of another Vietnam had made America 'ashamed of . . . [its] power, guilty about being strong' (19).

In the two Bush speeches from which I have quoted, and in many other similar speeches, Bush was articulating what many powerful American voices throughout the 1980s had sought to make the dominant meaning of the war: 'the Vietnam War as a noble cause betrayed – an American tragedy'. For example, in the 1980 presidential campaign Ronald Reagan declared, in an attempt to put an end to the Vietnam Syndrome, 'It is time we recognized that ours was, in truth, a noble cause' (quoted in John Carlos Rowe and Rick Berg, 1991: 10). Moreover, Reagan insisted, 'Let us tell those who fought in that war that we will never again ask young men to fight and possibly die in a war our government is afraid to let us win' (quoted in Stephen Vlastos, 1991: 69). In 1982 (almost a decade after the last US combat troops left Vietnam), the Vietnam Veterans' memorial was unveiled in Washington. Reagan observed that Americans were 'beginning to appreciate that [America's war in Vietnam] was a just cause' (quoted in Barbie Zelizer, 1995: 220). In 1984 (eleven years after the last US combat troops left Vietnam) the Unknown Vietnam Soldier was buried; at the ceremony President Reagan claimed, 'An American hero has returned home. . . . He accepted his mission and did his duty. And his honest patriotism overwhelms us' (quoted in Rowe and Berg, 1991: 10). In 1985 (twelve years after the last US combat troops left Vietnam), New York staged the first of the 'Welcome Home' parades for Vietnam veterans. In this powerful mix of political rhetoric and national remembering, there is a clear attempt to put in place a new 'consensus' about the meaning of America's war in Vietnam. It begins in 1980 in Reagan's successful presidential campaign, and ends in 1991 with the triumphalism of Bush after victory in the first Gulf War. Such speeches (and the reporting of such speeches) may have helped to shape understandings of the war. But the affective power of this way of understanding the war was undoubtedly given an enormous boost by Hollywood's Vietnam. Therefore, when, in the build-up to the Gulf War, Bush had asked Americans to remember the Vietnam War, the memories recalled by many Americans may have been of a war they had lived cinematically; a war of bravery and betrayal. Hollywood's Vietnam had provided the materials to rehearse, elaborate, interpret and retell an increasingly dominant memory of America's war in Vietnam.

This was a memory that had little relationship to the 'facts' of the war. Put simply, the United States deployed in Vietnam the most intensive firepower the world had ever witnessed. Hollywood narratives do not feature the deliberate defoliation of large areas of Vietnam, the napalm strikes, the search-and-destroy missions, the use of Free Fire Zones, the mass bombing. For example, during the 'Christmas bombing' campaign of 1972, the United States 'dropped more tonnage of bombs on Hanoi and Haiphong than Germany dropped on Great Britain from 1940 to 1945' (Franklin, 1993: 79). In total, the United States dropped three times the number of bombs on Vietnam as had been dropped anywhere during the whole of the Second World War (Pilger, 1990). In a memorandum to President Johnson in 1967, Secretary of Defense Robert McNamara wrote: '[The] picture of the world's greatest superpower killing or seriously injuring 1,000 noncombatants a week [his estimate of the human cost of the US bombing campaign], while trying to pound a tiny backward nation into submission on an issue whose merits are hotly disputed, is not pretty' (quoted in Martin, 1993: 19–20). This makes profoundly unconvincing Bush's claim (based on Hollywood rather than history) that the United States fought the war with one hand tied behind its back.

A second example of the consumption of Hollywood's Vietnam is provided by the comments of American Vietnam veterans. As Marita Sturken observes, 'Some Vietnam veterans say they have forgotten where some of their memories came from – their own experiences, documentary photographs, or Hollywood movies?' (1997: 20). For example, Vietnam veteran William Adams makes this telling point:

> When *Platoon* was first released, a number of people asked me, 'Was the war really like that?' I never found an answer, in part because, no matter how graphic and realistic, a movie is after all a movie, and war is only like itself. But I also failed to find an answer because what 'really' happened is now so thoroughly mixed up in my mind with what has been said about what happened that the pure experience is no longer there. This is odd, even painful, in some ways. But it is also testimony to the way our memories work. The Vietnam War is no longer a definite event so much as it is a collective and mobile script in which we continue to scrawl, erase, rewrite our conflicting and changing view of ourselves (quoted in Sturken, 1997: 86).

Similarly, academic and Vietnam veteran Michael Clark writes of how the ticker-tape welcome home parade for Vietnam veterans staged in New York in 1985, together with the media coverage of the parade and the Hollywood films that seemed to provide the context for the parade, had worked together to produce a particular memory of the war – a memory with potentially deadly effects:

> they had constituted our memory of the war all along . . . [They] healed over the wounds that had refused to close for ten years with a balm of nostalgia, and transformed guilt and doubt into duty and pride. And with a triumphant flourish [they] offered us the spectacle of [their] most successful creation, the veterans who will fight the next war (Clark, 1991: 180).

Moreover, as Clark is at pains to stress, 'the memory of Vietnam has ceased to be a point of resistance to imperialist ambitions and is now invoked as a vivid warning to do it right next time' (206). These concerns were fully justified by Bush's triumphalism at the end of the first Gulf War, when he boasted, as if the war had been fought for no other reason than to overcome a traumatic memory, 'By God, we've kicked the Vietnam Syndrome once and for all' (quoted in Franklin, 1993: 177). Echoing these comments, the *New York Times* (2 December 1993) featured an article with the title 'Is the Vietnam Syndrome Dead? Happily, It's Buried in the Gulf.' Vietnam, the sign of American loss and division, had been buried in the sands of the Persian Gulf. Kicking the Vietnam Syndrome (with the help of Hollywood's Vietnam) had supposedly liberated a nation from old ghosts and doubts; had made America once again strong, whole and ready for the next war.

Whiteness

In terms of the population of the world white people do not make up a significant number. Yet in terms of power and privilege they are the dominant colour. Of course this does not mean that all white people have power and privilege (whiteness is always articulated with, for example, social class, gender and sexuality).[6]

Part of the power of whiteness is that it seems to exist outside categories of 'race' and ethnicity. These categories appear to apply only to non-white people; whiteness seems to exist as a human norm from which races and ethnicities are a deviation. This is indeed a privileged position. As Richard Dyer (1997) makes clear,

> There is no more powerful position than that of being 'just human'. The claim to power is the claim to speak for the communality of humanity. Raced people can't do that – they can only speak for their race. But non-raced people can, for they do not represent the interests of a race. The point of seeing the racing of whites is to dislodge them/us from the position of power, with all the inequities, oppression, privileges and sufferings in its train, dislodging them/us by understanding the authority with which they/we speak in and on the world (2).

To understand the normative power of whiteness we have to forget about its biology and think about it as a cultural construct; that is, something that is presented as 'natural', 'normal' and 'universal'. What makes whiteness so powerful, therefore, is that it is more than the dominant colouring; it operates as an unmarked human norm, and it is against this norm that other ethnicities are invited to measure themselves. Put simply, white people are rarely thought of as white people; they are simply human without ethnicity. We see this every time, for example, we read about a white writer; he will be described as a writer; but if he is black he will often be described as a *black* writer. Blackness is a sign of ethnicity, whereas whiteness is supposedly just a sign of the human. Also, when a black person speaks she will be expected to speak on behalf of other black people, whereas a white person speaks as an individual or for humanity as a whole. When black people are discussed they are discussed as black people, whereas when white people are discussed they are discussed as people. In this way the ethnic invisibility of whiteness positions it as the normative human. Again, to quote Dyer, 'At the level of racial representation . . . whites are not of a certain race, they're just the human race' (3).

Many white people think of themselves as neutral and normal in terms of ethnicity and 'race'. They refer to other people's ethnic origins, while their own remains invisible and unmarked. When a white English person sees the terms 'ethnic fashion' or 'ethnic food', they would be amazed if this were a reference to white English food or fashion. By not being 'raced', they become the human race. To put an end to this privilege and power we have to see whiteness as the sign of just another ethnicity. Noticing difference is not the problem; it is how we make difference signify that may or may not be a problem.

Any discussion of 'race' and ethnicity, therefore, that does not include a discussion of whiteness will always, perhaps unknowingly and without intention, contribute to the power and privilege of whiteness. This is because its power and privilege is underpinned by its very unmarkness, its apparent universality as simply human and normal. To put it simply, white seems 'natural' and 'normal'. This will always be the case until whiteness is widely recognized as just the sign of another ethnicity.

Anti-racism and cultural studies

As was noted with both feminist and Marxist approaches to popular culture, discussions of 'race' and representation inevitably, and quite rightly, involve an ethical imperative to condemn the deeply inhuman discourses of racism. With this in mind, I want to end this section with two quotations, followed by a brief discussion and another quotation. The first quotation is from Stuart Hall and the second from Paul Gilroy.

> [T]he work that cultural studies has to do is to mobilise everything that it can find in terms of intellectual resources in order to understand what keeps making the

lives we live, and the societies we live in, profoundly and deeply antihumane in their capacity to live with difference. Cultural studies' message is a message for academics and intellectuals but, fortunately, for many other people as well. . . . I am convinced that no intellectual worth his or her salt, and no university that wants to hold up its head in the face of the twenty-first century, can afford to turn dispassionate eyes away from the problems of race and ethnicity that beset our world (Hall, 1996e: 343).

We need to know what sorts of insight and reflection might actually help increasingly differentiated societies and anxious individuals to cope successfully with the challenges involved in dwelling comfortably in proximity to the unfamiliar without becoming fearful and hostile. We need to consider whether the scale upon which sameness and difference are calculated might be altered productively so that the strangeness of strangers goes out of focus and other dimensions of basic sameness can be acknowledged and made significant. We also need to consider how a deliberate engagement with the twentieth century's history of suffering might furnish resources for the peaceful accommodation of otherness in relation to fundamental commonality. . . . [That is,] namely that human beings are ordinarily far more alike than they are unalike, that most of the time we can communicate with each other, and that the recognition of mutual worth, dignity, and essential similarity imposes restrictions on how we can behave if we wish to act justly (Gilroy, 2004: 3–4).

The work of cultural studies, like that of all reasonable intellectual traditions, is to intellectually, and by example, help to defeat racism, and by so doing, help to bring into being a world in which the term 'race' is little more than a long disused historical category, signifying in the contemporary nothing more than the human race. However, as Gilroy observed in 1987, and, unfortunately, as is still the case more than thirty years later, until that moment arrives,

'Race' must be retained as an analytic category not because it corresponds to any biological or epistemological absolutes, but because it refers investigation to the power that collective identities acquire by means of their roots in tradition. These identities, in the forms of white racism and black resistance, are the most volatile political forces in Britain today (2002: 339).

Notes

1. Early forms of humans ('hominins') first appeared in what is now Africa about 2.5 million years ago. Around 100,000 years ago a small group of Homo sapiens (our direct ancestors) migrated out of Africa. This group gradually populated all

parts of the earth. For a period of time early humans co-existed outside Africa with at least two other humanoid species, both of which became extinct, Neanderthals and Denisovans. Some present-day humans carry genes that prove our ancestors had children with these other species. However, people in the world today are descended from either this small group of migrants or from their fellow *Homo sapiens* who remained in Africa. Although, therefore, there is just one race, the human race, it is possible to group people into overlapping populations of bio-geographical clusters that are called 'ancestry groups' (marked by differences derived from tens of thousands of years experiencing the same diet and climate).

2. Hume is referring to Francis Williams, who graduated from Cambridge University with a degree in mathematics.

3. 'Race' and racism are not just manifested in representations and social actions and interactions; they also inhabit the inner landscapes of our psyches. For a discussion of this see Franz Fanon's *Black Skin, White Masks* (1986).

4. Chamberlain's speech finds a strange echo in a speech made by Tony Blair on confirming his resignation as prime minister, 'This country is a blessed nation. The British are special, the world knows it, in our innermost thoughts, we know it. This is the greatest nation on earth' (quoted in Storey, 2010b: 22).

5. For a fuller version of this argument, see Storey (2002b and 2010a).

6. Whiteness is divided not just by social class and gender (and other markers of social difference); it is also divided by distinctions within whiteness itself – who to include as white produces different answers at different moments in history.

Further reading

Storey, John (ed.), *Cultural Theory and Popular Culture: A Reader*, 4th edn, Harlow: Pearson Education, 2009. This is the companion volume to the previous edition of this book. A fully updated 5th edition containing further readings is due for publication in 2018. An interactive website is also available (www.routledge.com/cw/storey), which contains helpful student resources and a glossary of terms for each chapter.

Baker, Houston A. Jr, Manthia Diawara and Ruth H. Lindeborg (eds), *Black British Cultural Studies: A Reader*, Chicago: University of Chicago Press, 1996. A very interesting collection of essays.

Dent, Gina (ed.), *Black Popular Culture*, Seattle: Bay Press, 1992. A very useful collection of essays.

Dittmar, Linda and Gene Michaud (eds), *From Hanoi To Hollywood: The Vietnam War in American Film*, New Brunswick and London: Rutgers University Press, 1990. The best collection of work on Hollywood's Vietnam.

Dyer, Richard (1997), *White: Essays on Race and Culture*, London: Routledge. The classic account of whiteness and culture.

Fryer, Peter, *Staying Power: The History of Black People in Britain*, London: Pluto, 1984. A brilliant book.

Gandhi, Leela, *Postcolonial Theory: A Critical Introduction*, Edinburgh: Edinburgh University Press, 1998. A good introduction to post-colonial theory.

Gilroy, Paul, *There Ain't No Black in the Union Jack*, London: Routledge, 1987/2002. One of the classic cultural studies encounters with 'race'.

Gilroy, Paul, *The Black Atlantic*, London: Verso, 1993. A brilliant argument against 'cultural absolutism'.

Markus, Hazel Rose and Paula M.L. Moya, *Doing Race: 21 Essays for the 21st Century*, New York: Norton, 2010. An excellent collection of essays on 'doing race'.

Pitcher, Ben, *Consuming Race*, London: Routledge, 2014. A very interesting account of the role of 'race' in everyday life.

Williams, Patrick and Laura Chrisman (eds), *Colonial Discourse and Post-Colonial Theory: A Reader*, Harlow: Prentice Hall, 1993. An interesting collection of essays on post-colonial theory.

10 Postmodernism

Postmodernism is a term current inside and outside the academic study of popular culture. It has entered discourses as different as pop music journalism and Marxist debates on the cultural conditions of late or multinational capitalism. As Angela McRobbie (1994) observes,

> Postmodernism has entered into a more diverse number of vocabularies more quickly than most other intellectual categories. It has spread outwards from the realms of art history into political theory and onto the pages of youth culture magazines, record sleeves, and the fashion pages of Vogue. This seems to me to indicate something more than the mere vagaries of taste (13).

She also suggests that 'the recent debates on postmodernism possess both a positive attraction and a usefulness to the analyst of popular culture' (15). What is certainly the case is that as a concept postmodernism shows little sign of slowing down its colonial-like expansion. Here is Dick Hebdige's (1988) list of the ways in which the term has been used:

> When it becomes possible for people to describe as 'postmodern' the decor of a room, the design of a building, the diegesis of a film, the construction of a record, or a 'scratch' video, a television commercial, or an arts documentary, or the 'inter-textual' relations between them, the layout of a page in a fashion magazine or critical journal, an anti-teleological tendency within epistemology, the attack on the 'metaphysics of presence', a general attenuation of feeling, the collective chagrin and morbid projections of a post-War generation of baby boomers confronting disillusioned middle age, the 'predicament' of reflexivity, a group of rhetorical tropes, a proliferation of surfaces, a new phase in commodity fetishism, a fascination for images, codes and styles, a process of cultural, political, or existential fragmentation and/or crisis, the 'de-centring' of the subject, an 'incredulity towards metanarratives', the replacement of unitary power axes by a plurality of power/discourse formations, the 'implosion of meaning', the collapse of cultural hierarchies,

the dread engendered by the threat of nuclear self-destruction, the decline of the university, the functioning and effects of the new miniaturised technologies, broad societal and economic shifts into a 'media', 'consumer' or 'multinational' phase, a sense (depending on who you read) of 'placelessness' or the abandonment of placelessness ('critical regionalism') or (even) a generalised substitution of spatial for temporal coordinates – when it becomes possible to describe all these things as 'postmodern' . . . then it's clear we are in the presence of a buzzword (2009: 429).

For the purposes of this discussion I shall, with the exception of some necessary theoretical exposition, consider postmodernism only as it relates to the study of popular culture. To facilitate this I shall focus on the development of postmodern theory from its beginnings in the United States and Britain in the early 1960s, through its theorization in the work of Jean-François Lyotard, Jean Baudrillard and Fredric Jameson. This will be followed by a discussion of two examples of postmodern culture: pop music and television. The chapter will conclude with a discussion of three more general aspects of postmodernism: the collapse of absolute standards of value, the culture of globalization and convergence culture.

Postmodernism in the 1960s

Although the term 'postmodern' had been in cultural circulation since the 1870s (Best and Kellner, 1991), it is only in the 1960s that we see the beginnings of what is now understood as postmodernism. In the work of Susan Sontag (1966) and Leslie Fiedler (1971) we encounter the celebration of what Sontag calls a 'new sensibility' (1966: 296). It is in part a sensibility in revolt against the canonization of modernism's avant-garde revolution; it attacks modernism's official status, its canonization in the museum and the academy, as the high culture of the modern capitalist world. It laments the passing of the scandalous and bohemian power of modernism, its ability to shock and disgust the middle class. Instead of outraging from the critical margins of bourgeois society, the work of Pablo Picasso, James Joyce, T.S. Eliot, Virginia Woolf, Bertolt Brecht, Igor Stravinsky and others had not only lost the ability to shock and disturb, but had also become central, classical: in a word – canonized. Modernist culture has become bourgeois culture. Its subversive power has been drained by the academy and the museum. It is now the canon against which an avant-garde must struggle. As Fredric Jameson (1984) points out,

This is surely one of the most plausible explanations for the emergence of post-modernism itself, since the younger generation of the 1960s will now confront the formerly oppositional modern movement as a set of dead classics, which 'weigh like a nightmare on the brains of the living', as Marx [1977] once said in a different context (56).

Jameson (1988) argues that postmodernism was born out of

> the shift from an oppositional to a hegemonic position of the classics of modernism, the latter's conquest of the university, the museum, the art gallery network and the foundations, the assimilation . . . of the various high modernisms, into the 'canon' and the subsequent attenuation of everything in them felt by our grandparents to be shocking, scandalous, ugly, dissonant, immoral and antisocial (299).

For the student of popular culture perhaps the most important consequence of the new sensibility, with its abandonment of 'the Matthew Arnold notion of culture, finding it historically and humanly obsolescent' (Sontag, 1966: 299), is its claim that 'the distinction between "high" and "low" culture seems less and less meaningful' (302). In this sense, it is a sensibility in revolt against what is seen as the cultural elitism of modernism. Modernism, in spite of the fact that it often quoted from popular culture, was marked by a deep suspicion of all things popular. Its entry into the museum and the academy was undoubtedly made easier (regardless of its declared antagonism to 'bourgeois philistinism') by its appeal to, and homologous relationship with, the elitism of class society. The postmodernism of the 1960s was therefore in part a populist attack on the elitism of modernism. It signalled a refusal of what Andreas Huyssen (1986) calls 'the great divide . . . [a] discourse which insists on the categorical distinction between high art and mass culture' (viii). Moreover, according to Huyssen, 'To a large extent, it is by the distance we have travelled from this "great divide" between mass culture and modernism that we can measure our own cultural postmodernity' (57).

The American and British pop art of the 1960s presented a clear rejection of the 'great divide'. It rejected Arnold's definition of culture as 'the best that has been thought and said' (see Chapter 2), preferring instead Williams's social definition of culture as 'a whole way of life' (see Chapter 3). British pop art dreamed of America (seen as the home of popular culture) from the grey deprivation of early 1960s Britain. As Lawrence Alloway, the movement's first theorist, explains,

> The area of contact was mass produced urban culture: movies, advertising, science fiction, pop music. We felt none of the dislike of commercial culture standard among most intellectuals, but accepted it as a fact, discussed it in detail, and consumed it enthusiastically. One result of our discussions was to take pop culture out of the realm of 'escapism', 'sheer entertainment', 'relaxation', and to treat it with the seriousness of art (quoted in Frith and Horne, 1987: 104).

Andy Warhol was also a key figure in the theorizing of pop art. Like Alloway, he refuses to take seriously the distinction between commercial and non-commercial art. He sees 'commercial art as real art and real art as commercial art' (109). He claims that '"real" art is defined simply by the taste (and wealth) of the ruling class of the period. This implies not only that commercial art is just as good as "real" art – its value simply being defined by other social groups, other patterns of expenditure' (ibid.). We can of course object that Warhol's merging of high and popular is a little misleading.

Whatever the source of his ideas and his materials, once they are located in an art gallery the context locates them as art and thus high culture. John Rockwell argues that this was not the intention or the necessary outcome. Art, he argues, is what you perceive as art: 'A Brillo box isn't suddenly art because Warhol puts a stacked bunch of them in a museum. But by putting them there he encourages you to make your every trip to the supermarket an artistic adventure, and in so doing he has exalted your life. Everybody's an artist if they want to be' (120).

Huyssen (1986) claims that the full impact of the relationship between pop art and popular culture can be fully understood only when located within the larger cultural context of the American counterculture and the British underground scene: 'Pop in the broadest sense was the context in which a notion of the postmodern first took shape, and from the beginning until today, the most significant trends within postmodernism have challenged modernism's relentless hostility to mass culture' (188). In this way, then, postmodernism can be said to have been at least partly born out of a generational refusal of the categorical certainties of high modernism. The insistence on an absolute distinction between high and popular culture came to be regarded as the 'un-hip' assumption of an older generation. One sign of this collapse was the merging of pop art and pop music. For example, Peter Blake designed the Beatles' *Sergeant Pepper's Lonely Hearts Club Band* album; Richard Hamilton designed their 'white album'; Andy Warhol designed the Rolling Stones' album *Sticky Fingers*. Similarly, we could cite the new seriousness emerging in pop music itself, most evident in the work of performers such as Bob Dylan and the Beatles; there is a new seriousness in their work and their work is taken seriously in a way unknown before in considerations of pop music.

Huyssen also detects a clear relationship between the American postmodernism of the 1960s and certain aspects of an earlier European avant-garde; seeing the American counterculture – its opposition to the war in Vietnam, its support for black civil rights, its rejection of the elitism of high modernism, its birthing of the second wave of feminism, the welcome it gave to the gay liberation movement, its cultural experimentalism, its alternative theatre, its happenings, its love-ins, its celebration of the everyday, its psyche-delic art, its acid rock, its 'acid perspectivism' (Hebdige, 2009) – 'as the closing chapter in the tradition of avantgardism' (Huyssen, 1986: 195).

By the late 1970s the debate about postmodernism crossed the Atlantic. The next three sections will consider the responses of two French cultural theorists to the debate on the 'new sensibility', before returning to America and Fredric Jameson's account of postmodernism as the cultural dominant of late capitalism.

Jean-François Lyotard

Jean-François Lyotard's (1984) principal contribution to the debate on postmodernism is *The Postmodern Condition*, published in France in 1979, and translated into English in 1984. The influence of this book on the debate has been enormous. In many respects it was this book that introduced the term 'postmodernism' into academic circulation.

For Lyotard the postmodern condition is marked by a crisis in the status of knowledge in Western societies. This is expressed as an 'incredulity towards metanarratives' and what he calls 'the obsolescence of the metanarrative apparatus of legitimation' (xxiv). What Lyotard is referring to is the supposed contemporary collapse or widespread rejection of all overarching and totalizing frameworks that seek to tell universal stories ('metanarratives'): Marxism, liberalism, Christianity, for example. According to Lyotard, metanarratives operate through inclusion and exclusion, as homogenizing forces, marshalling heterogeneity into ordered realms, silencing and excluding other discourses, other voices in the name of universal principles and general goals. Postmodernism is said to signal the collapse of all metanarratives with their privileged truth to tell, and to witness instead the increasing sound of a plurality of voices from the margins, with their insistence on difference, on cultural diversity, and the claims of heterogeneity over homogeneity.[1]

Lyotard's particular focus is on the status and function of scientific discourse and knowledge. Science is important for Lyotard because of the role assigned to it by the Enlightenment.[2] Its task, through the accumulation of scientific knowledge, is to play a central role in the gradual emancipation of humankind. In this way, science assumes the status of a metanarrative, organizing and validating other narratives on the royal road to human liberation. However, Lyotard claims that since the Second World War, the legitimating force of science's status as a metanarrative has waned considerably. It is no longer seen to be slowly making progress on behalf of humankind towards absolute knowledge and absolute freedom. It has lost its way – its 'goal is no longer truth, but performativity' (46). Similarly, higher education is 'called upon to create skills, and no longer ideals' (48). Knowledge is seen no longer as an end in itself, but as a means to an end. Like science, education will be judged by its performativity; and as such it will be increasingly shaped by the demands of power. No longer will it respond to the question, 'Is it true?' It will hear only, 'What use is it?' 'How much is it worth?' and 'Is it saleable?' (51). Postmodern pedagogy would teach how to use knowledge as a form of cultural and economic capital without recourse to concern or anxiety about whether what is taught is true or false. At my own university the magic word is 'employability' – the absolute measure of all things academic.

Before leaving Lyotard, it is worth noting his own less than favourable response to the changed status of culture. The popular culture ('contemporary general culture') of the postmodern condition is for Lyotard an 'anything goes' culture, a culture of 'slackening', where taste is irrelevant, and money the only sign of value (79). The only relief is Lyotard's view that postmodernist culture is not the end of the much superior culture of modernism, but the sign of the advent of a new modernism. Postmodernism is that which breaks with one modernism to form a new modernism: 'A work can become modern only if it is first postmodern. Postmodernism thus understood is not modernism at its end but in the nascent state, and this state is constant' (ibid.).

Steven Connor (1989) suggests that *The Postmodern Condition* may be read 'as a disguised allegory of the condition of academic knowledge and institutions in the contemporary world' (41). Lyotard's 'diagnosis of the postmodern condition is, in one sense, the diagnosis of the final futility of the intellectual' (ibid.). Lyotard is himself aware of what he calls the contemporary intellectual's 'negative heroism'. Intellectuals have, he argues, been losing their authority since 'the violence and critique mounted against the academy during the sixties' (quoted in Connor, 1989: 41). As Iain Chambers (1988) observes,

> the debate over postmodernism can . . . be read as the symptom of the disruptive ingression of popular culture, its aesthetics and intimate possibilities, into a previously privileged domain. Theory and academic discourses are confronted by the wider, unsystemized, popular networks of cultural production and knowledge. The intellectual's privilege to explain and distribute knowledge is threatened; his authority, for it is invariably 'his', redimensionalized. This in part explains both the recent defensiveness of the modernist, particularly Marxist, project, and the cold nihilism of certain notorious strands in postmodernism (216).

Angela McRobbie (1994) claims that postmodernism has enfranchised a new body of intellectuals: 'the coming into being of those whose voices were historically drowned out by the (modernist) metanarratives of mastery, which were in turn both patriarchal and imperialist' (15). Moreover, as Kobena Mercer (1994) points out,

> While the loudest voices in the culture announced nothing less than the end of everything of any value, the emerging voices, practices and identities of dispersed African, Caribbean and Asian peoples crept in from the margins of postimperial Britain to dislocate commonplace certainties and consensual 'truths' and thus open up new ways of seeing, and understanding, the peculiarities of living in the twilight of an historic interregnum in which 'the old is dying and the new cannot be born' [Gramsci, 1971] (Mercer, 1994: 2).

Jean Baudrillard

Jean Baudrillard, according to Best and Kellner (1991), 'has achieved guru status throughout the English speaking world' (109). They claim that 'Baudrillard has emerged as one of the most high profile postmodern theorists' (111). His presence has not been confined to the world of academia; articles and interviews have appeared in many popular magazines.

Baudrillard claims that we in the West have reached a stage in social and economic development in which 'it is no longer possible to separate the economic or productive realm from the realms of ideology or culture, since cultural artefacts, images, representations, even feelings and psychic structures have become part of the world of the economic' (Connor, 1989: 51). This is partly explained, Baudrillard argues, by the fact that there has been a historical shift in the West, from a society based on the production of things to one based on the production of information. In *For a Critique of the Political Economy of the Sign*, he describes this as 'the passage from a metallurgic into a semiurgic society' (1981: 185). However, for Baudrillard, postmodernism is not simply a culture of the sign: rather it is a culture of the 'simulacrum'.

A simulacrum is an identical copy without an original. In Chapter 4, we examined Benjamin's claim that mechanical reproduction had destroyed the 'aura' of the work of art; Baudrillard argues that the very distinction between original and copy has itself now been destroyed. He calls this process 'simulation'. This idea can be demonstrated with reference to CDs and films. For example, when someone buys a copy of Steve Earle's *The Revolution Starts Now*, it makes little sense to speak of having purchased the original. Similarly, it would make no sense for someone having seen *The Eternal Sunshine of the Spotless Mind* in Newcastle to be told by someone having seen the film in Shanghai or Berlin that he had seen the original and she had not. Both would have witnessed an exhibition of a copy without an original. In both cases, film and CD, we see or hear a copy without an original. A film is a construction made from editing together film footage shot in a different sequence and at different times. In the same way, a music recording is a construction made from editing together sounds recorded in a different sequence and at different times.

Baudrillard (1983) calls simulation 'the generation by models of a real without origins or reality: a hyperreal' (2). Hyperrealism, he claims, is the characteristic mode of postmodernity. In the realm of the hyperreal, the distinction between simulation and the 'real' implodes; the 'real' and the imaginary continually collapse into each other. The result is that reality and simulation are experienced as without difference – operating along a roller-coaster continuum. Simulations can often be experienced as more real than the real itself – 'even better than the real thing' (U2). Think of the way in which *Platoon* has become the mark against which to judge the realism of representations of America's war in Vietnam (and increasingly its wars in Iraq and Afghanistan). Asking if it has the 'look' of *Platoon* is virtually the same as asking if it is realistic.

The evidence for hyperrealism is said to be everywhere. For example, we live in a society in which people write letters to characters in soap operas, making them offers of marriage, sympathizing with their current difficulties, offering them new accommodation, or just writing to ask how they are coping with life. Television villains are regularly confronted in the street and warned about the possible future consequences of not altering their behaviour. Television doctors, television lawyers and television detectives regularly receive requests for advice and help. I saw an American tourist on television enthusing about the beauty of the British Lake District. Searching for suitable words of praise, he said, 'It's just like Disneyland.' In the early 1990s the Northumbria police force introduced 'cardboard police cars' in an attempt to keep motorists within the law. I recently visited an Italian restaurant in Morpeth in which a painting of Marlon Brando as the 'Godfather' is exhibited as a mark of the restaurant's genuine *Italianicity*. Visitors to New York can do tours that bus them around the city, not as 'itself' but as it appears in *Sex and the City*. The riots following the acquittal of the four Los Angeles police officers captured on video physically assaulting the black motorist Rodney King were headlined in two British newspapers as 'LA Lawless' and in another as 'LA War' – the story anchored not by a historical reference to similar disturbances in Watts, Los Angeles, in 1965, or the implications of the words – 'No justice no peace' – chanted by demonstrators during the riots; the editors chose instead to locate the story within the fictional world of the American television series *LA Law*. Baudrillard calls this 'the dissolution of TV into life, the dissolution of life into TV' (55). Politicians increasingly play on this, relying on the conviction politics of the 'photo-opportunity' and the 'sound bite' in an attempt to win the hearts and minds of voters.

In New York in the mid-1980s the City Arts Workshop and Adopt a Building commissioned artists to paint murals on a block of abandoned buildings. After consultations with local residents it was agreed to depict images of what the community lacked: grocery store, newsstand, laundromat and record shop (Frith and Horne, 1987: 7). What the story demonstrates is something similar to the Northumbria police story – the substitution of an image for the real thing: instead of police cars, the illusion of police cars; instead of enterprise, the illusion of enterprise. Simon Frith and Howard Horne's (1987) rather patronizing account of working-class youth out at the weekend illustrates much the same point:

> What made it all real for them: the TAN. The tan courtesy of the sun bed. No one here had been on a winter break (this is the Tebbit generation); they'd bought their look across the counter of the hairdresser, the beauty parlour and the keep fit centre. And so every weekend they gather in dreary, drizzly York and Birmingham and Crewe and act not as if they were on holiday but as if they were in an advertisement for holidays. Shivering. A simulation, but for real (182).

The 1998 case of the imprisonment of *Coronation Street* character Deirdre Rachid is perhaps a classic example of hyperrealism (see Photo 10.1). The tabloid press not only covered the story, it campaigned for her release, in much the same way as if this was an incident from 'real life'. The *Daily Star* launched a campaign to 'Free the Weatherfield

Photo 10.1   An example of hyperrealism.

Source: Daily Express/N&S Syndication and Licensing

One', and invited readers to phone or fax them to register their protest. They also produced a free poster for readers to display in car windows. The *Sun* asked readers to sign their petition and invited them to buy specially produced campaign T-shirts. MPs were described as sympathetic to Deirdre's plight. The *Star* quoted Labour MP Fraser Kemp's intention to speak to Home Secretary Jack Straw: 'I will tell the Home Secretary that there has been an appalling miscarriage of justice. The Home Secretary should intervene to ensure justice is done and Deirdre is released.' Questions were asked in the Houses of Parliament. The broadsheets joined in (in the way they always do) by commenting on the tabloid stories.

In spite of all this, I think we can say with some confidence that the overwhelming majority of people who demonstrated their outrage at Deirdre Rachid's imprisonment and celebrated her release did so without believing that she was a real person, who had been unjustly sent to prison. What she is – and what they knew her to be – is a real character in a real soap opera (between 1972 and 2014), watched three times a week by millions of real viewers. It is this that makes her a significant cultural figure (and of significant cultural reality). If hyperrealism means anything, it cannot with any credibility signal a decline in people's ability to distinguish between fiction and reality. It is not, as some Baudrillardians seem to want to suggest, that people can no longer tell the difference between fiction and reality: it is that in some significant ways the distinction between the two has become less and less important. Why this has happened is itself an important question. But I do not think that hyperrealism really supplies us with the answer.

The answer may have something to do with the way in which, as noted by John Fiske (1994), the 'postmodern media' no longer provide 'secondary representations of reality; they affect and produce the reality that they mediate' (xv). He is aware that to make an event a media event is not simply in the gift of the media. For something to become a media event it must successfully articulate (in the Gramscian sense discussed in Chapter 4) the concerns of both public and media. The relationship between media and public is complex, but what is certain in our 'postmodern world' is that all events that 'matter' are media events. He cites the example of the arrest of O.J. Simpson: 'Local people watching the chase on TV went to O.J.'s house to be there at the showdown, but took their portable TVs with them in the knowledge that the live event was not a substitute for the mediated one but a complement to it. On seeing themselves on their own TVs, they waved to themselves, for postmodern people have no problem in being simultaneously and indistinguishably livepeople and mediapeople' (xxii). The people who watched the arrest seemed to know implicitly that the media do not simply report or circulate the news, they produce it. In order to be part of the news of O.J. Simpson's arrest it was not enough to be there, one had to be there on television. This suggests that there is no longer a clear distinction between a 'real' event and its media representation. O.J. Simpson's trial, for example, cannot be neatly separated into a 'real' event that television then represented as a media event. Anyone who watched the proceedings unfold on TV knows that the trial was conducted for the television audience as much as for those present in the court. Without the presence of the cameras this would have been a very different event indeed.

Baudrillard's (1983) own example of hyperrealism is Disneyland: he calls it 'a perfect model of all the entangled orders of simulation' (23). He claims that the success of Disneyland is due not to its ability to allow Americans a fantasy escape from reality, but to the fact that it allows them an unacknowledged concentrated experience of 'real' America.

> Disneyland is there to conceal the fact that it is the 'real' country, all of 'real' America, which is Disneyland (just as prisons are there to conceal the fact that it is the society in its entirety, in its banal omnipresence, which is carceral). Disneyland is presented as imaginary in order to make us believe that the rest is real, when in fact all of Los Angeles and the America surrounding it are no longer real, but of the order of the hyperreal and of simulation. It is no longer a question of a false representation of reality (ideology), but of concealing the fact that the real is no longer real (25).

He explains this in terms of Disneyland's social 'function': 'It is meant to be an infantile world, in order to make us believe that the adults are elsewhere, in the "real" world, and to conceal the fact that real childishness is everywhere' (ibid.). He argues that the reporting of 'Watergate' operated in much the same way. It had to be reported as a scandal in order to conceal the fact that it was a commonplace of American political life. This is an example of what he calls 'a simulation of a scandal to regenerative ends' (30). It is an attempt 'to revive a moribund principle by simulated scandal . . . a question of proving the real by the imaginary; proving truth by scandal' (36). In the same way, it could be argued that recent revelations about the activities of certain businessmen operating in the financial markets of London had to be reported as a scandal in order to conceal what Baudrillard calls capitalism's 'instantaneous cruelty; its incomprehensible ferocity; its fundamental immorality' (28–9). In other words, blame the bankers in order to protect the system that enables and encourages their greed and criminality. Or, as we are told in Bertolt Brecht's *The Threepenny Opera*, 'What's breaking into a bank compared with founding a bank?'

Baudrillard's general analysis supports Lyotard's central point about postmodernism, the collapse of certainty, and the dissolution of the metanarrative of 'truth'. God, nature, science, the working class, all have lost their authority as centres of authenticity and truth; they no longer provide the evidence on which to rest one's case. The result, he argues, is not a retreat from the 'real', but the collapse of the real into hyperrealism. As he says, 'When the real is no longer what it used to be, nostalgia assumes its full meaning. There is a proliferation of myths of origin and signs of reality . . . a panic stricken production of the real and the referential' (12–13). This is an example of the second historical shift identified by Baudrillard. Modernity was the era of what Paul Ricoeur (1981) calls the 'hermeneutics of suspicion',[3] the search for meaning in the underlying reality of appearances. Marx and Freud are obvious examples of this mode of thinking (see Chapters 4 and 5). Hyperreality thus calls into question the claims of representation, both political and cultural. If there is no real behind the appearance, no beyond or beneath, what can be called with validity a representation? For example, given this line of argument, *Rambo* does not represent a type of American thinking on

Vietnam, it *is* a type of American thinking on Vietnam; representation does not stand at one remove from reality, to conceal or distort, it *is* reality. The revolution proposed by Baudrillard's theory is a revolution against latent meaning (providing, as it does, the necessary precondition for ideological analysis). Certainly this is how the argument is often presented. But if we think again about his accounts of Disneyland and Watergate, does what he has to say about them amount to very much more than a rather traditional ideological analysis – the discovery of the 'truth' behind the appearance?

Baudrillard is ambivalent about the social and cultural changes he discusses. On the one hand, he appears to celebrate them. On the other, he suggests that they signal a form of cultural exhaustion: all that remains is endless cultural repetition. I suppose the truth of Baudrillard's position is a kind of resigned celebration. Lawrence Grossberg (1988) calls it 'celebration in the face of inevitability, an embracing of nihilism without empowerment, since there is no real possibility of struggle' (175). John Docker (1994) is more critical:

> Baudrillard offers a classic modernist narrative, history as a linear, unidirectional story of decline. But whereas the early twentieth-century high literary modernists could dream of an avant-garde or cultural elite that might preserve the values of the past in the hope of a future seeding and regrowth, no such hope surfaces in Baudrillard's vision of a dying, entropic world. It's not even possible to write in a rational argumentative form, for that assumes a remaining community of reason (105).

Fredric Jameson

Fredric Jameson is an American Marxist cultural critic who has written a number of very influential essays on postmodernism. Where Jameson differs from other theorists is in his insistence that postmodernism can best be theorized from within a Marxist or neo-Marxist framework.

For Jameson postmodernism is more than just a particular cultural style: it is above all a 'periodizing concept' (1985: 113). Postmodernism is 'the cultural dominant' of late or multinational capitalism. His argument is informed by Ernest Mandel's (1978) characterization of capitalism's three-stage development: 'market capitalism', 'monopoly capitalism' and 'late or multinational capitalism'. Capitalism's third stage 'constitutes . . . the purest form of capital into hitherto uncommodified areas' (Jameson, 1984: 78). He overlays Mandel's linear model with a tripartite schema of cultural development: 'realism', 'modernism' and 'postmodernism' (ibid.). Jameson's argument also borrows from Williams's (1980) influential claim that a given social formation will always consist of three cultural moments ('dominant', 'emergent' and 'residual'). Williams's argument is that the move from one historical period to another does not usually involve the complete collapse of one cultural mode and the installation of another. Historical change may simply bring about a shift in the relative place of different cultural modes. In a given social formation, therefore, different cultural modes will exist but only one will be dominant. It is on the basis of this claim that Jameson argues that postmodernism is 'the cultural dominant' of late or multinational capitalism (modernism is the residual; it is unclear what is the emergent).

Having established that postmodernism is the cultural dominant within Western capitalist societies, the next stage for Jameson is to outline the constitutive features of postmodernism. First, postmodernism is said to be a culture of pastiche: a culture, that is, marked by the 'complacent play of historical allusion' (Jameson, 1988: 105). Pastiche is often confused with parody; both involve imitation and mimicry. However, while parody has an 'ulterior motive', to mock a divergence from convention or a norm, pastiche is a 'blank parody' or 'empty copy', which has no sense of the very possibility of there being a norm or a convention from which to diverge. As he explains,

> Pastiche is, like parody, the imitation of a peculiar mask, speech in a dead language: but it is a neutral practice of such mimicry, without any of parody's ulterior motives, amputated of the satiric impulse, devoid of laughter and of any conviction that alongside the abnormal tongue you have momentarily borrowed, some healthy linguistic normality still exists. Pastiche is thus blank parody (1984: 65).

Rather than a culture of supposed pristine creativity, postmodern culture is a culture of quotations; that is, cultural production born out of previous cultural production.[4] It is therefore a culture 'of flatness or depthlessness, a new kind of superficiality in the most literal sense' (60). A culture of images and surfaces, without 'latent' possibilities, it derives its hermeneutic force from other images, other surfaces, the exhausted interplay of intertextuality. This is the world of postmodern pastiche, 'a world in which stylistic innovation is no longer possible, all that is left is to imitate dead styles, to speak through the masks and with the voices of the styles in the imaginary museum' (1985: 115).

Jameson's principal example of postmodern pastiche is what he calls the 'nostalgia film'. The category could include a number of films from the 1980s and 1990s: *Back to the Future I, II* and *III, Peggy Sue Got Married, Rumble Fish, Angel Heart, Blue Velvet*. He argues that the nostalgia film sets out to recapture the atmosphere and stylistic peculiarities of America in the 1950s. He claims that 'for Americans at least, the 1950s remain the privileged lost object of desire – not merely the stability and prosperity of a *pax Americana*, but also the first naive innocence of the countercultural impulses of early rock and roll and youth gangs' (1984: 67). He also insists that the nostalgia film is not just another name for the historical film. This is clearly demonstrated by the fact that his own list includes *Star Wars*. Now it might seem strange to suggest that a film about the future can be nostalgic for the past, but as Jameson (1985) explains, '[*Star Wars*] is metonymically a . . . nostalgia film . . . it does not reinvent a picture of the past in its lived totality; rather [it becomes a nostalgia film], by reinventing the feel and shape of characteristic art objects of an older period' (116).

Films such as *Raiders of the Lost Ark, Robin Hood: Prince of Thieves, The Mummy Returns* and *Lord of the Rings* operate in a similar way to evoke metonymically a sense of the narrative certainties of the past. Therefore, according to Jameson, the nostalgia film works in two possible ways: it recaptures and represents the atmosphere and stylistic features of the past; and/or it recaptures and represents certain styles of viewing of the past. What is of absolute significance for Jameson is that such films do not attempt to recapture or represent the 'real' past, but always make do with certain myths and stereotypes about the past. They offer what he calls 'false realism', films about other films, representations of other representations (what Baudrillard calls simulations: see discussion in the previous section): films 'in which the history of aesthetic styles displaces "real" history' (1984: 67). In this way, history is supposedly effaced by 'historicism . . . the random cannibalisation of all the styles of the past, the play of random stylistic allusion' (65–6). Here we might cite films like *True Romance*, *Pulp Fiction* and *Kill Bill*.

The failure to be historical relates to a second stylistic feature identified by Jameson: cultural 'schizophrenia'. He uses the term in the sense developed by Lacan (see Chapter 5) to signify a language disorder, a failure of the temporal relationship between signifiers. The schizophrenic, he claims, experiences time not as a continuum (past–present–future), but as a perpetual present that is only occasionally marked by the intrusion of the past or the possibility of a future. The 'reward' for the loss of conventional selfhood (the sense of self as always located within a temporal continuum) is an intensified sense of the present. Jameson explains it thus:

> Note that as temporal continuities break down, the experience of the present becomes powerfully, overwhelmingly vivid and 'material': the world comes before the schizophrenic with heightened intensity, bearing a mysterious and oppressive charge of affect, glowing with hallucinatory energy. But what might for us seem a desirable experience – an increase in our perceptions, a libidinal or hallucinogenic intensification of our normally humdrum and familiar surroundings – is here felt as loss, as 'unreality' (1985: 120).

To call postmodern culture schizophrenic is to argue that it has lost its sense of history (and its sense of a future different from the present). It is a culture suffering from 'historical amnesia', locked into the discontinuous flow of perpetual presents. The 'temporal' culture of modernism has given way to the 'spatial' culture of postmodernism.

Jim Collins (2009) has identified a similar trend in recent cinema, what he calls an 'emergent type of genericity' (470): popular films that 'quote' other films, self-consciously making reference to and borrowing from different genres of film. What makes Collins's position more convincing than Jameson's is his insistence on 'agency': the claim that such films appeal to (and help constitute) an audience of *knowing bricoleurs*, who take pleasure from this and other forms of bricolage. Moreover, while Jameson argues that such forms of cinema are characterized by a failure to be truly historical, Peter Brooker and Will Brooker (1997a), following Collins, see instead 'a new historical sense . . . the shared pleasure of intertextual recognition, the critical effect of play with narrative conventions, character and cultural stereotypes, and the power rather than passivity of nostalgia' (7). Brooker and Brooker argue that Quentin Tarantino's films, for example, can be seen as reactivating jaded conventions and audience alike, enabling a more active nostalgia and intertextual exploration than a term such as 'pastiche', which has nowhere to go but deeper into the recycling factory, implies. Instead of 'pastiche', we might think of 'rewriting' or 'reviewing' and, in terms of the spectator's experience, of the 'reactivation' and 'reconfiguration' of a given generational 'structure of feeling' within 'a more dynamic and varied set of histories' (ibid.).

They point to the ways in which Tarantino's work presents an 'aesthetic of recycling . . . an affirmative "bringing back to life", a "making new"' (Brooker and Brooker, 1997b: 56).

According to Collins (2009), part of what is postmodern about Western societies is the fact that the old media are not simply replaced by the new, but are recycled for circulation together with the new. As he explains, 'The ever-expanding number of texts and technologies is both a reflection of and a significant contribution to the "array" – the perpetual circulation and recirculation of signs that forms the fabric of postmodern cultural life' (457). He argues that 'This foregrounded, hyperconscious intertextuality reflects changes in terms of audience competence and narrative technique, as well as a fundamental shift in what constitutes both entertainment and cultural literacy in [postmodern culture]' (460). As a consequence of this, Collins argues, 'Narrative action now operates at two levels simultaneously – in reference to character adventure and in reference to a text's adventures in the array of contemporary cultural production' (464).

Jameson's final point, implicit in his claim that postmodernism is the 'cultural dominant' of late or multinational capitalism, is the claim that postmodernism is a hopelessly commercial culture. Unlike modernism, which taunted the commercial culture of capitalism, postmodernism, rather than resisting, 'replicates and reproduces – reinforces – the logic of consumer capitalism' (1985: 125). It forms the principal part of a process in which 'aesthetic production . . . has become integrated into commodity production generally' (1984: 56). Culture is no longer ideological, disguising the economic activities of capitalist society; it is itself an economic activity, perhaps the most important economic activity of all. Culture's changed situation can have a significant effect on cultural politics. No longer is it credible to see culture as ideological representation, an immaterial reflection of the hard economic reality. Rather, what we now witness is not just the collapse of the distinction between high and popular culture, but the collapse of the distinction between the realm of culture and the realm of economic activity.

According to Jameson, when compared to 'the Utopian "high seriousness" of the great modernisms', postmodern culture is marked by an 'essential triviality' (85). More than this, it is a culture that blocks 'a socialist transformation of society' (ibid.). Despite his rejection of a moral critique as inappropriate ('a category mistake'), and regardless of his citing of Marx's insistence on a dialectical approach, which would see postmodern culture as both a positive and a negative development, his argument drifts inexorably to the standard Frankfurt School critique of popular culture. The postmodern collapse of the distinction between high and popular has been gained at the cost of modernism's 'critical space'. The destruction of this critical space is not the result of an extinction of culture. On the contrary, it has been achieved by what he calls

> an 'explosion': a prodigious expansion of culture throughout the social realm, to the point at which everything in our social life from economic value and state power to practices and to the very structure of the psyche itself can be said to have become 'cultural' in some original and as yet unauthorised sense (89).

The thorough 'culturalization' or 'aestheticization' of everyday life is what marks postmodernism off from previous socio-cultural moments. Postmodernism is a culture, which offers no position of 'critical distance'; it is a culture in which claims of 'incorporation' or 'co-optation' make no sense, as there is no longer a critical space from which to be incorporated or co-opted. This is Frankfurt School pessimism at its most pessimistic (see Chapter 4). Grossberg (1988) sounds the critical note with economy:

> For Jameson . . . we need new 'maps' to enable us to understand the organisation of space in late capitalism. The masses, on the other hand, remain mute and passive, cultural dupes who are deceived by the dominant ideologies, and who respond to the leadership of the critic as the only one capable of understanding ideology and constituting the proper site of resistance. At best, the masses succeed in representing their inability to respond. But without the critic, they are unable even to hear their own cries of hopelessness. Hopeless they are and shall remain, presumably until someone else provides them with the necessary maps of intelligibility and critical models of resistance (174).

Although Jameson can be located within the traditions of Frankfurt School pessimism, there is a sense in which he is not quite as postmodern as one of the School's leading figures, Herbert Marcuse. Marcuse's (1968b) discussion of what he calls 'affirmative culture' (the culture or cultural space that emerged with the separation of 'culture' and 'civilization', discussed in Chapter 2) contains little of Jameson's enthusiasm for the historical emergence of culture as a separate sphere. As he explains,

> By affirmative culture is meant that culture of the bourgeois epoch, which led in the course of its own development to the segregation from civilisation of the mental and spiritual world as an independent realm of value that is also considered superior to civilisation. Its decisive characteristic is the assertion of a universally obligatory, eternally better and more valuable world that must be unconditionally affirmed: a world essentially different from the factual world of the daily struggle for existence, yet realisable by every individual for himself 'from within', without any transformation of the state of fact (95).

Affirmative culture is a realm we may enter in order to be refreshed and renewed in order to be able to continue with the ordinary affairs of everyday life. 'Affirmative' culture invents a new reality: 'a realm of apparent unity and apparent freedom was constructed within culture in which the antagonistic relations of existence were supposed to be stabilised and pacified. Culture affirms and conceals the new conditions of social life' (96). The promises made with the emergence of capitalism out of feudalism, of a society to be based on equality, justice and progress, were increasingly relegated from the world of the everyday to the realm of 'affirmative' culture. Like Marx and Engels (1957) on religion, Marcuse (1968b) argues that culture makes an unbearable condition bearable by soothing the ontological pain of existence.

> One of the decisive social tasks of affirmative culture is based on this contradiction between the insufferable mutability of a bad existence and the need for happiness in order to make such an existence bearable. Within this existence the resolution can be only illusory. And the possibility of a solution rests precisely on the character of artistic beauty as illusion.... But this illusion has a real effect, producing satisfaction . . . [in] the service of the status quo (118–24).

Something that produces satisfaction in the service of the status quo does not sound like something a Marxist would want to regret coming to an end. Moreover, does its demise really block, as Jameson claims, the transition to a socialist society? It might in fact be possible to argue just the opposite case.

Ernesto Laclau and Chantal Mouffe (2001) share some of Jameson's analysis of the postmodern, but unlike Jameson they recognize the possibility of agency.

> Today it is not only as a seller of labour-power that the individual is subordinated to capital, but also through his or her incorporation into a multitude of other social relations: culture, free time, illness, education, sex and even death. There is practically no domain of individual or collective life which escapes capitalist relations. But this 'consumer' society has not led to the end of ideology, as Daniel Bell announced, nor to the creation of a one-dimensional man, as Marcuse feared. On the contrary, numerous new struggles have expressed resistance against the new forms of subordination, and this from within the heart of the new society (161).

Laclau and Mouffe also refer to 'the new cultural forms linked to the expansion of the means of mass communication. These . . . make possible a new mass culture which . . . profoundly shake[s] traditional identities. Once again, the effects here are ambiguous, as along with the undeniable effects of massification and uniformization, this media-based culture also contains powerful elements for the subversion of inequalities' (163). This does not mean that there has necessarily been an increase in 'material' equality. Nevertheless,

> the cultural democratization which is the inevitable consequence of the action of the media permit the questioning of privileges based upon older forms of status. Interpellated as equals in their capacity as consumers, even more numerous groups are impelled to reject the real inequalities which continue to exist. This 'democratic

consumer culture' has undoubtedly stimulated the emergence of new struggles which have played an important part in the rejection of old forms of subordination, as was the case in the United States with the struggle of the black movement for civil rights. The phenomenon of the young is particularly interesting, and it is no cause for wonder they should constitute a new axis for the emergence of antagonisms. In order to create new necessities, they are increasingly constructed as a specific category of consumer, which stimulates them to seek a financial autonomy that society is in no condition to give them (164).

Postmodern pop music

A discussion of postmodernism and popular culture might highlight any number of different cultural texts and practices: for example, television, music video, advertising, film, pop music, fashion, new media, romantic love (Storey and McDonald, 2014a, 2014b, and Storey, 2014). I have space here to consider only two examples, television and pop music.

For Jameson (1984) the difference between modernist and postmodernist pop music is quite clear: the Beatles and the Rolling Stones represent a modernist moment against which punk rock (the Clash, for example) and new wave (Talking Heads, for example) can be seen as postmodernist. Andrew Goodwin (1991) has quite correctly pointed out that Jameson's compressed time-span solution – pop music culture's rapid progression through 'realism' (rock'n'roll), 'modernism', 'postmodernism' – enabling Jameson to establish a modernist moment against which to mark out a postmodernist response, is a very difficult argument to sustain. As Goodwin convincingly argues, the Beatles and the Rolling Stones are as different from each other as together they are different from the Clash and Talking Heads. In fact, it would be much easier to make an argument in which the distinction is made between the 'artifice' of the Beatles and Talking Heads and the 'authenticity' of the Rolling Stones and the Clash.

Goodwin himself considers a number of ways of seeing pop music and pop music culture as postmodernist. Perhaps its most cited aspect is the technological developments that have facilitated the emergence of 'sampling'. He acknowledges that the parallel with some postmodern theorizing is interesting and suggestive, but that is all it is – interesting and suggestive. What is often missed in such claims is the way in which sampling is used. As he explains, 'textual incorporation cannot be adequately understood as "blank parody". We need categories to add to pastiche, which demonstrate how contemporary pop opposes, celebrates and promotes the texts it steals from' (173). We also need to be aware of 'the historicizing function of sampling technologies in contemporary pop' (ibid.), the many ways in which sampling is 'used to invoke history and authenticity' (175). Moreover, in regard to Jameson's argument about nostalgia replacing history, 'it has often been overlooked that the "quoting" of sounds and styles acts to historicize contemporary culture' (ibid.). Rap is perhaps the best example of sampling being used in this way. When asked to name *the* black means of cultural expression, the African American cultural theorist Cornel West (2009), answered, 'music and preaching'. He went on to say,

> rap is unique because it combines the black preacher and the black music tradition, replacing the liturgical ecclesiastical setting with the African polyrhythms of the street. A tremendous articulateness is syncopated with the African drumbeat, the African funk, into an American postmodernist product: there is no subject expressing originary anguish here but a fragmented subject, pulling from past and present, innovatively producing a heterogeneous product. The stylistic combination of the oral, the literate, and the musical is exemplary . . . it is part and parcel of the subversive energies of black underclass youth, energies that are forced to take a cultural mode of articulation because of the political lethargy of American society (386).

This is a rejection of Jameson's claim that such work can be dismissed as an example of postmodern pastiche. The intertextual play of quotations in rap is not the result of aesthetic exhaustion; these are not the fragments of modernism shored against aesthetic ruin and cultural decline, but fragments combined to make a voice to be heard loudly within a hostile culture: the twisting of dismissal and denial into defiance.[5]

Postmodern television

Television, like pop music, does not have a period of modernism to which it can be 'post'. But, as Jim Collins (1992) points out, television is often seen as the 'quintessence' of postmodern culture. This claim can be made on the basis of a number of television's textual and contextual features. If we take a negative view of postmodernism, as the domain of simulations, then television seems an obvious example of the process – with its supposed reduction of the complexities of the world to an ever-changing flow of depthless and banal visual imagery. If, on the other hand, we take a positive view of postmodernism, then the visual and verbal practices of television can be put forward, say, as the knowing play of intertextuality and 'radical eclecticism' (Charles Jenks in Collins, 1992: 338), encouraging, and helping to produce, the 'sophisticated *bricoleur*' (Collins, 1992: 337) of postmodern culture. For example, a television series such as the now classic *Twin Peaks*[6] both helps to constitute an audience as bricoleurs and is watched in turn by an audience who celebrate the programme's bricolage. According to Collins,

> Postmodernist eclecticism might only occasionally be a preconceived design choice in individual programs, but it is built into the technologies of media sophisticated societies. Thus television, like the postmodern subject, must be conceived as a site – an intersection of multiple, conflicting cultural messages.

Only by recognising this interdependency of bricolage and eclecticism can we come to appreciate the profound changes in the relationship of reception and production in postmodern cultures. Not only has reception become another form of meaning production, but production has increasingly become a form of reception as it rearticulates antecedent and competing forms of representation (338).

Another divide within the approach to television as postmodern is between textual and 'economic' analysis. Instead of the semiotic sophistication of its intertextual play and radical eclecticism, television is condemned as hopelessly commercial. Collins uses *Twin Peaks* as a means of bringing together the different strands of the relationship between postmodernism and television. *Twin Peaks* is chosen because it 'epitomises the multiple dimensions of televisual postmodernism' (341). He argues that the postmodernism of the television series is the result of a number of interrelated factors: David Lynch's reputation as a film maker, the stylistic features of the series, and, finally, its commercial intertextuality (the marketing of related products: for example, *The Secret Diary of Laura Palmer*).

At the economic level, *Twin Peaks* marks a new era in network television's view of the audience. Instead of seeing the audience as a homogeneous mass, the series was part of a strategy in which the audience is seen as fragmented, consisting of different segments – stratified by age, class, gender, sexuality, geography, ethnicity and 'race' – each of interest to different advertisers. Mass appeal now involves attempts to intertwine the different segments to enable them to be sold to different sections of the advertising market. The significance of *Twin Peaks*, at least from this perspective, is that it represents an attempt by American network television to win back affluent sections of the television audience supposedly lost to cable, cinema and video – in short, the so-called 'yuppie' generation. Collins demonstrates this by addressing the way the series was promoted. First, there was the intellectual appeal – Lynch as auteur, *Twin Peaks* as avant-garde television. This was followed by *Twin Peaks* as soap opera. Together the two appeals soon coalesced into a postmodern reading formation in which the series was 'valorised as would-be cinema and would-be soap opera' (345). Similar marketing techniques have been used to promote many recent television programmes. The obvious examples are *Desperate Housewives, Sex and the City, Six Feet Under, The Sopranos, Lost, Mad Men, Boardwalk Empire, Borgen, The Bridge, Game of Thrones, Breaking Bad, The Wire, The Killing, Homeland,* and *Riviera*.

The marketing of *Twin Peaks* (and similar television programmes) is undoubtedly supported and sustained by the polysemic play of *Twin Peaks* itself. The series is, as Collins suggests, 'aggressively eclectic' (ibid.), not only in its use of conventions from Gothic horror, police procedural, science fiction and soap opera, but also in the different ways – from straight to parody – these conventions are mobilized in particular scenes. Collins also notes the play of 'tonal variations . . . within and across scenes' (ibid.). This has led some critics to dismiss *Twin Peaks* as 'mere camp'. But it is never simply camp – it is never simply anything – continually playing with our expectations, moving the audience, as it does, from moments of parodic distance to moments of emphatic intimacy. Although this is a known aspect of Lynch's filmic technique, more significantly it is also a characteristic 'reflective of changes in television entertainment and of viewer involvement in that entertainment' (347). As Collins explains,

> That viewers would take a great deal of pleasure in this oscillation and juxtaposition is symptomatic of the 'suspended' nature of viewer involvement in television that developed well before the arrival of *Twin Peaks*. The ongoing oscillation in discursive register and generic conventions describes not just *Twin Peaks* but the very act of moving up and down the televisual scale of the cable box. While watching *Twin Peaks*, viewers may be overtly encouraged to move in and out of an ironic position, but watching other television soap operas (nighttime or daytime) involves for many viewers a similar process of oscillation in which emotional involvement alternates with ironic detachment. Viewing perspectives are no longer mutually exclusive, but set in perpetual alternation (347–8).

Oscillation in discursive register and generic conventions is a primary factor in many recent television programmes. Again, the obvious examples are *Desperate Housewives*, *Sex and the City*, *Six Feet Under*, *Mad Men*, *Game of Thrones*, *Breaking Bad* and *The Sopranos*. The key point to understand with regard to *Twin Peaks* and postmodernism is that what makes the programme different from other television programmes is not that it produces shifting viewing positions, but that it 'explicitly acknowledges this oscillation and the suspended nature of television viewing. . . . [It] doesn't just acknowledge the multiple subject positions that television generates; it recognises that one of the great pleasures of the televisual text is that very suspension and exploits it for its own sake' (348).

Umberto Eco (1984) has identified a postmodern sensibility exhibited in an awareness of what he calls the 'already said'. He gives the example of a man who cannot tell his lover 'I love you madly', and says instead: 'As Barbara Cartland would put it, I love you madly' (39). Given that we now live in an increasingly media-saturated world, the 'already said' is, as Collins (1992) observes, 'still being said' (348). For example, we can identify this in the way that television, in a effort to fill the space opened up by the growth in satellite and cable channels, recycles its own accumulated past, and that of cinema, and broadcasts these alongside what is new in both media.[7] This does not mean that we must despair in the face of Jameson's postmodern 'structure'; rather we should think in terms of both 'agency' and 'structure' – which ultimately is always a question of 'articulation' (see Chapter 4). Collins provides this example of different strategies of articulation:

> The Christian Broadcasting Network and Nickelodeon both broadcast series from the late fifties and early sixties, but whereas the former presents these series as a model for family entertainment the way it used to be, the latter offers them as fun for the contemporary family, 'camped up' with parodic voice-overs, supergraphics, reediting designed to deride their quaint vision of American family life, which we all know never really existed even 'back then' (334).

There can be little doubt that similar things are happening in, for example, music, cinema, advertising, fashion, and in the different lived cultures of everyday life. It is not a sign that there has been a general collapse of the distinctions people make between, say, high culture/low culture, past/present, history/nostalgia, fiction/reality; but it is a sign that such distinctions (first noticed in the 1960s, and gradually more so ever since) are becoming increasingly less important, less obvious, less taken for granted. But this does not of course mean that such distinctions cannot be, and are not being, articulated and mobilized for particular strategies of social distinction. But above all, we should not take any of these changes at face value; we must always be alert to the what, why and for whom something is being articulated, and how it can always be articulated differently, in other contexts (see Chapter 12).

Postmodernism and the pluralism of value

Postmodernism has disturbed many of the old certainties surrounding questions of cultural value. In particular, it has problematized the question of why some texts are canonized, while others disappear without trace: that is, why only certain texts supposedly 'pass the test of time'. There are a number of ways to answer this question. First, we can insist that the texts which are valued and become part of what Williams (2009) calls the 'selective tradition' (see Chapter 3) are those that are sufficiently polysemic to sustain multiple and continuous readings.[8] The problem with this approach is that it seems to ignore questions of power. It fails to pose the question: 'Who is doing the valuing, in what context(s) and with what effects of power?' In short, it is very difficult to see how a process in which only certain people have the power and cultural authority to ensure the canonical reproduction of texts and practices can really be described as simply an effect of a text's polysemy.

Rather than begin with polysemy, cultural studies would begin with power. Put simply, a text will survive its moment of production if it is selected to meet the needs and desires of people with cultural power. Surviving its moment of production makes it available to meet the (usually different) desires and needs of other generations of people with cultural power. The selective tradition, as Williams (2009) points out, is 'governed by many kinds of special interests, including class interests'. Therefore, rather than being a natural repository of what Arnold (2009) thought of as 'the best that has been thought and said' (see Chapter 2), it 'will always tend to correspond to its *contemporary* system of interests and values, for *it* is not an absolute body of work but a continual selection and interpretation' (Williams, 2009: 38–9; original emphasis). Particular interests, articulated in specific social and historical contexts, always inform the selective tradition. In this way, what constitutes the selective tradition is as much about policing knowledge as it is about organizing terrains of critical inquiry.

It is not difficult to demonstrate how the selective tradition forms and re-forms in response to the social and political concerns of those with cultural power. We have only to think of the impact that, say, feminism, queer theory and post-colonial theory have had on the study of literature – women writers, gay writers, writers from the so-called colonial periphery have become a part of the institution of literature, not because their value has suddenly been recognized in some disinterested sweep of the field: they are there because power encountered resistance; even when the selected texts remain the same, how and why they are valued certainly changes; so much so that they are hardly the same texts from one historical moment to the next.[9] To paraphrase the Four Tops: 'It's the same old text / But with a different meaning since you achieved relative power'.[10] Or to put it in a less danceable discourse, a text is never really the issuing source of value, but always the site where the construction of value – variable values – can take place.

Of course, when we ascribe value to a text or practice, we are not (or rarely ever) saying this is only of value to me; our evaluation always (or usually always) includes the notion that the text or practice should also be of value to others. The trouble with some forms of evaluation is that they insist that their community of others is an ideal community, with absolute cultural authority over all other valuing communities. It is not that they insist that all others should consume what they value (it is usually better for 'value' if they do not), but they do insist on due deference for their judgements and absolute recognition of their cultural authority to judge (see discussion of the 'culture and civilization' tradition in Chapter 2).[11]

The postmodern return to questions of value has witnessed an increased interest in the work of Pierre Bourdieu (1984). As I pointed out in Chapter 1, Bourdieu argues that distinctions of 'culture' (whether understood as text, practice or way of living) are a significant aspect in the struggle between dominant and subordinate groups in society. He shows how arbitrary tastes and arbitrary ways of living are continually transmuted into legitimate taste and the only legitimate way of life. The consumption of culture is thus a means to produce and to legitimate social difference, and to secure social deference.

Bourdieu's project is to (re-)locate 'value' in the world of everyday experience, to suggest that similar things are happening when I 'value' a holiday destination or a particular mode of dress, as are happening when I 'value' a poem by T.S. Eliot or a song by Paul Robeson or a photograph by Cindy Sherman or a piece of music by Gavin Bryars. Such evaluations are never a simple matter of individual taste; cultural value operates both to identify and to maintain social difference and sustain social deference. Distinction is generated by learned patterns of consumption that are internalized as 'natural' preferences and interpreted and mobilized as evidence of 'natural' competences, which are, ultimately, used to justify forms of social and cultural domination. The cultural tastes of dominant groups are given institutional form, and then, with deft ideological sleight of hand, their taste for this institutionalized culture (i.e. their own) is held up as evidence of their cultural and, ultimately, their social, superiority. The effect of such cultural distinction is to produce and reproduce social distinction, social separation and social hierarchy. It becomes a means of establishing differences between dominated and dominant groups in society. The production and reproduction of cultural space thus produces and reproduces social space.

Bourdieu's purpose is not to prove the self-evident, that different classes have different lifestyles, different tastes in culture, but to identify and interrogate the processes by which the making of cultural distinctions secures and legitimates forms of power and control rooted in economic inequalities. He is interested not so much in the actual differences, but in how these differences are used by dominant groups as a means of social reproduction. The much heralded collapse of standards rehearsed (almost weekly) in the 'quality' media may be nothing more than a perceived sense that the opportunities to use culture to make and mark social distinction are becoming more and more difficult to find, as, for example, when Classic FM (both radio and magazine) continues to blur the once firm boundary between high and popular culture and Premier League football is, in many instances, as expensive as, say, ballet or opera.

Perhaps the most significant thing about postmodernism for the student of popular culture is the dawning recognition that there is no absolute categorical difference between high and popular culture. This is not to say that one text or practice might not be 'better' (for what/for whom, etc., must always be decided and made clear) than another text or practice. But it is to say that there are no longer any easy reference points to which we can refer, which will automatically preselect for us the good from the bad. Some might regard such a situation (or even the description of such a situation) with horror – the end of *Standards*. On the contrary, without easy recourse to fixed categories of value, it calls for rigorous, if always contingent, standards, if our task is to separate the good from the bad, the usable from the obsolete, the progressive from the reactionary. As John Fekete (1987) points out,

> By contrast [to modernism], postmodernism may be at last ready – or may, at least, represent the transition to a readiness – unneurotically, to get on without the Good-God-Gold Standards, once and for all, indeed without any capitalised Standards, while learning to be enriched by the whole inherited inventory once it is transferred to the lower case. . . . We need to believe and enact the belief that there are better and worse ways to live the pluralism of value. To see all cows as the same colour would truly amount to being lost in the night. But the prospect of learning to be at ease with limited warranties, and with the responsibility for issuing them, without the false security of inherited guarantees, is promising for a livelier, more colourful, more alert, and, one hopes, more tolerant culture that draws enjoyment from the dappled relations between meaning and value (17).

Fekete's point is not significantly different from the argument made by Susan Sontag (1966) at the birth of the postmodern 'new sensibility':

> The new sensibility is defiantly pluralistic; it is dedicated both to an excruciating seriousness and to fun and wit and nostalgia. It is also extremely history-conscious; and the voracity of its enthusiasms (and of the supercession of these enthusiasms) is very high-speed and hectic. From the vantage point of this new sensibility, the beauty of a machine or of the solution to a mathematical problem, of a painting by Jasper Johns, of a film by Jean-Luc Godard, and of the personalities and music of the Beatles is equally accessible (304).

The global postmodern

One way in which the world is said to be becoming postmodern is in its increasing globalization. Perhaps the dominant view of globalization, especially in discussions of globalization and culture, is to see it as the reduction of the world to an American 'global village': a global village in which everyone speaks English with an American accent, wears Levi jeans and Wrangler shirts, drinks Coca-Cola, eats at McDonald's, surfs the net on a computer overflowing with Microsoft software, listens to rock or country music, watches a mixture of MTV and CNN, Hollywood movies and reruns of *Dallas*, and then discusses the prophetically named World Series, while drinking a bottle of Budweiser and smoking a Marlboro cigarette. According to this scenario, globalization is the supposed successful imposition of American culture around the globe, in which the economic success of American capitalism is underpinned by the cultural work that its commodities supposedly do in effectively destroying indigenous cultures and imposing an American way of life on 'local' populations. Photo 10.2 presents a very succinct version of this argument. It is a photograph of a sculpture depicting people entering a Coca-Cola house as Chinese citizens and leaving as little Coca-Cola people. There are at least three problems with this view of globalization.

The first problem with globalization as cultural Americanization is that it operates with a very reductive concept of culture: it assumes that 'economic' success is the same as 'cultural' imposition. In other words, the recognition of the obvious success

Photo 10.2   The Coca-Colonization of China.

of American companies in placing products in most of the markets of the world is understood as self-evidently and unproblematically 'cultural' success. For example, American sociologist Herbert Schiller (1979) claims that the ability of American companies to successfully unload commodities around the globe is producing an American global capitalist culture. The role of media corporations, he claims, is to make programmes that 'provide in their imagery and messagery, the beliefs and per-spectives that create and reinforce their audiences' attachments to the way things are in the system overall' (30).

There are two overlapping problems with this position. First, it is simply assumed that commodities are the same as culture: establish the presence of the former and you can predict the details of the latter. But as John Tomlinson (1999) points out, 'if we assume that the sheer global presence of these goods is *in itself* token of a convergence towards a capitalist monoculture, we are probably utilising a rather impoverished concept of culture – one that reduces culture to its material goods' (83). It may be the case that certain commodities are used, made meaningful and valued in ways that promote American capitalism as a way of life, but this is not something that can be established by simply assuming that market penetration is the same as cultural assimilation.

Another problem with this position is that it is an argument that depends on the claim that commodities have inherent values and singular meanings, which can be imposed on passive consumers. In other words, the argument operates with a very discredited account of the flow of influence. It simply assumes that the dominant globalizing culture will be successfully injected into the weaker 'local' culture. That is, it is assumed that people are the passive consumers of the cultural meanings that supposedly flow directly and straightforwardly from the commodities they consume. To think that economic success is the same as cultural success is to work under the influence of what I shall call 'mode of production determinism' – that is, the argument that how something is made determines what it can mean or what it is worth (it is Hollywood, etc., what do you expect?). Such analysis always seems to want to suggest that 'agency' is always overwhelmed by 'structure'; that consumption is a mere shadow of production; that audience negotiations are fictions, merely illusory moves in a game of economic power. Moreover, 'mode of production determinism' is a way of thinking that seeks to present itself as a form of radical cultural politics. But all too often this is a politics in which attacks on power are rarely little more than self-serving revelations about how 'other people' are always 'cultural dupes' (see Chapters 4 and 12).

A second problem with globalization as cultural Americanization is that it oper-ates with a limited concept of the 'foreign'. First of all, it works with the assumption that what is foreign is always a question of national difference. But what is foreign can equally be a question of class, ethnicity, gender, sexuality, generation, or any other marker of social difference (see Figure 10.1). Moreover, what is foreign in terms of being imported from another country may be less foreign than differences already established by, say, class or generation. Furthermore, the imported foreign may be used against the prevailing power relations of the 'local' (see Photo 10.3 and Figure 10.2).

Local	*Locals*
national	class
	ethnicity
	gender
	generation
	'race'
	sexuality, etc.

Figure 10.1   The 'foreign'.

This is probably what is happening with the export of hip hop. What are we to make of the global success of hip hop? Are, for example, South African, French, Chinese or British rappers (and fans of hip hop) the victims of American cultural imperialism? Are they the cultural dupes of a transnational music industry? A more interesting approach would be to look at how South Africans, French, Chinese or British youth have 'appropriated' hip hop, used it to meet their local needs and desires. In other words, a more interesting approach would be one that looked at what they do with it, rather than only what it supposedly does to them. American culture is worked on; it is used to make space within what is perceived as the dominant national culture.

Photo 10.3   'Imagine there's no countries'.

THE LENNON

列儂餐吧

高 君
Steven Gao

- Yellow Submarine Bar
- Yoko Ono Bar
- Havana Lounge
- Strawberry Fields Dining Room
- Lucy's Sky Bar

青島・珠海路20號
#20 Zhuhai Road, TsingTao, P.R.C.
P.C.: 266071
Tel : 5893899
M.Tel: 13906393298
E-mail:stevengao@qdcnc.com

Figure 10.2   'Imagine there's no countries'.

Another problem with this very limited notion of the foreign is that it is always assumed that the 'local' is the same as the national. But within the national, there may well be many 'locals' (see Figure 10.1). Moreover, there may be considerable conflict between them, and between them and the dominant culture (i.e. 'the national'). Globalization can therefore both help confirm and help undo local cultures; it can keep one in place and it can make one suddenly feel out of place. For example, in 1946, addressing a conference of Spanish clerics, the Archbishop of Toledo wondered '[h]ow to tackle' what he called 'woman's growing demoralization – caused largely by American customs introduced by the cinematograph, making the young woman independent, breaking up the family, disabling and discrediting the future consort and mother with exotic practices that make her less womanly and destabilize the home' (quoted in Tomlinson, 1997: 123). Spanish women may have taken a different view.

A third problem with the model of globalization as cultural Americanization is that it assumes that American culture is monolithic. Even in the more guarded accounts of globalization it is assumed that we can identify something singular called American culture. George Ritzer (1999), for example, makes the claim that 'while we will continue to see global diversity, many, most, perhaps eventually all of those cultures will be affected by American exports: America will become virtually everyone's "second culture"' (89).

Globalization as cultural Americanization assumes that cultures can be lined up as distinct monolithic entities, hermetically sealed from one another until the fatal moment of the globalizing injection. Against such a view, Jan Nederveen Pieterse (1995) argues that globalization, as cultural Americanization,

> overlooks the countercurrents – the impact non-Western cultures have been making on the West. It downplays the ambivalence of the globalising momentum and ignores the role of local reception of Western culture – for example the indigenization of Western elements. It fails to see the influence non-Western cultures have been exercising on one another. It has no room for crossover culture – as in the development of 'third cultures' such as world music. It overrates the homogeneity of Western culture and overlooks the fact that many of the standards exported by

the West and its cultural industries themselves turn out to be of culturally mixed character if we examine their cultural lineages (53).

Moreover, the idea of globalization as the imposition of a singular and monolithic American culture (a middle-class culture of whiteness) begins to look very different, less monolithic, when we consider, for example, the fact that the United States has the third largest Hispanic population in the world. In addition, it is estimated that by 2076, the tricentennial of the American Revolution, people of Native American, African, Asian or Latin descent will make up the majority of its population.

Hall (1996b) has written that postmodernism 'is about how the world dreams itself to be American' (132). If this is the case, we may be all dreaming of many different Americas, depending on which bits of America we choose to consume. For example, if the material for our dreams is gathered from American popular music, the geography and geometry, the values, images, myths, styles, will be different depending on whether, for example, it is blues, country, dance, folk, heavy metal, jazz, rap, rock'n'roll, sixties rock, or soul. At the very least, each genre of music would produce different political articulations, in terms of class, gender, 'race', ethnicity, sexuality and generation. To recognize this is to recognize that cultures, even powerful cultures such as that of the USA, are never monolithic. As Said (1993) observes, '[A]ll cultures are involved in one another; none is single and pure, all are hybrid, heterogeneous, extraordinarily differentiated, and unmonolithic' (xxix). Moreover,

> [n]o one today is purely one thing. Labels like Indian, or woman, or Muslim, or American are now [no] more than starting points, which if followed into actual experience for only a moment are quickly left behind. Imperialism consolidated the mixture of cultures and identities on a global scale. But its worst and most paradoxical gift was to allow people to believe that they were only, mainly exclusively, White, or Black, or Western, or Oriental (407–8).

Globalization is much more complex and contradictory than the simple imposition of, say, American culture. It is certainly true that we can travel around the world while never being too far from signs of American commodities. What is not true, however, is that commodities equal culture. Globalization involves the ebb and flow of both homogenizing and heterogenizing forces, the meeting and the mingling of the 'local' and the 'global'. To understand this in a different way: what is exported always finds itself in the context of what already exists. That is, exports become imports, as they are incorporated into the indigenous culture. This can in turn impact on the cultural production of the 'local'. Ien Ang (1996) gives the example of the Cantonese Kung Fu movies that revitalized the declining Hong Kong film industry. The films are a mixture of 'Western' narratives and Cantonese values. As she explains:

> Culturally speaking, it is hard to distinguish here between the 'foreign' and the 'indigenous', the 'imperialist' and the 'authentic': what has emerged is a highly distinctive and economically viable hybrid cultural form in which the global

and the local are inextricably intertwined, in turn leading to the modernized reinvigoration of a culture that continues to be labelled and widely experienced as 'Cantonese'. In other words, what counts as 'local' and therefore 'authentic' is not a fixed content, but subject to change and modification as a result of the domestication of imported cultural goods (154–5).

Globalization may be making the world smaller, generating new forms of cultural hybridity, but it is also bringing into collision and conflict different ways of making the world mean. While some people may celebrate the opening up of new global 'routes', other people may resist globalization in the name of local 'roots'. Resistance in the form of a reassertion of the local against the flow of the global can be seen in the increase in religious fundamentalism (Christianity, Hinduism, Islam and Judaism) and the re-emergence of nationalism, most recently in the former Soviet Union and the former Yugoslavia. A more benign example of the insistence on 'roots' is the explosive growth in family history research in Europe and America. In all of these examples, globalization may be driving the search for 'roots' in a more secure past in the hope of stabilizing identities in the present.

Globalization is a complex process, producing contradictory effects, in changing relations of culture and power. One way to understand the processes of globalization is in terms of Gramsci's concept of hegemony. From the perspective of the post-Marxist cultural studies appropriation of hegemony theory, cultures are neither something 'authentic' (spontaneously emerging from 'below'), nor something which is simply imposed from 'above', but a 'compromise equilibrium' (Gramsci, 1971: 161) between the two; a contradictory mix of forces from both 'below' and 'above'; both 'commercial' and 'authentic'; both 'local' and 'global'; marked by both 'resistance' and 'incorporation', involving both 'structure' and 'agency'. Globalization can also be seen in this way. As Hall (1991) observes:

> what we usually call the global, far from being something which, in a systematic fashion, rolls over everything, creating similarity, in fact works through particularity, negotiates particular spaces, particular ethnicities, works through mobilizing particular identities and so on. So there is always a dialectic, between the local and the global (62).

Hegemony is a complex and contradictory process; it is not the same as injecting people with 'false consciousness'. It is certainly not explained by the adoption of the assumption (mocked by the authors) that 'hegemony is prepackaged in Los Angeles, shipped out to the global village, and unwrapped in innocent minds' (Liebes and Katz, 1993: xi). A better way of understanding the processes of globalization is one that takes seriously not just the power of global forces, but also those of the local. This is not to deny power but to insist that a politics in which 'local' people are seen as mute and passive victims of processes they can never hope to understand, a politics that denies agency to the vast majority, or at best recognizes only certain activities as signs of agency, is a politics that can exist without causing too much trouble to the prevailing structures of global power.

Convergence culture

Another aspect of the postmodern is convergence culture, 'where old and new media collide, where grassroots and corporate media intersect, where the power of the media producer and the power of the media consumer interact in unpredictable ways' (Henry Jenkins, 2006: 2). Convergence involves the flow of media content across a range of different platforms. This is not simply a matter of new technologies but a process that requires the active participation of consumers.

Convergence culture, like most popular culture discussed in this book, is a site of struggle and negotiation. It cannot be explained and understood as something imposed from 'above' or as something spontaneously emerging from 'below'; it is a complex and contradictory combination of both forces. As Jenkins observes,

> Convergence . . . is both a top–down corporate-driven process and a bottom–up consumer-driven process. Corporate convergence coexists with grassroots convergence. Media companies are learning how to accelerate the flow of media content across delivery channels to expand revenue opportunities, broaden markets, and reinforce viewer commitments. Consumers are learning how to use these different media technologies to bring the flow of media more fully under their control and to interact with other consumers (18).

Convergence culture is the result of three factors. The first is concentration of media ownership. Owning a range of different platforms encourages producers to distribute content across these different platforms. So, for example, a company may publish the book of the film, together with the game based on both and promote these in its magazines and newspapers and through its internet sites and mobile phone companies.

The second is technological change. This has created a new range of platforms for media content. For example, we can now do so many more things with a mobile phone than just make phone calls. We can take, send and receive photos and videos; make, send and receive sound files; send and receive text messages; download information from the internet; receive 'goal alerts'; play games; and use as a calendar, an alarm clock and a calculator (see Jewitt, 2005).

The third factor involves the consumers of media. I may, for example, choose to listen to my favourite music on my laptop, my CD or DVD player, my iPod, my car radio, on TV or radio, or on Youtube via my TV. The same music is made available on different platforms, but I have to actively participate to make the system work. Moreover, I select which platform best suits my pleasure and convenience.

The British science fiction television series *Doctor Who*, as Neil Perryman (2009) points out, 'embraces convergence culture on an unprecedented scale' (478). The BBC has made the programme available across a range of different platforms: mobile phones, podcasts, video blogs, websites, interactive red-button adventures and online games. In addition, it has launched two complementary series that take characters into other contexts. As Perryman observes,

Doctor Who is a franchise that has actively embraced both the technical and cultural shifts associated with media convergence since it returned to our television screens in 2005. Its producers have attempted to provide extra-value content and narrative complexity for both a hardcore fanbase and a mainstream audience by deploying a series of evolving and changing storytelling strategies across a wide range of media platforms (488).

Afterword

Postmodernism has changed the theoretical and the cultural bases of the study of popular culture. It raises many questions, not least the role that can be played by the student of popular culture: that is, what is our relationship to our object of study? With what authority, and for whom, do we speak? As Frith and Horne (1987) suggest,

> In the end the postmodern debate concerns the source of meaning, not just its relationship to pleasure (and, in turn, to the source of that pleasure) but its relationship to power and authority. Who now determines significance? Who has the right to interpret? For pessimists and rationalists like Jameson the answer is multinational capital – records, clothes, films, TV shows, etc. – are simply the results of decisions about markets and marketing. For pessimists and irrationalists, like Baudrillard, the answer is nobody at all – the signs that surround us are arbitrary. For optimists like Iain Chambers and Larry Grossberg the answer is consumers themselves, stylists and subculturalists, who take the goods on offer and make their own marks with them (169).

Chapter 12 will consist mostly of an attempt to find answers to some of these questions.

Notes

1. The rise of religious fundamentalism is difficult to locate in Lyotard's postmodern condition.
2. For a critical introduction to the Enlightenment, see Porter (1990).
3. See Ricoeur (1981).
4. In the eighteenth-century opera, pastiche was a very common practice. See Storey (2006 and 2010a).
5. For an interesting example of postmodern sampling that involves this book, listen to 'High Definition' by the Granite Countertops.
6. In 2017 Twin Peaks returned, screened on both television and Netflix. FBI Special Agent Dale Cooper (played once again by Kyle MacLachlan) goes back to the town where twenty-five years earlier he had investigated the murder of homecoming queen Laura Palmer.
7. The expansion of the market in DVD 'box sets' has undoubtedly contributed to this development.

8. See Easthope (1991), Connor (1992) and the debate on value between Easthope and Connor in *Textual Practice*, 4 (3), 1990 and 5 (3), 1991. See also Frow (1995).
9. See Tompkins (1985) and Smith (1988).
10. The Four Tops, 'It's The Same Old Song', *Four Tops Motown Greatest Hits*, Motown Record Company. The line should run as follows, 'It's the same old song / But with a different meaning since you've been gone.'
11. See Storey (2003).

Further reading

Storey, John (ed.), *Cultural Theory and Popular Culture: A Reader*, 4th edn, Harlow: Pearson Education, 2009. This is the companion volume to the previous edition of this book. A fully updated 5th edition containing further readings is due for publication in 2018. An interactive website is also available (www.routledge.com/cw/storey), which contains helpful student resources and a glossary of terms for each chapter.

Appignanesi, Lisa (ed.), *Postmodernism*, London: ICA, 1986. A collection of essays – mostly philosophical – on postmodernism. McRobbie's contribution, 'Postmodernism and popular culture', is essential reading.

Best, Steven, and Douglas Kellner, *Postmodern Theory: Critical Interrogations*, London: Macmillan, 1991. An excellent introduction to the debate about postmodernism.

Boyne, Roy and Ali Rattansi (eds), *Postmodernism and Society*, London: Macmillan, 1990. A useful collection of essays, with a very good introduction to the main issues in the debate about postmodernism.

Brooker, Peter and Will Brooker (eds), *Postmodern After-Images: A Reader in Film, Television and Video*, London: Edward Arnold, 1997. An excellent collection of essays, with very good introductory sections

Campbell, Neil, Jude Davies and George McKay, *Issues in Americanization*, Edinburgh: Edinburgh University Press, 2004. A very good collection of essays on a variety of topics relating to the idea of Americanization. The introduction is excellent.

Collins, Jim, *Uncommon Cultures: Popular Culture and Postmodernism*, London: Routledge, 1989. A very interesting book, situating popular culture in the debate about postmodernism.

Connor, Steven, *Postmodernist Culture: An Introduction to Theories of the Contemporary*, Oxford: Basil Blackwell, 1989. A comprehensive introduction to postmodernism: useful discussion of popular culture.

Docker, John, *Postmodernism and Popular Culture: A Cultural History*, Cambridge: Cambridge University Press, 1994. The aim of the book is to challenge the way a century of modernist theory has understood twentieth-century popular culture. Intelligent, polemical and very readable.

Featherstone, Mike, *Consumer Culture and Postmodernism*, London: Sage, 1991. An interesting sociological discussion of consumer culture and postmodernism. Essential reading.

Hebdige, Dick, *Hiding in the Light*, London: Comedia, 1988. A collection of essays mostly related to questions of postmodernism and popular culture. Essential reading.

Jenkins, Henry, *Convergence Culture: Where Old and New Media Collide*, New York: New York University Press, 2006. The key book on the emergence of 'convergence culture'.

Morris, Meaghan, *The Pirate's Fiancée: Feminism, Reading, Postmodernism*, London: Verso, 1988. A collection of essays concerned with both theory and analysis. Essential reading.

Ross, Andrew (ed.), *Universal Abandon: The Politics of Postmodernism*, Minneapolis: University of Minnesota Press, 1988. A useful collection of essays on postmodernism: some interesting discussion of popular culture.

Woods, Tim, *Beginning Postmodernism*, Manchester: Manchester University Press, 1999. Perhaps the best introduction to the debate that is postmodernism.

11 The materiality of popular culture

Materiality

This chapter will examine popular culture as material culture. However we define it, a great deal of popular culture takes material form. Even a few random examples should make this point: mobile phones, clothes, wedding rings, greetings cards, toys, bicycles, CDs (discs and players), DVDs (discs and players), cars, games consoles, televisions, radios, sporting equipment, computers, computer tablets (including the iPad), magazines, books, cinemas, football grounds, nightclubs and pubs. Youth subcultures are an obvious example of the visibility of materiality in popular culture. How we know a youth subculture is always through the materiality of what it consumes. There is always a drug of choice, a particular dress code, social spaces that are occupied, a particular music providing an aural landscape. It is the combination of these different forms of materiality that make a youth subculture visible to the wider society. But this is not just the case with youth subcultures; most people's lives are filled with material objects. We interact with material objects in many ways: we produce and consume them, we exchange them, we talk about them and admire them, and we use them to say things about ourselves. I type these words on my computer and you read them in the book you hold in your hands. These different forms of materiality have enabled our communication. If I know you I might send you an email from my laptop and you might respond with a text message from your mobile phone. We may then travel by bus, train or taxi to a pub and have a few bottles of beer or share a bottle or two of wine. In these different ways our encounter is enabled and constrained by the materiality that surrounds us.

Sometimes the material capacities of an object are such that they transform what we do. The car is an obvious example. It has helped bring about a fundamental change in the popular culture of shopping – not only how we shop, but also who shops. It has reshaped both the social practice of shopping and the built materiality of the shopping areas of towns and cities. Without the widespread use of the car it is very difficult to imagine the success of the out-of-town shopping centre, which always has as much space for cars as there is for shops and shoppers. Another obvious example is the mobile phone. They have changed many aspects of everyday life. For example, it is now impossible to walk down the high street of any town or city and not see people using mobile phones to talk, text, take photographs or listen to music. Text messaging has also significantly changed the development of romantic relationships (see Storey and McDonald 2014a, 2014b, and Storey 2014). The mobile phone's camera has 'democratized' the self-portrait – making possible the so-called 'selfie'.

There are different ways to think theoretically about the materiality of popular culture. In what follows I will briefly review just three: actor-network-theory, cultural studies, and material culture studies.

Materiality as actor

According to actor-network-theory popular culture is not just people acting and inter-acting, it is people acting and interacting with material objects and material objects interacting with each other. Many of our activities are mediated through material objects of a variety of kinds. Whether or not we use a bus or a car to travel to a concert or a football match, wear formal or casual clothes to meet friends at the pub, drink wine or water at a party, lager or real ale at a folk club, sleep on holiday in a tent or a hotel, these different material objects make a difference to the realization of our actions and interactions. And because they make a difference actor-network-theory regards them as 'actors' (Latour, 2007: 71). Against the idea of the non-acting material object Bruno Latour argues that 'any thing that does modify a state of affairs by making a difference is an actor... Thus, the questions to ask about any agent are simply the following: Does it make a difference in the course of some other agent's action or not?' (ibid.). Whether we choose to sleep in a tent rather than a hotel will always make it a very different holiday. The tent or the hotel becomes an actor in the drama of our vacation. Drinking lager rather than real ale at a folk club might make others think we do not really belong. Real ale or lager becomes an actor in a drama of social authenticity. Therefore, when we are trying to explain the materiality of popular culture we have to recognize the actions and interactions of both human and non-human actors. In other words, our experience of popular culture is constructed and mediated in part with the use of material objects.

The interaction between actors always takes place in networks. In other words, to understand one thing you have to see it in relation to other things; see it as part of a network. Such networks, as we have noted, will often include both humans and non-humans. However, such networks are always performed networks; there is nothing necessarily natural about the network in which a material object is situated; it might also find itself in other networks at other times. Furthermore, it is how something performs or is made to perform within a given network that determines its situated and therefore temporary meaning and significance. For example, if a public library exhibits a collection of photographs of a local community, these would temporarily exist in relation to each other, the exhibition space, and the local area. Although taken by different photographers for different purposes (a wedding, a sporting event, a children's picnic, a mining disaster, a landscape, a walk in the woods, a bonfire night, a carnival parade, an industrial strike) the gallery would situate them all in a network in which these differences of subject and purpose would be diminished, as they would all be, at least temporarily, of significance because of what they tell the exhibition's audience about the local area. Once removed from the public library, each photograph would return to other networks. Similarly, a bottle of beer is in one network when in a beach café it is handed by a woman to a man, but was in quite another when sold to the woman by a man behind the bar, and will be in yet another when collected by other bar staff. In each of these scenarios the bottle of beer is acting in a different drama.

Material objects can be both mediators and intermediaries. Intermediaries convey meaning unchanged, mediators, on the other hand, 'transform, translate, distort, and modify the meaning . . . they are supposed to carry' (39). Most media technologies are first encountered as mediators: that is, our inability to use them properly becomes a meaning in itself as they become actors in our drama of technological inadequacy. However, once we have mastered the technology they settle down as intermediaries. If the technology breaks down it has the potential to become a mediator again, once more an actor in the theatre of our everyday existence. When, for example, I give a lecture, the PowerPoint and the microphone I use mediate between the students and myself in the lecture theatre: both technologies are fundamental to the experience of our interaction. In other words, the interaction between us involves certain technologies and these technologies do not just work as intermediaries, they act as mediators – it makes a difference that a diagram is on PowerPoint and not just explained. Similarly, a bottle of beer is potentially an intermediary like the other drinks being consumed in the beach café. But because the woman knows that the man knows that the bottle of beer is an attempt to start a relationship, it becomes a mediator in that it conveys to both the potential beginning of a holiday romance.

A network is 'a string of actions where each participant is treated as a full-blown mediator' (128). In a network all the actors act: there is movement not between intermediaries but between mediators. 'As soon as actors are treated not as intermediaries but as mediators, they render the movement of the social visible' (ibid.). In a network there is not the transport of causality between intermediaries but a series of connections in which actors make other actors act. The materiality of the bottle of beer does not determine that a holiday romance will begin, but it does signal its possibility. There is a relationship (a potential network) between the giving of the bottle of beer and certain romantic possibilities, but it is not a simple relationship of cause and effect. The bottle of beer is acting in a drama of a possible relationship beginning in a beach café. It is by recognizing the interaction between the human and the material that popular culture and everyday life become fully visible to our analysis. According to Latour,

any human course of action might weave together in a matter of minutes, for instance, a shouted order to lay a brick, the chemical connection of cement with water, the force of a pulley unto a rope with a movement of the hand, the strike of a match to light a cigarette offered by a co-worker, etc. Here, the apparently reasonable division between material and social becomes just what is obfuscating any enquiry on how a collective action is possible (74).

In other words, if we are to understand everyday life, and popular culture as its primary feature, we have to fully recognize the role of material objects. As Latour argues, we should not think of the social and the material as separate categories. It is the weaving together of both material and social; that is, it is human-to-human, object-to-object, and human-to-object actions and interactions that make visible the materiality of popular culture.

Meaning and materiality

Everything said so far excludes how material objects are always inscribed with signification by human practice. As we noted in Chapter 4, cultural studies defines culture as a realized signifying system. Material objects surround us and we interact with them and we use them to interact with others. They accompany us through the shifting narratives of our lives, becoming the material of our emotions and our thoughts. But they always do this from within a particular regime of realized signification. Popular culture is never just the materiality of things; it is always a simultaneous entanglement of meaning, materiality and social practice. This admixture can take various forms: a text message written on an iPhone, musical sounds produced by the human body, graffiti painted on a wall, a toy loved by a child. When Roland Barthes writes about other similar examples, he says that what they have in common is that they are signs (1995: 157). 'When I walk through the streets – or through life – and encounter these objects, I apply to all of them, if need without realizing it, one and the same activity, which is that of a certain reading' (157). In other words, the material objects Barthes encounters are also signs to be read. They have materiality, but they also have meanings. Cultural studies shares with Barthes the insistence that 'All objects which belong to a society have a meaning' (182); that is, they have been transformed by the fact that 'humanity gives meaning to things' (179). In this way, then, the material objects that surround us do not issue their own meanings; they have to be made to mean and how they are made to signify informs how we think about them, value them, and use them.

Although material objects are always more than signs, more than symbolic representations of social relations, what they are for us is inconceivable outside a particular culture that entangles meaning, materiality and social practice. They are never things in themselves, but always objects that are articulated in relation to a particular regime of realized signification, enabling and constraining particular types of social practice. A mobile phone, a dress, a football, a wooden table, a CD, an advert in a magazine – what they all have in common is materiality and meaning produced by social practice. It is this combination that makes them examples of culture. Culture is not therefore something we 'have', it is something we 'do' – the social production and reproduction of meanings realized in materiality and social practice. Meanings are not in the materiality of things but in how things are constructed as meaningful in social practices of representation. As I have said a number of times in this book, the world and its contents has to be made to signify. Again to repeat, this is not a denial of the reality of material things but it is an insistence that such things are mute until made to signify in social practices of representation. This claim is sometimes misunderstood (often deliberately and mischievously) as a denial of the materiality of things. But to be absolutely clear the material properties of an object are not culturally constructed; what is constructed is its inscription and location in culture. Materiality is mute and outside culture until it is made to signify by human action. However, saying materiality is mute is not the same as saying it does not exist, nor is it the same as saying that it does not enable and constrain how it might be made to signify. In other words, culture is a social practice that entangles meaning with materiality.

It is sometimes claimed that cultural studies reduces material objects to a simple matter of meanings. The opposite is in fact true: the material object is not reduced; it is expanded to include what it means in human culture. Cultural studies has always been interested in the use of things and this interest has always involved a consideration of their materiality. In Chapter 4 I gave the example of passing and/or receiving a business card in China. In this example, the culture is not simply in the social act, nor in the materiality of the card, nor in the meaning of the card and act – it is in the entanglement of meaning, materiality and social practice. Moreover, the passing and/or receiving of a business card in China is not simply a symbolic performance in which meaning is represented, it is a performative event (see Chapter 8) in which meaning is enacted and realized. Similarly, a wedding ring represents the institution of marriage, but the act of wearing a wedding ring is also performatively articulating this institution. My wife and I grew up using different implements to eat our food – she chopsticks and I a knife and fork. This material difference impacted on the food we ate. To be able to eat with chopsticks entails a different method of cooking, different ingredients, and a very different way to serve the food. What is eaten and the experience of eating it are very different. But do chopsticks or a knife and fork determine these things or is it the culture of their use? My parents taught me how to use a knife and fork because *this is how you are supposed to eat*. My wife was taught by her parents to use chopsticks because *this is how you are supposed to eat*. Chopsticks or knife and fork did not do the teaching; parents guided by a long tradition of a culture of mealtime etiquette did it – a realized signifying system. It does not matter that chopsticks and knife and fork belong to different traditions, what matters is that each tradition depends on meaning entangled with materiality enabled in social practice.

Material objects have to be realized as meaningful by social practice. It is this process, human acts of making things mean that transforms them into cultural objects. In other words, they have to be culturally constructed. But as I said earlier, what is meant by cultural construction is often misunderstood. To be absolutely clear, it does not mean the making real of something. For example, nature is a cultural construct, but this does not mean that culture brings into actual being the things we call trees, rivers and mountains. What we refer to as trees, rivers and mountains have a real material existence outside of how they are constructed culturally. They are not cultural constructions in the sense that they only exist once framed within culture. Before its encounter with human culture the tree did not exist as a tree, but it did exist as a living organism. What was culturally constructed was not this living organism but its conceptualization as a tree. Over the years this conceptualization has grown deeper and richer, as a result of, for example, the discourses of artists, novelists, botanists and poets. Cultural construction, therefore, does not mean the bringing into being of a material object; rather it points to how material objects are made meaningful and understood as meaningful in the particular regimes of realized signification we call culture. The material world is always framed by culture (this determines our experience of it, our understanding of it, and the questions we ask when we encounter it – in this sense it is a cultural construct), but the ontology of the material world is not in doubt (this is not a cultural construct).

I used to live near a wood and it is a magical place to walk and daydream. But I do not think this magic is something intrinsic to the trees themselves. I have no doubt that their type, size and shape enables and constrains this magic, but I do not think they produce it. In my view the magic is a result of the entanglement of trees with human culture. The magic depends on the existence of the woods, but it is only really made to happen because of how woods in general have been made to signify, how they have been realized in signification – fairy tales, children's adventure stories, gothic horror, etc. When Little Redcape, for example (see Chapter 5), is told not 'to stray from the path', the imaginative power of this injunction derives from the possibilities of danger and excitement conjured up by the narrative connotations of the surrounding woods. Although they exist outside culture, woods are cultural constructs. However, what is constructed is not the trees themselves, but what the trees signify. This means that when we go into a wood we encounter it as already entangled with meaning – even the simple idea that a wood is a good place to relax is a cultural construct. So when we say something is a cultural construct we are not saying that culture brought it into being, we are saying that there is nothing natural about what it means and how it is understood as meaningful, this is always the result of the work of a particular culture – realized signification. However, to repeat, material reality is not an effect of signification, it can exist perfectly well without being made to mean and being understood as meaningful, but for us it always exists realized in signification, and it is this entanglement of signification and materiality enabled by a social practice that cultural studies calls culture.

To describe the moon as a cultural construct might sound slightly ridiculous. Surely it is a natural satellite in synchronous rotation with the earth? Yes, it is, but from the beginning of human history people have looked up at the moon and inscribed meaning on it and in this way it has also become a cultural object, represented in, for example, songs, poetry, stories, paintings, mythologies. It is this ascription of signification that has culturally constructed the moon as an entanglement of meaning and materiality. But these representations, these modes of signification, did not construct the moon's material existence, an existence that predates human beings by more than four billion years. Similarly, the universe as the *universe* is a cultural construct. It is human culture that gives it meaning as *the universe*. However, this is not to deny that

Photo 11.1 Begin the revolution.

what we call the universe has an existence outside signification. In other words, what we call the universe exists prior to its realization in signification, but it does not exist as *the universe* (i.e. as an aspect of human culture). When thinking critically about a material object we have to distinguish between its undeniable materiality and its variable meanings. Moreover, to focus our critical gaze on its variable meanings does not in any way deny its undeniable materiality. This is not to conflate culture with the material reality of the world. The materiality of the moon can exist just fine without human culture. To describe the moon as a cultural construct is not to claim that it is culture that brought it into being. Rather it is the claim that what the moon signifies and how this signification helps organize our relations with the moon is always a matter of culture. The moon is real enough but for us its reality is entangled with signification and this signification frames our interactions with the moon. Once it is caught in the human gaze it becomes a cultural object – a significant object in popular culture. It existed perfectly well before this moment, but it is only with this moment that it begins to exist as the moon.

When I was in Tarragona for a conference in 2008 I was shown around the excavations of the Roman Forum. At one point I noticed a part of the wall had been covered by glass. When I asked why, I was told that it was to protect some graffiti dating from the beginning of the Spanish Civil War (see Photo 11.1). At some point after the graffiti was written someone had taken the trouble to hide it behind a brick wall. During the excavations the wall had been removed and the graffiti discovered. Then the decision was made to protect it and make it available to tourists. As an example of culture, the graffiti exists in at least four moments. In each of these moments its materiality deteriorates a little, but what changes, and changes significantly, is what the graffiti signifies. In each of these moments a different social practice comes into play. In the first moment, that of production, someone decided to paint the words on the wall. According to the date, this was the night when the Spanish Civil War began. Written in Catalan the words translate as *Begin the Revolution*. The call for revolution might have been deeply serious or an example of drunken bravado. The second is the most interesting and the most politically unambiguous moment. Someone, the writer or another person, made the decision to conceal the graffiti. We can assume a number of things about the act of concealment. It was done when fascism was either victorious or close to victory. The graffiti was concealed to stop it being destroyed by the fascists. Taking the trouble to conceal it with a brick wall put the person doing the work in potential danger. The person risked this danger because they wanted the words to survive as evidence of resistance to be read again after the fall of fascism. The third moment is when the graffiti was discovered. Fascism had gone and the excavators saw the words as historical evidence of opposition to its victory in the Spanish Civil War. The fourth moment, the moment of tourism, was when it became available to people like myself to encounter it on a tour of the Roman Forum. In each of these moments materiality, meaning and social practice are combined in a different way. From moments one to four the graffiti's materiality changes very little, but what does change is what it signifies, and its changing signification is always a result of social practice.

Materiality without meaning

Those working in material culture studies often accuse cultural studies of ignoring the materiality of things to focus instead on their meanings. Contrary to cultural studies, they seem to think that objects exist in the world as meaningful before they are made meaningful by human practice. Material culture studies seem to take for granted the material object as only ever a thing in itself. What is missing from this analysis is the recognition that the material object always exists for us in terms of how it has been realized in culture and realization always involves signification. The human making of meaning is presented by material culture studies, as a secondary process that always occurs after a natural meaning has been constituted. But there are no natural meanings, only meanings produced by human practice. Meaning is not found waiting to be discovered, it is a human production.

Paul Graves-Brown, in what I take to be a misplaced critique of cultural studies, makes this claim, 'if meaning is only ever "read into" things, there can be no common basis for understanding' (2000: 4). He seems to assume that our common basis for understanding is produced by the materiality of things – they produce their own meanings. But materiality is always mute until made to signify in a particular social practice. Therefore, any common basis for understanding cannot emerge from their muteness; it can only emerge through a shared regime of realized signification within which the material object is situated and made meaningful. In other words, our common basis for understanding derives from the regime of realized signification in which the object and we exist. Moreover, regimes of realized signification are always structured by power. As we have seen in Chapters 4 and 6, we might call this 'ideology' (Althusser), 'common sense' (Gramsci) or a 'regime of truth' (Foucault). But these meanings, meanings that organize and regulate social practice, do not come from the materiality of things; they come from those with the power to make things mean in particular ways. Material culture studies seem to think that things just signify in themselves or that signification is just not that important. Both positions are very unhelpful if we are trying to understand the relations between culture and power.

In Daniel Miller's little manifesto for material culture studies (Miller, 2009) he uses *The Emperor's New Clothes*[1] as a means to demonstrate why semiotics (which seems to be code for cultural studies) is incapable of really understanding materiality. First published in 1837, it is a story by Danish writer Hans Christian Andersen in which two swindlers present themselves as master weavers, and promise to make the Emperor a beautiful set of clothes that will be 'invisible to anyone who was unfit for his office, or who was unusually stupid'. Of course it quickly becomes clear that the clothes do not exist. People therefore have a choice: either to acknowledge the Emperor's nakedness or pretend he is wearing beautiful clothes. Out of fear of seeming unfit for office, the Emperor and the court officials admire the beautiful clothes. Not wishing to seem stupid, the town's people choose the same option. It is only the little boy who shouts out that the Emperor is in fact naked.

According to Miller, semiotics believes that clothes represent 'a real or true self which lies deep within us' (2009: 13). Semiotics supposedly sees clothing 'as the surface that represents, or fails to represent, the inner core of true being' (ibid.). Heroically challenging the idea of an inner self, Miller concludes that the real meaning of the story is this: 'But what was revealed by the absence of clothes was not the Emperor's inner self but his outward conceit' (ibid.). Therefore what we have is 'a morality tale of pretentiousness and vanity' (ibid.). I am not sure which semioticians actually believe in an inner self that is represented by clothes, but I think it is possible, from the perspective of cultural studies, to produce a very different reading of Andersen's story.

With the exception of the recognition of the little boy, the Emperor, the court officials, and the town's people are all trapped in the 'common sense' of a realized signifying system in which the Emperor's position of power is simply taken for granted. However, to recognize that he is naked (as a result of his own stupidity) is to threaten the legitimacy of this power. As we observed in Chapter 4, 'one man is king only because other men stand in the relation of subjects to him. They, on the contrary, imagine that they are subjects because he is king' (Marx, 1976c: 149). The Emperor's absence of clothes threatens to break this relationship and end the misrecognition that sees being an emperor as a gift of nature and royal subjecthood as a natural consequence of this gift. What is revealed is the fact that the Emperor really is naked, in that there is no natural substance to his authority to command. As Slavoj Žižek explains,

'Being-a-king' is an effect of the network of social relations between a 'king' and his 'subjects'; but – and here is the fetishistic misrecognition – to the participants of this social bond, the relationship appears necessarily in an inverse form: they think that they are subjects giving the king royal treatment because the king is already himself outside the relationship to his subjects, a king; as if the determination of 'being-a-king' were a 'natural' property of the person of a king (1989: 20).

In other words, the Emperor's nakedness threatens this misrecognition. Clothing, here and elsewhere, is cultural not because it represents an inner self (whatever this might be) but because it is part of how the self is produced and reproduced. In order to understand this we have to pay attention not just to meanings or materiality, but also to how meanings and materiality are entangled together by social practice. Moreover, to focus only on materiality or only on meanings would blind us to the many ways the entanglement is structured by relations of power.

Miller argues that, 'in material culture we are concerned . . . with how things make people' (2009: 42). Although I would not disagree – 'clothes maketh the man', this making is always, and fundamentally, inseparable from realized signification and social practice. We have seen this already in the case of the Emperor. In other words, using an object is always entangled with the meaning of the object. But Miller remains quite adamant that 'we cannot regard clothing as a form of representation, a semiotic sign or symbol of the person' (40). While it is true that we cannot regard clothing as *just* a form of representation, a semiotic sign or symbol of the person, it is also always true that clothing *is* a form of representation, a semiotic sign, a symbol of the person. It is never a question of either one or the other; it is always both. Again, we have to recognize the entanglement of meaning, materiality and social practice. Miller's dress code as a student is a clear example of the need to fully recognize this entanglement. He provides the example of what he was routinely wearing when he met his wife at Cambridge University: 'When I met my wife as fellow students, my trousers were held up at the top with string and their hem at the base with staples' (14).

Miller's mode of dress at Cambridge means something quite specific. It is a visible identification with the rather conservative and middle class idea that intellectuals are too concerned with matters of the intellect to be bothered about what they wear. To dress in this way is not a sign of casual neglect, it is a sign of a very studied disrepair – identification with a very old image of the serious student as would-be intellectual. But this dress code can also be found in less privileged places. It is not difficult to find in any city men who dress in a way similar to how Miller dressed at Cambridge – but here we will find not studied disrepair but an increasing inability, through lack of alternatives and the imperatives of drugs and alcohol, to pay attention to how one looks. In both cases the dress code seems the same, but in each example the cultural significance, the entanglement of materiality, meaning and social practice is literally worlds apart – the same dress code but very different meanings. If we pay attention only to the materiality of the clothes we would not be able to understand the difference between the privileged culture of a Cambridge student and the often inescapable hopelessness of being what George Orwell called 'down and out'.[2] To pay attention to only the materiality of the clothes, without locating their materiality in a particular realized regime of signification, would produce a very impoverished understanding. Moreover, by paying attention to the entanglement of materiality, meaning and social practice, we are at the start of an analysis that can expand from dress code to wider questions of why students dress the way they do and why the sixth richest economy in the world should have people sleeping rough on its streets.

It is, therefore, only partly true to say that 'Culture comes above all from stuff' (Miller, 2009: 54). When culture does come from stuff it is always stuff entangled in meaning and social practice. Material culture studies' endless descriptions of the materiality of stuff are always accompanied by the claim that addressing questions of meaning is superficial. The irony here of course is that all the interesting things it has to say about materiality are always about its meaning. For example, in an attempt to explain why in so many rooms allocated to au pairs the furniture of choice is white melamine IKEA furniture, Miller moves quickly away from mute materiality to matters of meaning.

> Just like the au pair herself, white melamine from IKEA is generally seen as inexpensive, generically European in a young, modern poise, characterized by cleanliness, functionality and efficiency. Hopefully reasonably long-lasting, and quite easy to replace (90).

Regardless of what we might think of this analysis, it is dependent on a series of assumptions about what white melamine IKEA furniture signifies. Put simply, it is an analysis of the au pair's room that depends on the entanglement of materiality, meaning and social practice.

Material objects in a global world

When different cultures share the same material objects, what marks cultural difference is obviously not these objects but the different meanings of these objects and how these meanings are realized in social practice. People from different societies use many of the same material objects, yet what they signify varies enormously (see Chapter 10). What Miller says about Coca-Cola is a very good example. 'Coca-Cola is everywhere, but means slightly different things in each locality' (9). What marks this difference is not its materiality, but how it is made to signify in particular social practices. The materiality of the drink is always entangled with meaning.

Coca-Cola likes to present itself as more than a sweet, fizzy drink – drinking it supposedly offers entry into the American global village. Perhaps the most famous manifestation of this idea is the television advert made in 1971. It featured 200 young people on a hill at sunrise, each wearing some version of national dress, each holding up a bottle of Coca-Cola and singing with the New Seekers:

> I'd like to buy the world a home and furnish it with love
> Grow apple trees and honeybees and snow-white turtle doves
> I'd like to teach the world to sing in perfect harmony
> I'd like to buy the world a Coke and keep it company
> It's the real thing[3]

This might be a compelling invitation to the paradise that is the American global village, but this is by no means the universal meaning of the drink. In China, for example, it can mean US imperialism (see Photo 10.2 in Chapter 10), the promise of capitalist modernity or simply the basis for a drink to cure the common cold (in which it is boiled with fresh ginger). The drink may have a single materiality but what it signifies is different depending on its location in a particular social practice (i.e. on who is consuming it and where). While it is true that its iconic bottle and its distinctive typography are globally recognized, to understand its global status we have to move beyond its materiality and address it as an object of culture in which materiality and meaning are entangled and enabled by social practice.

Another example of the entanglement of materiality with variable meaning is the global success of Christmas. In China, a country that is officially atheist, the Christian

Photo 11.2 Christmas in China.

festival is becoming more and more visible. This is certainly not a sign of an interest in Christianity or the weakening of official atheism. What we see is a festival that has been completely drained of its Christian significance. Promoted by the new department stores, it has been absorbed and repurposed in order to encourage people to consume. The material trappings of the festival may look similar (see Photo 11.2), but what it means and how these meanings organize social practice is very different from, for example, what it is supposed to mean in the UK (see Storey, 2010a).

Culture is about making the world signify. It matters because signification helps organize and regulate social practice. Such a concept of culture does not deny the existence of the materiality of things, but it does insist that this materiality is mute, it does not issue its own meanings, and it is therefore always made meaningful by human agency entangled in relations of power. Although how something is made meaningful is always enabled and constrained by the materiality of the thing itself, culture is not a property of mere materiality; it is the entanglement of meaning, materiality and social practice; variable meanings in a range of different contexts and social practices. In other words, culture is never merely mute materiality; it is always social, material and semiotic.

Notes

1. The story can be found online at http://www.andersen.sdu.dk/vaerk/hersholt/TheEmperorsNewClothes_e.html.
2. See George Orwell's *Down and Out in Paris and London*.
3. The video can be found on YouTube (https://www.youtube.com/watch?v=ib-Qiyklq-Q).

Further reading

Storey, John (ed.), *Cultural Theory and Popular Culture: A Reader*, 4th edn, Harlow: Pearson Education, 2009. This is the companion volume to the previous edition of this book. A fully updated 5th edition containing further readings is due for publication in 2018. An interactive website is also available (www.routledge.com/cw/storey), which contains helpful student resources and a glossary of terms for each chapter.

Barthes, Roland, *The Semiotic Challenge*, Berkeley: University of California Press, 1995. Contains some of the key essays on semiology and materiality.

Baudrillard, Jean, *The System of Objects*, London: Verso, 2005. Although not discussed in this chapter, it is a very influential account of the material object.

Berger, Arthur Asa, *What Objects Mean*, Walnut Creek, CA: Left Coast Press, 2014. A very good introduction to a range of theories of materiality.

Bryant, Levi R., *The Democracy of Objects*, Michigan: Open Humanities Press, 2011. A very interesting philosophical account of the material object.

Dant, Tim, *Material Culture in the Social World*, Milton Keynes: Open University Press, 1999. A very good introduction to issues around materiality and culture.

Latour, Bruno, *Reassembling the Social*, Oxford: Oxford University Press, 2007. An excellent introduction to actor-network-theory, written by the founder of this approach.

Malinowska, Anna and Karolina Lebek (eds.), *Materiality and Popular Culture*, Abingdon: Abingdon: Routledge, 2017. An excellent collection of essays discussing popular culture in relation to materiality.

Marx, Karl, *Early Writings*, Harmondsworth: Penguin, 1992. Marx's theory of the production of material life forms the foundation for most work on materiality in cultural studies. See 'Preface to *A Contribution to the Critique of Political Economy*'.

Miller, Daniel, *Stuff*. Cambridge: Polity Press, 2009. Offers a clear account of material culture studies.

12 The politics of the popular

I have tried in this book to outline something of the history of the relationship between cultural theory and popular culture. In the main I have tended to focus on the theoretical and methodological aspects and implications of the relationship, as this, in my opinion, is the best way in which to *introduce* the subject.[1] However, I am aware that this has been largely at the expense of, on the one hand, the historical conditions of the production of theory about popular culture, and on the other, the political relations of its production and reproduction (these are analytical emphases and not separate and distinct 'moments').

Something I hope I have demonstrated, however, is the extent to which popular culture is a concept of ideological contestation and variability, to be filled and emptied, articulated and disarticulated, in a range of different and competing ways. Even my own truncated and selective history of the study of popular culture shows that 'studying' popular culture can be a very serious business indeed – a serious political business.

Take, for example, Jim McGuigan's (1992) claim that the study of popular culture within contemporary cultural studies is in the throes of a paradigm crisis. This is supposedly nowhere more clearly signalled than in the widespread political practice of 'cultural populism'. McGuigan defines cultural populism as 'the intellectual assumption, made by some students of popular culture, that the symbolic experiences and practices of ordinary people are more important analytically and politically than Culture with a capital C' (4). On the basis of this definition, I am a cultural populist, and, moreover, so is McGuigan. However, the purpose behind his argument is to challenge not cultural populism as such, but what he calls 'an *uncritical* populist drift in the study of popular culture' (ibid.), with its supposed fixation on strategies of interpretation at the expense of an adequate grasp of the historical and economic conditions of consumption. He contends that cultural studies has increasingly narrowed its focus to questions of interpretation without situating such questions within a context of material relations of power.

He claims that cultural populism's exclusive focus on consumption and a corresponding uncritical celebration of popular reading practices has produced a 'crisis of qualitative judgment' (79). What he means by this is that there are no longer absolutist criteria of judgement. What is 'good' and what is 'bad' are now open to dispute. He blames postmodern uncertainty fostered by cultural populism, claiming that 'the reinsertion of aesthetic and ethical judgment into the debate is a vital rejoinder to the uncritical drift of cultural populism and its failure to dispute laissez-faire conceptions of consumer sovereignty and quality' (159). Clearly unhappy with the intellectual uncertainties of postmodernism, he desires a return to the full authority of the modernist intellectual: always ready to make clear and comprehensive that which the ordinary mind is unable to grasp. He seeks a return to the Arnoldian certainties – culture is the best that has been thought and said (and the modernist intellectual will tell us what this is). He seems to advocate an intellectual discourse in which the university lecturer is the guardian of the eternal flame of Culture, initiating the uninitiated into the glow of its absolute moral and aesthetic value; students assume the role of passive consumers of an already constituted knowledge – fixed, formulated and administered by the professorial guardians of the flame.

The refusal to privilege aesthetic judgement is not in my opinion a crisis, but a welcome recognition that there are other, sometimes far more interesting, questions to be asked (see Chapter 10). What is aesthetically 'good' and what is aesthetically 'bad' change and change again in context after context. Moreover, what is 'good' aesthetically may be 'bad' in terms of politics; what is 'bad' aesthetically may be 'good' politically. Rather than become trapped by a hopeless quest for abstract certainty, it is much more productive to recognize that it is only in grounded contexts that these questions can be really answered. But more than this, cultural studies should be little concerned with making speculative value judgements about the inherent qualities of commodities and focus its time instead on what people do with them, make from them, etc., in the constraining and enabling structures of everyday life. These are what I mean by more interesting questions. Those who insist on a return to absolute standards are saying little more than that it is too confusing now: I want back my easy and unquestioned authority to tell ordinary people what it is worth and how it should be done.[2]

> That ordinary people use the symbolic resources available to them under present conditions for meaningful activity is both manifest and endlessly elaborated upon by new revisionism [uncritical cultural populism]. Thus emancipatory projects to liberate people from their alleged entrapment, whether they know they are entrapped or not, are called into question by this fundamental insight. Economic exploitation, racism, gender and sexual oppression, to name but a few, exist, but the exploited, estranged and oppressed cope, and, furthermore, if such writers as John Fiske and Paul Willis are to be believed, they cope very well indeed, making valid sense of the world and obtaining grateful pleasure from what they receive. Apparently, there is so much action in the micro-politics of everyday life that the Utopian promises of a better future, which were once so enticing for critics of popular culture, have lost all credibility (171).

Most of this is simply untrue. Even Fiske (his prime example) celebrates not an achieved utopia, but the active struggle of men and women to make sense of and make space in a world structured around exploitation and oppression. McGuigan seems to be saying that pleasure (and its identification and celebration) is in some fundamental sense counter-revolutionary. The duty and historical destiny of ordinary men and women is to suffer and be still, until moral leftists reveal what is to be enjoyed on the glorious morning of the long day after the Revolution. Feminists, unwilling to lie back and think about the determining role of production, exposed the rhetorical vacuousness of this kind of thinking a long time ago. It simply is not the case that claims that audiences produce meaning are in some profound sense a denial of the need for political change. We can celebrate symbolic resistance without abandoning our commitment to radical politics. This is in effect the core of Ang's point (see Chapter 8).

As McGuigan names John Fiske and Paul Willis as perhaps the most 'guilty' of uncritical cultural populists, I shall outline some of the key features of their work to explain what is at issue in what is so far a rather one-sided debate. In order to facilitate this, I shall introduce two new concepts that have their provenance in the work of Pierre Bourdieu: the 'cultural field' and the 'economic field'.

The cultural field

John Fiske is generally seen as the epitome of the uncritical drift into cultural populism. According to McGuigan, 'Fiske's position is . . . indicative of the critical decline of British cultural studies' (85). Fiske is said to continually sacrifice economic and technological determinations to make space for *interpretation* – a purely hermeneutic version of cultural studies. For example, he is accused of reducing the study of television 'to a kind of subjective idealism' (72), in which the popular reading is king or queen, always 'progressive' – untroubled by questions of sexism or racism, and always ungrounded in economic and political relations. In short, Fiske is accused of an uncritical and unqualified celebration of popular culture; he is the classic example of what happened to cultural studies following the supposed collapse of hegemony theory and the consequent emergence of what McGuigan refers to as the 'new revisionism', the reduction of cultural studies to competing hermeneutic models of consumption. New revisionism, with its supposed themes of pleasure, empowerment, resistance and popular discrimination, is said to represent a moment of 'retreat from more critical positions' (75). In political terms, it is at best an uncritical echo of liberal claims about the 'sovereignty of the consumer', and at worst it is uncritically complicit with prevailing 'free market' ideology.

Fiske would not accept 'new revisionism' as an accurate description of his position on popular culture. He would also reject absolutely two assumptions implicit in the attack on his work. First, he would dismiss totally the view that 'the capitalist culture industries produce only an apparent variety of products whose variety is finally illusory for they all promote the same capitalist ideology' (Fiske, 1987: 309). Second, he is emphatic in his refusal of any argument that depends for its substance on the claim 'that "the people" are "cultural dupes" . . . a passive, helpless mass incapable of discrimination and thus at the economic, cultural, and political mercy of the barons of the industry' (ibid.). Against these assumptions, Fiske argues that the commodities from which popular culture is made circulate in two simultaneous economies: the financial and the cultural.

> The workings of the financial economy cannot account adequately for all cultural factors, but it still needs to be taken into account in any investigation. . . . But the cultural commodity cannot be adequately described in financial terms only: the circulation that is crucial to its popularity occurs in the parallel economy – the cultural (311).

While the financial economy is primarily concerned with exchange value, the cultural is primarily focused on use – 'meanings, pleasures, and social identities' (ibid.). There is of course dialogical interaction between these separate, but related, economies. Fiske gives the example of the American television programme *Hill Street Blues*. The programme was made by MTM and sold to NBC. NBC then 'sold' the potential audience to Mercedes-Benz, the sponsors of the programme. This all takes place in the financial economy. In the cultural economy, the television series changes from commodity (to be sold to NBC) to a site for the production of meanings and pleasures for its audience. And in the same way, the audience changes from a potential commodity (to be sold to Mercedes-Benz) to a producer (of meanings and pleasures). He argues that 'the power of audiences-as-producers in the cultural economy is considerable' (313). The power of the audience, he contends,

> derives from the fact that meanings do not circulate in the cultural economy in the same way that wealth does in the financial. They are harder to possess (and thus to exclude others from possessing), they are harder to control because the production of meaning and pleasure is not the same as the production of the cultural commodity, or of other goods, for in the cultural economy the role of consumer does not exist as the end point of a linear economic transaction. Meanings and pleasures circulate within it without any real distinction between producers and consumers (ibid.).

The power of the consumer derives from the failure of producers to predict what will sell. 'Twelve out of thirteen records fail to make a profit, TV series are axed by the dozen, expensive films sink rapidly into red figures (*Raise the Titanic* is an ironic example – it nearly sank the Lew Grade empire)' (ibid.). In an attempt to compensate for failures, the culture industries produce 'repertoires' of goods in the hope of attracting an audience; while the culture industries seek to incorporate audiences as commodity consumers, the audience often excorporates the text to its own purposes. Fiske cites the example of the way Australian Aboriginal viewers appropriated Rambo as a figure of resistance, relevant to their own political and cultural struggles. He also cites the example of Russian Jews watching *Dallas* in Israel and reading it as 'capitalism's self-criticism' (320).[3]

Fiske argues that resistance to the power of the powerful by those without power in Western societies takes two forms, semiotic and social. The first is mainly concerned with meanings, pleasures and social identities; the second is dedicated to transformations of the socio-economic system. He contends that 'the two are closely related, although relatively autonomous' (316). Popular culture operates mostly, 'but not exclusively', in the domain of semiotic power. It is involved in 'the struggle between homogenisation and difference, or between consensus and conflict' (ibid.). In this sense, popular culture is a semiotic battlefield in which audiences constantly engage in 'semiotic guerrilla warfare' (316) in a conflict fought out between the forces of incorporation and the forces of resistance: between an imposed set of meanings, pleasures and social identities, and the meanings, pleasures and social identities produced in acts of semiotic resistance, where 'the hegemonic forces of homogeneity are always met by the resistances of heterogeneity' (Fiske, 1989a: 8). In Fiske's semiotic war scenario, the two economies favour opposing sides of the struggle: the financial economy is more supportive of the forces of incorporation and homogenization; the cultural economy is more accommodating to the forces of resistance and difference. Semiotic resistance, he argues, has the effect of undermining capitalism's attempt at ideological homogeneity: dominant meanings are challenged by subordinate meanings; thus, the dominant class's intellectual and moral leadership is challenged. Fiske states his position without apology and with absolute clarity:

> It . . . sees popular culture as a site of struggle, but, while accepting the power of the forces of dominance, it focuses rather upon the popular tactics by which these forces are coped with, are evaded or are resisted. Instead of tracing exclusively the processes of incorporation, it investigates rather the popular vitality and creativity that makes incorporation such a constant necessity. Instead of concentrating on the omnipresent, insidious practices of the dominant ideology, it attempts to understand the everyday resistances and evasions that make that ideology work so hard and insistently to maintain itself and its values. This approach sees popular culture as potentially, and often actually, progressive (though not radical), and it is essentially optimistic, for it finds in the vigour and vitality of the people evidence both of the possibility of social change and of the motivation to drive it (20–1).

Fiske also locates popular culture in what Pierre Bourdieu (1984) calls 'the cultural field' (113–20), in which takes place a cultural struggle between dominant or official culture and popular culture abstracted from economic and technological determinations, but ultimately over-determined by them. The historical creation of a unique space – the cultural field – in which Culture with a capital C could develop above and beyond the social has for Bourdieu the purpose, or at least the consequence, of reinforcing and legitimizing class power as cultural and aesthetic difference. The class relations of the cultural field are structured around two divisions: on the one hand, between the dominant classes and the subordinate classes, and on the other, within the dominant classes between those with high economic capital as opposed to high cultural capital, and those with high cultural capital as opposed to high economic capital. Those whose power stems primarily from cultural rather than economic power are engaged in a constant struggle within the cultural field 'to raise the social value of the specific competences involved in part by constantly trying to raise the scarcity of those competences. It is for this reason that . . . they will always resist as a body moves towards cultural democracy' (220).[4]

As we noted in Chapter 1 (see also Chapter 10), for Bourdieu (1984) the category of 'taste' functions as a marker of 'class' (using the word in a double sense to mean both a socio-economic category and the suggestion of a particular level of quality). At the pinnacle of the hierarchy of taste is the 'pure' aesthetic gaze – a historical invention – with its emphasis on form over function. The 'popular aesthetic' reverses this emphasis, subordinating form to function. Accordingly, popular culture is about performance, high culture is about contemplation; high culture is about representation, popular culture is about what is represented. As he explains, 'Intellectuals could be said to believe in the representation – literature, theatre, painting – more than in the things represented, whereas the people chiefly expect representations and the conventions which govern them to allow them to believe "naively" in the things represented' (5).

Aesthetic 'distance' is in effect the denial of function: it insists on the 'how' and not the 'what'. It is analogous to the difference between judging a meal good because it was economically priced and filling, and judging a meal good on the basis of how it was served, where it was served. The 'pure' aesthetic or cultured gaze emerges with the emergence of the cultural field, and becomes institutionalized in the art museum. Once inside the museum art loses all prior functions (except that of being art) and becomes pure form: 'Though originally subordinated to quite different or even incompatible functions (crucifix and fetish, Pieta and still life), these juxtaposed works tacitly demand attention to form rather than function, technique rather than theme' (30). For example, an advertisement for soup displayed in an art gallery becomes an example of the aesthetic, whereas the same advertisement in a magazine is an example of commerce. The effect of the distinction is to produce 'a sort of ontological promotion akin to a transubstantiation' (6).

As Bourdieu says, 'it is not easy to describe the "pure" gaze without also describing the naive gaze which it defines itself against' (32). The naive gaze is of course the gaze of the popular aesthetic:

> The affirmation of continuity between art and life, which implies the subordina-
> tion of form to function . . . a refusal of the refusal which is the starting point of
> the high aesthetic, i.e. the clear cut separation of ordinary dispositions from the
> specially aesthetic disposition (ibid.).

The relations between the pure gaze and the popular/naive gaze are needless to say not those of equality, but a relation of dominant and dominated. Moreover, Bourdieu argues that the two aesthetics articulate relations of power. Without the required cultural capital to decipher the 'code' of art we are made socially *vulnerable* to the condescension of those who have the required cultural capital. What is cultural (i.e. acquired) is presented as natural (i.e. innate), and is, in turn, used to justify what are social relations. In this way, 'art and cultural consumption are predisposed . . . to fulfil a social function of legitimating social differences' (7). Bourdieu calls the operation of such distinctions the 'ideology of natural taste' (68). According to the ideology, only a supposedly instinctively gifted minority armed against the mediocrity of the masses can attain genuine 'appreciation'. Ortega y Gasset makes the point with precision: 'art helps the "best" to know and recognise one another in the greyness of the multitude and to learn their mission, which is to be few in number and to have to fight against the multitude' (31). Aesthetic relations both mimic and help reproduce social relations of power. As Bourdieu observes,

> Aesthetic intolerance can be terribly violent. . . . The most intolerable thing for those who regard themselves as the possessors of legitimate culture is the sacrilegious reuniting of tastes which taste dictates shall be separated. This means that the games of artists and aesthetes and their struggles for the monopoly of artistic legitimacy are less innocent than they seem. At stake in every struggle over art there is also the imposition of an art of living, that is, the transmutation of an arbitrary way of living into the legitimate way of life which casts every other way of living into arbitrariness (57).

Like other ideological strategies, 'The ideology of natural taste owes its plausibility and its efficacy to the fact that . . . it naturalises real differences, converting differences in the mode of acquisition of culture into differences of nature' (68).

In an argument that draws heavily on the work of Bourdieu, Paul Willis (1990) argues that the aesthetic appreciation of 'art' has undergone an 'internal hyperinstitutionalization' (2) – the dissociation of art from life, a stress on form over function – in a further attempt to distance itself and those who 'appreciate' it from the 'uncultured mass'. Part of this process is the denial of the necessary relationship between aesthetics and 'education' (understood in its broadest sense to include both formal and informal): the production and reproduction of the necessary 'knowledge' on which aesthetic appreciation is founded. In denial of such a relationship, aesthetic appreciation is presented as something innate, rather than something learned. Rather than seeing this as a question of non-access to knowledge – they have not been 'educated' in the necessary code to 'appreciate' the formal qualities of high culture – the majority of the population are encouraged to view 'themselves as ignorant, insensitive and without the finer sensibilities of those who really "appreciate". Absolutely certainly they're not the "talented" or "gifted", the elite minority held to be capable of performing or creating "art"' (3). This manufactures a situation in which people who make culture in their everyday lives see themselves as uncultured. Against the strategies of the 'internal hyperinstitutionalization' of culture, Willis argues the case for what he calls 'grounded aesthetics': the process through which ordinary people make cultural sense of the world, 'the ways in which the received natural and social world is made human to *them* and made, to however small a degree (even if finally symbolic), controllable by them' (22).

> [Grounded aesthetics] is the creative element in a process whereby meanings are attributed to symbols and practices and where symbols and practices are selected, reselected, highlighted and recomposed to resonate further appropriate and particularised meanings. Such dynamics are emotional as well as cognitive. There are as many aesthetics as there are grounds for them to operate in. Grounded aesthetics are the yeast of common culture (21).

Grounded aesthetic value is never intrinsic to a text or practice, a universal quality of its form; it is always inscribed in the 'sensuous/emotive/cognitive' (24) act of consumption (how a commodity is appropriated, 'used' and made meaningful). This is an argument against those who locate creativity only in the act of production, consumption being merely the recognition or misrecognition of the aesthetic intention. Against such claims, Willis insists that consumption is a symbolic act of creativity. His 'fundamental point . . . is that "messages" are not now so much "sent" and "received" as *made* in reception. . . . "Sent message" communication is being replaced by "made message" communication' (135). Cultural communication is ceasing to be a process of listening to the voices of others. Grounded aesthetics is the insistence that commodities are consumed (and made into culture) on the basis of use, rather than in terms of supposed inherent and ahistorical qualities (textual or authorial). In grounded aesthetics, meanings or pleasures are undecidable in advance of the practices of 'production in use'. This of course means that a commodity or a commodified practice that is judged to be banal and uninteresting (on the basis of textual analysis or an analysis of its mode of production) may be made to bear or to do, in its 'production in use', all sorts of interesting things within the lived conditions of a specific context of consumption. In this way, Willis's argument is a rebuke to both textualism, which makes judgements on the basis of formal qualities, and the political economy of culture approach, which makes judgements on the basis of the relations of production. The 'symbolic work' of consumption, he maintains, is never a simple repetition of the relations of production, nor is it a direct confirmation of the semiotic certainties of the lecture theatre.

> People bring living identities to commerce and the consumption of cultural commodities as well as being formed there. They bring experiences, feelings, social position and social memberships to their encounter with commerce. Hence they bring a necessary creative symbolic pressure, not only to make sense of cultural commodities, but partly through them also to make sense of contradiction and

structure as they experience them in school, college, production, neighbourhood, and as members of certain genders, races, classes and ages. The results of this necessary symbolic work may be quite different from anything initially coded into cultural commodities (21).

The French cultural theorist Michel de Certeau (1984, 2009) also interrogates the term 'consumer', to reveal the activities that lie within the act of consumption or what he prefers to call 'secondary production' (2009: 547). Consumption, as he says, 'is devious, it is dispersed, but it insinuates itself everywhere, silently and almost invisibly, because it does not manifest itself through its own products, but rather through its ways of using the products imposed by a dominant economic order' (546). For de Certeau, the cultural field is a site of continual conflict (silent and almost invisible) between the 'strategy' of cultural imposition (production) and the 'tactics' of cultural use (consumption or 'secondary production'). The cultural critic must be alert to 'the difference or similarity between . . . production . . . and . . . secondary production hidden in the process of . . . utilisation' (547).[5] He characterizes the active consumption of texts as 'poaching': 'readers are travellers; they move across lands belonging to someone else, like nomads poaching their way across the fields they did not write' (1984: 174).

The idea of reading as poaching is clearly a rejection of any theoretical position that assumes that the 'message' of a text is something which is imposed on a reader. Such approaches, he argues, are based on a fundamental misunderstanding of the processes of consumption. It is a 'misunderstanding [which] assumes that "assimilating" necessarily, means "becoming similar to" what one absorbs, and not "making something similar" to what one is, making it one's own, appropriating or reappropriating it' (166).

Acts of textual poaching are always in potential conflict with the 'scriptural economy' (131–76) of textual producers and those institutional voices (professional critics, academics, etc.) who, through an insistence on the authority of authorial and/or textual meaning, work to limit and to confine the production and circulation of 'un-authorized' meanings. In this way, de Certeau's notion of 'poaching' is a challenge to traditional models of reading, in which the purpose of reading is the passive reception of authorial and/or textual intent: that is, models of reading in which reading is reduced to a question of being 'right' or 'wrong'. He makes an interesting observation about how the notion of a text containing a hidden meaning may help sustain certain relationships of power in matters of pedagogy:

This fiction condemns consumers to subjection because they are always going to be guilty of infidelity or ignorance when confronted by the mute 'riches' of the treasury. . . . The fiction of the 'treasury' hidden in the work, a sort of strong-box full of meaning, is obviously not based on the productivity of the reader, but on the social institution that overdetermines his relation with the text. Reading is as it were overprinted by a relationship of forces (between teachers and pupils . . .) whose instrument it becomes (171).

This may in turn produce a teaching practice in which 'students . . . are scornfully driven back or cleverly coaxed back to the meaning "accepted" by their teachers' (172).[6] This is often informed by what we might call 'textual determinism':[7] the view that the value of something is inherent in the thing itself. This position can lead to a way of working in which certain texts and practices are prejudged to be beneath the legitimate concerns of the academic gaze. Against this way of thinking, I would contend that what really matters is not the object of study, but how the object is studied.

Many areas of everyday life could be said to illustrate de Certeau's account of the practice of consumption, but perhaps none more so than the consumption practices of fan cultures. Together with youth subcultures, fans are perhaps the most visible part of the audience for popular texts and practices. In recent years fandom has come increasingly under the critical gaze of cultural studies. Traditionally, fans have been treated in one of two ways – ridiculed or pathologized. According to Joli Jenson (1992), 'The literature on fandom is haunted by images of deviance. The fan is consistently characterised (referencing the term's origins) as a potential fanatic. This means that fandom is seen as excessive, bordering on deranged, behaviour' (9). Jenson suggests two typical types of fan pathology: 'the obsessed individual' (usually male) and 'the hysterical crowd' (usually female). She contends that both figures result from a particular reading and 'unacknowledged critique of modernity', in which fans are viewed 'as a psychological symptom of a presumed social dysfunction' (ibid.). Fans are presented as one of the dangerous 'others' of modern life. 'We' are sane and respect-able; 'they' are either obsessed or hysterical.

This is yet another discourse on other people. Fandom is what 'other people' do. This can be seen clearly in the way in which fandom is assigned to the cultural activities of popular audiences, while dominant groups are said to have cultural interests, tastes and preferences. Moreover, as Jenson points out, this is a discourse that seeks to secure and police distinctions between class cultures. This is supposedly confirmed by the object(s) of admiration that mark off the tastes of dominant groups from those of popular audiences,[8] but it is also supposedly sustained by the methods of appreciation – popular audiences are said to display their pleasure to emotional excess, whereas the audience for dominant culture is always able to maintain respectable aesthetic distance and control.[9]

Perhaps one of the most interesting accounts of a fan culture from within cultural studies is Henry Jenkins's (1992) *Textual Poachers*. In an ethnographic investigation of a fan community (mostly, but not exclusively, white middle-class women), he approaches fandom as 'both . . . an academic (who has access to certain theories of popular culture, certain bodies of critical and ethnographic literature) and as a fan (who has access to the particular knowledge and traditions of that community)' (5).

Fan reading is characterized by an intensity of intellectual and emotional involve-ment. 'The text is drawn close not so that the fan can be possessed by it but rather so that the fan may more fully possess it. Only by integrating media content back into their everyday lives, only by close engagement with its meanings and materials, can fans fully consume the fiction and make it an active resource' (62). Arguing against textual determinism (the text determines how it will be read and in so doing positions the reader in a particular ideological discourse), he insists that '[t]he reader is drawn not into the preconstituted world of the fiction but rather into a world she has created from textual materials. Here, the reader's pre-established values are at least as important as those preferred by the narrative system' (63).

Fans do not just read texts, they continually re-read them. This changes profoundly the nature of the text–reader relationship. Re-reading undermines the operations of what Barthes (1975) calls the 'hermeneutic code' (the way a text poses questions to generate the desire to keep reading). Re-reading in this way thus shifts the reader's attention from 'what will happen' to 'how things happen', to questions of character relations, narrative themes, the production of social knowledges and discourses.

While most reading is a solitary practice, performed in private, fans consume texts as part of a community. Fan culture is about the public display and circulation of meaning production and reading practices. Fans make meanings to communicate with other fans. The public display and circulation of these meanings are crucial to a fan culture's reproduction. As Jenkins explains, 'Organised fandom is, perhaps first and foremost, an institution of theory and criticism, a semistructured space where competing interpretations and evaluations of common texts are proposed, debated, and negotiated and where readers speculate about the nature of the mass media and their own relationship to it' (86).

Fan cultures are not just bodies of enthusiastic readers; they are also active cultural producers. Jenkins notes ten ways in which fans rewrite their favourite television shows (162–77):

1. *Recontextualization* – the production of vignettes, short stories and novels that seek to fill in the gaps in broadcast narratives and suggest additional explanations for particular actions.
2. *Expanding the series timeline* – the production of vignettes, short stories, novels that provide background history of characters, etc., not explored in broadcast narratives or suggestions for future developments beyond the period covered by the broadcast narrative
3. *Refocalization* – this occurs when fan writers move the focus of attention from the main protagonists to secondary figures. For example, female or black characters are taken from the margins of a text and given centre stage.
4. *Moral realignment* – a version of refocalization in which the moral order of the broadcast narrative is inverted (the villains become the good guys). In some versions the moral order remains the same but the story is now told from the point of view of the villains.
5. *Genre shifting* – characters from broadcast science fiction narratives, say, are relocated in the realms of romance or the Western, for example.
6. *Cross-overs* – characters from one television programme are introduced into another. For example, characters from *Doctor Who* may appear in the same narrative as characters from *Star Wars*.
7. *Character dislocation* – characters are relocated in new narrative situations, with new names and new identities.

8. *Personalization* – the insertion of the writer into a version of their favourite television programme. For example, I could write a short story in which I am recruited by the Doctor to travel with him in the Tardis on a mission to explore what has become of Manchester United in the twenty-fourth century. However, as Jenkins points out, many in the fan culture discourage this subgenre of fan writing.

9. *Emotional intensification* – the production of what are called 'hurt-comfort' stories in which favourite characters, for example, experience emotional crises.

10. *Eroticization* – stories that explore the erotic side of a character's life. Perhaps the best known of this subgenre of fan writing is 'slash' fiction, so called because it depicts same-sex relationships (as in Kirk/Spock, etc.).

In addition to fan fiction, fans make music videos in which images from favourite programmes are edited into new sequences to a soundtrack provided by a popular song; they make fan art; they produce fanzines; they engage in 'filking' (the writing and performing at conferences of songs – filk songs – about programmes, characters or the fan culture itself); and they organize campaigns to encourage television networks to bring back favourite programmes or to make changes in existing ones.[10] As Jenkins points out, echoing de Certeau, 'Fans are poachers who get to keep what they take and use their plundered goods as the foundations for the construction of an alternative cultural community' (223).

In his discussion of filking, Jenkins draws attention to a common opposition within filk songs between fandom and 'Mundania' (the world in which non-fans – 'mundane readers' or 'mundanes' – live). The difference between the two worlds is not simply one of intensity of response: 'Fans are defined in opposition to the values and norms of everyday life, as people who live more richly, feel more intensely, play more freely, and think more deeply than "mundanes"' (268). Moreover, 'Fandom constitutes . . . a space . . . defined by its refusal of mundane values and practices, its celebration of deeply held emotions and passionately embraced pleasures. Fandom's very existence represents a critique of conventional forms of consumer culture' (283).

What he finds particularly empowering about fan cultures is their struggle to create 'a more participatory culture' from 'the very forces that transform many Americans into spectators' (284). It is not the commodities that are empowering, it is what the fans do with them that empowers. As Jenkins explains,

> I am not claiming that there is anything particularly empowering about the texts fans embrace. I am, however, claiming that there is something empowering about what fans do with those texts in the process of assimilating them to the particulars of their lives. Fandom celebrates not exceptional texts but rather exceptional readings (though its interpretive practices make it impossible to maintain a clear or precise distinction between the two) (ibid.).

In a way reminiscent of the classic cultural studies model of subcultural reading, fan cultures, according to Jenkins, struggle to resist the demands of the ordinary and the everyday. While youth subcultures define themselves against parent and dominant cultures, fan cultures define themselves in opposition to the supposed everyday cultural passivities of 'Mundania'.

Grossberg (1992) is critical of the 'subcultural' model of fan cultures, in which 'fans constitute an elite fraction of the larger audience of passive consumers' (52).

> Thus, the fan is always in constant conflict, not only with the various structures of power, but also with the vast audience of media consumers. But such an elitist view of fandom does little to illuminate the complex relations that exist between forms of popular culture and their audiences. While we may all agree that there is a difference between the fan and the consumer, we are unlikely to understand the difference if we simply celebrate the former category and dismiss the latter one (ibid.).

In a similar way, subcultural analysis has always tended to celebrate the extraordinary against the ordinary – a binary opposition between resistant 'style' and conformist 'fashion'. Subcultures represent youth in resistance, actively refusing to conform to the passive commercial tastes of the majority of youth. Once resistance has given way to incorporation, analysis stops, waiting for the next 'great refusal'. Gary Clarke (1990) draws attention to the London-centredness of much British subcultural theory, with its suggestion that the appearance of a given youth subculture in the provinces is a telling sign of its incorporation. It is not surprising, then, that he also detects a certain level of cultural elitism structuring much of the classic cultural studies work on youth subcultures.

> I would argue generally that the subcultural literature's focus on the stylistic deviance of a few contains (albeit implicitly) a similar treatment of the rest of the working class as unproblematically incorporated. This is evident, for example, in the distaste felt for youth deemed as outside subcultural activity – even though most 'straight' working-class youths enjoy the same music, styles, and activities as the subcultures – and in the disdain for such cults as glam, disco, and the Ted revival, which lack 'authenticity'. Indeed, there seems to be an underlying contempt for 'mass culture' (which stimulates the interest in those who deviate from it) that stems from the work of the Marxism of the Frankfurt School and, within the English tradition, to the fear of mass culture expressed in *The Uses of Literacy* (90).

If subcultural consumption is to remain an area of concern in cultural studies, Clarke suggests that future analysis 'should take the breakthrough of a style as its starting point' (92), rather than seeing this as the defining moment of incorporation. Better still, cultural studies should focus on 'the activities of all youths to locate continuities and discontinuities in culture and social relations and to discover the meaning these activities have for the youths themselves' (95).

The economic field

There is now a whole genre of articles and conference papers by people working in media and communications (i.e. academics, almost all male, outside cultural studies) that is totally dedicated to endlessly publishing and presenting the proposition that cultural studies, if it is to remain politically credible, must, without delay, fully embrace the working methods of political economy.[11] McGuigan (1992) has the credit of being an early and serious exponent of this genre:

> In my view, the separation of contemporary cultural studies from the political economy of culture has been one of the most disabling features of the field of study. The core problematic was virtually premised on a terror of economic reductionism. In consequence, the economic aspects of media institutions and the broader economic dynamics of consumer culture were rarely investigated, simply bracketed off, thereby severely undermining the explanatory and, in effect, critical capacities of cultural studies (40–1).

Nicholas Garnham (2009) makes a similar point: 'the project of cultural studies can only be successfully pursued if the bridge with political economy is rebuilt' (619). Work on consumption in cultural studies has, or so the argument goes, vastly over-estimated the power of consumers, by failing to keep in view the 'determining' role production plays in limiting the possibilities of consumption.

So, what can political economy offer to cultural studies? Here is Peter Golding and Graham Murdock's (1991) outline of its protocols and procedures:

> What distinguishes the critical political economy perspective . . . is precisely its focus on the interplay between the symbolic and economic dimensions of public communications [including popular culture]. It sets out to show how different ways of financing and organising cultural production have traceable consequences for the range of discourses and representations in the public domain and for audiences' *access* to them (15; my italics).

It is clearly important to address such questions in a world in which the culture industries are owned and controlled by fewer and fewer powerful individuals and institutions. It is now quite common for the power of a culture industry to stretch well beyond its most publicly visible point. A company known for making films may also own the company that owns the book on which the film is based and the company that owns the music of the soundtrack and the newspapers and magazines in which the film is reviewed. These 'synergies' give particular culture industries enormous power over what we view, read and listen to and, moreover, how we are encouraged to listen, view and read.

But how does the political economy of culture address such questions? The significant word in the quotation above is 'access' (privileged over 'use' and 'meaning'). This reveals the limitations of the approach: good on the economic dimensions but weak on the symbolic. Golding and Murdock suggest that the work of theorists such as Willis and Fiske in its 'romantic celebration of subversive consumption is clearly at odds with cultural studies' long-standing concern with the way the mass media operate ideologically, to sustain and support prevailing relations of domination' (17). What is particularly revealing about this claim is not the critique of Willis and Fiske, but the assumptions about the purposes of cultural studies. They seem to be suggesting that unless the focus is firmly and exclusively on domination and manipulation, cultural studies is failing in its task. There are only two positions: on the one hand, romantic celebration, and on the other, the recognition of ideological power – and only the second is a serious scholarly pursuit. Are all attempts to show people resisting ideological manipulation forms of romantic celebration? Are left pessimism and moral leftism the only guarantees of political and scholarly seriousness?

Political economy's idea of cultural analysis seems to involve little more than detailing access to, and availability of, texts and practices. Nowhere do they actually advocate a consideration of what these texts and practices might mean (textually) or be made to mean in use (consumption). As Golding and Murdock point out,

> in contrast to recent work on audience activity within cultural studies, which concentrates on the negotiation of textual interpretations and media use in immediate social settings, critical political economy seeks to relate variations in people's responses to their overall location in the economic system (27).

This seems to suggest that the specific materiality of a text is unimportant, and that audience negotiations are mere fictions, illusory moves in a game of economic power.

While it is clearly important to locate the texts and practices of popular culture within the field of their economic conditions of existence, it is clearly insufficient to do this in the way advocated by political economy and to think then that you have also analysed and answered important questions to do with both the specific materiality of a text, and audience appropriation and use. It seems to me that post-Marxist hegemony theory still holds the promise of keeping in active relationship production, text and consumption, whereas political economy threatens, in spite of its admirable intentions, to collapse everything back into the economic.

It is Willis's attitude to the capitalist market that most offends political economy, especially his claim that the capitalist drive for profit produces the very conditions for the production of new forms of common culture.

> No other agency has recognised this realm [common culture] or supplied it with usable symbolic materials. And commercial entrepreneurship of the cultural field has discovered something real. For whatever self-serving reasons it was accomplished, we believe that this is an historical recognition. It counts and is irreversible. Commercial cultural forms have helped to produce an historical present from which we cannot now escape and in which there are many more materials – no matter what we think of them – available for necessary symbolic work than ever

there were in the past. Out of these come forms not dreamt of in the commercial imagination and certainly not in the official one – forms which make up common culture (1990: 19).

Capitalism is not a monolithic system. Like any 'structure' it is contradictory in that it both constrains and enables 'agency'. For example, while one capitalist bemoans the activities of the latest youth subculture, another embraces it with economic enthusiasm, and is prepared to supply it with all the commodities it is able to desire. It is these, and similar, contradictions in the capitalist market system that have produced the possibility of a common culture.

Commerce and consumerism have helped to release a profane explosion of everyday symbolic life and activity. The genie of common culture is out of the bottle – let out by commercial carelessness. Not stuffing it back in, but seeing what wishes may be granted, should be the stuff of our imagination (27).

This entails what Willis knows will be anathema for many, not least the advocates of political economy, the suggestion of 'the possibility of cultural emancipation working, at least in part, through ordinary, hitherto uncongenial economic mechanisms' (131). Although it may not be entirely clear what is intended by 'cultural emancipation', beyond, that is, the claim that it entails a break with the hegemonic exclusions of 'official culture'. What is clear, however, and remains anathema to political economy, is that he sees the market, in part, because of its contradictions – 'supplying materials for its own critique' (139) – and despite its intentions and its distortions, as facilitating the symbolic creativity of the realm of common culture.

People find on the market incentives and possibilities not simply for their own confinement but also for their own development and growth. Though turned inside out, alienated and working through exploitation at every turn, these incentives and possibilities promise more than any visible alternative. . . . Nor will it suffice any longer in the face of grounded aesthetics to say that modern 'consumer identities' simply repeat 'inscribed positions' within market provided texts and artefacts. Of course the market does not provide cultural empowerment in anything like a full sense. There are choices, but not choices over choices – the power to set the cultural agenda. Nevertheless the market offers a contradictory empowerment that has not been offered elsewhere. It may not be the best way to cultural emancipation for the majority, but *it may open up the way to a better way* (160; my italics).

Like capitalism, the culture industries, which supply the commodities from which people make culture, are themselves not monolithic and non-contradictory. From the very first of the culture industries, nineteenth-century stage melodrama, to perhaps one of the most powerful in the twenty-first century, pop music, cultural commodities have been 'articulated' in ways which 'may open the way to a better future'. For example, Photo 12.1 is a poster for a benefit organized at the Queen's Theatre (a commercial site

Photo 12.1 For the benefit of striking bookbinders.

Source: Arts Library Manchester

established to sell commodified entertainment) in Manchester. The poster shows how the theatre had given itself over (or had been taken over) for a benefit performance in support of bookbinders striking in London.[12] Another significant example is the fact that Nelson Mandela's first major public appearance, following his release in 1990, was to attend a concert to thank a pop music audience (consumers of the commodified practice that is pop music) because they 'chose to care'.[13] Both examples challenge the idea that capitalism and the capitalist culture industries are monolithic and non-contradictory.

Willis also makes the point that it is crude and simplistic to assume that the effects of consumption must mirror the intentions of production. As Terry Lovell (2009) points out, drawing on the work of Marx (1976c), the capitalist commodity has a double existence, as both use value and exchange value. Use value refers to 'the ability of the commodity to satisfy some human want' (539). Such wants, says Marx, 'may spring from the stomach or from the fancy' (ibid.). The exchange value of a commodity is the amount of money realized when the commodity is sold in the market. Crucial to Willis's argument is the fact, as pointed out by Lovell, that 'the use value of a commodity cannot be known in advance of investigation of actual use of the commodity' (540). Moreover, as Lovell indicates, the commodities from which popular culture is made

> have different use values for the individuals who use and purchase them than they have for the capitalists who produce and sell them, and in turn, for capitalism as a whole. We may assume that people do not purchase these cultural artefacts in order to expose themselves to bourgeois ideology . . . but to satisfy a variety of different wants which can only be guessed at in the absence of analysis and investigation. There is no guarantee that the use-value of the cultural object for its purchaser will even be compatible with its utility to capitalism as bourgeois ideology (542).

Almost everything we buy helps reproduce the capitalist system economically. But everything we buy does not necessarily help secure us as 'subjects' of capitalist ideology. If, for example, I go to an anti-capitalist demonstration, my travel, food, accommodation, clothing, etc., all contribute to the reproduction of the system I would like to over-throw. Therefore, although most of, if not all, my consumption is 'capitalist', this does not prevent me from being anti-capitalist. There is always a potential contradiction between exchange value and use value.

The primary concern of capitalist production is exchange value leading to surplus value (profit). This does not mean, of course, that capitalism is uninterested in use value: without use value, commodities would not sell (so every effort is made to stimulate demand). But it does mean that the individual capitalist's search for surplus value can often be at the expense of the general ideological needs of the system as a whole. Marx was more aware than most of the contradictions in the capitalist system. In a discussion of the demands of capitalists that workers should save in order to better endure the fluctuations of boom and slump, he points to the tension that may exist between 'worker as producer' and 'worker as consumer':

each capitalist does demand that his workers should save, but only his own, because they stand towards him as workers; but by no means the remaining world of workers, for these stand towards him as consumers. In spite of all 'pious' speeches he therefore searches for means to spur them on to consumption, to give his wares new charms, to inspire them with new needs by constant chatter, etc. (Marx, 1973: 287).

The situation is further complicated by tensions between particular capitals and capitalism as a whole. Common class interests – unless specific restraints, censorship, etc., are imposed – usually take second place to the interests of particular capitals in search of surplus value.

If surplus value can be extracted from the production of cultural commodities which challenge, or even subvert, the dominant ideology, then all other things being equal it is in the interests of particular capitals to invest in the production of such commodities. Unless collective class restraints are exercised, the individual capitalist's pursuit of surplus value may lead to forms of cultural production which are against the interests of capitalism as a whole (Lovell, 2009: 542–3).

To explore this possibility would require specific focus on consumption as opposed to production. This is not to deny the claim of political economy that a full analysis must take into account economic determinations. But it is to insist that if our focus is consumption, then our focus must be consumption as it is experienced and not as it should be experienced given a prior analysis of the relations of production.

Those on the moral and pessimistic left who attack the capitalist relations of consumption miss the point: it is the capitalist relations of production that are oppressive and exploitative and not the consumer choice facilitated by the capitalist market. This also seems to be Willis's point. Moral leftists and left pessimists have allowed themselves to become trapped in an elitist and reactionary argument that claims more (quantity) always means less (quality).

It is important to distinguish between the power of the culture industries and the power of their influence. Too often the two are conflated, but they are not necessarily the same. The trouble with the political economy approach is that too often it is assumed that they are the same. This, all too often, produces a simple logic: the culture industries are purveyors of capitalist ideology; those who buy their products are in effect buying capitalist ideology; being duped by a capitalist multinational; being reproduced as capitalist subjects, ready to spend more and more money and consume more and more ideology. The problem with this approach is that it fails to acknowledge fully that capitalism produces commodities on the basis of their exchange value, whereas people tend to consume the commodities of capitalism on the basis of their use value. There are two economies running in parallel courses: the economy of use, and the economy of exchange – we do not understand one by interrogating only the other. We cannot understand consumption by collapsing it into production, nor will we understand production by reading it off consumption. Of course the difficulty is not in keeping them apart, but in bringing them into a relationship that can be meaningfully analysed. However, if when studying popular culture our interest is the repertoire of products available for consumption, then production is our primary concern, whereas, if we are interested in discovering the particular uses of a specific text or practice, our primary focus should be on consumption. In both instances, our approach would be determined by the questions we seek to answer. Although it is certainly true that in an ideal research situation – given adequate time and funding – cultural analysis would remain incomplete until production and consumption had been dialectically linked, in the real world of study this is not always going to be the case. In the light of this, political economy's insistence that it offers the only really valid approach to the study of popular culture is not only untrue, but, if widely believed, could result in either a reductive distortion, or a complete stifling, of cultural studies research.

Post-Marxist cultural studies: hegemony revisited

The critique of cultural studies offered by political economy is important not for what it says but because it draws attention to a question, which, needless to say, it does not itself answer. The question is how to keep in analytical view the 'conditions of existence' of the texts and practices of everyday life. The problem with the mode of analysis advocated by political economy is that it addresses only the beginning of the process of making culture. What it describes is better understood, to borrow Stuart Hall's (1996c) phrase, as 'determination by the economic in the *first* instance' (45; original emphasis). There are economic conditions, and fear of economic reductionism cannot just will them away. However, the point is not simply to detail these conditions, to produce an understanding of how these conditions generate a repertoire of commodities; what is also required is an understanding of the many ways in which people select, appropriate and use these commodities, and make them into culture. In other words, what is needed is an understanding of the relationship between 'structure' and 'agency'. This will not be achieved by abandoning one side of the relationship. Hall (1996d) is undoubtedly right to suggest that a number of people working in cultural studies have at times turned away from 'economic' explanations:

> What has resulted from the abandonment of deterministic economism has been, not alternative ways of thinking questions about the economic relations and their effects, as the 'conditions of existence' of other practices . . . but instead a massive, gigantic, and eloquent disavowal. As if, since the economic in the broadest sense, definitely does not, as it was once supposed to do, 'determine' the real movement of history 'in the last instance', it does not exist at all! (258).

Hall describes this as 'a failure of theorisation so profound, and . . . so disabling, that . . . it has enabled much weaker and less conceptually rich paradigms to continue to flourish and dominate the field' (ibid.). A return there must be to a consideration of the 'conditions of existence', but it cannot be a return to the kind of analysis canvassed by political economy, in which it is assumed that 'access' is the same as appropriation and use, and that production tells us all we need to know about textuality and consumption. Nor is it a matter of having to build bridges to political economy; what is required, as McRobbie and others have canvassed, is a return to what has been, since the 1970s, the most convincing and coherent theoretical focus of (British) cultural studies – hegemony theory.

McRobbie accepts that cultural studies has been radically challenged as debates about postmodernism and postmodernity have replaced the more familiar debates about ideology and hegemony. She argues that it has responded in two ways. On the one hand, there have been those who have advocated a return to the certainties of Marxism, while on the other, there have been those who have turned to consumption (understood *too* exclusively in terms of pleasure and meaning-making). In some ways, as she recognizes, this is almost a rerun of the structuralism/culturalism debate of the late 1970s and early 1980s. It could also be seen as yet another performance of the playing of one side of Marx's (1977) dialectic against the other (we are made by history/we make history). McRobbie (1994) rejects a return 'to a crude and mechanical base–superstructure model, and also the dangers of pursuing a kind of cultural populism to a point at which anything that is consumed and is popular is also seen as oppositional' (39). Instead, she calls for 'an extension of Gramscian cultural analysis' (ibid.); and for a return to ethnographic cultural analysis which takes as its object of study 'the lived experience which breathes life into [the] . . . inanimate objects [the commodities supplied by the culture industries]' (27).

Post-Marxist hegemony theory at its best insists that there is always a dialogue between the processes of production and the activities of consumption. The consumer always confronts a text or practice in its material existence as a result of determinate conditions of production. But in the same way, the text or practice is confronted by a consumer who in effect *produces in use* the range of possible meaning(s) – these cannot just be read off from the materiality of the text or practice, or the means or relations of its production.[14]

The ideology of mass culture

We have to start from here and now, and acknowledge that we (all of us) live in a world dominated by multinational capitalism, and will do so for the foreseeable future – 'pessimism of the intelligence, optimism of the will', as Gramsci said (1971: 175). We need to see ourselves – all people, not just vanguard intellectuals – as active participants in culture: selecting, rejecting, making meanings, attributing value, resisting and, yes, being duped and manipulated. This does not mean that we forget about 'the politics of representation'. What we must do (and here I agree with Ang) is see that although pleasure is political, pleasure and politics can often be different. Liking *The Killing* or *Game of Thrones* does not determine my politics, making me more left-wing or less left-wing. There is pleasure and there is politics: we can laugh at the distortions, the evasions, the disavowals, while still promoting a politics that says these are distortions, evasions, disavowals. We must teach each other to know, to politicize for, to recognize the difference between different *versions* of reality, and to know that each can require a different politics. This does not mean the end of a feminist or a socialist cultural politics, or the end of struggles around the representations of 'race', class, gender, disability or sexuality, but it *should* mean the final break with the 'culture and civilization' problematic, with its debilitating insistence that particular patterns of consumption determine the moral and political worth of an individual.

In many ways, this book has been about what Ang calls 'the ideology of mass culture'. Against this ideology, I have posed consumption and use and historical contingency. Ultimately, I have argued that popular culture is what we make from the commodities and commodified practices made available by the culture industries. To paraphrase what I said in the discussion of post-Marxist cultural studies, *making* popular culture ('production in use')[15] can be empowering to subordinate and resistant to dominant understandings of the world. But this is not to say that popular culture is always empowering and resistant. To deny the passivity of consumption is not to deny that sometimes consumption is passive; to deny that the consumers of popular culture are cultural dupes is not to deny that the culture industries seek to manipulate. But it is to deny that popular culture is little more than a degraded landscape of commercial and ideological manipulation, imposed from above in order to make profit and secure social control. Post-Marxist cultural studies insists that to decide these matters requires vigilance and attention to the details of production, textuality and consumption. These are not matters that can be decided once and for all (outside the contingencies of history and politics) with an elitist glance and a condescending sneer. Nor can they be read off from the moment of production (locating meaning, pleasure, ideological effect, the probability of incorporation, the possibility of resistance, in, variously, the intention, the means of production or the production itself): these are only aspects of the contexts for 'production in use'; and it is, ultimately, in 'production in use' that questions of meaning, pleasure, ideological effect, incorporation or resistance can be (contingently) decided.

Such an argument will not satisfy those ideologues of mass culture whose voices seemed to grow suddenly louder, more insistent, during the period of writing the first edition of this book. I am thinking of the British and American media panic about the threat to high culture's authority – the debates about dumbing down, 'political correctness' and multiculturalism. The canon is wielded like a knife to cut away at critical thinking. They dismiss with arrogance what most of us call culture. Saying popular culture (or more usually, mass culture) and high culture (or more usually, just culture) is just another way of saying 'them' and 'us'. They speak with the authority and support of a powerful discourse behind them. Those of us who reject this discourse, recognizing its thinking and unthinking elitism, find ourselves often with only the discursive support of the (often equally disabling) ideology of populism. The task for new pedagogies of popular culture is to find ways of working which do not fall victim to the disabling tendencies of, on the one hand, a dismissive elitism, and on the other, a disarming anti-intellectualism. Although this book has not established any new ways of working, I hope it has at least mapped the existing approaches in such a way as to help make future discoveries a real possibility for other students of popular culture.

Notes

1. The book is an introduction in that it tries to be accessible in terms of subject matter, but it is also an introduction in the sense that it introduces something new. That is to say, although all the work discussed here has a previous existence, it is not a body of work that previously existed as a tradition of cultural theory and popular culture. The originality of this book is to bring this work together as a way of understanding popular culture.
2. Leonard Cohen's *The Future* expresses the point perfectly, 'Give me back the Berlin Wall, give me Stalin and St Paul / I've seen the future, brother: it's murder.'
3. Fiske is citing Liebes and Katz (1993).
4. Operating in a slightly different register, but making the same point, two friends at the university where I work, who, to be fair, have had to endure much mocking with regard to their long-term devotion to *Doctor Who*, have recently shown signs of resentment at the new popularity of the TV series. It would seem that the new democracy of enjoyment threatens their, admittedly embattled, 'ownership' of all things *Doctor Who*.
5. Here is an example of the 'tactics' of secondary production: although my parents always voted for the Labour Party, for many years at elections they invariably voted separately. The reason is that my father always accepted a lift to the polling station in a large grey Bentley driven by a Conservative member of the local council. My mother, born and brought up in a mining village in the Durham coalfield, who had lived through the bitter aftermath of the General Strike of 1926, refused to even countenance the prospect of riding in a Tory's Bentley – 'I would not be seen dead in that car.' My father, who had grown up amidst the general hardship of life in the part of Salford depicted in Walter Greenwood's *Love on the Dole*, always responded in the same way: he would insist that there was much humour to be had from 'being driven by a Tory to vote Labour'.
6. Andy Medhurst (1999) describes this way of teaching, quite accurately I think, as the 'missionary imposition' (98).
7. See Storey (2017).
8. Jenson (1992: 19–20) argues convincingly that it is possible to be a fan of James Joyce in much the same way as it is possible to be a fan of Barry Manilow.
9. Audiences for classical music and opera had to learn the aesthetic mode of consumption. See Storey (2006 and 2010a).

10. See Perryman (2009) for a discussion of how *Doctor Who* fans helped to bring back the programme to television.
11. For an informed and polemical debate between cultural studies and the political economy of culture, see *Critical Studies in Mass Communication*, 12, 1995. See also Part Seven of *Cultural Theory and Popular Culture: A Reader*, 4th edn, edited by John Storey, Harlow: Pearson Education, 2009.
12. See Storey (1992 and 2010a).
13. See Storey (1994).
14. The 'circuit of culture' model developed by Gay et al. (1997) is undoubtedly a tremendous contribution to work in post-Marxist cultural studies.
15. Marx (1976a) makes the point that 'a product only obtains its last finish in consumption. . . . For example, a dress becomes a real dress only in the act of being worn; a house which is uninhabited is in fact no real house; in other words, a product, as distinct from a mere natural object, proves itself as such, becomes a product, only in consumption' (19). This is the difference between a book and a text; the first is produced by a publisher, the second is produced by a reader.

Further reading

Storey, John (ed.), *Cultural Theory and Popular Culture: A Reader*, 4th edn, Harlow: Pearson Education, 2009. This is the companion volume to the previous edition of this book. A fully updated 5th edition containing further readings is due for publication in 2018. An interactive website is also available (www.routledge.com/cw/storey), which contains helpful student resources and a glossary of terms for each chapter.

Bennett, Tony, *Culture: A Reformer's Science*, London: Sage, 1998. A collection of essays, ranging across the recent history and practice of cultural studies, by one of the leading figures in the field.
During, Simon (ed.), *The Cultural Studies Reader*, 2nd edn, London: Routledge, 1999. A good selection of material from many of the leading figures in the field.
Gilroy, Paul, Lawrence Grossberg and Angela McRobbie (eds), *Without Guarantees: In Honour of Stuart Hall*, London: Verso, 2000. An excellent collection of essays engaging with the work of Stuart Hall.
Gray, Ann and Jim McGuigan (eds), *Studying Culture: An Introductory Reader*, London: Edward Arnold, 1993. A good selection of material from many of the leading figures in the field.
Grossberg, Lawrence, *Bringing it all Back Home: Essays on Cultural Studies*, Durham, NC: Duke University Press, 1997. An excellent collection of theoretical essays by one of the leading figures in cultural studies.
Grossberg, Lawrence, *Dancing in Spite of Myself: Essays on Popular Culture*, Durham, NC: Duke University Press, 1997. An excellent collection of essays on popular culture by one of the leading figures in cultural studies.

Grossberg, Lawrence, Cary Nelson and Paula Treichler (eds), *Cultural Studies*, London: Routledge, 1992. The collection consists of forty essays (most followed by discussion). An excellent introduction to relatively recent debates in cultural studies.

Morley, David and Kuan-Hsing Chen (eds), *Stuart Hall: Critical Dialogues in Cultural Studies*, London: Routledge, 1995. This is a brilliant book. It brings together interviews and essays (on and by Stuart Hall). Together they weave an image of the past, present and possible future of cultural studies.

Munns, Jessica and Gita Rajan, *A Cultural Studies Reader: History, Theory, Practice*, New York: Longman, 1995. Well organized, with a good selection of interesting essays.

Storey, John (ed.), *What is Cultural Studies? A Reader*, London: Edward Arnold, 1996. An excellent collection of essays that in different ways attempt to answer the question, 'What is cultural studies?'

Storey, John, *Inventing Popular Culture*, Malden, MA: Blackwell, 2003. An historical account of the concept of popular culture.

Storey, John, *Culture and Power in Cultural Studies: The Politics of Signification*, Edinburgh: Edinburgh University Press, 2010. Extends many of the arguments in this book into more detailed areas of research.

Storey, John, *From Popular Culture to Everyday Life*, London: Routledge, 2014. The book moves the critical focus of cultural studies from popular culture to everyday life.

Bibliography

Acred, Cara (2016), *Today's Social Classes*, Cambridge: Independence Educational Publishers.

Adorno, Theodor (1991a), 'How to look at television', in *The Culture Industry*, London: Routledge.

Adorno, Theodor (1991b), 'The schema of mass culture', in *The Culture Industry*, London: Routledge.

Adorno, Theodor (2009), 'On popular music', in *Cultural Theory and Popular Culture: A Reader*, 4th edn, edited by John Storey, Harlow: Pearson Education.

Adorno, Theodor and Max Horkheimer (1979), *Dialectic of Enlightenment*, London: Verso.

Althusser, Louis (1969), *For Marx*, London: Allen Lane.

Althusser, Louis (1971), *Lenin and Philosophy*, New York: Monthly Review Press.

Althusser, Louis (2009), 'Ideology and ideological state apparatuses', in *Cultural Theory and Popular Culture: A Reader*, 4th edn, edited by John Storey, Harlow: Pearson Education.

Althusser, Louis and Etienne Balibar (1979), *Reading Capital*, London: Verso.

Anderson, Perry (1980), *Arguments within English Marxism*, London: Verso.

Ang, Ien (1985), *Watching Dallas: Soap Opera and the Melodramatic Imagination*, London: Methuen.

Ang, I. (1996), 'Culture and communication: towards an ethnographic critique of media consumption in the transnational media system', in *What is Cultural Studies? A Reader*, edited by John Storey, London: Edward Arnold.

Ang, Ien (2009), 'Feminist desire and female pleasure', in *Cultural Theory and Popular Culture: A Reader*, 4th edn, edited by John Storey, Harlow: Pearson Education.

Arnold, Matthew (1896), *Letters 1848–1888*, Volume I, London: Macmillan.

Arnold, Matthew (1954), *Poetry and Prose*, London: Rupert Hart Davis.

Arnold, Matthew (1960), *Culture and Anarchy*, London: Cambridge University Press.

Arnold, Matthew (1960–77), *Complete Prose Works*, Volume III, Ann Arbor: University of Michigan Press.

Arnold, Matthew (1973), *On Education*, Harmondsworth: Penguin.

Arnold, Matthew (2009), 'Culture and Anarchy', in *Cultural Theory and Popular Culture: A Reader*, 4th edn, edited by John Storey, Harlow: Pearson Education.

Austin, J.L. (1962), *How to Do Things with Words*, Oxford: Clarendon Press.

Ball, Vicky (2012a), 'The "feminization" of British television and the re-traditionalization of gender', *Feminist Media Studies* 12 (2).

Ball, Vicky (2012b), 'Sex, class and consumerism in British television drama', in *Renewing Feminism: Stories, Fantasies and Futures*, edited by H. Thornham and E. Weissmann, London: IB Tauris.

Barrett, Michèle (1982), 'Feminism and the definition of cultural politics', in *Feminism, Culture and Politics*, edited by Rosalind Brunt and Caroline Rowan, London: Lawrence & Wishart.

Barthes, Roland (1967), *Elements of Semiology*, London: Jonathan Cape.

Barthes, Roland (1973), *Mythologies*, London: Paladin.

Barthes, Roland (1975), *S/Z*, London: Jonathan Cape.

Barthes, Roland (1977a), 'The photographic message', in *Image–Music–Text*, London: Fontana.

Barthes, Roland (1977b), 'Rhetoric of the image', in *Image–Music–Text*, London: Fontana.

Barthes, Roland (1977c), 'The death of the author', in *Image–Music–Text*, London: Fontana.

Barthes, Roland (1995), *The Semiotic Challenge*, Berkeley: University of California Press.

Barthes, Roland (2009), 'Myth today', in *Cultural Theory and Popular Culture: A Reader*, 4th edn, edited by John Storey, Harlow: Pearson Education.

Baudrillard, Jean (1981), *For a Critique of the Political Economy of the Sign*, St Louis, MD: Telos Press.

Baudrillard, Jean (1983), *Simulations*, New York: Semiotext(e).

Baudrillard, Jean (2009), 'The precession of simulacra', in *Cultural Theory and Popular Culture: A Reader*, 4th edn, edited by John Storey, Harlow: Pearson Education.

Beauvoir, Simone de (1984), *The Second Sex*, New York: Vintage.

Beaver, Harold (1999), 'Homosexual signs: in memory of Roland Barthes', in *Camp: Queer Aesthetics and the Performing Subject: A Reader*, edited by Fabio Cleto, Edinburgh: Edinburgh University Press.

Beck, Ulrich and Elisabeth Beck-Gernsheim (2002), *Individualization*, London: Sage.

Benjamin, Walter (1973), 'The work of art in the age of mechanical reproduction', in *Illuminations*, London: Fontana.

Bennett, Tony (1977), 'Media theory and social theory', in *Mass Communications and Society*, DE 353, Milton Keynes: Open University Press.

Bennett, Tony (1979), *Formalism and Marxism*, London: Methuen.

Bennett, Tony (1980), 'Popular culture: a teaching object', *Screen Education*, 34.

Bennett, Tony (1982a), 'Popular culture: defining our terms', in *Popular Culture: Themes and Issues 1*, Milton Keynes: Open University Press.

Bennett, Tony (1982b), 'Popular culture: themes and issues', in *Popular Culture*, U203, Milton Keynes: Open University Press.

Bennett, Tony (1983), 'Text, readers, reading formations', *Literature and History*, 9 (2).

Bennett, Tony (1986), 'The politics of the popular', in *Popular Culture and Social Relations*, Milton Keynes: Open University Press.

Bennett, Tony (2009), 'Popular culture and the turn to Gramsci', in *Cultural Theory and Popular Culture: A Reader*, 4th edn, edited by John Storey, Harlow: Pearson Education.

Bentham, Jeremy (1995), *The Panopticon Writings*, edited and introduced by Miran Bozovic, London: Verso

Bernstein, J.M. (1978), 'Introduction', in *The Culture Industry*, London: Routledge.

Best, Steven and Douglas Kellner (1991), *Postmodern Theory: Critical Interrogations*, London: Macmillan.

Bloch, Ernst (1995), *The Principle of Hope*, volume two, Cambridge, MA: MIT Press.

Bourdieu, Pierre (1992), *Distinction: A Social Critique of the Judgement of Taste*, translated by Richard Nice, Cambridge, MA: Harvard University Press.

Brecht, Bertolt (1978), *On Theatre*, translated by John Willett, London: Methuen.

Brogan, D.W. (1978), 'The problem of high and mass culture', in *Literary Taste, Culture, and Mass Communication*, Volume I, edited by Peter Davison, Rolf Meyersohn and Edward Shils, Cambridge: Chadwyck Healey.

Brooker, Peter and Will Brooker (1997a), 'Introduction', in *Postmodern After-Images: A Reader in Film*, edited by Peter Brooker and Will Brooker, London: Edward Arnold.

Brooker, Peter and Will Brooker (1997b), 'Styles of pluralism', in *Postmodern After-Images: A Reader in Film*, edited by Peter Brooker and Will Brooker, London: Edward Arnold.

Brooks, Peter (1976), *The Melodramatic Imagination*, New Haven, CT: Yale University Press.

Brunsdon, Charlotte (1991), 'Pedagogies of the feminine: feminist teaching and women's genres', *Screen*, 32 (4).

Burke, Peter (1994), *Popular Culture in Early Modern Europe*, Aldershot: Scolar Press.

Burston, Paul and Colin Richardson (1995), 'Introduction', in *A Queer Romance: Lesbians, Gay Men and Popular Culture*, edited by Paul Burston and Colin Richardson, London: Routledge.

Butler, Judith (1993), *Bodies That Matter: On the Discursive Limits of Sex*, New York: Routledge.

Butler, Judith (1999), *Gender Trouble: Feminism and the Subversion of Identity*, 10th anniversary edn, New York: Routledge.

Butler, Judith (2000), 'Restaging the universal', in *Contingency, Hegemony, Universality: Contemporary Dialogues on the Left*, by Judith Butler, Ernesto Laclau and Slavoj Žižek, London: Verso.

Butler, Judith (2009), 'Imitation and gender insubordination', in *Cultural Theory and Popular Culture: A Reader*, 4th edn, edited by John Storey, Harlow: Pearson Education.

Butler, Judith, Ernesto Laclau and Slavoj Žižek (2000), *Contingency, Hegemony, Universality: Contemporary Dialogues on the Left*, London: Verso.

Canaan, Joyce and Christine Griffin (1990), 'The new men's studies: part of the problem or part of the solution', in *Men, Masculinities and Social Theory*, edited by Jeff Hearn and David Morgan, London: Unwin Hyman.

Carey, James W. (1996), 'Overcoming resistance to cultural studies', in *What Is Cultural Studies? A Reader*, edited by John Storey, London: Edward Arnold.

Certeau, Michel de (1984), *The Practice of Everyday Life*, Berkeley: University of California Press, 1984.

Certeau, Michel de (2009), 'The practice of everyday life', in *Cultural Theory and Popular Culture: A Reader*, 4th edn, edited by John Storey, Harlow: Pearson Education.

Chambers, Iain (1986), *Popular Culture: The Metropolitan Experience*, London: Routledge.

Chauncey, George (1994), *Gay New York: Gender, Urban Culture, and the Making of the Gay Male World, 1890–1940*, New York: Basic Books.

Chinn, Sarah E. (1997), 'Gender performativity', in *The Lesbian and Gay Studies Reader: A Critical Introduction*, edited by Andy Medhurst and Sally R. Munt, London: Cassell.

Chodorow, Nancy (1978), *The Reproduction of Mothering: Psychoanalysis and the Sociology of Gender*, Berkeley: University of California Press.

Clark, Michael (1991), 'Remembering Vietnam', in *The Vietnam War and American Culture*, edited by John Carlos Rowe and Rick Berg, New York: Columbia University Press.

Clarke, Gary (1990), 'Defending ski-jumpers: a critique of theories of youth subcultures', in *On Record*, edited by Simon Frith and Andrew Goodwin, New York: Pantheon.

Cleto, Fabio (ed.) (1999), *Camp: Queer Aesthetics and the Performing Subject*, Edinburgh: Edinburgh University Press.

Coleridge, Samuel Taylor (1972), *On the Constitution of the Church and State*, London: Dent.

Collins, Jim (1992), 'Postmodernism and television', in *Channels of Discourse, Reassembled*, edited by Robert C. Allen, London: Routledge, 1992.

Collins, Jim (2009), 'Genericity in the nineties', in *Cultural Theory and Popular Culture: A Reader*, 4th edn, edited by John Storey, Harlow: Pearson Education.

Connor, Steven (1989), *Postmodernist Culture: An Introduction to Theories of the Contemporary*, Oxford: Blackwell.

Connor, Steven (1992), *Theory and Cultural Value*, Oxford: Blackwell.

Coward, Rosalind (1984), *Female Desire: Women's Sexuality Today*, London: Paladin.

Creekmur, Corey K. and Alexander Doty (1995), 'Introduction', in *Out in Culture: Gay, Lesbian, and Queer Essays on Popular Culture*, edited by Corey K. Creekmur and Alexander Doty, London: Cassell.

Curtin, Philip (1964), *The Image of Africa*, Wisconsin: University of Wisconsin Press.

Derrida, Jacques (1973), *Speech and Phenomena*, Evanston, IL: North Western University Press.

Derrida, Jacques (1976), *Of Grammatology*, Baltimore, MD: Johns Hopkins University Press.

Derrida, Jacques (1978a), *Writing and Difference*, London: Routledge & Kegan Paul.

Derrida, Jacques (1978b), *Positions*, London: Athlone Press.

Derrida, Jacques (1982), *Margins of Philosophy*, Chicago: University of Chicago Press.

Descartes, Rene (1993), *Meditations on First Philosophy*, London: Hackett.

Disraeli, Benjamin (1980), *Sybil, or the Two Nations*, Harmondsworth: Penguin.

Dittmar, Linda, and Gene Michaud (1990) (eds), *From Hanoi To Hollywood: The Vietnam War in American Film*, New Brunswick, NJ and London: Rutgers University Press.

Docker, John (1994), *Postmodernism and Popular Culture: A Cultural History*, Cambridge: Cambridge University Press.

Doty, Alexander (1995), 'Something queer here', in *Out in Culture: Gay, Lesbian and Queer Essays on Popular Culture*, edited by Corey K. Creekmur and Alexander Doty, London: Cassell.

Dunning, Eric (1971), 'The development of football', in *The Sociology of Sport*, edited by Eric Dunning, London: Frank Cass.

Dyer, Richard (1990), 'In defence of disco', in *On Record: Rock, Pop, and the Written Word*, edited by Simon Frith and Andrew Goodwin, London: Routledge.

Dyer, Richard (1997), *White: Essays on Race and Culture*, London: Routledge.

Dyer, Richard (1999), 'Entertainment and utopia', in *The Cultural Studies Reader*, 2nd edn, edited by Simon During, London: Routledge.

Eagleton, Terry (1983), *Literary Theory: An Introduction*, Oxford: Blackwell.

Easthope, Antony (1986), *What a Man's Gotta Do: The Masculine Myth in Popular Culture*, London: Paladin.

Easthope, Antony (1991), *Literary into Cultural Studies*, London: Routledge.

Eco, Umberto (1984), *Postscript to The Name of the Rose*, New York: Harcourt Brace Jovanovich.

Engels, Frederick (2009), 'Letter to Joseph Bloch', in *Cultural Theory and Popular Culture: A Reader*, 4th edn, edited by John Storey, Harlow: Pearson Education.

Fanon, Franz (1986), *Black Skin, White Masks*, London: Pluto.

Fekete, John (1987), 'Introductory notes for a postmodern value agenda', in *Life After Postmodernism*, edited by John Fekete, New York: St. Martin's Press.

Fiedler, Leslie (1957), 'The middle against both ends', in *Mass Culture: The Popular Arts in America*, edited by Bernard Rosenberg and David Manning White, New York: Macmillan.

Fiedler, Leslie (1971), *The Collected Essays of Leslie Fiedler*, Volume 2, New York: Stein and Day.

Fischer, Ernst (1973), *The Necessity of Art*, Harmondsworth: Penguin.

Fiske, John (1987), *Television Culture*, London: Routledge.

Fiske, John (1989a), *Understanding Popular Culture*, London: Unwin Hyman.

Fiske, John (1989b), *Reading the Popular*, London: Unwin Hyman.

Fiske, John (1994), *Media Matters: Everyday Culture and Media Change*, Minnesota: University of Minnesota Press.

Foucault, Michel (1979), *Discipline and Punish*, Harmondsworth: Penguin.

Foucault, Michel (1981), *The History of Sexuality*, Harmondsworth: Penguin.

Foucault, Michel (1989), *The Archaeology of Knowledge*, London: Routledge.

Foucault, Michel (2002a), 'Truth and power', in *Michel Foucault Essential Works: Power*, edited by James D. Faubion, Harmondsworth: Penguin.

Foucault, Michel (2002b), 'Question of method', in *Michel Foucault Essential Works: Power*, edited by James D. Faubion, Harmondsworth: Penguin.

Foucault, Michel (2002c), 'Truth and juridical forms', in *Michel Foucault Essential Works: Power*, edited by James D. Faubion, Harmondsworth: Penguin.

Foucault, Michel (2009), 'Method', in *Cultural Theory and Popular Culture: A Reader*, 4th edn, edited by John Storey, Harlow: Pearson Education.

Franklin, H. Bruce (1993), *M.I.A. or Mythmaking in America*, New Brunswick, NJ: Rutgers University Press.

Freud, Sigmund (1973a), *Introductory Lectures on Psychoanalysis*, Harmondsworth: Pelican.

Freud, Sigmund (1973b), *New Introductory Lectures on Psychoanalysis*, Harmondsworth: Pelican.

Freud, Sigmund (1975), *The Psychopathology of Everyday Life*, Harmondsworth: Pelican.

Freud, Sigmund (1976), *The Interpretation of Dreams*, Harmondsworth: Pelican.

Freud, Sigmund (1977), *On Sexuality*, Harmondsworth: Pelican.

Freud, Sigmund (1984), *On Metapsychology: The Theory of Psychoanalysis*, Harmondsworth: Pelican.

Freud, Sigmund (1985), *Art and Literature*, Harmondsworth: Pelican.

Freud, Sigmund (1986), *Historical and Expository Works on Psychoanalysis*, Harmondsworth: Pelican.

Freud, Sigmund (2009), 'The Dream-Work', in *Cultural Theory and Popular Culture: A Reader*, 4th edn, edited by John Storey, Harlow: Pearson Education.

Frith, Simon (1983), *Sound Effects: Youth, Leisure and the Politics of Rock*, London: Constable.

Frith, Simon (2009), 'The good, the bad and the indifferent: defending popular culture from the populists', in *Cultural Theory and Popular Culture: A Reader*, 4th edn, edited by John Storey, Harlow: Pearson Education.

Frith, Simon and Howard Horne (1987), *Art into Pop*, London: Methuen.

Frow, John (1995), *Cultural Studies and Value*, New York: Oxford University Press.

Fryer, Peter (1984), *Staying Power: The History of Black People in Britain*, London: Pluto.

Gamman, Lorraine and Margaret Marshment (1988), 'Introduction', in *The Female Gaze, Women as Viewers of Popular Culture*, edited by Lorraine Gamman and Margaret Marshment, London: The Women's Press.

Garnham, Nicholas (2009), 'Political economy and cultural studies: reconciliation or divorce', in *Cultural Theory and Popular Culture: A Reader*, 4th edn, edited by John Storey, Harlow: Pearson Education.

Garnham, Nicholas and Raymond Williams (1980), 'Pierre Bourdieu and the sociology of culture: an introduction', *Media, Culture and Society*, 2 (3).

Gay, Paul du, Stuart Hall, Linda Janes, Hugh Mackay and Keith Negus (1997), *Doing Cultural Studies*, London: Sage.

Giddens, Anthony (1992), *The Transformation of Intimacy*, Cambridge: Polity.

Gill, Rosalind (2007), 'Postfeminist media culture: elements of a sensibility', in *European Journal of Cultural Studies*, 10, 147–66.

Gilroy, Paul (2002), *There Ain't No Black in the Union Jack*, London: Routledge Classics.

Gilroy, Paul (2004), *After Empire*, London: Routledge.

Gilroy, Paul (2009), '"Get up, get into it and get involved" – soul, civil rights and black power', in *Cultural Theory and Popular Culture: A Reader*, 4th edn, edited by John Storey, Harlow: Pearson Education.

Gilroy, Paul, Lawrence Grossberg and Angela McRobbie (2000) (eds), *Without Guarantees: In Honour of Stuart Hall*, London: Verso.

Gledhill, Christine (2009), 'Pleasurable negotiations', in *Cultural Theory and Popular Culture: A Reader*, 4th edn, edited by John Storey, Harlow: Pearson Education.

Golding, Peter and Graham Murdock (1991), 'Culture, communications and political economy', in *Mass Media and Society*, edited by James Curran and Michael Gurevitch, London: Edward Arnold.

Goodwin, Andrew (1991), 'Popular music and postmodern theory', *Cultural Studies*, 5 (2).

Gramsci, Antonio (1968), *The Modern Prince and Other Writings*, New York: International Publishers.

Gramsci, Antonio (1971), *Selections from Prison Notebooks*, London: Lawrence & Wishart.

Gramsci, Antonio (2007), *Prison Notebooks*, volume III, New York: Columbia University Press.

Gramsci, Antonio (2009), 'Hegemony, intellectuals, and the state', in *Cultural Theory and Popular Culture: A Reader*, 4th edn, edited by John Storey, Harlow: Pearson Education.

Graves-Brown, Paul (2000), *Matter, Materiality and Modern Culture*, London: Routledge.

Gray, Ann (1992), *Video Playtime: The Gendering of a Leisure Technology*, London: Routledge.

Gray, Thomas (1997), 'Elegy Written in a Country Churchyard', in *Selected Poems of Thomas Gray*, London: Bloomsbury.

Green, Michael (1996), 'The Centre for Contemporary Cultural Studies', in *What is Cultural Studies? A Reader*, edited by John Storey, London: Edward Arnold.

Grossberg, Lawrence (1988), *It's a Sin: Essays on Postmodernism, Politics and Culture*, Sydney: Power Publications.

Grossberg, Lawrence (1992), 'Is there a fan in the house?', in *The Adoring Audience*, edited by Lisa Lewis, London: Routledge.

Grossberg, Lawrence (2009), 'Cultural studies vs. political economy. is anybody else bored with this debate?', in *Cultural Theory and Popular Culture: A Reader*, 4th edn, edited by John Storey, Harlow: Pearson Education.

Haag, Ernest van den (1957), 'Of happiness and despair we have no measure', in *Mass Culture: The Popular Arts in America*, edited by Bernard Rosenberg and David Manning White, New York: Macmillan.

Haines, Harry W. (1990), 'They were called and they went': the political rehabilitation of the Vietnam veteran', in Linda Dittmar and Gene Michaud (eds), *From Hanoi To Hollywood: The Vietnam War in American Film*, New Brunswick, NJ and London: Rutgers University Press.

Hall, Stuart (1978), 'Some paradigms in cultural studies', *Annali*, 3.

Hall, Stuart (1980a), 'Encoding/decoding', in *Culture, Media, Language*, edited by Stuart Hall, Dorothy Hobson, Andrew Lowe and Paul Willis, London: Hutchinson.

Hall, Stuart (1980b), 'Cultural studies and the Centre; some problematics and problems', in *Culture, Media, Language*, edited by Stuart Hall, Dorothy Hobson, Andrew Lowe and Paul Willis, London: Hutchinson.

Hall, Stuart (1991), 'Old and new ethnicities', in *Culture, Globalization and the World-System*, edited by Anthony Smith, London: Macmillan.

Hall, Stuart (1992), 'Cultural studies and its theoretical legacies', in *Cultural Studies*, edited by Lawrence Grossberg, Cary Nelson and Paula Treichler, London: Routledge.

Hall, Stuart (1996a), 'Cultural studies: two paradigms', in *What is Cultural Studies? A Reader*, edited by John Storey, London: Edward Arnold.

Hall, Stuart (1996b), 'On postmodernism and articulation: an interview with Stuart Hall', in *Stuart Hall: Cultural Dialogues in Cultural Studies*, edited by David Morley and Kuan-Hsing Chen, London: Routledge.

Hall, Stuart (1996c), 'The problem of ideology: Marxism without guarantees', in *Stuart Hall: Cultural Dialogues in Cultural Studies*, edited by David Morley and Kuan-Hsing Chen, London: Routledge.

Hall, Stuart (1996d), 'When was the "post-colonial"? Thinking at the limit', in *The Postcolonial Question*, edited by L. Chambers and L. Curti, London: Routledge.

Hall, Stuart (1996e), 'Race, culture, and communications: looking backward and forward at cultural studies', in *What is Cultural Studies: A Reader*, edited by John Storey, London: Edward Arnold.

Hall, Stuart (1997a), 'Introduction', in *Representation*, edited by Stuart Hall, London: Sage.

Hall, Stuart (1997b), 'The spectacle of the "other"', in *Representation*, edited by Stuart Hall, London: Sage.

Hall, Stuart (2009a), 'The rediscovery of ideology: the return of the repressed in media studies', in *Cultural Theory and Popular Culture: A Reader*, 4th edn, edited by John Storey, Harlow: Pearson Education.

Hall, Stuart (2009b), 'Notes on deconstructing "the popular"', in *Cultural Theory and Popular Culture: A Reader*, 4th edn, edited by John Storey, Harlow: Pearson Education.

Hall, Stuart (2009c), 'What is this "black" in black popular culture?', in *Cultural Theory and Popular Culture: A Reader*, 4th edn, edited by John Storey, Harlow: Pearson Education.

Hall, Stuart and Paddy Whannel (1964), *The Popular Arts*, London: Hutchinson.

Harvey, Adrian (2005), *Football: The First Hundred Years*, London: Routledge.

Harvey, David (1989), *The Condition of Postmodernity*, Oxford: Blackwell.

Hawkes, Terence (1977), *Structuralism and Semiotics*, London: Methuen.

Hebdige, Dick (1979), *Subculture: The Meaning of Style*, London: Methuen.

Hebdige, Dick (1988), 'Banalarama, or can pop save us all?' *New Statesman & Society*, 9 December.

Hebdige, Dick (2009), 'Postmodernism and "the other side"', in *Cultural Theory and Popular Culture: A Reader*, 4th edn, edited by John Storey, Harlow: Pearson Education.

Hermes, Joke (1995), *Reading Women's Magazines*, Cambridge: Polity Press.

Hoggart, Richard (1970), 'Schools of English and contemporary society', in *Speaking to Each Other*, Volume II, edited by Richard Hoggart, London: Chatto and Windus.

Hoggart, Richard (1990), *The Uses of Literacy*, Harmondsworth: Penguin.

hooks, bell (1989), *Talking Back: Thinking Feminist, Thinking Black*, London: Sheba Feminist Publishers.

hooks, bell (2009), 'Postmodern blackness', in *Cultural Theory and Popular Culture: A Reader*, 4th edn, edited by John Storey, Harlow: Pearson Education.

Horkheimer, Max (1978), 'Art and mass culture', in *Literary Taste, Culture and Mass Communication*, Volume XII, edited by Peter Davison, Rolf Meyersohn and Edward Shils, Cambridge: Chadwyck Healey.

Huyssen, Andreas (1986), *After the Great Divide: Modernism, Mass Culture and Postmodernism*, London: Macmillan.

Jameson, Fredric (1981), *The Political Unconscious*, London: Methuen.

Jameson, Fredric (1984), 'Postmodernism, or the cultural logic of late capitalism', *New Left Review*, 146.

Jameson, Fredric (1985), 'Postmodernism and consumer society', in *Postmodern Culture*, edited by Hal Foster, London: Pluto.

Jameson, Fredric (1988), 'The politics of theory: ideological positions in the postmodernism debate', in *The Ideologies of Theory Essays*, Volume 2, London: Routledge.

Jeffords, Susan (1989), *The Remasculinization of America: Gender and the Vietnam War*, Bloomington and Indianapolis: Indiana University Press.

Jenkins, Henry (1992), *Textual Poachers*, New York: Routledge.

Jenkins, Henry (2006), *Convergence Culture: Where Old and New Media Collide*, New York: New York University Press.

Jenson, Joli (1992), 'Fandom as pathology', in *The Adoring Audience*, edited by Lisa Lewis, London: Routledge.

Jewitt, Robert (2005), 'Mobile networks: globalisation, networks and the mobile phone', in *Culture and Power: Culture and Society in the Age of Globalisation*, edited by Chantal Cornut-Gentille, Zaragoza: Zaragoza University Press.

Johnson, Richard (1979), 'Three problematics: elements of a theory of working-class culture', in *Working Class Culture: Studies in History and Theory*, edited by John Clarke et al., London: Hutchinson.

Johnson, Richard (1996), 'What is cultural studies anyway?' in *What is Cultural Studies? A Reader*, edited by John Storey, London: Edward Arnold.

Klein, Michael (1990), 'Historical memory, film, and the Vietnam era', in *From Hanoi To Hollywood: The Vietnam War in American Film*, edited by Linda Dittmar and Gene Michaud, New Brunswick, NJ and London: Rutgers University Press.

Lacan, Jacques (1989), *Four Fundamental Concepts in Psychoanalysis*, New York: Norton.

Lacan, Jacques (2001), *Ecrits*, London: Routledge.

Lacan, Jacques (2009), 'The mirror stage', in *Cultural Theory and Popular Culture: A Reader*, 4th edn, edited by John Storey, Harlow: Pearson Education.

Laclau, Ernesto (1979), *Politics and Ideology in Marxist Theory*, London: Verso.

Laclau, Ernesto (1993), 'Discourse', in *A Companion to Contemporary Political Philosophy*, edited by R.E. Goodin and P. Pettit, London: Blackwell.

Laclau, Ernesto and Chantal Mouffe (2001), *Hegemony and Socialist Strategy: Towards a Radical Democratic Politics*, 2nd edn, London: Verso.

Laclau, Ernesto and Chantal Mouffe (2009), 'Post-Marxism without apologies', in *Cultural Theory and Popular Culture: A Reader*, 4th edn, edited by John Storey, Harlow: Pearson Education.

Latour, Bruno (2007), *Reassembling the Social*, Oxford: Oxford University Press.

Leavis, F.R. (1933), *For Continuity*, Cambridge: Minority Press.

Leavis, F.R. (1972), *Nor Shall My Sword*, London: Chatto and Windus.

Leavis, F.R. (1984), *The Common Pursuit*, London: Hogarth.

Leavis, F.R. (2009), 'Mass civilisation and minority culture', in *Cultural Theory and Popular Culture: A Reader*, 4th edn, edited by John Storey, Harlow: Pearson Education.

Leavis, F.R. and Denys Thompson (1977), *Culture and Environment*, Westport, CT: Greenwood Press.

Leavis, Q.D. (1978), *Fiction and the Reading Public*, London: Chatto and Windus.

Levine, Lawrence (1988), *Highbrow/Lowbrow: The Emergence of Cultural Hierarchy in America*, Cambridge, MA: Harvard University Press.

Lévi-Strauss, Claude (1968), *Structural Anthropology*, London: Allen Lane.

Liebes, T. and E. Katz (1993), *The Export of Meaning: Cross-cultural Readings of Dallas*, 2nd edn, Cambridge: Polity Press.

Light, Alison (1984), '"Returning to Manderley": romance fiction, female sexuality and class', *Feminist Review*, 16.

Littler, Jo (2013), 'Meritocracy as plutocracy: the marketising of "equality" within neoliberalism', *New Formations*, pp. 52–72.

Littler, Jo (2017), *Against Meritocracy*, London: Routledge.

Lovell, Terry (2009), 'Cultural production', in *Cultural Theory and Popular Culture: A Reader*, 4th edn, edited by John Storey, Harlow: Pearson Education.

Lowenthal, Leo (1961), *Literature, Popular Culture and Society*, Palo Alto, CA: Pacific Books.

Lyotard, Jean-François (1984), *The Postmodern Condition: A Report on Knowledge*, Manchester: Manchester University Press.

Macdonald, Dwight (1998), 'A theory of mass culture', in *Cultural Theory and Popular Culture: A Reader*, 2nd edn, edited by John Storey, Harlow: Prentice Hall.

Macherey, Pierre (1978), *A Theory of Literary Production*, London: Routledge & Kegan Paul.

Maltby, Richard (1989), 'Introduction', in *Dreams for Sale: Popular Culture in the 20th Century*, edited by Richard Maltby, London: Harrap.

Mandel, Ernest (1978), *Late Capitalism*, London: Verso.

Marcuse, Herbert (1968a), *One Dimensional Man*, London: Sphere.

Marcuse, Herbert (1968b), *Negations*, London: Allen Lane.

Markus, Hazel Rose, and Paula M.L. Moya (2010), *Doing Race: 21 Essays for the 21st Century*, Norton: New York.

Martin, Andrew (1993), *Receptions of War: Vietnam in American Culture*, Norman: University of Oklahoma Press.

Marx, Karl (1951), *Theories of Surplus Value*, London: Lawrence & Wishart.

Marx, Karl (1963), *Selected Writings in Sociology and Social Philosophy*, Harmondsworth: Pelican.

Marx, Karl (1973), *Grundrisse*, Harmondsworth: Penguin.

Marx, Karl (1976a), 'Preface' and 'Introduction', in *Contribution to the Critique of Political Economy*, Peking: Foreign Languages Press.

Marx, Karl (1976b), 'Theses on Feuerbach', in *Ludwig Feuerbach and the End of Classical German Philosophy*, by Frederick Engels, Peking: Foreign Languages Press.

Marx, Karl (1976c), *Capital*, Volume I, Harmondsworth: Penguin.

Marx, Karl (1977), *The Eighteenth Brumaire of Louis Bonaparte*, Moscow: Progress Publishers.

Marx, Karl and Friedrich Engels (1957), *On Religion*, Moscow: Progress Publishers.

Marx, Karl and Frederick Engels (1974), *The German Ideology* (student edn), edited and introduced by C.J. Arthur, London: Lawrence & Wishart.

Marx, Karl, and Friedrich Engels (1998), *The Communist Manifesto*, Peking: Foreign Languages Press.

Marx, Karl and Frederick Engels (2009), 'Ruling class and ruling ideas', in *Cultural Theory and Popular Culture: A Reader*, 4th edn, edited by John Storey, Harlow: Pearson Education.

McGuigan, Jim (1992), *Cultural Populism*, London: Routledge.

McLellan, Gregor (1982), 'E.P. Thompson and the discipline of historical context', in *Making Histories: Studies in History Writing and Politics*, edited by Richard Johnson, London: Hutchinson.

McRobbie, Angela (1992), 'Post-Marxism and cultural studies: a post-script', in *Cultural Studies*, edited by Lawrence Grossberg, Cary Nelson and Paula Treichler, London: Routledge.

McRobbie, Angela (1994), *Postmodernism and Popular Culture*, London: Routledge.

McRobbie, Angela (2004), 'Post-Feminism and Popular Culture', in *Feminist Media Studies*, 4 (3), 255–64.

Medhurst, Andy (1999), 'Teaching queerly: politics, pedagogy and identity in lesbian and gay studies', in *Teaching Culture: The Long Revolution in Cultural Studies*, Leicester: NIACE Press.

Mercer, Kobena (1994), *Welcome to the Jungle: New Positions in Black Cultural Studies*, London: Routledge.

Miller, Daniel (2009), *Stuff*, Cambridge: Polity.

Mills, Sara (2004), *Discourse*, 2nd edn, London: Routledge.

Modleski, Tania (1982), *Loving with a Vengeance: Mass Produced Fantasies for Women*, Hamden, CT: Archon Books.

Morley, David (1980), *The Nationwide Audience*, London: BFI.

Morley, David (1986), *Family Television: Cultural Power and Domestic Leisure*, London: Comedia.

Morris, R.J. (1979), *Class and Class Consciousness in the Industrial Revolution 1780–1850*, London: Macmillan.

Morris, William (1979), 'Art Labour and Socialism', in *Marxism and Art*, by Maynard Solomon, Brighton: Harvester.

Morris, William (1986), *News From Nowhere and Selected Writings and Designs*, Harmondsworth: Penguin.

Morris, William (2003), *News From Nowhere*, Oxford: Oxford World's Classics.

Mouffe, Chantal (1981), 'Hegemony and ideology in Gramsci', in *Culture, Ideology and Social Process*, edited by Tony Bennett, Colin Mercer and Janet Woollacott, Milton Keynes: Open University Press.

Mulvey, Laura (1975), 'Visual pleasure and narrative cinema', in *Screen*, 16 (3).

Myers, Tony (2003), *Slavoj Žižek*, London: Routledge.

Nederveen Pieterse, J. (1995), 'Globalisation as hybridisation', in *International Sociology*, 9 (2), 161–84.

New Left Review (eds) (1977), *Aesthetics and Politics*, London: Verso.

Newton, Esther (1972), *Mother Camp: Female Impersonators in America*, Englewood Cliffs, NJ: Prentice Hall.

Newton, Esther (1999), 'Role models', in *Camp: Queer Aesthetics and the Performing Subject: A Reader*, edited by Fabio Cleto, Edinburgh: Edinburgh University Press.

Nixon, Richard (1986), *No More Vietnams*, London: W.H. Allen.

Nixon, Sean (1996), *Hard Looks: Masculinities, Spectatorship and Contemporary Consumption*, London: UCL Press.

Nowell-Smith, Geoffrey (1987), 'Popular culture', *New Formations*, 2.

O'Connor, Alan (1989), *Raymond Williams: Writing, Culture, Politics*, Oxford: Basil Blackwell.

Orwell, George (2001), *Down and Out in Paris and London*, Harmondsworth: Penguin.

Parker, Ian (2004), *Slavoj Žižek: A Critical Introduction*, London: Pluto Press.

Perryman, Neil (2009), 'Doctor Who and the convergence of media', in *Cultural Theory and Popular Culture: A Reader*, 4th edn, edited by John Storey, Harlow: Pearson Education.

Pilger, John (1990), 'Vietnam movies', *Weekend Guardian*, 24–5 February.

Pitcher, Ben (2014), *Consuming Race*, London: Routledge.

Polan, Dana (1988), 'Complexity and contradiction in mass culture analysis: on Ien Ang *Watching Dallas*', Camera Obscura, 16.

Porter, Roy (1990), *The Enlightenment*, Basingstoke: Macmillan.

Propp, Vladimir (1968), *The Morphology of the Folktale*, Austin: Texas University Press.

Radway, Janice (1987), *Reading the Romance: Women, Patriarchy, and Popular Literature*, London: Verso.

Radway, Janice (1994), 'Romance and the work of fantasy: struggles over feminine sexuality and subjectivity at the century's end', in *Viewing, Reading, Listening: Audiences and Cultural Reception*, edited by Jon Cruz and Justin Lewis, Boulder, CO: Westview Press.

Rakow, Lana F. (2009), 'Feminist approaches to popular culture: giving patriarchy its due', in *Cultural Theory and Popular Culture: A Reader*, 4th edn, edited by John Storey, Harlow: Pearson Education.

Ricoeur, Paul (1981), *Hermeneutics and the Human Sciences*, New York: Cambridge University Press.

Ritzer, G. (1999), *The McDonaldization Thesis*, London: Sage.

Rosenberg, Bernard (1957), 'Mass culture in America', in *Mass Culture: The Popular Arts in America*, edited by Bernard Rosenberg and David Manning White, New York: Macmillan.

Ross, Andrew (1989), *No Respect: Intellectuals and Popular Culture*, London: Routledge.

Rowe, John Carlos and Rick Berg (eds) (1991), *The Vietnam War and American Culture*, New York: Columbia University Press.

Said, Edward (1985), *Orientalism*, Harmondsworth: Penguin.

Said, Edward (1993), *Culture and Imperialism*, New York: Vintage Books.

Samuel, Raphael (1981), *Peoples' History and Socialist Theory*, London: Routledge & Kegan Paul.

Saussure, Ferdinand de (1974), *Course in General Linguistics*, London: Fontana.

Schiller, Herbert (1978), 'Transnational media and national development', in *National Sovereignty and International Communication*, edited by K. Nordenstreng and Herbert Schiller, Norwood, NJ: Ablex.

Schiller, Herbert (1979), 'Translating media and national development', in *National Sovereignty and International Communication*, edited by K. Nordenstreng and Herbert Schiller.

Shils, Edward (1978), 'Mass society and its culture', in *Literary Taste, Culture, and Mass Communication*, Volume I, edited by Peter Davison, Rolf Meyersohn and Edward Shils, Cambridge: Chadwyck Healey.

Showalter, Elaine (1990), 'Introduction', in *Speaking of Gender*, edited by Elaine Showalter, London: Routledge.

Smith, Barbara Herrnstein (1988), *Contingencies of Value*, Cambridge, MA: Harvard University Press.

Sontag, Susan (1966), *Against Interpretation*, New York: Deli.

Stacey, Jackie (1994), *Star Gazing: Hollywood and Female Spectatorship*, London: Routledge.

Stedman Jones, Gareth (1998), 'Working-class culture and working-class politics in London, 1870–1900: notes on the remaking of a working class', in *Cultural Theory and Popular Culture*, 2nd edn, edited by John Storey, Harlow: Prentice Hall.

Storey, John (1985), 'Matthew Arnold: the politics of an organic intellectual', *Literature and History*, 11 (2).

Storey, John (1992), 'Texts, readers, reading formations: My Poll and My Partner Joe in Manchester in 1841', *Literature and History*, 1 (2).

Storey, John (1994), '"Side-saddle on the golden calf": moments of utopia in American pop music and pop music culture', in *An American Half Century: Postwar Culture and Politics in the USA*, edited by Michael Klein, London: Pluto Press.

Storey, John (ed.) (1996), *What is Cultural Studies: A Reader*, London: Edward Arnold.

Storey, John (2001a), 'The sixties in the nineties: Pastiche or hyperconsciousness', in *Tough Guys, Smooth Operators and Foxy Chicks*, edited by Anna Gough-Yates and Bill Osgerby, London: Routledge.

Storey, John (2001b), 'The social life of opera', in *European Journal of Cultural Studies*, 6 (1).

Storey, John (2002a), 'Expecting rain: opera as popular culture', in *High-Pop*, edited by Jim Collins, Oxford: Blackwell.

Storey, John (2002b), 'The articulation of memory and desire: from Vietnam to the war in the Persian Gulf', in *Film and Popular Memory*, edited by Paul Grainge, Manchester: Manchester University Press.

Storey, John (2003), *Inventing Popular Culture: From Folklore to Globalisation*, Malden, MA: Blackwell.

Storey, John (2005), 'Popular', in *New Key Words: A Revised Vocabulary of Culture and Society*, edited by Tony Bennett et al., Oxford: Blackwell.

Storey, John (2006), 'Inventing opera as art in nineteenth-century Manchester', in *International Journal of Cultural Studies*, 9 (4).

Storey, John (2008), 'The invention of the English Christmas', in *Christmas, Ideology and Popular Culture*, edited by Sheila Whiteley, Edinburgh: Edinburgh University Press.

Storey, John (2009), *Cultural Theory and Popular Culture: A Reader*, 4th edn, Harlow: Pearson Education.

Storey, John (2010a), *Culture and Power in Cultural Studies: The Politics of Signification*, Edinburgh: Edinburgh University Press.

Storey, John (2010b), 'Becoming British', in *The Cambridge Companion to Modern British Culture*, edited by Michael Higgins, Clarissa Smith and John Storey, Cambridge: Cambridge University Press.

Storey, John (2010c), *Cultural Studies and the Study of Popular Culture*, 3rd edn, Edinburgh: Edinburgh University Press.

Storey, John (2011), 'Postmodernism and popular culture', in *The Routledge Companion to Postmodernism*, edited by Stuart Sim, London: Routledge.

Storey, John (2014), *From Popular Culture to Everyday Life*, London: Routledge.

Storey, John (2016), 'Class and the Invention of Tradition: the cases of Christmas, football and folksong', in *The Making of English Popular Culture*, edited by John Storey, London: Routledge.

Storey, John (2017), *Theories of Consumption*, London: Routledge.

Storey, John (2018), *Utopian Desire*, London: Routledge.

Storey, John, and Katy McDonald (2014a), 'Love's best habit: the uses of media in romantic relationships', in *International Journal of Cultural Studies*, 17(2), 113–25.

Storey, John, and Katy McDonald (2014b), 'Media love: intimacy in mediatized worlds', in *Mediatized Worlds*, edited by A. Hepp and F. Krotz, London: Palgrave, 221–32.

Sturken, Marita (1997), *Tangled Memories: The Vietnam War, the AIDS Epidemic, and the Politics of Remembering*, Berkeley: University of California Press.

Taylor, Matthew (2013), *The Association Game*, London: Routledge.

Thompson, E.P. (1976), 'Interview', *Radical History Review*, 3.

Thompson, E.P. (1976), William Morris: *Romantic to Revolutionary*, New York: Pantheon.

Thompson, E.P. (1980), *The Making of the English Working Class*, Harmondsworth: Penguin.

Thompson, E.P. (1995), *The Poverty of Theory*, 2nd edn, London: Merlin Press.

Tomlinson, John (1997), 'Internationalism, globalization and cultural imperialism', in *Media and Regulation*, edited by Kenneth Thompson, London: Sage.

Tomlinson, John (1999), *Globalization and Culture*, Cambridge: Polity Press.

Tompkins, Jane (1985), *Sensational Designs: The Cultural Work of American Fiction, 1790–1860*, New York: Oxford University Press.

Tong, Rosemary (1992), *Feminist Thought: A Comprehensive Introduction*, London: Routledge.

Tumin, Melvin (1957), 'Popular culture and the open society', in *Mass Culture: The Popular Arts in America*, edited by Bernard Rosenberg and David Manning White, New York: Macmillan.

Turner, Graeme (2003), *British Cultural Studies: An Introduction*, 3rd edn, London: Routledge.

Vlastos, Stephen (1991), 'America's "enemy": the absent presence in revisionist Vietnam War history', in *The Vietnam War and American Culture*, edited by John Carlos Rowe and Rick Berg, New York: Columbia University Press.

Volosinov, Valentin (1973), *Marxism and the Philosophy of Language*, New York: Seminar Press.

Walby, Sylvia (1990), *Theorising Patriarchy*, Oxford: Blackwell.

Walton, David (2008), *Introducing Cultural Studies: Learning Through Practice*, London: Sage.

Walton, John K and James Walvin (1988) (eds), *Leisure in Britain 1780–1939*, Manchester: Manchester University Press.

Walvin, James (2000), *The People's Game*, Edinburgh: Mainstream Publishing Company

Warner, Michael (1993), 'Introduction', in *Fear of a Queer Planet*, edited by Michael Warner, Minneapolis: Minnesota University Press.

West, Cornel (2009), 'Black postmodernist practices', in *Cultural Theory and Popular Culture: A Reader*, 4th edn, edited by John Storey, Harlow: Pearson Education.

White, David Manning (1957), 'Mass culture in America: another point of view', in *Mass Culture: The Popular Arts in America*, edited by Bernard Rosenberg and David Manning White, New York: Macmillan.

Williams, Raymond (1957), 'Fiction and the writing public', *Essays in Criticism*, 7.

Williams, Raymond (1963), *Culture and Society*, Harmondsworth: Penguin.

Williams, Raymond (1965), *The Long Revolution*, Harmondsworth: Penguin.

Williams, Raymond (1980), 'Base and superstructure in Marxist cultural theory', in *Problems in Materialism and Culture*, London: Verso.

Williams, Raymond (1981), *Culture*, London: Fontana.

Williams, Raymond (1983), *Keywords*, London: Fontana.

Williams, Raymond (2009), 'The analysis of culture', in *Cultural Theory and Popular Culture: A Reader*, 4th edn, edited by John Storey, Harlow: Pearson Education.

Williamson, Judith (1978), *Decoding Advertisements*, London: Marion Boyars.

Willis, Paul (1990), *Common Culture*, Buckingham: Open University Press.

Willis, Susan (1991), *A Primer for Daily Life*, London: Routledge.

Winship, Janice (1987), *Inside Women's Magazines*, London: Pandora.

Wright, Will (1975), *Sixguns and Society: A Structural Study of the Western*, Berkeley: University of California Press.

Zelizer, Barbie (1995), 'Reading the past against the grain: the shape of memory studies', in *Critical Studies in Mass Communication*, June.

Žižek, Slavoj (1989), *The Sublime Object of Ideology*, London: Verso.

Žižek, Slavoj (1991), *Looking Awry: An Introduction to Jacques Lacan through Popular Culture*, Cambridge, MA: MIT Press.

Žižek, Slavoj (1992), *Enjoy Your Symptom: Jacques Lacan in Hollywood and Out*, London: Routledge.

Žižek, Slavoj (2009), 'From reality to the real', in *Cultural Theory and Popular Culture: A Reader*, 4th edn, edited by John Storey, Harlow: Pearson Education.

Index

Above Suspicion (TV drama) 177
access to texts and practices 265, 271
actor-network theory 238–40
Adams, William 198
Adorno, Theodor 53, 66, 68–70, 73
advertising: art and 69; cars 77; and
    consumption 82–3, 171–3; as ideological
    82–3; and Leavisism 25–6; and 'new man'
    masculinity 178; post-feminist 176–7; for
    teaching profession 130–3; in women's
    magazines 170–1; Wonderbra campaign
    176–7, **176**, *see also* television commercials
aesthetic gaze 256–7
aesthetic judgement 28, 168, 252
aesthetic(s): distance 256–7, 260; and gender
    154; grounded 145, 258; and politics 256;
    popular 168; postmodern 209, 216–18,
    221; and taste 145; and television 165; and
    working class 40
affirmative culture 218–19
agency 51, 216, 219, 232, 249; and structure
    63, 223, 228, 232, 270
alienation of labour 64–5
Alloway, Lawrence 206
Althusser, Louis 4, 58, 74–83, 116, 133, 138n2
Althusserianism 74–83
American counterculture 29, 89–90, 207
American culture 8; Disneyland 213–14;
    as mass culture 29–34; as monolithic
    230–1; Watergate scandal 213–14,
    see also American Westerns; Americanization;
    Vietnam War
American Westerns: and the American Dream
    122–3; classic 120–2; and myth 122–3;

narrative functions 120–1; professional
    120–3; structuring oppositions 120, *121–2*;
    transition theme 120–3
Americanization 8, 227–31
The Analysis of Culture (Williams) 45–50
anarchy 13, 20–1, 25, 66
anchorage 128
Anderson, Perry 51
Ang, Ien 163, 165–9, 173, 231, 253, 271–2
Angel Heart (film) 215
anti-capitalism 89–90
anti-racism 200–1
Apocalypse Now (film) 192
appropriation 41, 156, 162, 173, 228, 265,
    271
aristocracy 20 1
Arnold, Malcolm 53
Arnold, Matthew 7, 13, 19–24, 45, 66, 74, 85,
    206, 224
art 39, 55, 64, 67, 206–7; and advertising
    69; aesthetic appreciation of 256–8;
    form versus function in 256–7; mass 55;
    mechanical reproduction of 73; museum
    256; pop 206–7; popular 54–5, 65;
    'real' 206
articulation 10, 89–90, 223–4
Aston Villa 148
audience(s) 3, 5; as community 55;
    fragmented 222; and performer relationship
    55; power 254; ratings 5; size of 5
aura, of texts and practices 72–3, 210
austerity 141
Austin, J.L. 180–1
authentic culture 66–9, 232

authority 21; collapse of 24–5; of intellectuals 209; of literature 28
avant-garde 154, 205, 207, 214, 222

Back to the Future films 215
Ball, Vicky 177
banking scandals 213
Barbarians, Philistines and Populace 20
Barnsley 148
Barrett, Michèle 153
Barthes, Roland 4, 116, 118, 123–31, 240, 261
base/superstructure relationship 3, 61–3, 74, 142–3, 271
Baudrillard, Jean 209–14, 216
the Beatles 207, 220
Beauvoir, Simone de 179
Beaver, Harold 185n9
Beck, Ulrich 177
Beck-Gernsheim, Elisabeth 177
Beethoven, Ludwig van 54
Benefits Street (TV programme) 140
Benjamin, Walter 66, 72–4, 210
Bennett, Tony 5, 9–11, 13, 28, 35, 69
Bentham, Jeremy 135–6
Berg, Rick 197
Bernstein, J.M. 74
Best, Steven 205, 209
Big Brother (TV programme) 137
Biressi, Anita 140–2
Birmingham City 148
Blackburn Olympic 147
Blackburn Rovers 147–8
blackness 200
Blackpool **36**, 148
Blake, Peter 207
Bloch, Ernest 150
Bloch, Joseph 62
Blue Velvet (film) 215
Boardwalk Empire (TV series) 222
Bolton Wanderers 148
Borgen (TV series) 222
Born on the Fourth of July (film) 194
Bourdieu, Pierre 6, 140, 144–6, 168, 225–6, 253, 255–7
Bourne, George 27

Breaking Bad (TV series) 222–3
Brecht, Bertolt 3, 67, 205, 213
bricolage 85, 216, 221–2
bricoleurs 216, 221
The Bridge (TV series) 222
British underground scene 207
Broadhurst, Thomas 81
Brogan, D.W. 32–3
Brooker, Peter 216–17
Brooker, Will 216–17
Brooks, Peter 166
Brunsdon, Charlotte 163
Burke, Peter 12
Burnley 147–8
Burston, Paul 179
Bush, George H.W. 197–9
Butler, Judith 179–83, 184n8

Cambridge 147
Canaan, Joyce 178–9
capital, forms of 144, 146
capitalism 67, 69, 72, 74, 142, 149, 213, 268–9; American 227–8; anti-capitalism 89–90; and common culture 265–6; feminist analyses of 152, 154; and gay culture 183; hegemony of 84; ideology of 3, 253, 268; industrial 18, 21, 64; late or multinational 204, 214–15, 217–18, 234, 271; market 214; monopoly 214; and music 89–90
Carey, James W. 2
Caribbean, British hegemony in 84
Carlyle, Thomas 13, 191
cars: advertisements for 77; and social practice of shopping 237
Casualties of War (film) 194
CCTV 137
celebrity surveillance magazines 138
Centre for Contemporary Cultural Studies 39, 56–7, 59
Certeau, Michel de 259–60
Chamberlain, Joseph 192
Chambers, Iain 209, 234
Charterhouse 147
Chartism 19
Chauncey, George 59n1

Chinn, Sarah E. 181–2
Chodorow, Nancy 159–60
choice, consumer 177
Christmas 4, 9, 248–9
cinema 25; cine-psychoanalysis 109–11,
    156–7; women at the cinema 153–7,
    see also film
civil service 150
civilization: Coleridge on 22; mass 25, 28,
    see also culture and civilization tradition
civilizing mission 191–2
Clarendon Commission 147
Clark, Michael 198–9
Clarke, Gary 263
the Clash 9, 220
class 3, 6, 24, 50, 140–51; class for itself 143;
    class in itself 143; consciousness 50, 141–3;
    and consumption 34, 144–6; distinction
    144–6; dominant 3, 10, 12–13, 18, 48, 63,
    83–4, 143–6, 149, 151, 225; segregation
    13, 18; struggle 63, 140–4, 146; and taste
    144–5, see also middle class; working class
classical music 57, 69, 70, see also opera
clothing 245–7
Coca Cola 247–8
Cocker, Jarvis 112
Cold War 29, 34
Coleridge, Samuel Taylor 22
Collins, Jim 216–17, 221–3
colonialism 84, 127, 147, 188, 191–3
commercial culture 8, 12, 42, 206, 217–18
commodification 68–9
commodities: American 227–8, 231;
    consumption 85, 92, 228, 258; exchange
    value 166, 254, 268–9; production 92, 166,
    217, 269–70; use value 166, 268; youth
    culture, re-articulation of 85
common culture 12–13, 27, 49, 265–6
communism 65, 141
community: audience as 55; of experience 46;
    fan 260–2; organic 8, 27–8, 45, 54–5; sense
    of 40
competition 149
concentration of ownership 233, 264
conformity 33, 66; gender 181

Connor, Steven 209
connotation 4, 124, 128–9, 165
Conrad, Joseph, Heart of Darkness 192
conscious 95
consciousness: class 50; false 3, 67, 154, 173,
    232; political 169; social 62
consensus, hegemony and 83–4
conservatism 49, 74n2, 246; neo- 68–9
Conservative Party 4, 10–11, 84, 124
constative language 180
consumer society 29
consumers: choice 177; power of 254;
    sovereignty of 253
consumption 29, 145, 251; active versus
    passive 8, 71–3, 92, 272; and advertising
    82–3, 171–3; cinema spectators 156–7; and
    class 34, 141; commodity 85, 92, 228, 258;
    and creativity 258–9; fan cultures 260–3;
    and femininity 170; and gay culture 183; of
    Hollywood's Vietnam 196–9; and meaning
    73–4, 265; and mode of production 73;
    and pleasure 170–1; politics of 73–4,
    258–64, 269–72; of romantic fiction 159; of
    women's magazines 174–5
containment, ideology of 29, 34
convergence culture 233–4
Coronation Street 211–12
Cosmopolitan (magazine) 172
counterculture, American 29, 89–90, 207
Coventry City 148
Coward, Rosalind 157–8, 160, 177
Creekmur, Corey K. 183
Crewe Alexandria 148
cricket 147–9
critical theory 66
cross-overs, TV programme 261
cultural capital 144–6, 208
cultural construction 240–4
cultural decline 23–4, 35, 39, 44
cultural economy 254–5
cultural emancipation 266
cultural field 253–63
cultural imperialism 164
cultural industries see culture industries
cultural modes 214–15

cultural populism 168, 251–3, 271
cultural power 224–5, 256, 266
cultural repertoires 126, 129
cultural studies 38–9, 58, 140; and anti-racism
    200–1; British 141; and class 140–1;
    post-Marxist 86–93, 270–1
cultural theory 5, 12–13, 34, 45, 73–4, 83;
    and class 140, 144; and gender 164, 173;
    and politics 251, 273n1; and psychoanalysis
    111
cultural value 224–6
culturalism 13, 38–60, 86; Hall and Whannel:
    The Popular Arts 38, 52–7; Hoggart, *The Uses
    of Literacy* 38–45; Thompson: *The Making
    of the English Working Class* 50–2; Williams,
    'The Analysis of Culture' 45–50
culture: affirmative 218–19; 'authentic'
    66–9, 232; as body of knowledge 19;
    circuit of 274n14; commercial 8, 12, 42,
    206, 217–18; common 12–13, 27, 49,
    265–6; convergence 233–4; democratic
    definition of 48–9; democratization of
    69; documentary 45–7; dominant 1, 10,
    178, 228, 230, 260; European or Western
    192, 230–1; folk 1, 8–9, 30–2; 'ideal'
    45–6; as intellectual/spiritual/aesthetic
    development 1; local 228, 230, 232; of
    other people 34–5, 74; as a particular way
    of life 1–2, 46–8; political economy of 183,
    258, 264–70; reflection theory of 62; of
    the selective tradition 47–8, 57, 224–5; as
    signifying practices 2; 'social' definition of
    46, 58, 90, 206; working class 1, 9, 18, 20,
    22, 39–45, 48–9, *see also* American culture;
    high culture; mass culture
culture and civilization tradition 13, 18–38,
    86; and Frankfurt School 74; Leavisism
    23–9, 35; Matthew Arnold 19–23
culture industries 11, 41, 44, 66–9, 85–6,
    253–4; and ideology 92, 253; manipulation
    by 42, 66–7, 86, 272; as not monolithic and
    non-contradictory 266, 268; ownership of
    264; power of 101, 264, 269
culture shock 91
Culture and Society (Williams) 38, 45, 48–9

Curtin, Philip 191
customs 4, 81
Cutter's Way (film) 194

Daily Mirror 7
Daily Star 211–12
Daily Telegraph 128
Dallas (TV programme) 164–9, 254;
    denotative and connotative reading of 165;
    fans 167–8; haters of 166–7; and ideology
    of mass culture 166–9; ironizing viewers
    of 166–8; melodramatic imagination 166;
    pleasure(s) of watching 164–9; and populist
    ideology 168; and realism 165–6
Dances with Wolves (film) 122–3, 133
Dante Alighieri 31
David-Neel, Alexandra 81
deconstruction 133
defining popular culture 5–14
deindustrialization 141
democracy 21, 24–5
democratization of culture 69
denotation *124*, 128–9, 165
Department of Education and Science 130–3
Derby County 148
Derrida, Jacques 131–3, 181
Descartes, René 108
desire 68, 109–10; and fantasy 112–13; female
    157–8; Freudian 97, 101–2; sexual 158,
    185n9
Desperate Housewives (TV series) 222–3
determinism 62, 87, 154, 228, 260, 270
Dickens, Charles 6
différance 131
difference 144; and 'race' 187, 189
disciplinary society 137
discourse 11, 87–9, 133–5; hegemonic 92;
    language as 133; scientific 208; of sexuality
    134–5
discrimination 53–4, 57, 253
Disneyland 213–14
Disraeli, Benjamin 19
Dittmar, Linda 195
Docker, John 36n1, 214
Doctor Who (TV series) 233–4

dominant class 3, 10, 12–13, 18, 48, 63, 83–4, 225, 255–6
dominant culture 1, 10, 178, 228, 230, 260
dominant ideology 10, 255, 269
dominant meanings 255
dominant reading 11
Doty, Alexander 183
Downton Abbey (TV programme) 140
Dracula (Stoker) 14–16
drag 182
dreams 9, 97–101, 104–5, 112; and associations 99–100, 104; and displacement 99; latent and manifest content 98–9; secondary revision 100; and symbolization 99–100
dual-systems theory 152
dumbing down 272
Dyer, Richard 72, 155, 199–200
Dylan, Bob 207

Eagleton, Terry 107–9, 111, 116
Easthope, Antony 178
Eastwick, Samuel 190
Eco, Umberto 223
economic capital 144–6, 208
economic determinism 62, 74–5, 270
economic field 253, 264–73
economic power 228, 256, 265
economy: and American Western 122; cultural 254–5; financial 254–5
education 21, 144, 208, 257; and class 149–50, 151n1
ego 96–8, 100, 107
Eliot, T.S. 205
elitism 23, 26, 31, 51, 59n1, 85, 90, 92, 123; and class 147, 149; and cultural field 263; and economic field 269; and politics 258, 272–3; and popular culture 6, 12; and postmodernism 206–7, 214
emotional intensification 262
emotional realism 165–6
The Emperor's New Clothes 233–4
empowerment 175; and fan cultures 262; and women's magazines 175
Engels, Frederick 62–3, 65, 146, 219

eroticization 262
escapism 9, 39, 154–6, 161–2
Eton 147, 151n1
European culture 192
Everton 148
exchange value 166, 254, 268–9
exclusion 6, 35, 57, 208

FA Cup 147–9
Faith, Adam 53
false consciousness 3, 67, 154, 173, 232
family history research 232
fan cultures 260–3
fantasy 102, 169; Lacanian notion of 112–13; and romantic fiction 158–60, 163
Fekete, John 226
female gaze 154
feminine identity, de/re-traditionalization of 177
femininity 158, 179, 182; and Hollywood cinema 156; and women's magazines 170–1
feminism/feminist analysis 3, 11, 15, 152–3, 207, 224, 253; cine-psychoanalysis 109–11, 156–7; dual-systems theory 152; fiction 25, 43, 169; liberal 152; and literary theory 153; Marxist 152; and men's studies 178–9; post-feminism 152, 172, 175–8; radical 152; reading romance 157–64; reading women's magazines 170–5; watching *Dallas* 164–9; women at the cinema 153–7
feudalism 21, 24, 61–2, 74, 142, 219
fiction 25, 43, 169; imperial 192–3; moral tone 43; nineteenth-century 47; 'slash' 262; and women's magazines 170–2, *see also* romantic fiction
Fiedler, Leslie 33–4, 205
figuration, as distinct from representation 80
filking 262
films 73, 210, 216–17; Cantonese Kung Fu 231–2; film noir 6, 16n2, 111; intertextuality 216–17; nostalgia 215–16; as an object of study 133, *134*, 155, *see also* American Westerns; cinema; Vietnam War, film representations of
financial crash 141

financial economy 254–5
Fischer, Ernst 143
Fiske, John 8, 11, 212, 252–5
folk culture 1, 8–9, 30–2
folk music 41
food 61, 66, 114n4, 140, 142, 145, 157, 171,
    200, 241, 268
football 87–8, 119, 146–50, 226, 237–8, 240
Football Association 147
Football League 148
forces of production 3, 62
the foreign, limited notion of 228–30
form and function 256–7
'fort-da' game 105, 107
Foucault, Michel 116, 133–7, 193
Four Tops 225, 235n8
Frankfurt School 8, 66–74, 217–18, 263;
    'authentic' culture 66–9; and capitalism
    67, 69, 72, 74; commodification 68–9;
    and consumption 71–3; and culture and
    civilization tradition 74; and culture
    industry 66–9; and manipulation 66–7,
    86; and mass culture 66, 68–9, 72, 74;
    and mechanical reproduction 721–3; and
    popular music 69–73
Franklin, Aretha 182–3
Franklin, H. Bruce 194, 198–9
French imperialism 80, 126–7
Freud, Sigmund 32, 36n3, 79, 95–106, 109,
    113n1, 114n4, 213; dreams 97–101,
    104–5, 112; id, ego and super-ego 96–8,
    100; model of the psyche 95–7; Oedipus
    complex 96, 100–1, 114n7, 114n8;
    pleasure principle 96–7; reality principle
    96–7; repression 97; sexual instincts 95;
    and textual analysis 101–5; unconscious,
    conscious and preconscious 95, 98
Frith, Simon 8, 72–3, 206, 211, 234
Fryer, Peter 189, 191
function and form 256–7

Game of Thrones (TV series) 222–3
Gamman, Lorraine 154
Garnham, Nicholas 144, 264
Gay, Paul du 274n14

gays/gay culture see queer theory
gaze: aesthetic 256–7; female 154; male
    109–11, 154, 177; popular/naive 256–7
gender 3, 59n1; conformity 181;
    performativity 180–3; and sex distinction
    179–80, see also femininity; feminism/
    feminist analysis; masculinity; men's studies
genre shifting 261
Giddens, Anthony 177
Gill, Rosalind 177
Gilroy, Paul 187–9, 201
Gledhill, Christine 154
globalization 227–32
Golding, Peter 264–5
Goodwin, Andrew 220
Gosse, Edmund 24
Gramsci, Antonio 10, 56, 58, 83, 85–6, 88,
    144, 146, 209, 232, 271
gratifications, substitute versus real 32
Graves-Brown, Paul 244
Gray, Ann 173
Gray, Thomas 150
Green, Michael 39, 58
Greenberg, Clement 53
Gresham's Law of culture 31
Griffin, Christine 178–9
Grossberg, Lawrence 214, 218, 234, 263
grounded aesthetics 258
Gulf War (1991) 197–9

Haag, Ernest van den 31–2
Haines, Harry W. 195
Hall, Stuart 4, 7–8, 11, 38, 45, 50, 52–8, 74,
    86–7, 91–2, 188, 200–1, 231–2, 270–1
Hamilton, Richard 207
Harrow 147, 151n1
Harvey, David 86
Hawkes, Terence 119–20
Heart of Darkness (Conrad) 192
Hebdige, Dick 13, 85, 204–5, 207
Hegel, G.W.F. 112
hegemony 9–11, 56, 83–6, 88–9, 146–7,
    178, 232, 253; of capitalism 84; and class
    141; and consensus 83–4; discourse 92;
    English language 84; and negotiation 84–6;

post-Marxist theory of 265, 271; Western 192; and youth subcultures 85

Hermes, Joke 172–5

heterosexuality 178–80, 182

hierarchies 27, 33, 49, 54, 132–4, 184n8, 187–8; and class 144–5, 150; and politics 256; and postmodernism 204, 225

high culture 5–6, 8, 29–30, 35, 53–4, 67, 74, 141, 206–7, 257, 272; absorption into mass culture 31–2; and popular culture, division between 6–7, 12, 169, 207, 217–18, 226; and representation 256

Highsmith, Patricia 113

Hill Street Blues (TV programme) 254

hip hop culture 229

Hirsch, Paul 72

history, Marxist approach to 61, 63–4

Hoggart, Richard 38–45, 49, 54, 58, 140–1

holiday destinations 140

Homeland 222

homogeneity/homogenization 8, 10, 31, 66, 68, 126, 144, 208, 231, 255

homosexuality 59n1, 183, *see also* queer theory

hooks, bell 152–3

Horkheimer, Max 66–9

Horne, Howard 206, 211, 234

human nature 97, 114n4

Human Nature (film) 113n1

Hume, David 191

Hunt, James 191–2

'hurt-comfort' stories 262

Huyssen, Andreas 206–7

hyperrealism 210–14

id 96–8

ideal, in defining culture 45–6; ego 110; romance narrative 159–60; self 174–5

identification, cinematic 156

Ideological State Apparatuses (ISAs) 81, 85

ideology 2–5, 63, 79; and advertising 82–3; Althusser's theory of 74–6; as a body of ideas 2, 124; capitalist 3, 253, 268; and class 141, 145; as concealment/distortion 2–3; connotation 4; and culture industries 92, 94; dominant 10, 255, 269; of mass

culture 166–9, 271–3; as material practice 4; and meritocracy 149–51; of natural taste 257; patriarchal 3; populist 168; of racism 189–91; of romantic fiction 162; and texts 3–4, 80–1

I'm a Celebrity, Get Me Out of Here (TV programme) 137

the Imaginary 107

immigration 188, 190–1

imperialism 188, 191–3, 231; cultural 164; French 80, 126–7

inclusion 35, 208

incorporation 11, 83–6, 232, 255, 263, 272

individualism 177

industrial capitalism 18, 21, 64

Industrial Revolution 27, 50, 141, 146, 148

industrialization 12–13, 18, 146

inequalities 3–4, 145, 149–51, 188, 219, 226

institutionalization 145, 188, 225, 256

intellectuals: American 29, 32, 34; authority of 209; clothing 246; organic 85

interpellation 81–3, 138n2, 171

interpretation 251, 253

interpretative fallacy 77

intertextuality 216–17, 221–2

irony 166–8

the Jam 9

Jameson, Fredric 61, 86, 205–6, 214–20, 234

jazz music 56–7

Jefferson Airplane 89–90

Jeffords, Susan 194

Jenkins, Henry 233, 260–3

Jenks, Charles 221

Jenson, Joli 260

Jeremy Kyle Show 138

Jerry Springer Show 138

Johnny Guitar (film) 122

Johnson, Richard 38, 52

Johnston, Sir Harry 191

Joyce, James 205

juke box boys 43–4

Katz, E. 232

Kellner, Douglas 209

Kill Bill (film) 216
The Killing (TV series) 222
Klein, Michael 196
knowledge 23, 79; and aesthetic appreciation
  257; constituted 252; culture as body of 19;
  as form of cultural/economic capital 208;
  and power 133–5, 192; practical 174–5;
  scientific 208; social 129, 261
Knox, Robert 191
Kung Fu movies 231–2

labour: alienation of 64–5; division of 65
Labour Party 83
Lacan, Jacques 105–10, 112–13, 116
lack 105, 107
Laclau, Ernesto 87–9, 107, 219
Lang, Jack 164
language 114n6; and advertising 25–6;
  constative 180; diachronic approach to 118;
  as a discourse 133; Lacan on 107–8; *langue*
  and *parole* 116, 119–20, 129; performative
  180–1; and reality 118; and structuralism
  116–19; synchronic approach to 118–19;
  syntagmatic and paradigmatic axes of
  117–18
langue 116, 119–20, 129
Latour, Bruno 238–9
Leavis, F.R. 23–8, 36n2, 49, 66
Leavis, Q.D. 24–5, 27, 54
Leavisism 23–9, 35, 38, 44–5, 57, 74; and
  advertising 25–6; and common culture
  27; and cultural decline 23–4, 35, 44; and
  literature 24, 28; and mass culture 25, 28,
  53; and organic communities 27–8; and
  popular fiction 25; and taste 24
Leicester City 148
leisure 27–8, 69
Levi jeans 9
Lévi-Strauss, Claude 116, 119–20
liberal feminism 152
Liebes, T. 232
lifestyle 140, 150, 174, 225
Light, Alison 164
literary criticism, feminist 153
literature 24, 28

Littler, Jo 149
lived cultures or practices 2, 14, 39, 47, 49, 58
local culture 228, 230, 232
Long, Edward 189–90
Lord of the Rings (film) 215
Los Angeles riots 198–9
love, romantic 109
Lovell, Terry 268–9
Lowenthal, Leo 66
Lynch, David 222
Lyotard, Jean-François 207–9

Macdonald, Dwight 30–1, 33
McDonald, Katy 220, 238
McGuigan, Jim 251–3, 264
Macherey, Pierre 77–81, 116, 184n7
McLellan, Gregor 51, 65
McNamara, Robert 198
McRobbie, Angela 86, 176–7, 204, 209,
  271
Mad Men (TV series) 222–3
magazines: celebrity surveillance 138, *see also*
  Paris Match; women's magazines
The Making of the English Working Class
  (Thompson) 50–2
male gaze 109–11, 154, 177
Maltby, Richard 8–9
Manchester City 148
Manchester United 148
Mandel, Ernest 214
Mandela, Nelson 268
manipulation 42, 66–7, 86, 272
Marcuse, Herbert 66–9, 178, 218–19
marketing, of TV programmes 222
Markus, Hazel Rose 188
Marley, Bob 89
Marshment, Margaret 154
Martin, Andrew 198
Marx, Karl 3, 51, 61–5, 75–6, 91, 112, 114n4,
  140–4, 146, 157, 166, 213, 219, 245,
  268–9, 274n15
Marxisms 3, 38, 52, 58, 86–7, 263, 271;
  Althusserianism 74–83; and class
  144; classical Marxism 61–4; English
  Marxism 64–5; Frankfurt School 66–74;

and hegemony theory 83–6, *see also* post-Marxism
Marxist feminism 152
masculinity 91, 178–9, 182; dominant 178; 'new man' 178
mass art 55
mass culture 1, 8–9, 11, 53, 55, 206, 219, 263; in America 29, 34; and Frankfurt School 66, 68–9, 72, 74; Hoggart on 40, 42, 44; ideology of 166–9, 271–3; as imported American culture 8; Leavisism 25, 28, 53; as 'pre-digested' 53, 71
mass production 6, 31
materiality 237–50; as actor 238–40; and meaning 240–8
meaning 2, 90–2, 234, 254, 272; aesthetics 258; and combination 117–19; and consumption 73–4, 265; contextuality of 14–16; deferment of 131–2; and discourse 87–9; dominant 255; and grounded aesthetics 258; and materiality 240–8; 'oppositional' 85; and process of selection and combination 117–19; as result of difference and relationships 116–17; and social practice 240–2, 247–9; and structure 119, 131; subordinate 255; of texts 14–16, 77–9, 101–66, 173–5, 265; and women's magazines 173–5
mechanical reproduction 72–3, 210
Medhurst, Andy 273n6
media 81; convergence 233, 264; events 212; media-based culture 219; ownership 233; platforms 233–4; recycling 217; surveillance 137–8
melodrama, nineteenth-century 63–4, 266
melodramatic imagination 166
men's studies 178–9
Mercer, Kobena 209
meritocracy 140, 149–51
metanarratives 208
Michaud, Gene 195
middle class 18, 20–1, 48, 141, 146–7, 151
military 150
Miller, Daniel 245–7
Mills, Sara 81

mirror stage 105–7, 110
Missing in Action films 193–5
mobile phones 237–8
mode of production 3, 61–3, 73, 75, 142–3, 258
mode of production determinism 228
modernism 205–8, 214, 216, 220, 252
modernity 213
Modleski, Tania 157, 163–4
moral realignment 261
moral tone 43
Morley, David 11, 173
morphemes 120
Morris, R.J. 8, 13
Morris, William 54, 64–5
Mother Courage and Her Children (Brecht) 67
Mouffe, Chantal 10, 87–9, 219
Moya, Paula M.L. 188
multinational capitalism 204, 214–15, 217–18, 234, 271
Mulvey, Laura 109–11, 153–4
The Mummy Returns (film) 215
mundanes/Mundania 262–3
Murdock, Graham 264–5
music: American counterculture 89–90; and capitalism 89–90; and class 140; classical 6–7, 57, 69, 70; folk 41; jazz 56–7; opera 6–7, 69, 70; rap 220–1; recordings 210; reggae 89; rock'n'roll 220, *see also* pop music; popular music
music hall 54, 63–4
Myers, Tony 111
mythemes 120
Mythologies (Barthes) 123–4
myths 4, 120, 122–4, 126–7

narcissism 110
nationalism 232
nature 241–2
Nederveen Pieterse, J. 230–1
negotiated reading 11
negotiation, hegemony and 84–6
neo-conservatism 68–9
neoliberalism 141, 149, 177
networks, actors and 238–40

new revisionism 253
New York Times 199
News From Nowhere (Morris) 65
newspapers 128, 140; popular/tabloid 7, 25, 211–12; *see also individual titles*
Newsweek 197
Newton, Esther 184–5n9, 185n10
Nixon, Richard 197
Nixon, Sean 178
nostalgia 215–17, 220
Notts County 148
Nowell-Smith, Geoffrey 13
Nunn, Heather 140–2

objectification, sexual 109, 111
O'Connor, Alan 45
Oedipus complex 96, 100–1, 105, 108–9, 114n7, 114n8, 160
Old Etonians 147
opera 6–7, 69, *70*
organic communities 8, 27–8, 45, 54–5
Orientalism 192–200
Ortega y Gasset, José 257
Orwell, George 247
other/otherness 1, 13–14
ownership, concentration of 233, 264
Oxford 147

panoptic machine 135–8
Paris Match (magazine) 124, **125**, 126–7
Paris, Texas (film) 109
Parker, Ian 111
parody 215, 220, 222–3
parole 116, 119–20, 129
passive consumption 8, 71–3, 92, 272
pastiche 215–17, 220–1
patriarchy 3, 109, 152–4, 156, 178–9; and romantic fiction 158, 161
Pavarotti, Luciano 6–7
peasants 143
Peggy Sue Got Married (film) 215
performative language 180–1
performativity 208, 241; of education 208; gender 180–3
Perryman, Neil 233–4

personalization 262
petit bourgeoisie 142
phonemes 120
photographs 124–9
Picasso, Pablo 205
Pilger, John 198
Platoon (film) 194–6, 210
pleasure 234, 252–4, 271–2; and consumption 170–1; fore- 102; grounded aesthetics 258; of looking (scopophilia) 109–11; reading romantic fiction 157–8, 161, 163; visual 170–1; watching *Dallas* 164–9
pleasure principle 96–7
plutocracy 149
poaching (textual) 259–60
Polan, Dana 169
political consciousness 169
political economy of culture 183, 258, 264–71
politics 5, 144, 149–50; anti-capitalist 89–90; and class 141, 143, 145; and 'race' 188; of signification 4, *see also* politics of the popular
politics of the popular: and aesthetic judgement 251–2, 256–8; and consumption 73–4, 258–64, 269–72; and cultural field 253, 255–64; and cultural populism 251–3, 271; and economic field 264–70; and fan culture 260–3; and ideology of mass culture 271–3; and post-Marxist cultural studies 270–1
pop art 206–7
pop music 9, 55–8, 207, 266; postmodern 220–1; sampling technologies 220–1; in television commercials 9, 12
popular art 54–5, 65
The Popular Arts (Hall and Whannel) 38, 52–7
popular culture: and class 140–1; and class struggle 146–9; ways of defining 5–14
popular music 41–2, 69–73; active versus passive consumption of 71–2; as social cement 71–2; standardization 69–71, *see also* jazz; pop music
populism 168, 251–3, 271–2
Porter, Cole 54

post-feminism 152, 172, 175–8
post-Marxism 86–93, 270–1
post-structuralism 2, 9, 131–8; and Lacanian psychoanalysis 105–9
The Postmodern Condition (Lyotard) 207–9
postmodern pop music 220–1
postmodern television 221–4
postmodernism 12, 204–36, 251–2; in the 1960s 205–7; Baudrillard 209–14; and class 141; as commercial culture 233–4; and convergence culture 233–4; as cultural dominant of late capitalism 214–15, 217; and globalization 227–32; Jameson 205–6, 214–20; Lyotard 207–9; and metanarratives 208; and pastiche 215–17, 220–1; and pluralism of value 224–6; and pop art 206–7; and simulation 210–11, 213, 216, 221; use of the term 204–5; and women's magazines 173
POW, The Escape (film) 194
power 3–5, 9, 11, 18, 124, 246; in binary oppositions 132; consumer 254, 264; cultural 224–5, 256, 266; of culture industries 101, 264, 269; economic power 228, 256, 265; ideological, of romantic fiction 162; and knowledge 133–5, 192; local 228, 232; middle-class 21; modernism 205; narrative, of Westerns 120; and Orientalism 192; and panopticism 136–7; patriarchal 3, 152, 157–8; as productive 135, 193; of racism 188–9; and signification 245; of whiteness 199 200; working class 21, 39
preconscious 95
press *see* newspapers
Preston North End 148
'primitive' societies 119–20
production 258–9, 264, 271; and class 141–2, 146; commodity 92, 166, 217, 269–70; forces of 3, 62; mass 6, 31; means of 75, 92, 142, 272; mode of 3, 61–3, 73, 75, 228, 258; relations of 3, 62, 75, 258, 269; secondary 259, 273n5; in use 92, 258, 272
Propp, Vladimir 120
pseudo-individualization 70–1

psyche, Freudian model of 95–7
psychoanalysis 15; cine- 109–11, 156, 167; Freudian 95–105; Lacanian (post-structuralist) 105–9
public schools 147–9
Pulp Fiction (film) 216

queer theory 179–84, 224

'race' and racism 3, 187–203; anti-racism 200–1; and colonialism and imperialism 188, 191–3; ideology of racism 189–92; and Orientalism 192–200; and power 188–9; and signification 187–8; and slavery and slave trade 188, 190–1; and whiteness 199–200
radical feminism 152
radicalism 13, 29, 50
Radway, Janice 159–64, 173
Raiders of the Lost Ark (film) 215
Raise the Titanic (film) 254
Rakow, Lana F. 153
Rambo (film) 193–5, 213–14
rap music 220–1
Rastafarian culture 89
reading: deconstructive 133; dominant 11; fan cultures 260–1; negotiated 11; as poaching 259–60; positions 9, 11, 127; queer 183; romantic fiction 25, 157–64; subordinate reading 11; symptomatic 76–81; women's magazines 170–5
Reagan, Ronald 197 8
the Real 105–6, 108, 112, 210
realism 214; *Dallas* (TV programme) 165–6; emotional 165–6; false 216; hyperrealism 210–14; pop music 220
reality 108, 112, 210, 213 14; and language 1, 18
reality principle 96–7
recontextualization 261
reflection theory of culture 62
refocalization 261
reggae music 89
Reilly, Kelly 177
relations of production 3, 62, 75, 258, 269

religious fundamentalism 232
representation(s) 158, 212–14, 216, 222,
    241–2, 246; as distinct from figuration 80;
    and high culture 256; and ideology 75, 81;
    politics of 271–2; racial *see* 'race' and racism
repression 32, 97, 114n2
reproduction, mechanical 72–3, 210
resistance 11, 84–6, 162, 232, 253, 272;
    and class 141; and new revisionism 253;
    semiotic 254–5; social 254–5; youth
    (sub)culture 85, 263
Richards, Keith 90
Richardson, Colin 179
Ricoeur, Paul 213
rituals 4, 81
Ritzer, G. 230
Riviera 222
Robin Hood, Prince of Thieves (film) 215
rock'n'roll 220
Rockwell, John 207
Rolling Stones 207, 220
romantic fiction 25, 157–64; consumption
    159; and emotional fulfilment 160–1;
    and emotional reproduction 161; as
    escapism 161–2; and fantasy 158–60,
    163; ideological power of 162; and male
    violence 160–2; and oppositional practices
    in reading 162; and patriarchy 158,
    161–2; pleasure in reading 157–8, 161, 163;
    utopian longing in reading 162–3
Rosenberg, Bernard 30
Ross, Andrew 8, 29, 34
Rowe, John Carlos 197
Rumble Fish (film) 215

Said, Edward 192, 231
Samuel, Raphael 52
Saussure, Ferdinand de 116–19, 131
Scattergood, John 190
Schiller, Herbert 228
schizophrenia (cultural) 216
Schwenger, Peter 178
scientific knowledge and discourse 208
scopophilia 109–11
The Secret Diary of Laura Palmer 222

selective tradition 47–8, 57, 224–5
semiotic resistance 254–5
semiotics/semiology 123–4, 127, 245
Sergeant Pepper's Lonely Hearts Club Band
    (Beatles) 207
sex, and gender distinction 179–80
Sex and the City (TV series) 210, 222–3
sexual desire 158, 185n9
sexual instincts 95
sexual objectification 109, 111
sexuality 59n1; discourse of 134–5; female
    158, 160, *see also* heterosexuality;
    homosexuality; queer theory
Shakespeare, William 6, 27
Shane (film) 121
Sharp, Cecil 41
Sheffield Wednesday 148
Shils, Edward 32–4
Showalter, Elaine 152–3, 178
signification 2, 4, 80, 90–1, 123–4, 126–7,
    169, 240–5; and power 245; and 'race' and
    racism 187–8
signifier/signified 108, 116–17, 123, *124*,
    126–7, 131–2
signs 123, *124*, 131, 240; polysemic nature of
    124, 128
Simpson, O.J. 212
simulacrum 210
simulation 210–11, 213, 216, 221
situation comedy 66–7
Six Feet Under (TV series) 222–3
'slash' fiction 262
slavery and slave trade 188, 190–1
soap operas 42, 157, 210–12, *see also Dallas*
    (TV programme)
social capital 144–6
social consciousness 62
social control 29, 63
social formation 74–5, 214–15, 255–6
social knowledge 129, 261
social mobility 149–50
social practice, and meaning 240–2, 247–9
socialism 29, 64–5
Socialist Worker 128
sociology 6, 52, 58, 146

Sontag, Susan 205–6, 226
The Sopranos (TV series) 222–3
Soviet Union 30–1
Spare Rib (magazine) 170, 172
Stacey, Jackie 154–7
standardization 67, 69–71
standards 226
the *Star* 212
Star Wars (film) 215
Starkey, David 132
State 21
Sticky Fingers (Rolling Stones) 207
Stoke City 148
Stoker, Bram, *Dracula* 14–16
Storey, John 11–12, 41, 85, 220, 238, 249
Stravinsky, Igor 205
structuralism 2, 9, 86, 116–31; and language
    116–19; and myths 120, 122–4, 126–7; and
    Westerns 120–3, *see also* post-structuralism
structure, and agency 63, 223, 228, 232, 270
structure of feeling 46–7, 58
Sturken, Marita 198
subcultures 85
subjectivity 11
subordinate groups/cultures 3, 10, 18, 76,
    83–5, 225, 256
subordinate meaning 255
subordinate reading 11
the *Sun* 7, 212
Sunderland 148
super-ego 96–7
superstructure 3, 61–3, 74, 142–3, 271
surplus value 268–9
surveillance 136–8
the Symbolic 106, 108
symbolization, dreams 99–100

Talking Heads 220
Tarantino, Quentin 216–17
taste 6, 24, 31, 56, 168, 206, 208, 225, 256;
    natural, ideology of 257
Taxi Driver (film) 77
technological change 233
Teddy boys 43–4
teenagers *see* youth (sub)culture

television: and class 140; context and
    viewing of 15; economic analysis 222;
    fan culture rewriting of 261–2; female
    identity constructions 177; and financial
    economy 254; and hyperrealism 210–12;
    intertextuality 220–1; make-over shows
    138; marketing techniques 222; news 7;
    postmodern 221–4; rewriting of 261–2;
    situation comedy 66–7; soap operas 42,
    157, 210–12; surveillance programmes
    137–8; talk shows 138, *see also Dallas*;
    television commercials
television commercials: opera and classical
    music in 69, *70*; pop music in 9, 12
Ten Years Younger (TV programme) 138
texts 2, 14; access to 264–5, 271; aura 72–3,
    210; context and meaning of 14–16;
    cultural value of 224–6; as decentred
    77; and Freudian psychoanalysis 101–5;
    as ideological forms 3–4, 80–1; and
    interpretative fallacy 77; meaning of
    14–16, 77–9, 101–5, 119, 131, 173–5,
    265; poaching of 259–60; problematic
    76–7; symptomatic reading of 76–81;
    unconscious of 79–80
textual determinism 260–1
Thatcher, Margaret 141
Thickness, Philip 190
Thompson, Denys 24–8
Thompson, E.P. 18, 38, 50–2, 58, 63, 65,
    140–1, 143–4
The Threepenny Opera (Brecht) 213
Time Magazine 196
Tomlinson, John 228, 230
Tong, Rosemary 152
trade unionism 13, 21
True Romance (film) 216
truth, regimes of 135, 137, 193, 196
Tumin, Melvin 34
Turner, Graeme 2, 11
Twin Peaks (TV series) 221–3

Uncommon Valor (film) 193–4
unconscious: Freudian 95, 98; of texts 79–80
underground scene 207

United Kingdom (UK) 150–1
upper class 141, 147, 150
urbanization 12–13, 18, 146
The Uses of Literacy (Hoggart) 38–45

value 54; cultural 224–6; exchange value 166,
    254, 268–9; surplus value 268–9; use value
    166, 268
Verne, Jules 80–1
Vietnam War 89–90, 207; 'Americanization
    of the war' narrative paradigm 195–6; bad
    leadership 193–4; consumption of 196–9;
    film representations of 193–9, 210; and
    first Gulf War 197–9; 'inverted firepower
    syndrome' narrative paradigm 194–5, 199;
    loss as theme in 194; as reality 213–14; as
    regimes of truth 193, 196; and Vietnam
    veterans 198–9; 'war as betrayal' narrative
    paradigm 193–4
violence, male 160–2
Vlastos, Stephen 197
Volosinov, Valentin 89

Walby, Sylvia 152
Walvin, James 147
Warhol, Andy 206–7
Warner, Michael 183
West Bromwich Albion 148
West, Cornel 221
Western culture 192, 230–1
Westerns *see* American Westerns
Westminster 147
Whannel, Paddy 38, 52–8
What Not To Wear (TV programme) 138
White, Charles 189–90
White, David Manning 30
whiteness 187–8 202n6

Williams, Raymond 1–2, 5, 11–12, 22, 28, 38,
    41–2, 45–51, 54, 58, 90, 140–1, 144, 206,
    214
Williamson, Judith 82
Willis, Paul 11, 252–3, 257–9, 265–6, 268–9
Willis, Susan 73
Winship, Janice 170–2, 175
Winstanley, Gerard 184n7
The Wire (TV series) 222
Wolverhampton Wanderers 148
Woman's Own (magazine) 170, 172
women at the cinema 153–7
women reading romantic fiction 157–64
women's magazines 170–5; advertisements
    170–1; and consumption 170–1; femininity
    and 170–1; fictions of 170–2; and meaning
    production 173–5; postmodern perspective
    on 173; problem pages 172, 175; repertoires
    of consumption 174–5; as survival manuals
    170
Wonderbra advertising campaign 176–7, **176**
Woolf, Virginia 205
working class 8, 13, 19–21, 23, 50–2, 74, 92,
    141, 146–8, 150; aesthetic 40; culture 1, 9,
    18, 20, 22, 39–45, 48–9; education of 21;
    power 21, 39
Wright, Will 120–3

Young, G.M. 51
youth (sub)culture 55–6; and class 141; and
    hegemony 85; juke box boys (Teddy boys)
    43–4; and materiality 237; resistance 85,
    263
YouTube 233

Zelizer, Barbie 197
Žižek, Slavoj 1, 16n2, 83